ASCENT®
CENTER FOR TECHNICAL KNOWLEDGE

3DEXPERIENCE SIMULIA 2023x
Linear Structural Validation

Learning Guide
1ˢᵗ Edition

ASCENT - Center for Technical Knowledge®
3DEXPERIENCE SIMULIA 2023x
Linear Structural Validation
1st Edition

Prepared and produced by:

ASCENT Center for Technical Knowledge
630 Peter Jefferson Parkway, Suite 175
Charlottesville, VA 22911

866-527-2368
www.ASCENTed.com

ASCENT - Center for Technical Knowledge (a division of Rand Worldwide Inc.) is a leading developer of professional learning materials and knowledge products for engineering software applications. ASCENT specializes in designing targeted content that facilitates application-based learning with hands-on software experience. For over 25 years, ASCENT has helped users become more productive through tailored custom learning solutions.

We welcome any comments you may have regarding this guide, or any of our products. To contact us please email: feedback@ASCENTed.com.

Contents

Preface

The *3DEXPERIENCE SIMULIA 2023x: Linear Structural Validation* guide covers the fundamentals of the Linear Structural Validation (LSV) app. It provides you with the knowledge to effectively use 3DEXPERIENCE 2023x for structural finite element analysis and simulation, thereby reducing design time. This is an extensive hands-on guide, which enables you to apply your knowledge through real-world scenarios and examples.

Topics Covered

- Introduction to 3DX simulation

- Basic structural simulation

- Loads and boundary conditions

- Mesh refinement

- Assembly analysis

- Fasteners

- Frequency analysis

- Buckling analysis

- Thermal Analysis

Prerequisites

- Access to the 3DEXPERENCE CATIA 2023x version of the software, to ensure compatibility with this guide. Future software updates that are released by Dassault Systèmes may include changes that are not reflected in this guide. The practices and files included with this guide might not be compatible with prior versions (i.e., 3DEXPERENCE CATIA 2022x).

- Completion of the *3DEXPERENCE CATIA 2022x: Introduction to Modeling* course or equivalent CATIA experience is recommended. Any knowledge of FEA is beneficial, but is not a mandatory requirement.

Note on Software Setup

This guide assumes a standard installation of the software using the default preferences during installation. Lectures and practices use the standard software templates and default options for the Content Libraries.

Note on Learning Guide Content

ASCENT's learning guides are intended to teach the technical aspects of using the software and do not focus on professional design principles and standards. The exercises aim to demonstrate the capabilities and flexibility of the software, rather than following specific design codes or standards, which can vary between regions

In This Guide

The following highlights the key features of this guide.

Feature	Description
Practice Files	The Practice Files page includes a link to the practice files and instructions on how to download and install them. The practice files are required to complete the practices in this guide.
Chapters	A chapter consists of the following: Learning Objectives, Instructional Content, Practices, Chapter Review Questions, and Command Summary. • **Learning Objectives** define the skills you can acquire by learning the content provided in the chapter. • **Instructional Content**, which begins right after Learning Objectives, refers to the descriptive and procedural information related to various topics. Each main topic introduces a product feature, discusses various aspects of that feature, and provides step-by-step procedures on how to use that feature. Where relevant, examples, figures, helpful hints, and notes are provided. • **Practice** for a topic follows the instructional content. Practices enable you to use the software to perform a hands-on review of a topic. It is required that you download the practice files (using the link found on the Practice Files page) prior to starting the first practice.

Practice Files

To download the practice files for this guide, use the following steps:

1. Type the URL *exactly as shown below* into the address bar of your Internet browser to access the Course File Download page.

    Note: If you are using the ebook, you do not have to type the URL. Instead, you can access the page by clicking the URL below.

    https://www.ascented.com/getfile/id/lemboglossumPF

    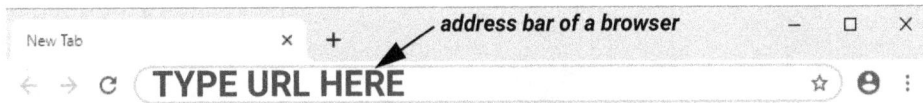

2. On the Course File Download page, click the **DOWNLOAD NOW** button, as shown below, to download the .ZIP file that contains the practice files.

3. Once the download is complete, unzip the file and extract its contents.

    The recommended practice files folder location is:
    C:\Simulia Linear Structural Validation Practice Files

    Note: It is recommended that you do not change the location of the practice files folder. Doing so may cause errors when completing the practices.

Stay Informed!

To receive information about upcoming events, promotional offers, and complimentary webcasts, visit:

www.ASCENTed.com/updates

Introduction to 3DEXPERIENCE Simulation

The Simulation solution (SIMULIA) in 3DEXPERIENCE platform is a powerful software tool that enables you to simulate structural and thermal behavior of your design to help you understand and improve the design's performance.

Learning Objectives

- 3DEXPERIENCE platform for Simulation and Analysis.
- Structural Simulation Roles and Apps.
- Linear Structural Validation App
- Understand the concept of FEA.
- Understand the FEA solution refinement.
- Linear structural analysis assumptions and limitations.
- Review the FEA process.

1.1 3DEXPERIENCE Platform for Simulation and Analysis

The 3DEXPERIENCE platform provides a unified user interface with software apps for every department in your company, including marketing, sales, and engineering. The app suite includes:

- Modeling
- Simulation and Analysis
- Automation and Optimization
- Design Review and Decision Making
- Data Management

3DEXPERIENCE Simulation integrates powerful analysis solutions with the CAD data created and managed on the platform. The benefits of simulation on the platform include:

- Product Modeling and Simulation that are fully associative
- State-of-the-art Solvers for all types of simulation
- Automated model creation and meshing for components and assemblies
- Coupled multi-physics simulations
- Simulation data management
- High-performance Result Visualization
- Remote HPC and cloud computing

Modeling and Simulation work together on the 3DEXPERIENCE platform:

- Engineers and users of all levels always have access to the latest model
- If the product geometry changes, you can automatically update the simulation
- Model geometry is parametric, allowing design exploration and optimization

The simulation suite includes apps for a wide range of physics domains:

- Structural simulation
- Thermal simulation
- Motion simulation
- Fluid flow simulation
- Vibro-acoustics

1.2 Structural Simulation Roles and Apps

Structural Simulation solutions in the 3DEXPERIENCE platform enable assessing the structural integrity of products subject to various environmental, boundary, and loading conditions, in order to guide the design decisions.

3DEXPERIENCE is a 'role' based platform, which means you can customize the level of capability that each user needs based on the role the user is assigned. 3DEXPERIENCE analysis and simulation portfolio includes a variety of user roles, for users of all skill levels. The summary, from entry-level to high-end, is presented in the following table.

Role	Apps	Description
Structural Designer (SRD)	Linear Structural Validation Physics Results Explorer Material Definition	• Easy-to-use app for design engineers • Enables quick evaluation of strength and stiffness of products and components • Linear simulations only
Structural Engineer (SLL)	Linear Structural Scenario Creation Physics Results Explorer Material Definition	• Comprehensive linear structural analysis • Includes static, buckling, and linear dynamics
Structural Performance Engineer (SFO)	Structural Model Creation Structural Scenario Creation Physics Results Explorer Material Definition	• Adds non-linear structural, implicit dynamics, and transient thermal simulations • Enables multi-step analysis process
Structural Mechanics Engineer (SSU)	Structural Model Creation Simulation Model Preparation Mechanical Scenario Creation Physics Results Explorer Material Definition	• Full FEA capability within the 3DEXPERIENCE • Enables explicit dynamics, random response, and all the advanced modeling tools
Structural Analysis Engineer (SYE)	Structural Model Creation Simulation Model Preparation Mechanical Scenario Creation Physics Results Explorer Material Definition	• Similar to Structural Mechanics Engineer but acts as a standalone FEA solution • Essentially, it is an enhanced pre- and post-processing FEA tool Computation must be performed remotely or on the cloud, using tokens

This learning content covers the **Linear Structural Validation** app; therefore, ensure that you have the **Structural Designer** role assigned to you to be able to perform the hands-on practices in this book.

1.3 Linear Structural Validation App

The Linear Structural Validation app provides easy-to-use simulation capabilities for the conceptual and early-stage design, allowing virtual product testing before physical prototype is available.

The app is very user-friendly, greatly reducing the need for the user to understand the complexities of the underlying simulation technology. The tools and options are intuitive and explained in the language of product designers, while the complex FEA features are applied automatically behind the scenes.

The user receives continuous guidance about the tasks, so there is never any confusion as what to do next to complete the simulation set up. The simulation and its results are associated with the product and are managed in the PLM database.

The Linear Structural Validation app enables the following types of simulations for design engineers:

- Linear static
- Buckling
- Natural frequency
- Steady-state thermal

1.4 Finite Element Analysis (FEA)

Structural simulations in the 3DEXPERIENCE platform are executed using the proven Abaqus FEA solver technology.

Finite Element Analysis is a numerical mathematical method based on the following process:

1. Discretize (i.e., divide) the model into smaller and more simplified volumes (tetrahedra, bricks, wedges, etc.) called *finite elements*. The collection of finite elements approximates the shape of the model, and is called *finite element mesh*, or just *mesh*. An example of a meshed model is shown in Figure 1–1.

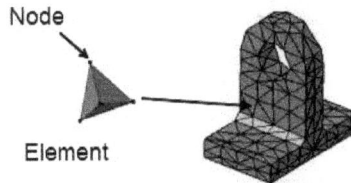

Figure 1–1

2. Approximate the variation of the principal quantity of interest (such as displacement, stress, etc.), within each finite element with polynomials. These polynomials are typically called *local approximation functions* or *shape functions*.

3. Connect the finite elements across the inter-element boundaries, thus effectively *sewing* elemental polynomials together. The *sewn* local polynomials now approximate a variation of the quantity of interest over the entire model, and therefore comprise the global approximation function in the form of a piece-wise polynomial.

4. Solve the governing equations and boundary conditions (i.e., a boundary value problem) for the global approximation function and find the best fitting solution. In linear structural mechanics, the principle of minimum total potential energy is typically used to find the best fitting solution, which results in solving a large number (sometimes hundreds of thousands) of simultaneous linear equations.

5. Present the results for this approximate solution.

The key FEA concept is the use of piece-wise polynomials to approximate the sought field quantity in the model, which effectively replaces a continuum problem with an infinite number of degrees of freedom (DOF) by a discrete problem with a finite number of DOF (hence the terms *finite elements* and *discretization*).

For example, consider how the FEA method works when applied to calculate deflections in a simple beam as shown in Figure 1−2. The beam is clamped at the left end, has a couple of supports in the middle, and is loaded by a couple of transversal forces and a moment. The bottom graph shown in Figure 1−2 represents the unknown true deflection of the beam, which you are trying to determine using the FEA method.

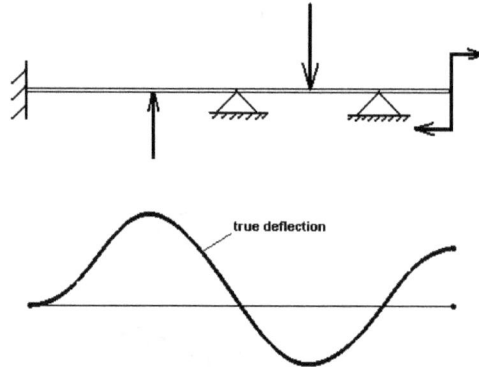

Figure 1−2

The first step in the process (shown in the example in Figure 1−3) is to mesh the beam by breaking it into a collection of shorter pieces (i.e., finite elements) connected at their ends (i.e., the nodes).

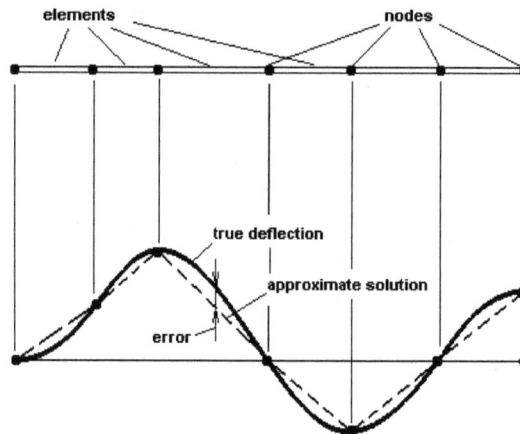

Figure 1−3

Next, the deflection *Y* within each finite element is approximated by a polynomial. In this example, you use linear polynomial $Y = a_0 + a_1X$, which means that deflection within each element is approximated by essentially a straight line.

Next, the local linear polynomials are sewn together at the nodes, creating a global approximation function in the form of a piece-wise linear polynomial, which is a polyline.

> **Note:** *Sewing local polynomials at the nodes ensures continuity of the global approximation function, and therefore of the FEA solution for the deflection over the entire beam.*

Finally, the global approximation function is best-fit to satisfy both the bending differential equations and beam boundary conditions (loads and constraints). The resulting function (the dashed line shown in Figure 1–3) now represents the FEA solution for the true deflection (the solid line shown in Figure 1–3) in the beam.

It is important to note that your FEA result contains a certain amount of error, which is the deviation between the true deflection (the solid line shown in Figure 1–3) and the FEA solution (the dashed line shown in Figure 1–3), which is called the *discretization error*.

Any FEA solution is just an approximation, which means it always contains a discretization error. Therefore, in the FEA process, it is critical to know how to estimate, how to control, and how to reduce this unavoidable approximation error to acceptable levels.

1.5 FEA Solution Refinement

The process of bringing the FEA approximation error to acceptable levels is typically called *solution refinement*, and it involves making the finite elements in the mesh progressively smaller.

Consider the example of the beam shown in Figure 1–3. If you make the finite elements smaller without changing anything else, the approximation error becomes smaller as well, as shown in Figure 1–4.

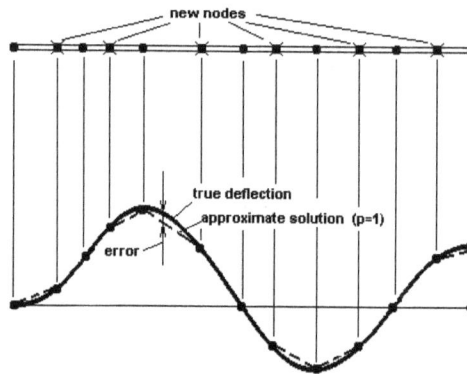

Figure 1–4

This approach is the one that is used in the Linear Structural Validation app for improving the FEA solution.

1.6 Linear Structural Analysis Assumptions and Limitations

The intended users for Linear Structural Validation are design engineers rather than FEA experts. To simplify the simulation, the assumed response of all components in the simulation is **linear**. As such, its use is subject to the following assumptions and limitations.

Linear material model

The materials in the analysis are assumed to be linear elastic, i.e., the relationship between the stress and the strain following the Hooke's law. The elastic materials are characterized by two properties: Young's Modulus (also called Modulus of Elasticity) and Poisson's Ratio.

The non-linear material behaviors such as plasticity, hyper-elasticity, or visco-elasticity (or creep) are not supported.

Small displacements and strains

All translations and rotations in the model are assumed small, which means that the equilibrium equations in the analysis are solved on the original, i.e., undeformed, geometry. Also, the strains are assumed small, i.e., under 2000 microstrain.

The geometrically nonlinear simulations involving large displacements and rotations are not supported.

Geometrically linear contact

The word "contact" in FEA usually refers to varying with the load, i.e., nonlinear, boundary conditions and interactions between the parts. A simple example of such a condition would be an assembly in which initially there's a clearance between the parts, but this clearance gets eliminated and the parts start pressing against each other once the load exceeds a certain magnitude.

Although Linear Structural Validation app has some contact analysis capabilities, it is limited to only geometrically linear contact, in which the sliding between the parts in contact is negligible.

Geometrically non-linear contact, such as with finite sliding, is not supported.

1.7 FEA Process

A typical FEA analysis process consists of three main steps, as shown in Figure 1–5:

- **Pre-processing:** All input data for the analysis is prepared, such as material properties, loads, and restraints.

- **Solution:** The model is checked for errors, and the analysis computation is performed.

- **Post-processing:** The analysis results are reviewed and verified. A report is prepared.

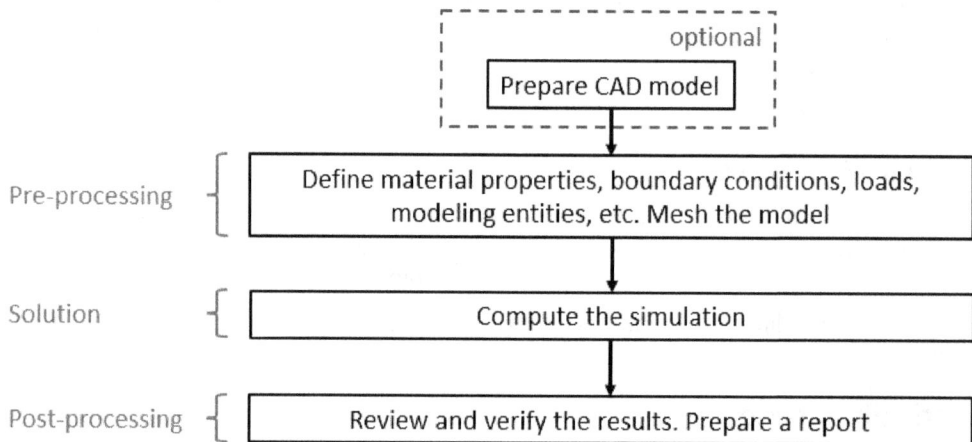

Figure 1–5

The CAD model preparation step is optional. It might not be required, depending on the complexity of the model.

1.8 CAD Model Preparation

A CAD model is developed to provide detailed information for manufacturing. All of the required information related to fillets, rounds, holes, and threads must be included. Processing steps and surface finishes are indicated, and dimensions are fully specified.

A FEA model is developed to determine model behavior under a specific set of loading and boundary conditions. To analyze a model effectively, a FEA model is often different from a model developed for manufacturing. The symmetry of a model can often be exploited. Minor features, such as rounds, fillets, chamfers, and holes, can often be ignored unless they are expected to have a large effect on the result. Therefore, the general recommendation is to use the simplest model possible that is going to yield reliable results at the lowest computational time and cost.

In the example shown in Figure 1−6, the area of interest is the stress in the weld between two pipes due to high pressure. The FEA model for the component is shown on the right. In this case, the symmetry of the component (1/2 of the component) is used for the FEA model. The minor rounds, fillets, chamfers, and holes are also ignored.

Note that the FEA model would be different if the area of interest was the stress at the intersection of lips and pipes.

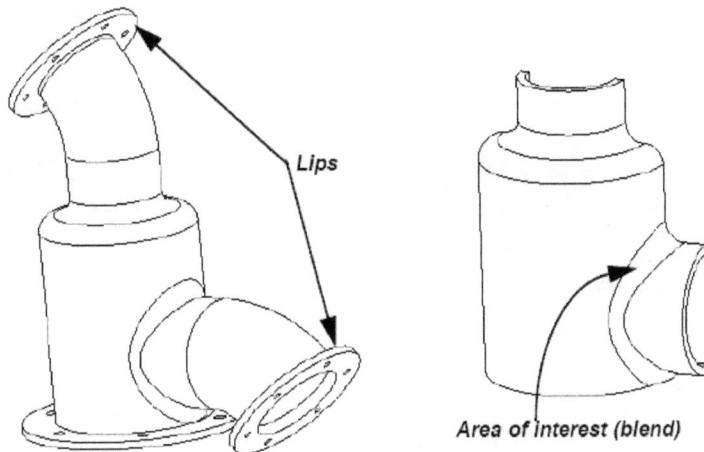

Lips

Area of interest (blend)

Figure 1−6

It must be emphasized that CAD model simplification is **optional**. If your model is not overly complex, and could be computed within a reasonable time, it is best to solve it "as is", without any simplification or defeaturing.

Chapter

2

Basic Structural Simulation

In this chapter, you learn about the tools and processes required to setup your model for a basic static stress analysis. You also learn how to run the computation and then view the results.

Learning Objectives

- Understand the Finite Element Analysis (FEA) process.
- Import and prepare CAD model.
- Launch the Linear Structural Validation app.
- Apply materials.
- Mesh the model.
- Apply boundary conditions and loads.
- Run the analysis.
- Visualize the simulation results.
- Create analysis report.

2.1 Simulation Process in Linear Structural Validation App

The simulation process in Linear Structural Validation (LSV) app contains three different components: pre-processing, computation, and post-processing. Each component contains several steps, as shown in Figure 2–1.

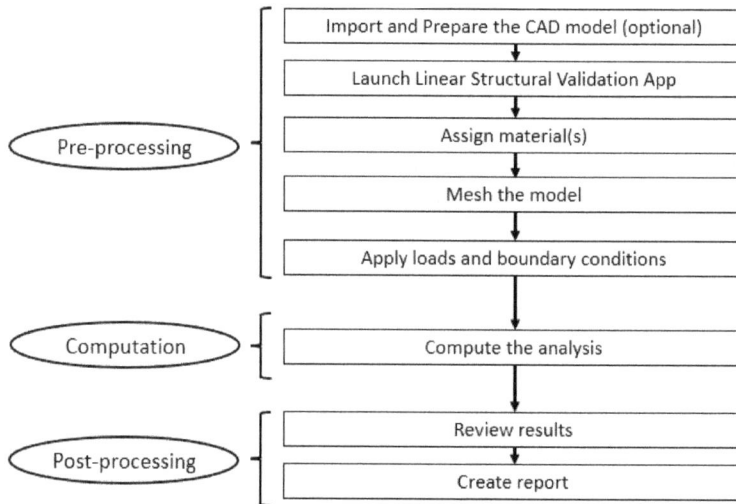

Figure 2–1

The pre-processing involves preparing all the data necessary for the simulation, such as mesh, material properties, loads, restraints, etc. This stage may optionally involve CAD model import and preparation, such as simplification and defeaturing.

The computation stage is a batch-like process. Once the model is prepared and checked for errors, the computation is done by the FEA solver automatically, without any user involvement. Computation time may vary from seconds to hours to days. The major contributing factor is the number of finite elements in the model, and therefore care should be taken as not to create a mesh with too many elements.

The post-processing stage involves visualization and validation of the analysis results. Should the accuracy of the results be inadequate, the user might have to go back to the pre-processing stage and modify the model, such as adjust the mesh, modify the simulation features, etc., and then re-compute the analysis and check the results again. This process may take several iterations, until the desired accuracy is attained.

Lastly, once the analysis is validated, the analysis report is issued.

2.2 Importing and Preparing CAD Model

If not yet stored in the 3DEXPERIENCE PLM database, geometry for the simulation can be imported using many different formats, as shown in Figure 2–2.

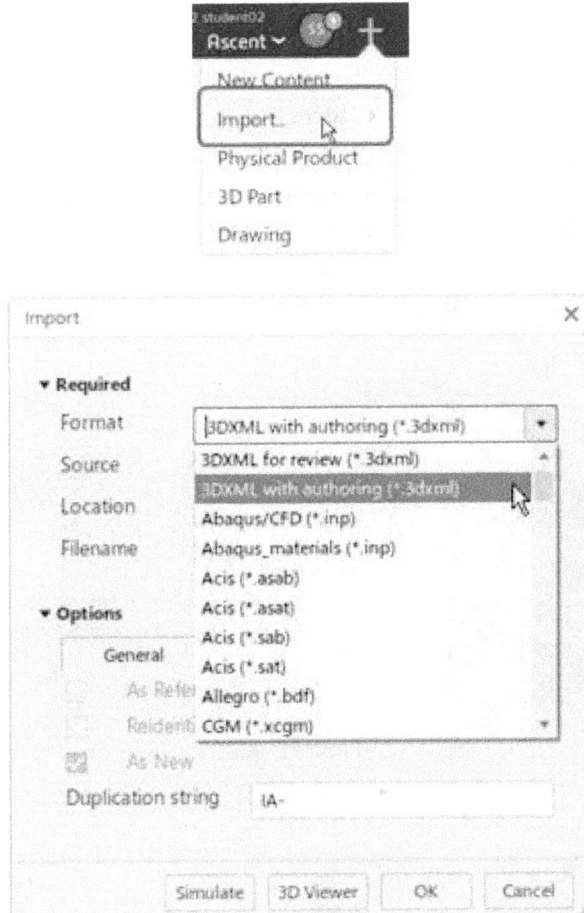

Figure 2–2

When importing the geometry, pay attention to the model units. The imported geometry dimensions will be interpreted by the platform according to the current units as set in **Preferences>Common Preferences>Parameters, Measures, and Units** (default is **mm**).

Once imported, you can verify the model's dimensions using the (Measure Item) or (Measure Between) tools.

To migrate models from CATIA V4 or V5 to the 3DEXPERIENCE platform, select **Add>Import>CATIA File**, as shown in Figure 2−3.

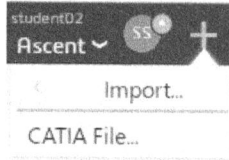

Figure 2−3

Be aware that small geometric features in the analysis model will need small mesh size to capture the details, which can lead to large meshes and long simulation times. It is recommended that you remove small features and details that are not needed for the simulation.

For example, lettering and embossing should be removed from the geometry, as shown in Figure 2−4.

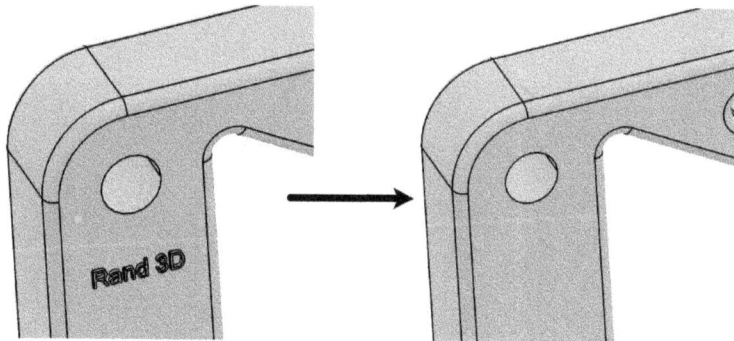

Figure 2−4

2.3 Launching Linear Structural Validation App

To access the app, select the outer ring of the Compass and search for **Linear Structural Validation**, as shown in Figure 2–5. Note that if this app is not found, this means you have not been assigned an appropriate 3DEXPERIENCE role.

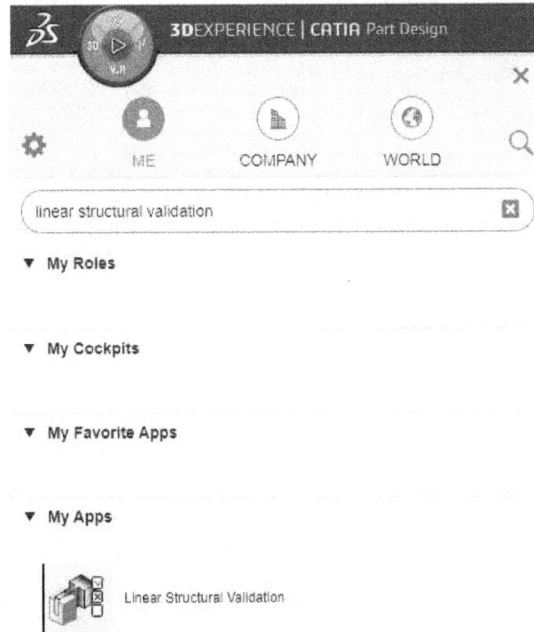

Figure 2–5

The *Simulation Initialization* dialog box opens, as shown in Figure 2–6. Select the *Analysis type* from the list and click **OK** to enter the app.

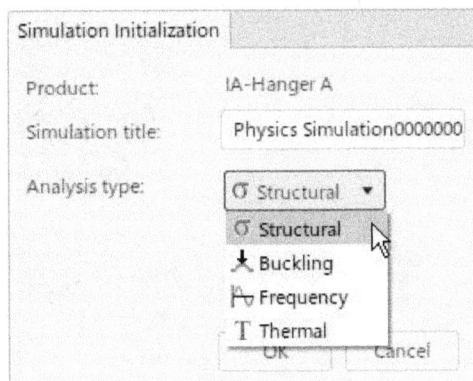

Figure 2–6

The simulation document consists of three containers, as shown in Figure 2-7.

- **Model**: Contains the model geometry, finite element mesh, and material properties
- **Scenario**: Contains various simulation features, such as loads, boundary conditions, and connections
- **Result**: Contains simulation results and plots

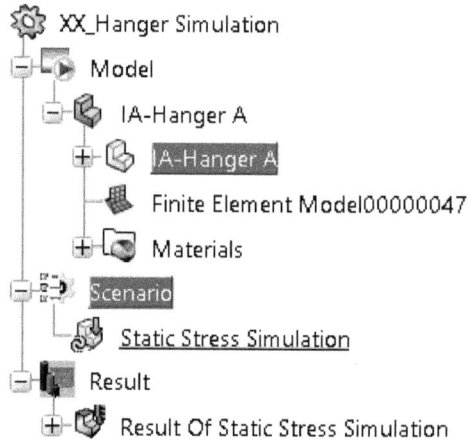

Figure 2-7

2.4 Applying Materials

Before performing a simulation, a material must be applied to all parts in the model. A material characterizes, among other things, the part's mechanical properties (elasticity, plasticity, etc.) as well as its visual appearance, which is done using material *domains*. The typical material domains include *Appearance*, *Simulation*, and *Drafting*.

The material models used in the Structural analysis are captured in the *Simulation* domain. If a material doesn't have the Simulation domain, it is not valid for simulation.

A material can be created in the 3DEXPERIENCE platform from the **Material Definition** app.

Multiple mechanical properties and behaviors can be defined for a material, as shown in Figure 2–8. The following material properties are required for the LSV app: Density, Proof (Yield) Stress, Young's Modulus, Poisson's Ratio.

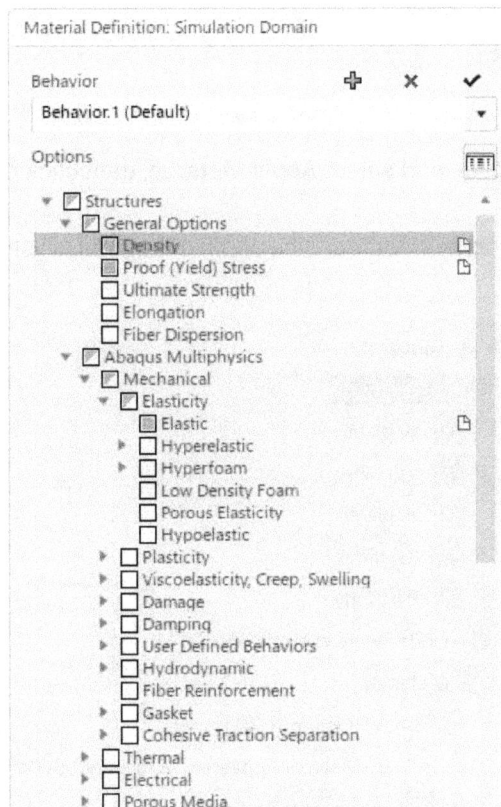

Figure 2–8

There are two applications in which you can apply the material for the analysis:

*   In the Part Design app

*   In the LSV app

Applying Material in the Part Design app

- In the *Tools* section of the Action Bar, click ⬭ (Material Browser). The window with the list of materials in the database opens as shown in Figure 2-9.

3DSearch - Search results for "flattenedtaxonomies:types/CATMatReference"

2 Re...   🕔   ℹ   ⫬ Relevancy ▼   ⊞   ⌄

🔵 XX_Steel
student02 student02 | | student02 student02   ⌄

🔵 IA-Aluminium A
student02 student02 | 06/03/2023 | ⌄

Figure 2-9

- Select a material, right-click and select **Apply Material**, then click on the part body.

- Click ✔ (Close) in the context toolbar. The applied material is listed in the tree, as shown in Figure 2-10.

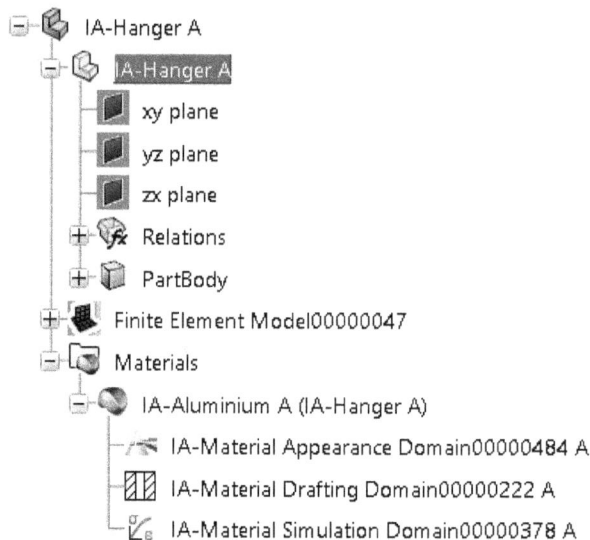

- IA-Hanger A
  - IA-Hanger A
    - xy plane
    - yz plane
    - zx plane
    - Relations
    - PartBody
  - Finite Element Model00000047
  - Materials
    - IA-Aluminium A (IA-Hanger A)
      - IA-Material Appearance Domain00000484 A
      - IA-Material Drafting Domain00000222 A
      - IA-Material Simulation Domain00000378 A

Figure 2-10

Applying Material in the Linear Structural Validation app

- In the *Setup* section of the Action Bar, click 🔵 (Material Palette).

- The *Material Palette* dialog box opens. In the drop-down menu in the top left corner of the dialog box, select whether to browse **All** materials, the **Recently Applied**, or the **In-Session** materials, as shown in Figure 2–11.

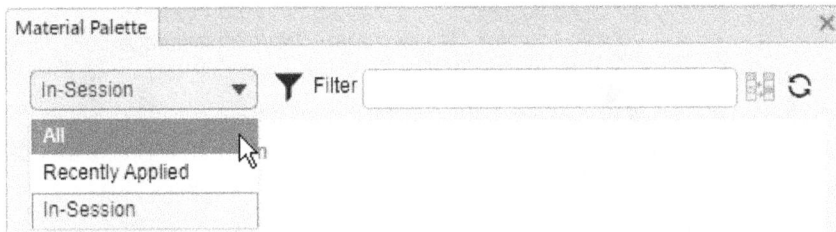

Figure 2–11

- Drag and drop a material from the Material Palette onto the part body. Click ✔ (Close) in the context toolbar to confirm the operation.

2.5 Simulation Assistant

The LSV app provides the Assistant tool, which serves as the simulation guide. To open the Assistant, select ⊞ (Assistant) in the *Setup* section of the Action Bar. The *Assistant* dialog box displays, as shown in Figure 2-12.

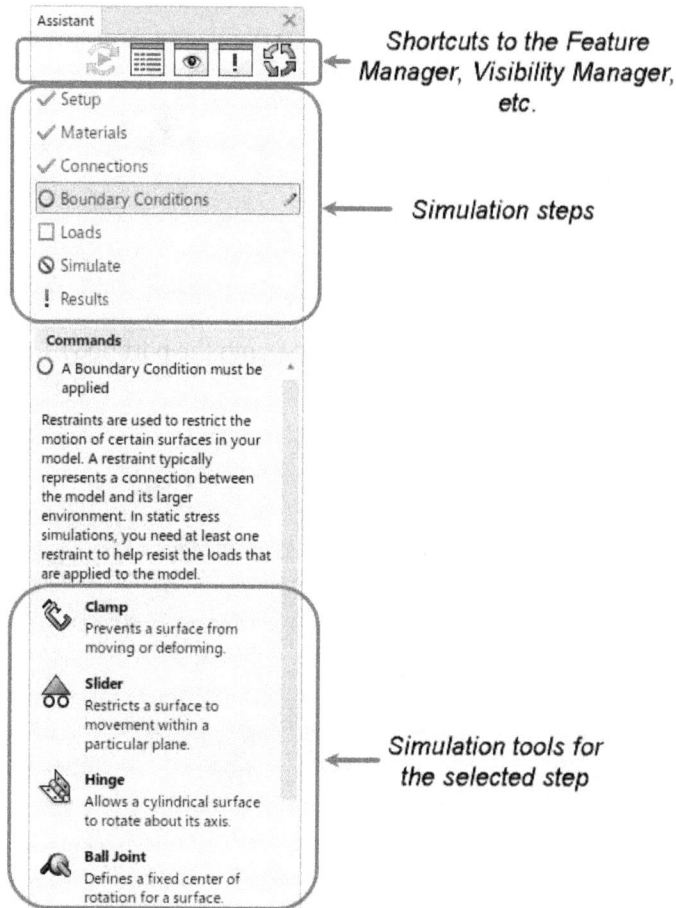

Figure 2-12

The Assistant displays the list of the simulation steps, with various symbols indicating the state of the step (i.e., the green checkmark means the step has been completed). Once a simulation step is selected in the list, the bottom section of the dialog box displays the most frequently used tools and commands for that step. Lastly, the very top section of the dialog box contains the shortcut icons for Update, Feature Manager, Visibility Manager, etc.

Using the Assistant, however, is optional. All the simulation tools can also be found in the Action Bar.

2.6 Meshing the Model

LSV app automatically creates a finite element model for the part upon launching the app, as shown in Figure 2-13.

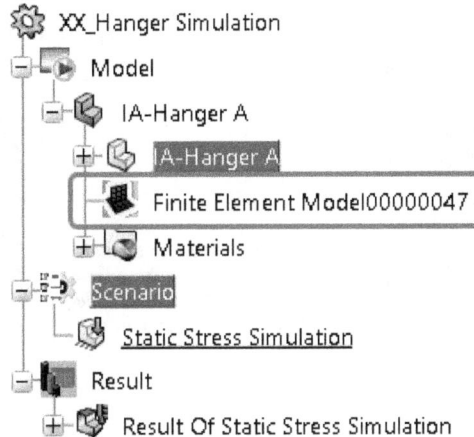

Figure 2-13

Usually, you can run your simulation without changing the default mesh specification. However, mesh parameters can be modified if needed, such as when desiring a better analysis accuracy.

There are two global meshing parameters:

*   **Element Size**: This is the characteristic size of the elements in the mesh, which is defined as the length of the longest edge in an element, as shown in Figure 2-14. Using a smaller element size results in a greater number of elements in the model and thus in a more accurate analysis, but at the cost of longer computation time. The recommendation is to try to strike a balance between the two – use the fewest number of elements in the model that would yield acceptable analysis accuracy.

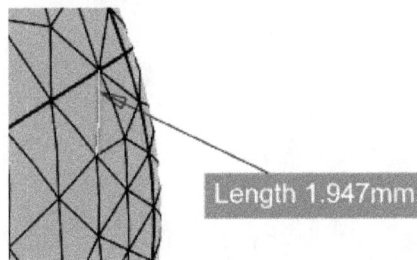

Figure 2-14

- **Elements per Hole**: This specifies the minimum number of elements around the holes, fillets, or other rounded surfaces, as shown in Figure 2–15. A higher number results in smaller elements, thus better accuracy around holes and other curved features.

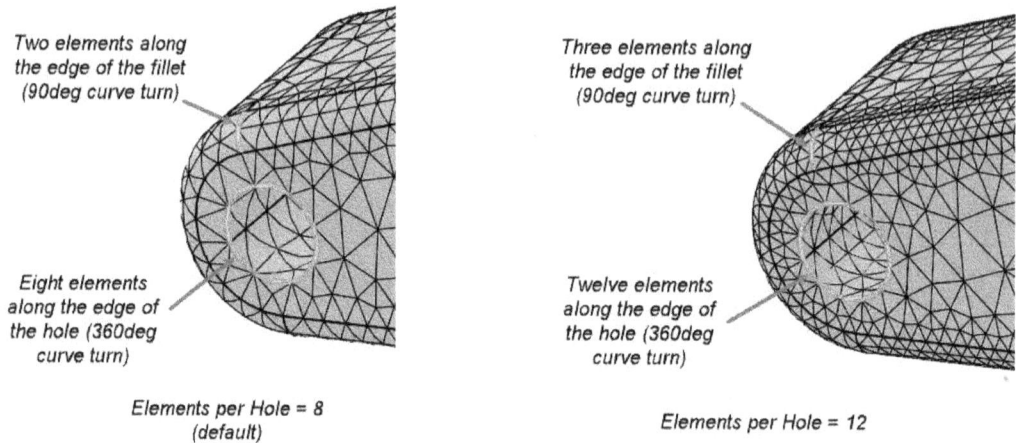

Two elements along the edge of the fillet (90deg curve turn)

Eight elements along the edge of the hole (360deg curve turn)

Elements per Hole = 8 (default)

Three elements along the edge of the fillet (90deg curve turn)

Twelve elements along the edge of the hole (360deg curve turn)

Elements per Hole = 12

Figure 2–15

To modify the meshing parameters, select (Mesh Specifications) in the *Mesh* section of the Action Bar. The *Mesh Specifications* dialog box opens, as shown in Figure 2–16.

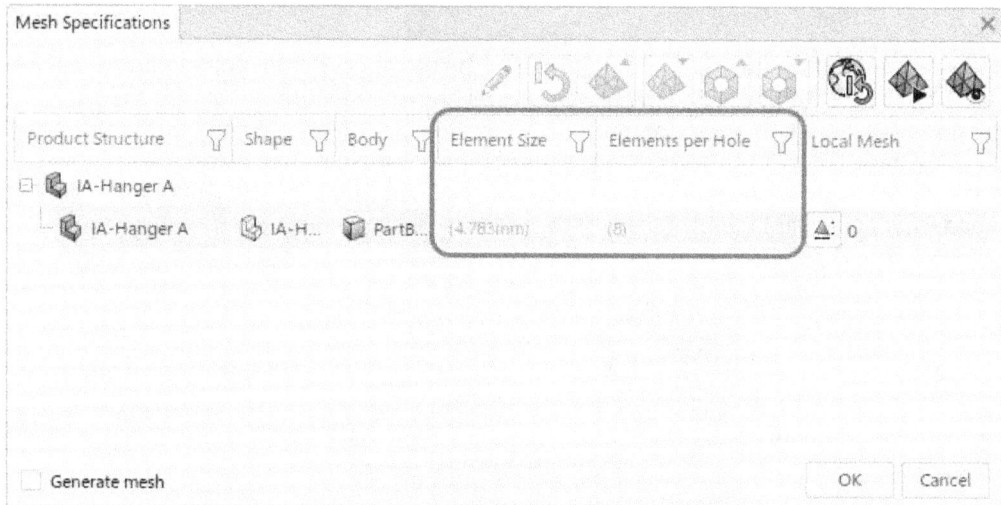

Figure 2–16

To generate the mesh, select (Generate Mesh) in the *Mesh* section of the Action Bar. Once generated, the mesh is displayed as shown in Figure 2-17.

Figure 2-17

To hide or show the mesh, select (Hide/Show Mesh) in the Action Bar.

2.7 Applying Loads and Boundary Conditions

Simulation entities such as Loads and Boundary Conditions in LSV cannot be applied directly to the mesh. Instead, they must be applied to the model geometry, such as surfaces, edges, or points.

If you try to apply simulation entities to the mesh, the mouse cursor displays the "no entry" symbol, as shown in Figure 2–18. Hide the mesh to return to the model view, then apply the load or boundary condition to the part geometry.

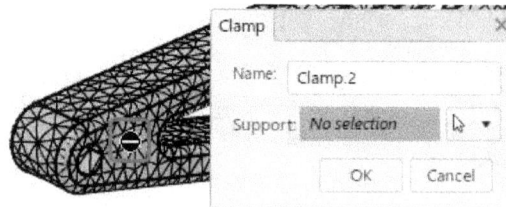

Figure 2–18

Boundary conditions restrict the motion of your model and are necessary to resist loads. Boundary conditions are used to simulate supports, such as when the part is attached to a solid foundation, or to model conditions such as symmetry. The following table presents the summary of the boundary conditions that can be created in LSV.

Restraint	Description
Clamp	Models "immovable" boundary condition, with all motions restrained.
Fixed Displacement	Allows restraining a surface in any of the coordinate directions.
Applied Translation	Applies a prescribed non-zero displacement.
Planar Symmetry	Reduces model size for models with *reflective* symmetry, in which geometry, loads, and boundary conditions on one side of the symmetry plane is mirrored on the other side of the symmetry plane.
Ball Joint	Models a ball joint.
Slider	Restrains motion in normal to the planar surface direction, while allowing the surface to translate in tangent directions.
Hinge	Allows rotation of a cylindrical surface about its axis, while restraining all other degrees of freedom.

Loads are intended to simulate the external loading conditions in your model, from applied weights and pressures to interactions with other parts. The analysis then calculates how your model responds to the applied loads. The following table presents the summary of the loads that can be applied in LSV.

Load	Description
Pressure	Applies pressure load on surfaces, in normal to the surface direction.
Force	Applies either a distributed force on a surface, or a concentrated force on a point.
Gravity	Applies gravity load.
Centrifugal Force	Applies centrifugal load.
Remote Force	Transmits force from a point to a surface.
Remote Torque	Applies a twisting load.
Bearing Load	Simulates contact load applied to a cylindrical hole by a rigid pin or shaft.

2.8 Feature Manager

The Feature Manager allows you to review, edit, or hide simulation features. To open the

Feature Manager, select ⊞ (Feature Manager) either in the *Assistant* dialog box, or in the *Setup* section of the Action Bar. The *Feature Manager* dialog box opens, as shown in Figure 2–19

- Select a feature to highlight the geometry in the model.

- Double-click to edit the definition, such as modify the magnitude of the load.

- Use the Hide/Show icon to hide or show a feature.

- Select multiple features and right-click to manage multiple items.

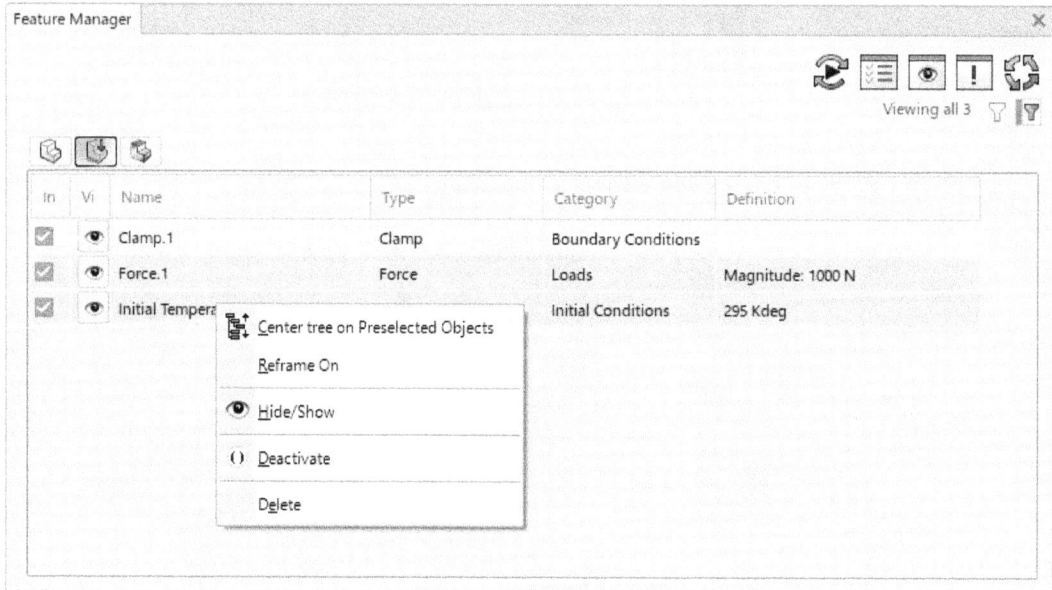

Figure 2–19

2.9 Visibility Manager

The Visibility Manager allows you to control the display status of various items in your model.

To open the Visibility Manager, select ⬚ (Visibility Manager) in the *Assistant* dialog box. The *Visibility Manager* dialog box opens, as shown in Figure 2–20.

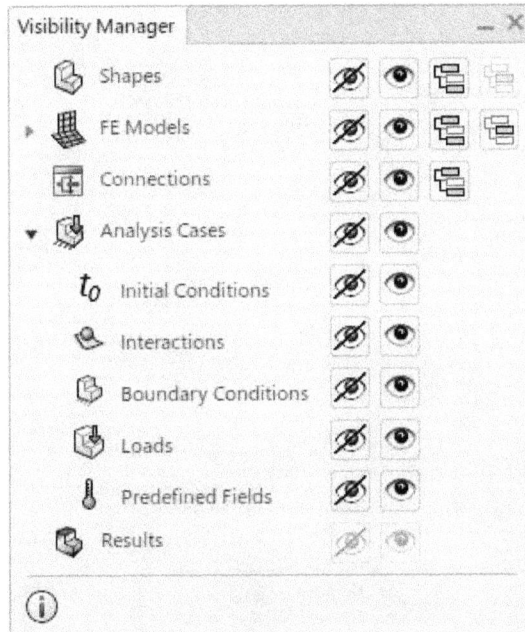

Figure 2–20

2.10 Computation

Once you have completed all the pre-processing steps, which is indicated by green checkmarks in the *Assistant* dialog box, you can compute the simulation.

To start the computation, select 🔁 (Simulate) either in the *Assistant* dialog box, as shown in Figure 2–21, or in the *Results* section of the Action Bar.

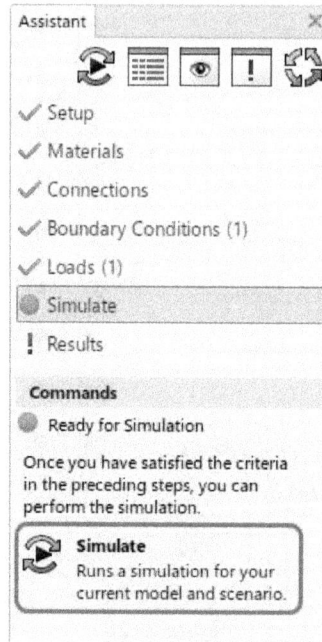

Figure 2–21

The *Simulate* dialog box opens, as shown in Figure 2–22. Select whether to overwrite the previous analysis result, if any, and leave all other options at defaults.

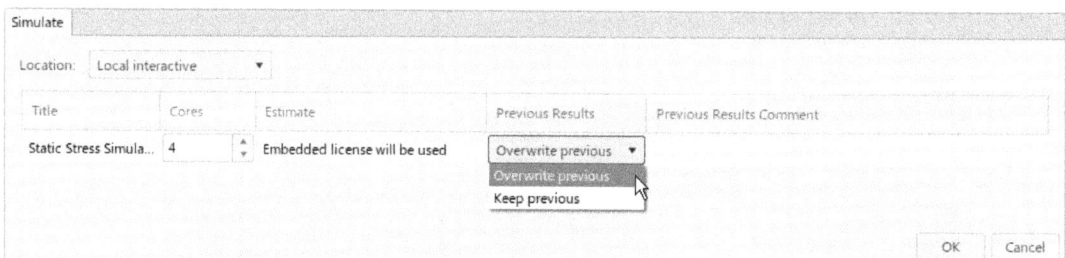

Figure 2–22

Click **OK** to proceed with the computation. The *Simulation Status* dialog box opens, informing you of the progress. Once the computation is completed, the message in the dialog box displays "Static Stress Simulation completed", as shown in Figure 2–23. Close the *Simulation Status* dialog box.

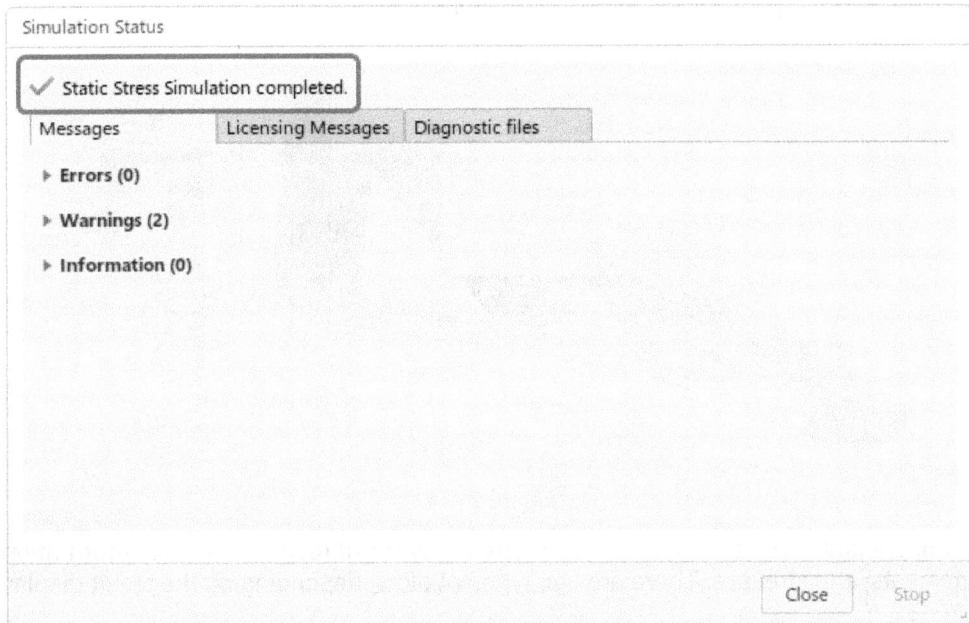

Simulation Status

✓ Static Stress Simulation completed.

Messages	Licensing Messages	Diagnostic files

▶ **Errors (0)**

▶ **Warnings (2)**

▶ **Information (0)**

Close   Stop

Figure 2–23

2.11 Results Visualization

Once the simulation is computed, the *Von Mises stress* result is automatically displayed. From there, you can visualize a different result plot using the *Plot* drop-down menu that usually floats in the middle of the screen, as shown in Figure 2-24.

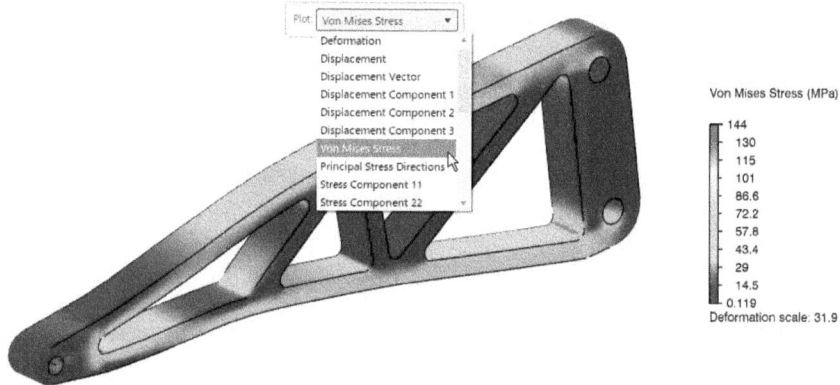

Figure 2-24

The LSV app enables you to visualize many different types of results, such as deformations, displacements, and stresses. There are two types of plots, depending on the result displayed:

- **Color plot**: The surface of the model is colored, with the color coding indicating the magnitude of the result.

- **Vector plot**: The plot uses a combination of color coding and arrows to indicate the magnitude and direction of the results.

The summary is presented in the following table.

Result Plot	Description
Deformation	Deformed model
Displacement	Color plot of displacement magnitude
Displacement Vectors	Vector plot of model displacements
Displacement Component 1	Color plot of displacement in X-direction
Displacement Component 2	Color plot of displacement in Y-direction
Displacement Component 3	Color plot of displacement in Z-direction
Von Mises Stress	Color plot of Von Mises stress
Principal Stress Directions	Vector plot of principal stresses
Stress Component 11	Color plot of normal stress Sxx

Result Plot	Description
Stress Component 22	Color plot of normal stress Syy
Stress Component 33	Color plot of normal stress Szz
Stress Component 12	Color plot of shear stress Txy
Stress Component 13	Color plot of shear stress Txz
Stress Component 23	Color plot of shear stress Tyz
Factor of Safety	Color plot of factor of safety, calculated as: <Materia Yield (Proof) Stress> / <Von Mises Stress>
Compression - Tension	Color plot of tension and compression areas
Reaction Force	Color plot of reaction force magnitude at boundary conditions
Reaction Force Vector	Vector plot of reaction force at boundary conditions
Reaction Force Component 1	Color plot of reaction force Fx at boundary conditions
Reaction Force Component 2	Color plot of reaction force Fy at boundary conditions
Reaction Force Component 3	Color plot of reaction force Fz at boundary conditions
Simulation Accuracy (%)	Color plot of simulation accuracy, calculated as: <Energy Density Error> / <Maximum Energy Density>

Once a result plot is displayed, double-clicking it opens the *Contour Plot* dialog box, which reveals additional visualization options such as deformation scale factor, display threshold, and edge visualization, as shown in Figure 2–25.

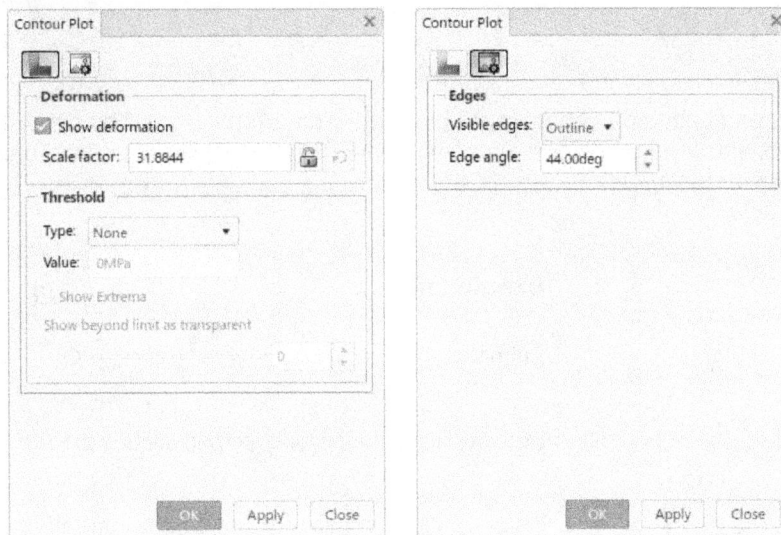

Figure 2–25

You can also customize the result plot transparency, whether to show the original geometry, etc., by clicking (Rendering Settings) in the Action Bar, as shown in Figure 2-26.

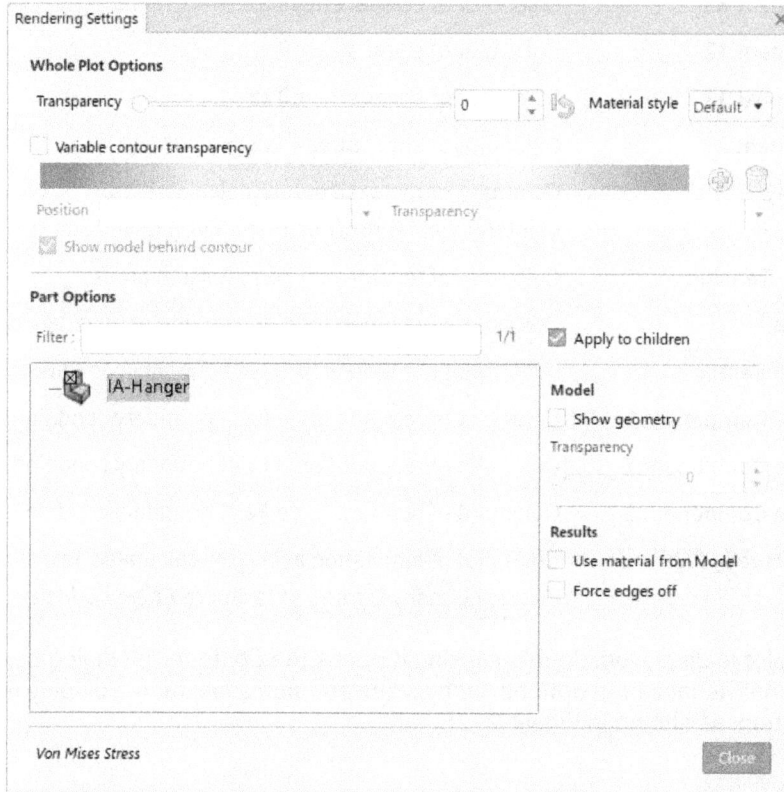

Figure 2-26

In addition, the result plots can be animated for better understanding of model deformation, cross-sectioned with a cut plane, annotated with the minimum and maximum labels, etc. These tools are located in the *Results* section of the Action Bar, and their summary is presented in the following table.

Tool	Description
Play Animation	Animates the result image
View Cut	Cuts the result image with a cross-section plane
Show Min/Max Values	Finds locations of minimum and maximum values in the image

2.12 Result Sensors

The result sensors are maximum quantities for the following results:

- Displacement Magnitude

- Von Mises Stress

- Reaction Force

To display the sensors, open the Feature Manager, and make the *Results* section active. The list in the dialog box displays the result sensors, as shown in Figure 2–27.

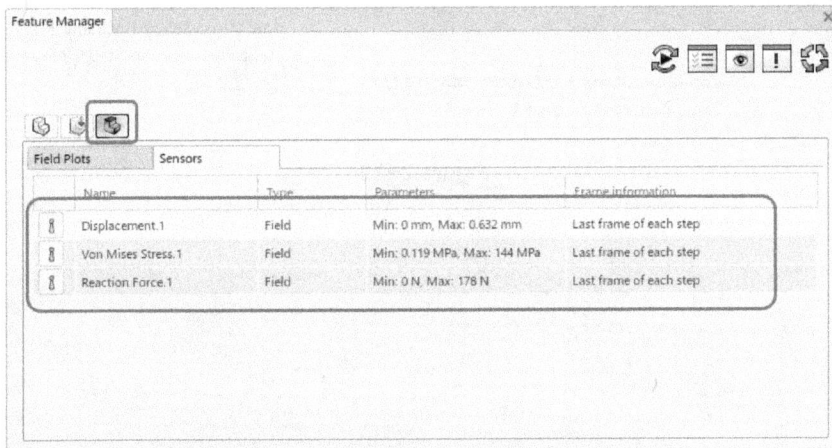

Figure 2–27

To display the sensor, right-click the sensor in the list and select **Show/Hide annotation,** as shown in Figure 2–28.

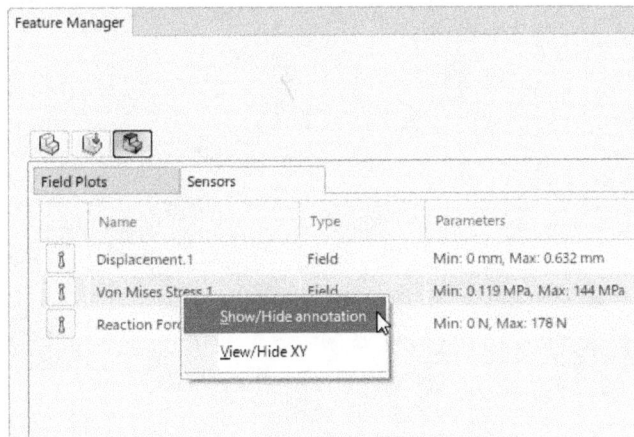

Figure 2–28

The sensor is displayed in the result plot, as shown in Figure 2–29.

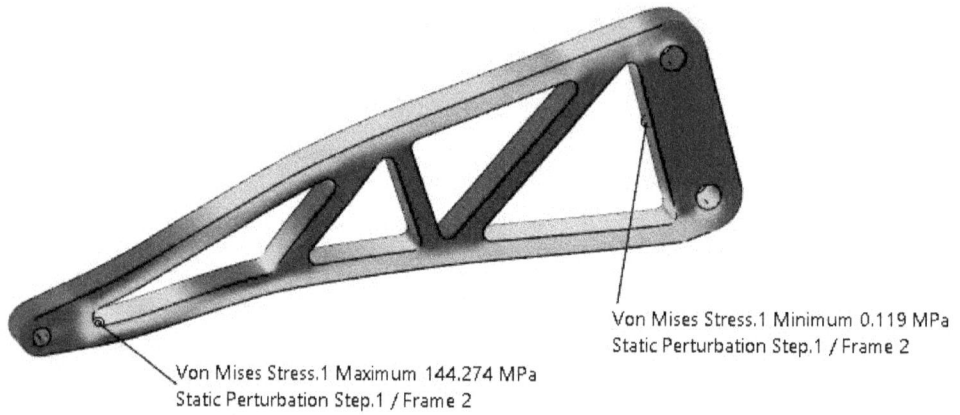

Von Mises Stress.1 Minimum 0.119 MPa
Static Perturbation Step.1 / Frame 2

Von Mises Stress.1 Maximum 144.274 MPa
Static Perturbation Step.1 / Frame 2

Figure 2–29

2.13 Creating a Report

To create the analysis report, click ▢ (Report) in the *Results* section of the Action Bar. The *Report Definition* dialog box opens, as shown in Figure 2–30.

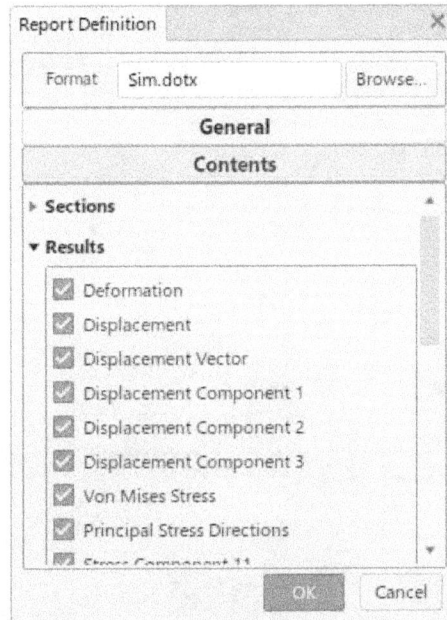

Figure 2–30

If required, click **Browse** and select the report template file.

Select **General**, and enter information such as company name and logo, engineer's name, phone, email, etc., as shown in Figure 2–31.

Figure 2–31

Click **Contents** and select the images you want to include in the report, as shown in Figure 2-32.

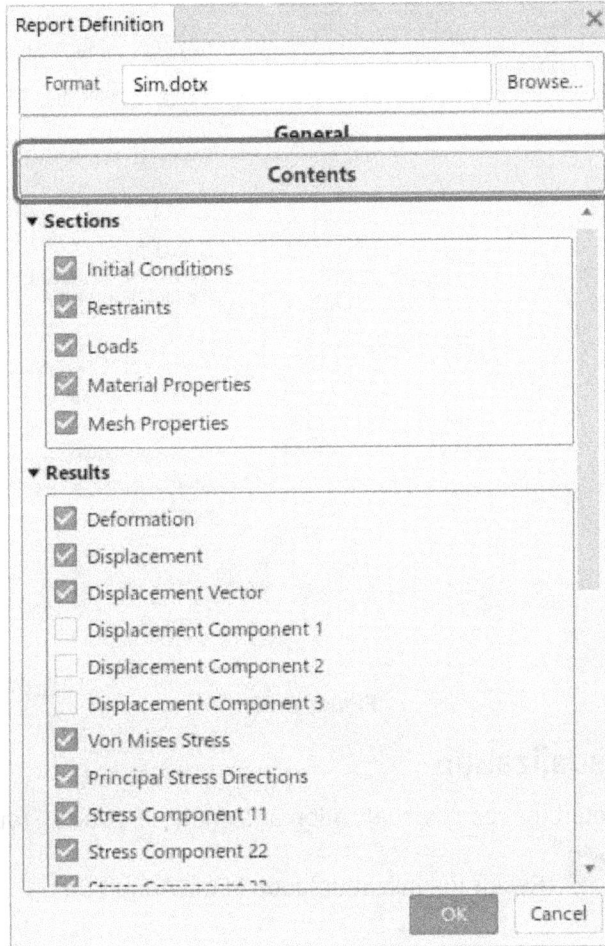

Figure 2-32

Click **OK** to generate and display the report, as shown in Figure 2–33.

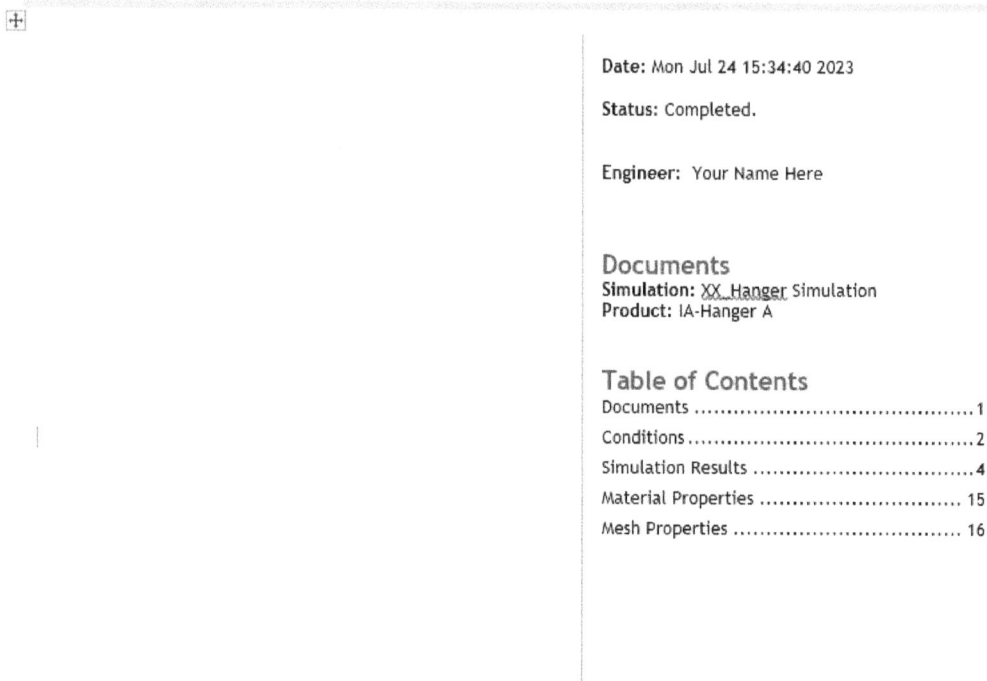

Date: Mon Jul 24 15:34:40 2023

Status: Completed.

Engineer: Your Name Here

Documents
Simulation: XX_Hanger Simulation
Product: IA-Hanger A

Table of Contents

Figure 2–33

Exiting Result Visualization

When you have completed the result visualization and analysis, you can return to the model

view by selecting the ⬚ (Result Visualization) icon in the Action Bar.

Practice 2a
Static Stress Analysis of a Bracket

Practice Objectives

- Apply the material.
- Mesh the model.
- Set up loads and boundary conditions.
- Compute the analysis.
- Display results.
- Modify the part dimensions and recompute the analysis.
- Create analysis report.

In this practice, you will set up and run a static stress analysis on a simple bracket part shown in Figure 2-34. You will also examine the analysis results, make a design change, and re-run the analysis to validate the design change.

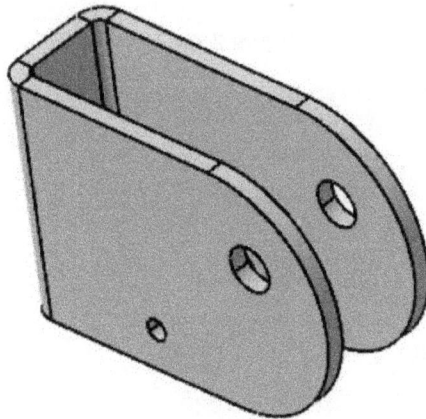

Figure 2-34

Task 1: Open the part.

1. Import with your initials and open **UFR-723_02.3dxml**.

2. Set the View Mode as ⬭ (Shading with Sharp and Smooth Edges). The part displays as shown in Figure 2–35.

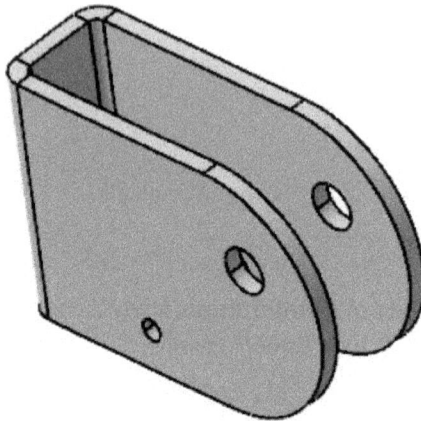

Figure 2–35

3. Select **Preferences>Common Preferences>Parameters, Measures, and Units>Units** and set the units as follows:

   - *Length:* **Millimeter (mm)**
   - *Force:* **Newton (N)**
   - *Moment:* **Newton x Meter (Nxm)**
   - *Pressure:* **Megapascal (MPa)**
   - *Stress:* **Megapascal (MPa)**

Task 2: Launch the Linear Structural Validation app.

1. Click the outer ring of the Compass, and in the list of *My Apps,* select **Linear Structural Validation**, as shown in Figure 2−36.

   Note: If this app is not available, this means that you do not have a proper license.

Figure 2−36

2. In the *Physics Simulation* dialog box, enter **<*Your Initials*>_UFR Bracket Analysis** for the *Title* and click **OK**, as shown in Figure 2−37.

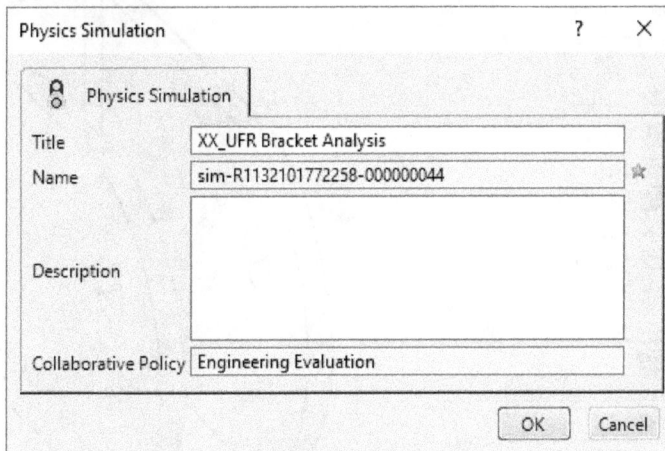

Figure 2−37

3. In the *Simulation Initialization* dialog box that opens, select **Structural** for *Analysis* type, and click **OK**, as shown in Figure 2–38.

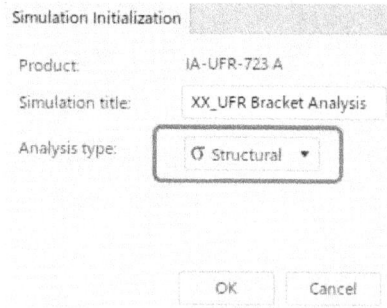

Simulation Initialization

Product: IA-UFR-723 A

Simulation title: XX_UFR Bracket Analysis

Analysis type: σ Structural ▾

OK   Cancel

Figure 2–38

4. 3DEXPERIENCE opens a new window, named *UFR Bracket Analysis*.

5. Examine the specification tree and note that the following simulation entities have been created, as shown in Figure 2–39:

- **Finite Element Model**: This is the part mesh.

- **Static Stress Simulation**: This is the container for the boundary conditions and loads. Note that it is empty since you have not applied any loads or boundary conditions yet.

- **Result Of Static Stress Simulation**: This is the container for the analysis results.

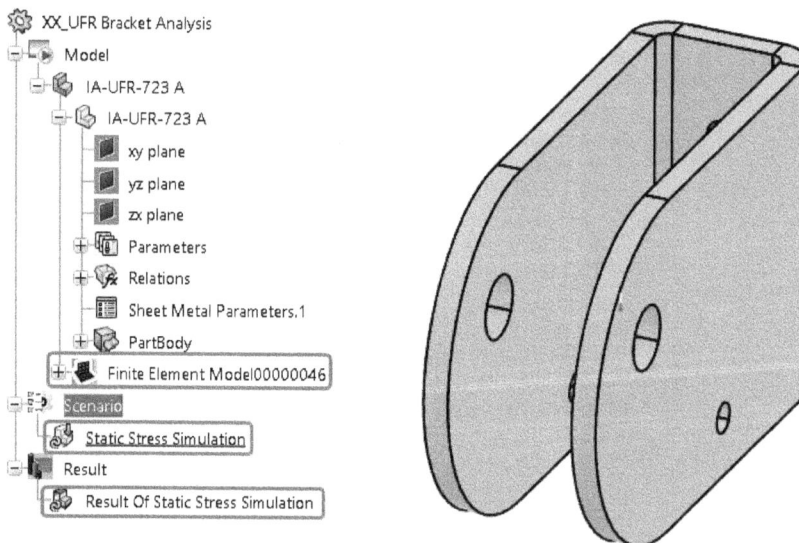

Figure 2–39

Task 3: Create material definition.

Before performing the simulation, a material must be applied to the part. The material definition can be created prior to running a simulation, then selected from the 3DEXPERIENCE database. Alternatively, the material definition can be created during the analysis setup.

In this task, you will create a new material definition for the bracket.

1. Click the outer ring of the Compass, and in the list of *My Apps,* select the **Material Definition** app.

2. In the *Core Material* dialog box, enter **<Your Initials>_Aluminum** for the *Title* and click **OK**, as shown in Figure 2−40.

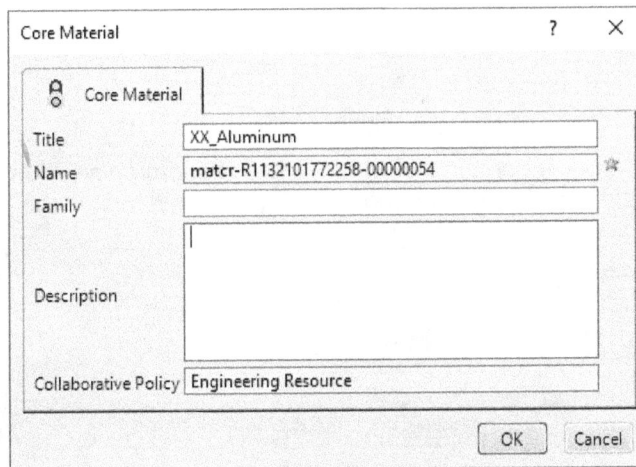

Figure 2−40

3. The *Material Editor* window opens. Select **Aluminum** material in the tree, and in the Action Bar, click (Add Domain).

4. In the *Add Domain* dialog box, select **Simulation Domain** and click **OK**, as shown in Figure 2–41.

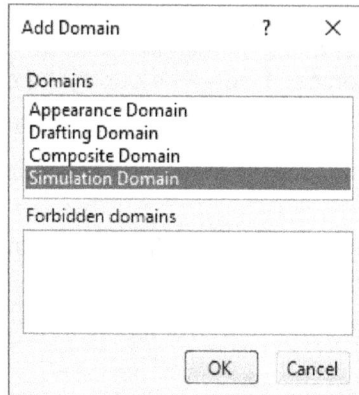

Figure 2–41

5. In the *Material Simulation Domain* dialog box, enter **<*Your Initials*>_Aluminum Simulation Domain** for the *Title* and click **OK**, as shown in Figure 2–42.

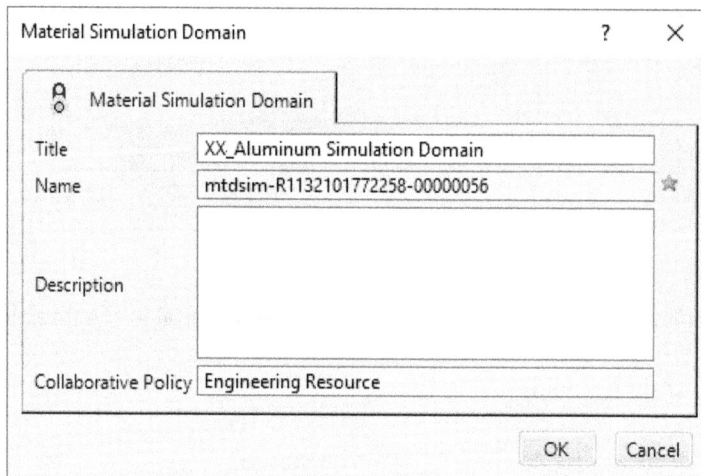

Figure 2–42

6. Double-click **Aluminum Simulation Domain** in the tree. The *Material Definition: Simulation Domain* dialog box opens, as shown in Figure 2–43.

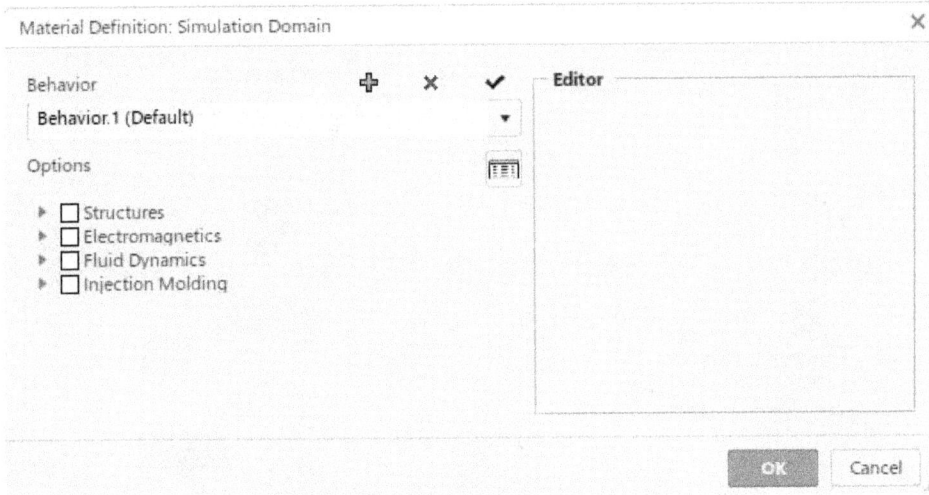

Figure 2–43

7. Expand the *Structures* section and select the **Density** checkbox. Enter **2710kg_m3** as the material density, as shown in Figure 2–44.

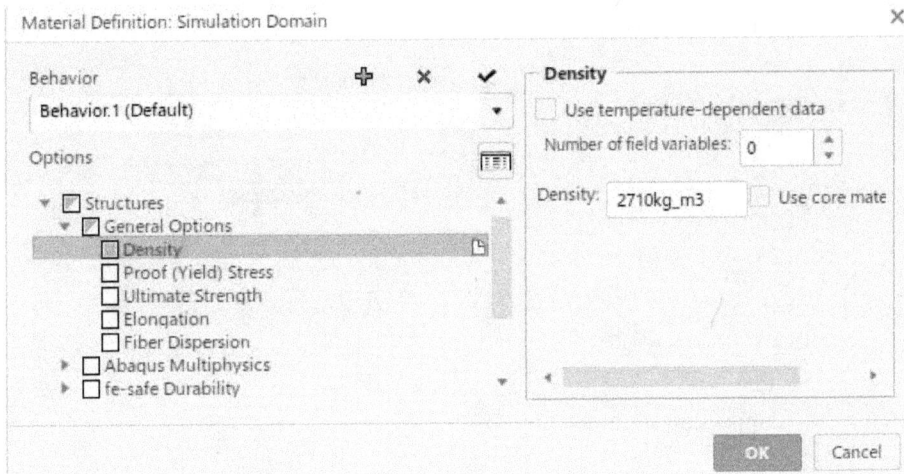

Figure 2–44

8. Select the **Proof (Yield) Stress** checkbox and enter **95MPa** as the material yield stress, as shown in Figure 2-45.

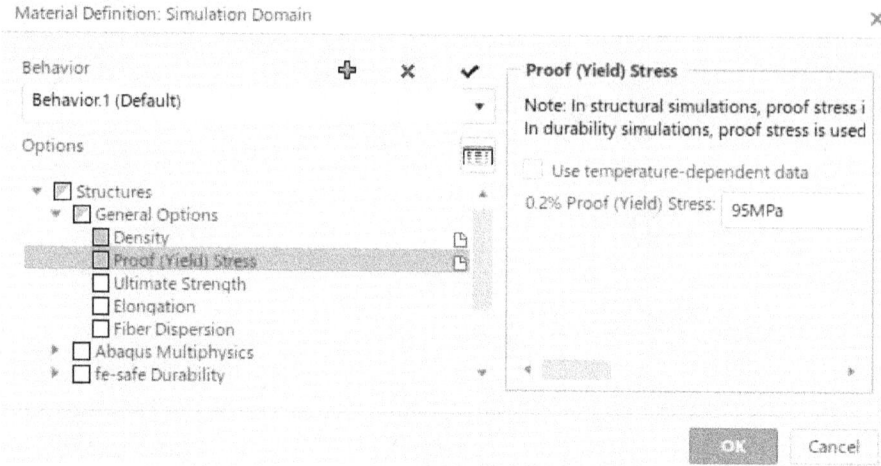

Figure 2-45

9. Expand the *Abaqus Multiphysics>Mechanical>Elasticity* section and select the **Elastic** checkbox. Enter **70000MPa** for the *Young's Modulus* and **0.346** for the *Poisson's Ratio*, as shown in Figure 2-46.

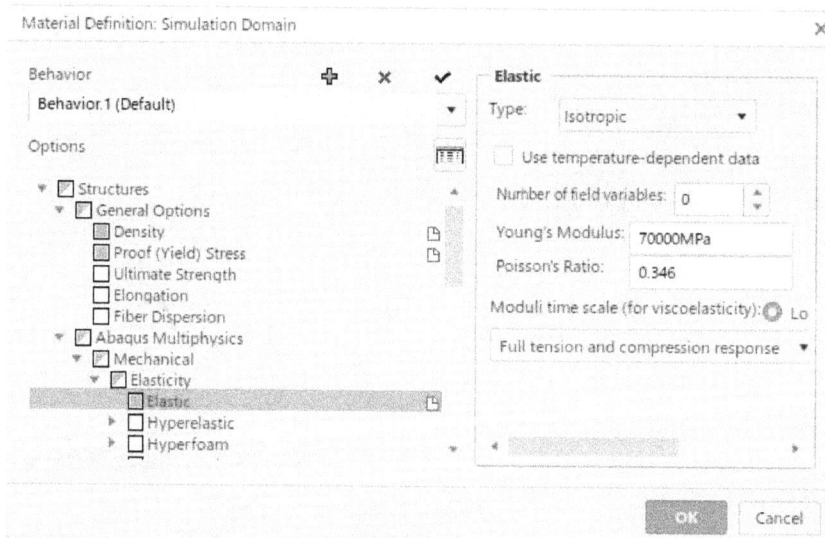

Figure 2-46

10. Click **OK** to complete the material definition.

11. Save the material to the 3DEXPERIENCE database, but do not close the *Material Editor* window.

Task 4: Apply the material.

In this task, you will apply the material to the bracket.

1. Activate the *UFR Bracket Analysis* window.

2. In the *Setup* section of the Action Bar, click ⬤ (Material Palette). In the drop-down menu in the top left corner of the *Material Palette* dialog box, select **In-Session**. The *Material Palette* dialog box opens as shown in Figure 2–47.

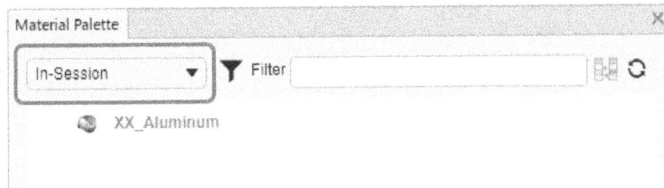

Figure 2–47

3. Drag and drop the **Aluminum** from the *Material Palette* dialog box onto the part body. Click

    ✔ (Close) in the context toolbar to confirm the operation.

4. Close the *Material Palette* dialog box. Note that the applied material displays in the specification tree, as shown in Figure 2–48.

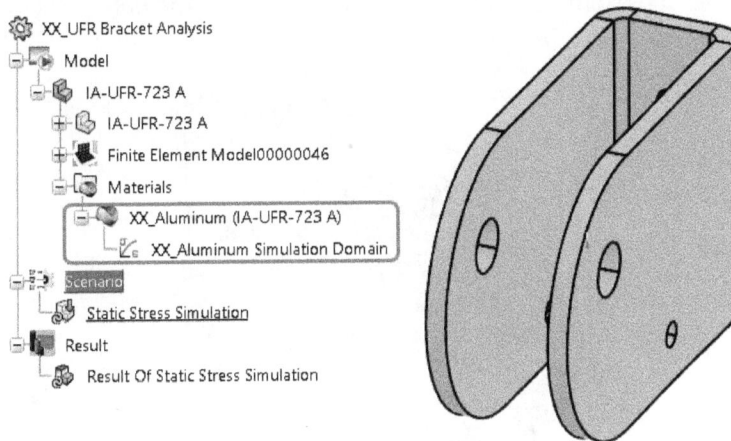

Figure 2–48

Task 5: Mesh the part.

In this task, you will generate and visualize the finite element mesh for the bracket.

1. In the *Mesh* section of the Action Bar, select ◆ (Mesh Specifications). The *Mesh Specifications* dialog box opens, as shown in Figure 2–49, which displays the default mesh size and number of elements per hole.

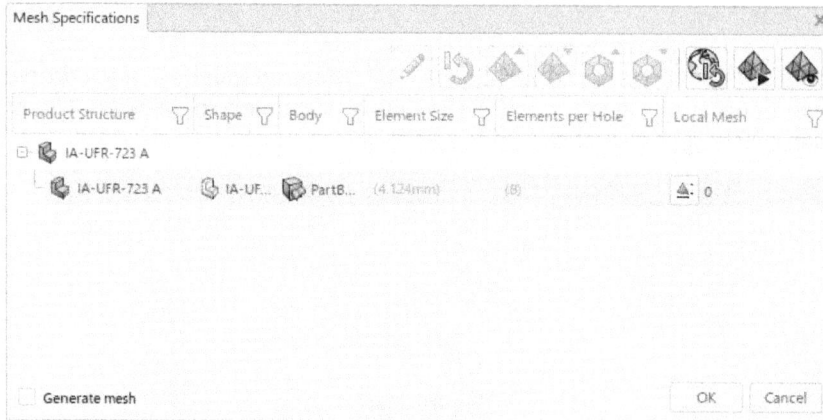

Figure 2–49

2. In this practice, you will use the default element size. Click **OK** to close the *Mesh Specifications* dialog box.

3. Select ◆ (Generate Mesh). The mesh for the part is displayed, as shown in Figure 2–50. Rotate the model and examine the mesh in various areas of the part.

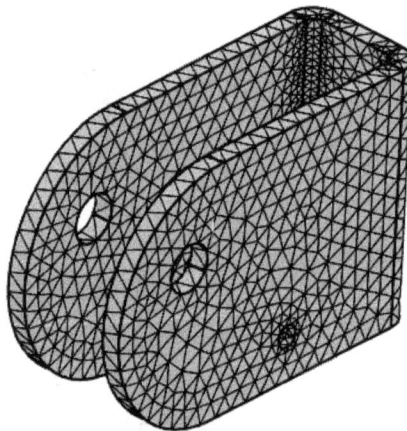

Figure 2–50

4. Select ◆ (Hide/Show Mesh) to hide the mesh.

Task 6: Apply Clamp.

In this task, you will apply the **Clamp** boundary condition to the two holes in the middle of the bracket. This models the bracket being rigidly bolted to the adjoining structure.

In the *Linear Structural Validation* app, loads and boundary conditions can be applied either by selecting relevant icons in the Action Bar, or by using the Simulation Assistant. In this task, you will use the Assistant tool.

1.   In the Action Bar, select ⊞ (Assistant). The *Assistant* dialog box opens, as shown in Figure 2−51.

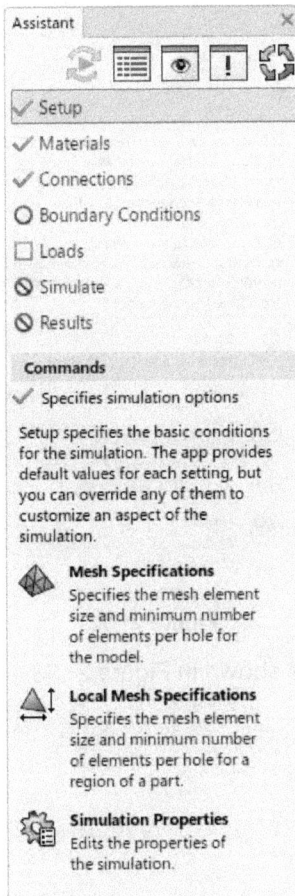

Figure 2−51

2. Select the *Boundary Conditions* section and click ![clamp icon] (Clamp), as shown in Figure 2–52.

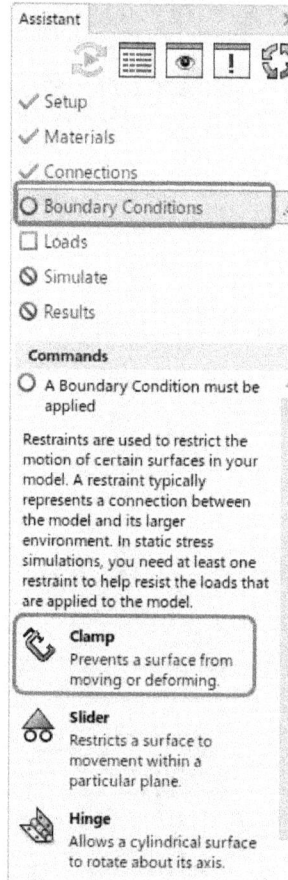

Figure 2–52

3. The *Clamp* dialog box opens, as shown in Figure 2–53.

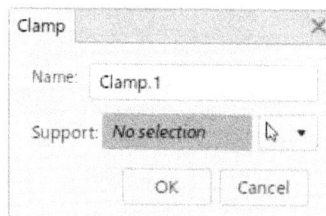

Figure 2–53

4. Select the inside surfaces of the two holes, as shown in Figure 2–54.

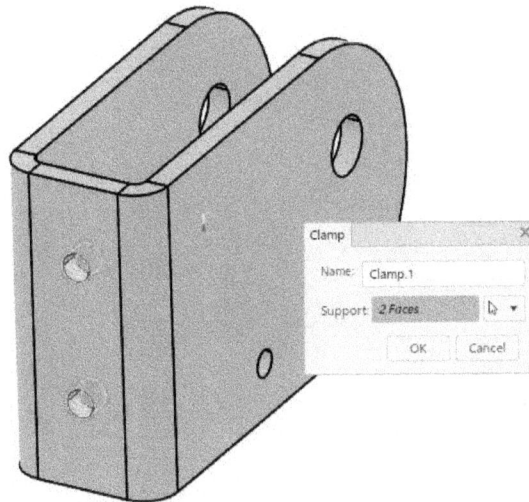

Figure 2–54

5. Click **OK** to close the *Clamp* dialog box.

Task 7: Apply loads.

In this task, you will apply a **500N** vertical force to the bracket.

1. In the *Assistant* dialog box, select the *Loads* section and click ✎ (Force). The *Force* dialog box opens, as shown in Figure 2–55.

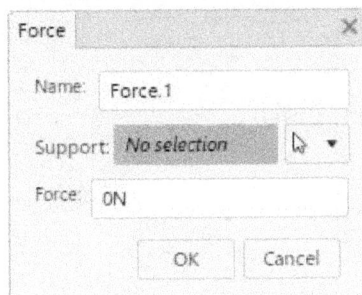

Figure 2–55

2. Select the inside surfaces of both large holes in the flanges of the part.

3. The force direction is always aligned with the **W** axis of the robot. To align the **W** axis of the robot with the **Z** direction in the model, select 👆 (Align Triad Handle with the Global Axis System) in the context toolbar.

4. Enter **-500N** as the *Force* value. The model displays, as shown in Figure 2−56.

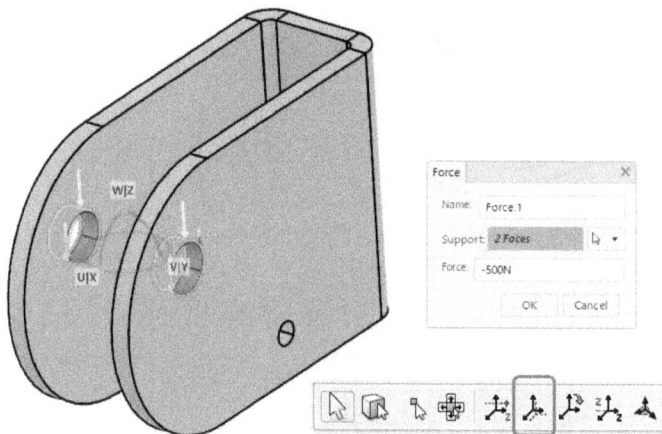

Figure 2−56

5. Click **OK** to close the *Force* dialog box. The model displays as shown in Figure 2−57.

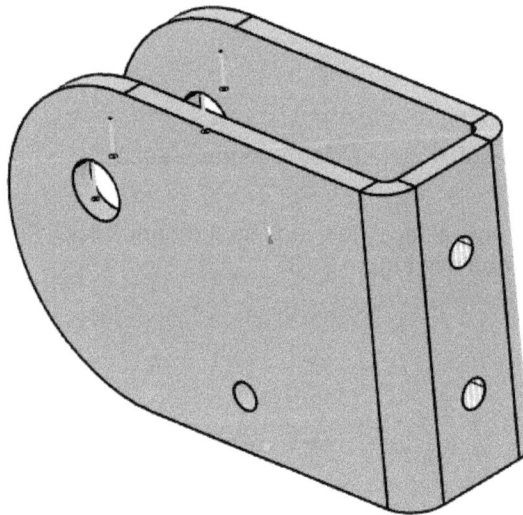

Figure 2−57

Task 8: Run the analysis.

1. Select the *Simulate* section in the *Assistant* dialog box and click ⟳ (Simulate), as shown in Figure 2–58.

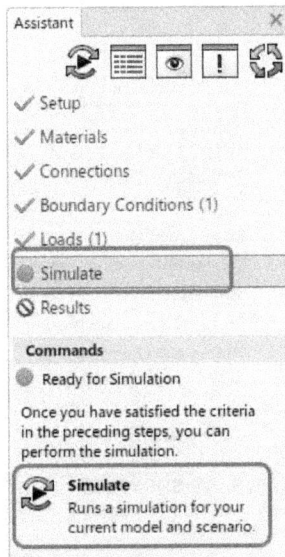

Figure 2–58

2. The *Simulate* dialog box opens, as shown in Figure 2–59.

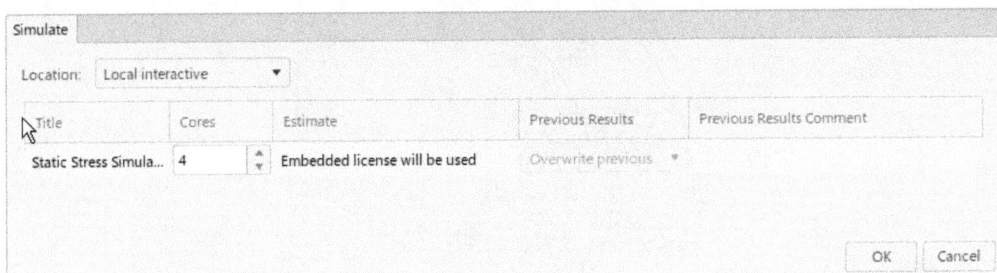

Figure 2–59

3. Accept all the default settings and click **OK** to continue with the computation. 3DEXPERIENCE displays the *Simulation Status* dialog box, informing you of the progress.

4. This particular simulation should take under 30sec to solve. In the end, the *Simulation Status* dialog box should display the message, "Static Stress Simulation completed".

5. Close the *Simulation Status* and the *Assistant* dialog boxes.

Task 9: Display the deformed mesh.

Once the computation completes, by default, 3DEXPERIENCE displays the *Von Mises Stress* result plot. In this task, you will display the model deformation as computed in the analysis.

1. On the screen, locate the *Plot* drop-down menu and select **Deformation**, as shown in Figure 2–60.

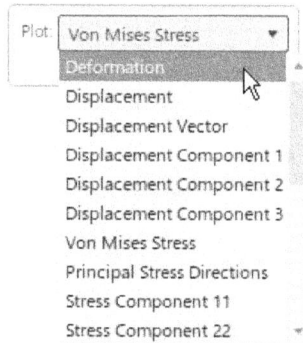

Figure 2–60

2. The deformed model image displays, as shown in Figure 2–61.

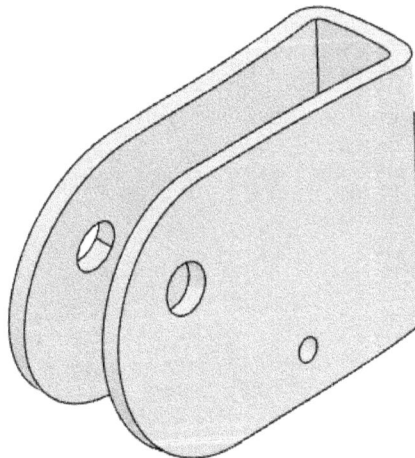

Figure 2–61

3. In the tree, right-click the **Model** object and select **Hide/Show** in the contextual menu, as shown in Figure 2−62.

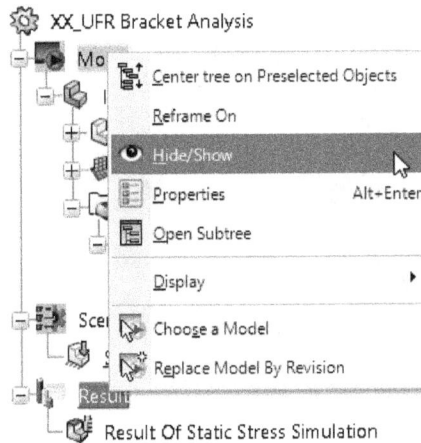

Figure 2−62

4. The deformed model is now overlaid over the undeformed, as shown in Figure 2−63.

    Note: Overlaying the deformed over the undeformed model helps you visualize the overall shape and direction of the model deformation under the applied loads.

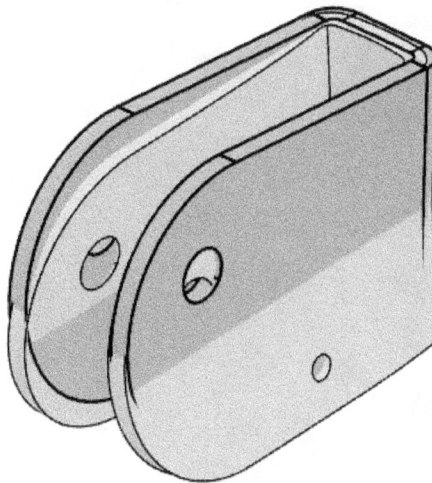

Figure 2−63

5. Select the deformed image in the window, then select ✏️ (Plot options) in the context toolbar, as shown in Figure 2−64.

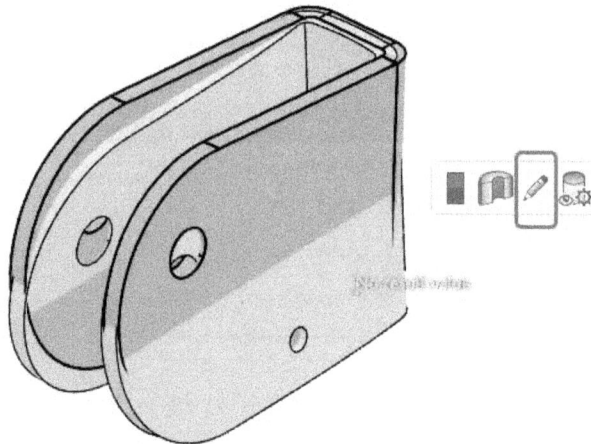

Figure 2−64

6. In the *Contour Plot* dialog box, set the *Scale factor* value to **50**, as shown in Figure 2−65.

*Note: CATIA scales up (i.e., exaggerates) the displayed deformation of the model. Setting the **Scale factor** to **50** means that the displayed deformation will be 50 times the actual deformation under the given loads.*

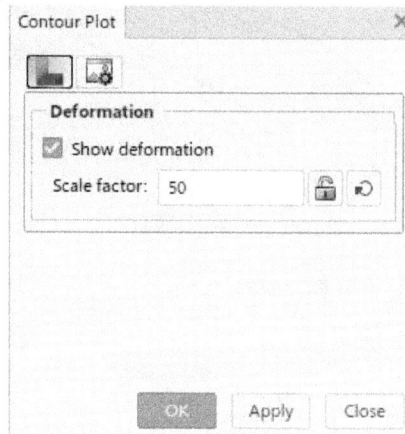

Figure 2−65

7. Switch to the *Rendering* section in the *Contour Plot* dialog box. Select **Mesh** in the *Visible edges* drop-down menu, as shown in Figure 2–66.

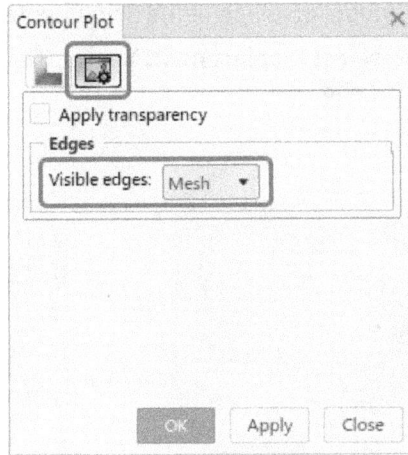

Figure 2–66

8. Click **OK** to close the dialog box. The model displays as shown in Figure 2–67.

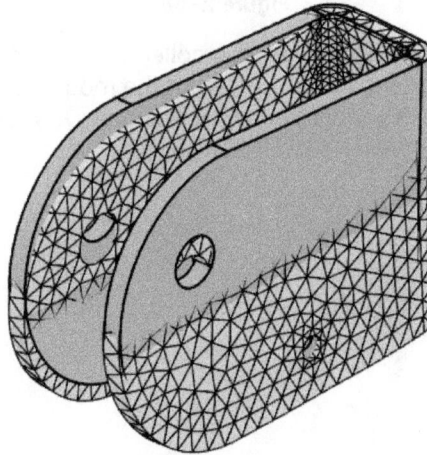

Figure 2–67

9. Right-click the **Model** object in the tree and select **Hide/Show** to hide the undeformed model.

Task 10: Display the displacements.

In this task, you will display the model displacements as computed in the analysis.

1. In the *Plot* drop-down menu, select **Displacement Vector**. The displacement vector image displays, as shown in Figure 2–68.

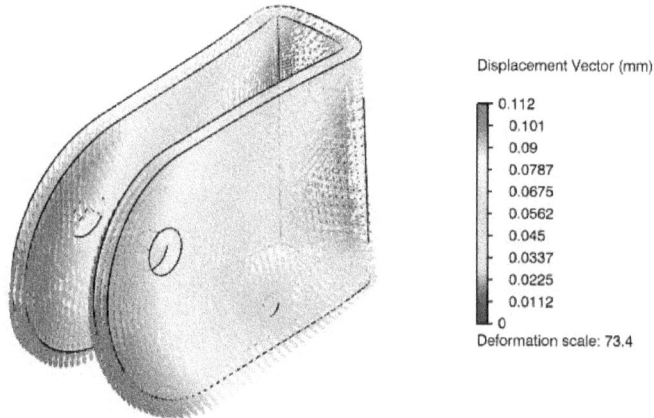

Displacement Vector (mm)

```
0.112
0.101
0.09
0.0787
0.0675
0.0562
0.045
0.0337
0.0225
0.0112
0
```
Deformation scale: 73.4

Figure 2–68

2. The model displacements are displayed as a collection of vectors, each vector originating at a mesh node. Zoom in on the image and point the mouse to any of the vectors. The mouse tooltip displays the displacement components in **X**, **Y**, and **Z** directions, as shown in Figure 2–69.

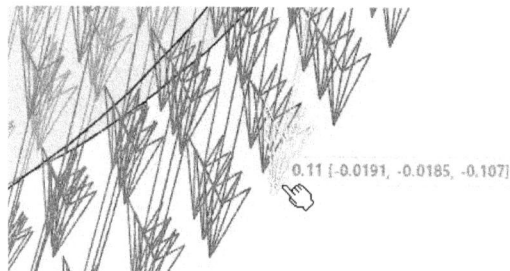

0.11 [-0.0191, -0.0185, -0.107]

Figure 2–69

3. Select **Displacement** in the *Plot* drop-down menu. The image is now displayed as a color plot of the translational displacement magnitude, as shown in Figure 2–70.

    Note: *The displacement magnitude D is computed from the nodal displacement components D_x, D_y, and D_z with the following equation:*

    $$D = \sqrt{D_x^2 + D_y^2 + D_z^2}$$

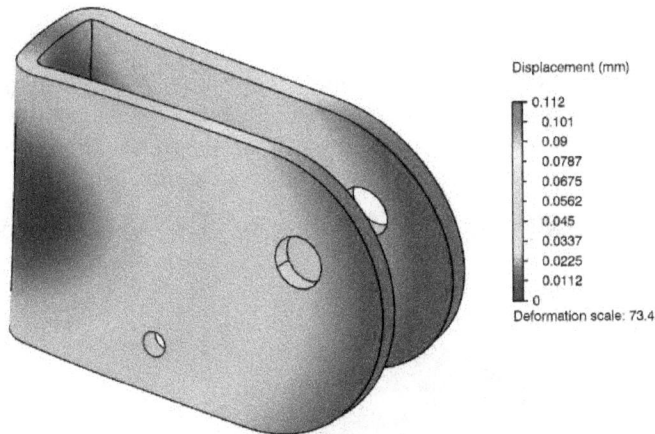

Figure 2-70

4. Note that the maximum displacement magnitude under the *500N* load is **0.112mm**. In the next step, you will display the vertical displacement D_z alone.

5. Select **Displacement Component 3** object in the *Plot* drop-down menu. The image is displayed as shown in Figure 2-71.

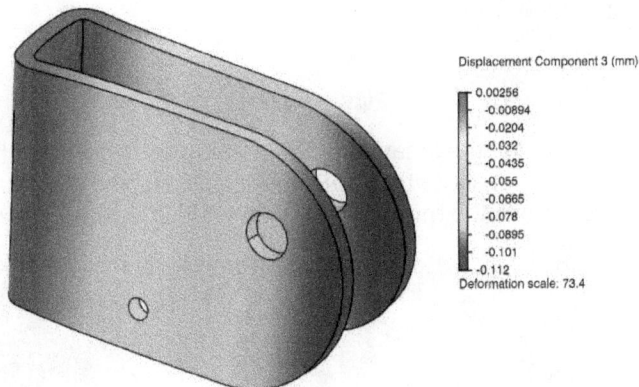

Figure 2-71

*   Note that the maximum displacement in vertical Z-direction is **-0.112mm**. This is the same as the maximum displacement magnitude, which indicates that vertical displacement is the dominant mode of deformation in the bracket under the given load.

Task 11: Display the Stresses.

In this task, you will display the *Von Mises stress* in the model. *Von Mises stress* is a criterion used to determine if the material will yield and is mostly used for ductile materials such as metals. The bracket is made of Aluminum, which is a ductile metal, therefore *Von Mises stress* would be an appropriate criterion to predict the bracket's failure.

1. In the *Plot* drop-down menu, select **Von Mises Stress**. The stress image displays, as shown in Figure 2−72.

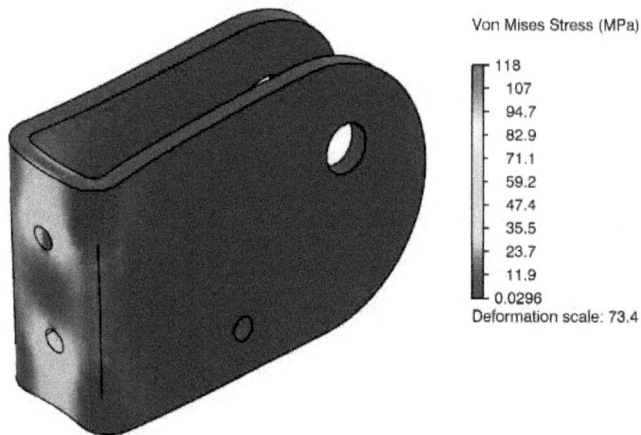

Von Mises Stress (MPa)

    118
    107
    94.7
    82.9
    71.1
    59.2
    47.4
    35.5
    23.7
    11.9
    0.0296
Deformation scale: 73.4

Figure 2−72

2. Rotate the model to examine the location of the maximum stress, which is around the clamped holes in the bracket. Note that 3DEXPERIENCE displays the stress values at the mesh nodes when you move the mouse pointer over the image, as shown in Figure 2−73.

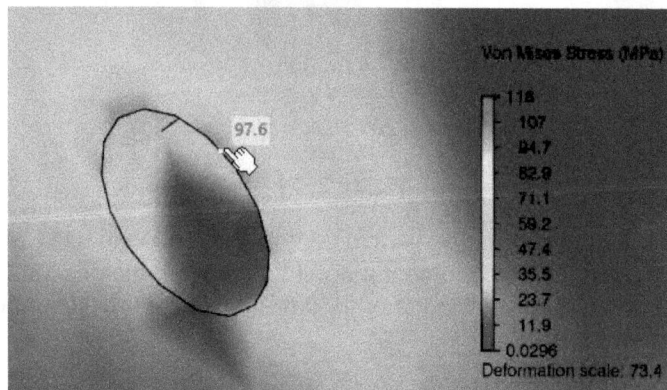

Figure 2−73

3. Note that the *Yield Strength* of the material is **95MPa**, while the maximum stress in the model is **118MPa**, which is greater than the material's *Yield Strength*. Therefore, the bracket is predicted to fail under the given loading. In the following steps, you will locate the areas in the model that should fail.

4. In the *Results* section of the Action Bar, select ▉ (Show Min/Max Values). In the context toolbar, select ▢ (Show only Max value), then ✅, as shown in Figure 2−74.

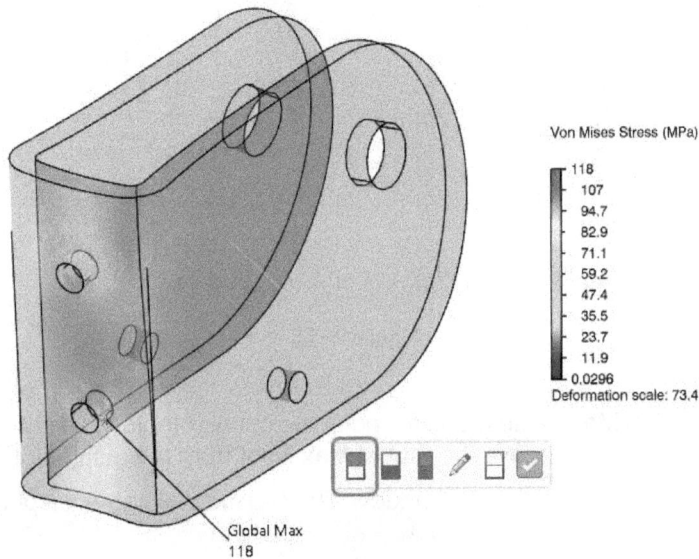

Von Mises Stress (MPa)

118
107
94.7
82.9
71.1
59.2
47.4
35.5
23.7
11.9
0.0296
Deformation scale: 73.4

Global Max
118

Figure 2−74

5. The result is displayed, as shown in Figure 2–75. The maximum *Von Mises stress* occurs at the lower clamped hole.

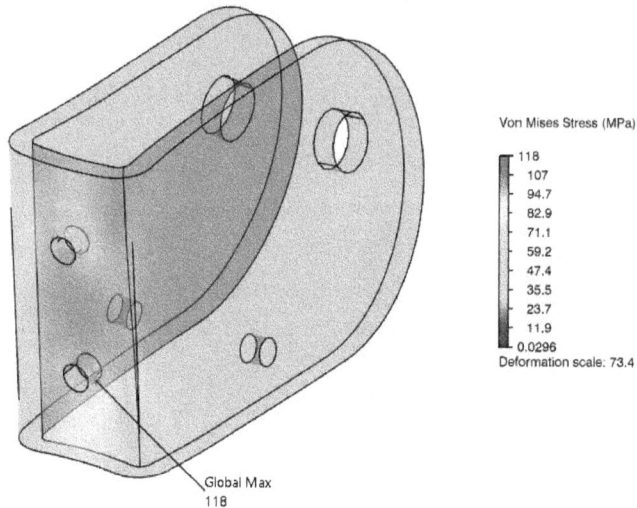

Figure 2–75

6. Click ▪ (Show Min/Max Values) again, and in the context toolbar, select ⊟ (Hide Max or Min values and close) to remove the **Global Max** label from the result plot.

7. Double-click the result legend in the window. The *Legend* dialog box displays, as shown in Figure 2–76.

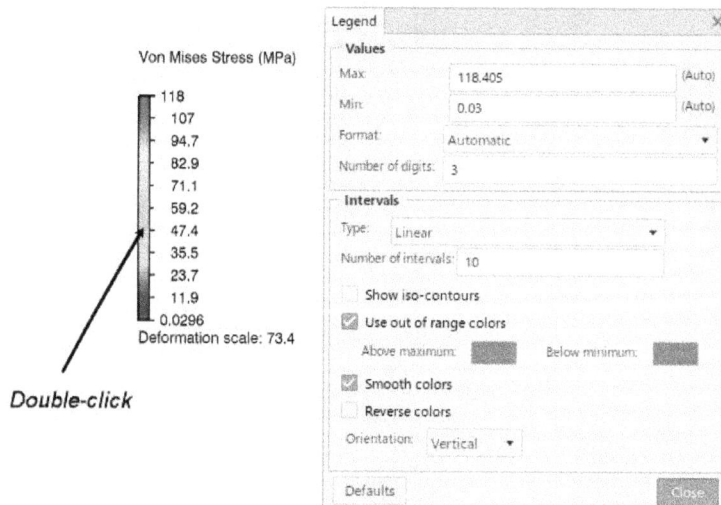

Figure 2–76

8. Deactivate the **Smooth colors** option.

   *Note: Unselecting the **Smooth** option helps visually discern the areas of different stress levels in the model.*

9. Enter **95** as the *Max* value and **0** as the *Min* value. The dialog box displays as shown in Figure 2–77.

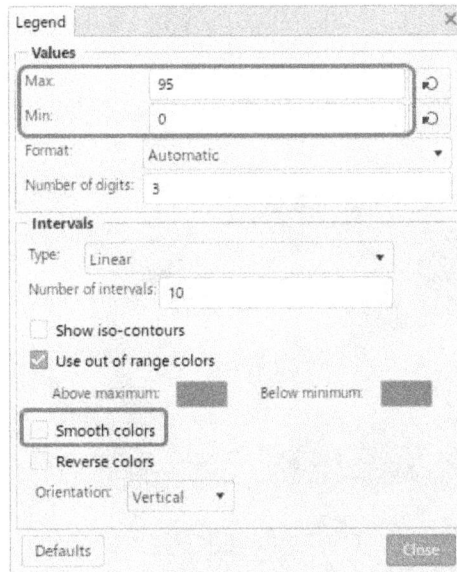

Figure 2–77

10. Click **Close** to close the *Legend* dialog box. Zoom in on one of the clamped holes. The dark grey color now indicates the areas where the stress exceeds **95MPa**, which is the yield strength of the material, as shown on Figure 2–78.

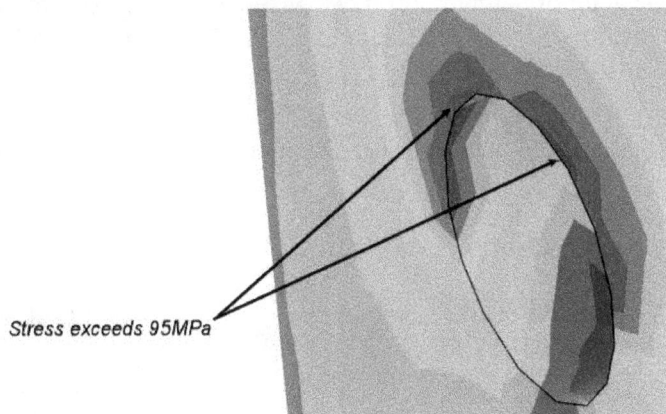

Stress exceeds 95MPa

Figure 2–78

Task 12: Display the Factor of Safety plot.

The Factor of Safety (FoS) value indicates whether the stress, as calculated in the analysis, exceeds the material strength, using the following formula:

$$FoS = <material\_yield\_strength> / <stress\_in\_analysis>$$

Therefore, **FoS > 1** indicates that the maximum stress doesn't exceed the material strength, and the part is safe under the given loads. Alternatively, **FoS < 1** indicates that part is predicted to fail.

1. In the *Plot* drop-down menu, select **Factor of Safety**. The Factor of Safety plot displays, as shown in Figure 2–79.

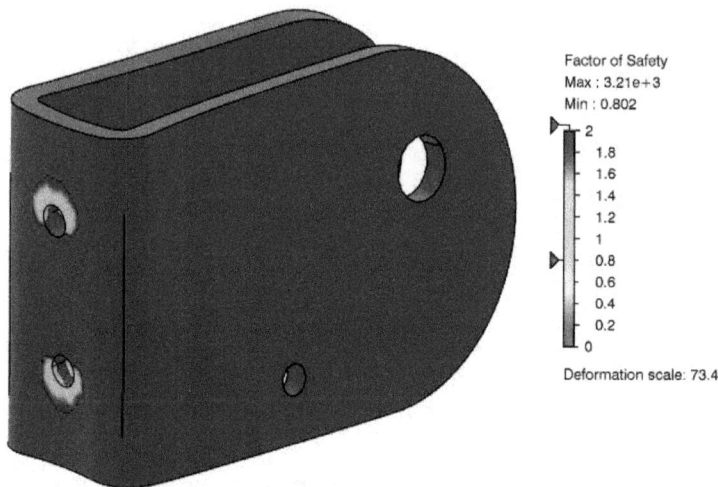

Figure 2–79

*   Note that the Factor of Safety value is below **1** in the areas close to the clamped holes. This means that the material in those areas is predicted to yield and potentially rupture under the given load.

2. In the Action Bar, select ⬚ (Results Visualization) to exit the analysis results visualization.

Task 13: Modify the bracket thickness.

In this task, you will modify the bracket dimensions in order to bring the stress levels to below the yield strength of the material.

1. Activate the *UFR-723* window and double-click the **UFR-723** 3D Shape, as shown in Figure 2–80. This automatically activates the **Part Design** app.

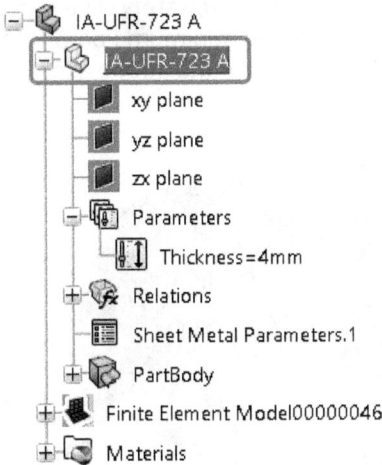

Figure 2–80

2. Double-click **Thickness** in the *Parameters* node in the tree and change the value from **4mm** to **5mm**, as shown in Figure 2–81.

    Note: *It is impossible to predict how thick the bracket should be to make it strong enough. Therefore, several design-analysis iterations might be required here.*

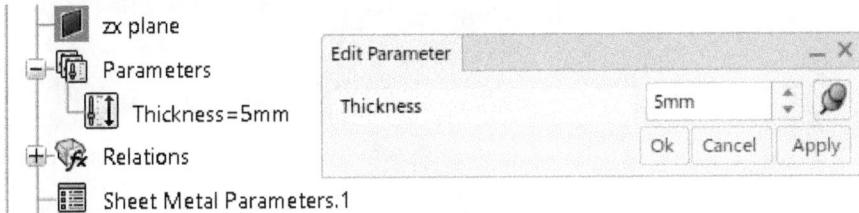

Figure 2–81

3. Click **OK** to close the *Edit Parameter* dialog box. 3DEXPERIENCE regenerates the model, so the bracket part is now **5mm** thick.

Task 14: Re-run the analysis.

1. Activate the *UFR Bracket Analysis* window.

2. In the Action Bar, select 🔄 (Simulate) and re-run the analysis.

Task 15: Display the Factor of Safety plot.

1. In the *Plot* drop-down menu, select **Factor of Safety**. The Factor of Safety plot displays, as shown in Figure 2–82. Note that now the minimum Factor of Safety value is **1.08**, which means there are no areas in the part where the stress exceeds the material's yield strength.

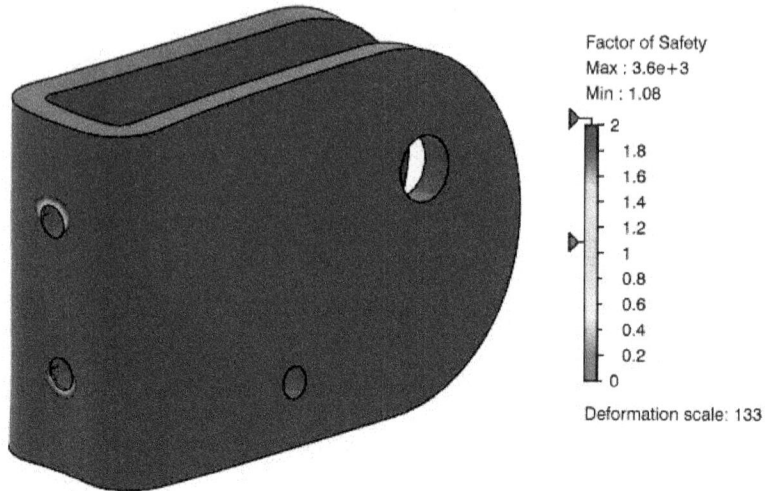

Factor of Safety
Max : 3.6e+3
Min : 1.08

2
1.8
1.6
1.4
1.2
1
0.8
0.6
0.4
0.2
0

Deformation scale: 133

Figure 2–82

Task 16: Create the analysis report.

1. In the *Results* section of the Action Bar, select [icon] (Report). The *Report Definition* dialog box opens as shown in Figure 2–83.

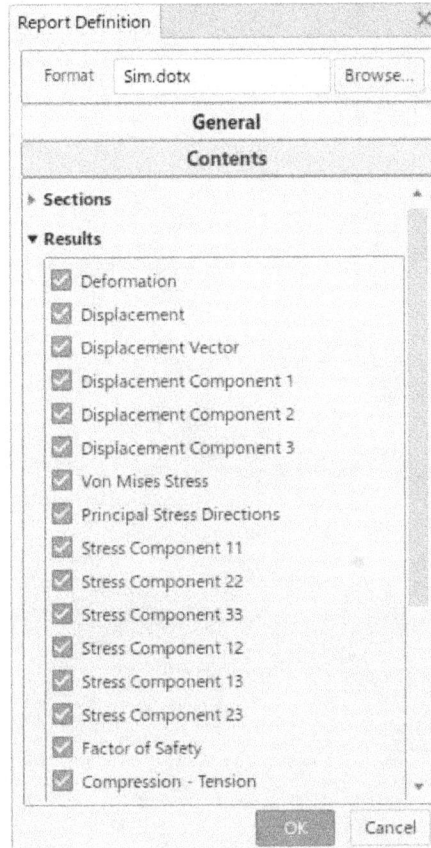

Report Definition   ✕

| Format | Sim.dotx | Browse... |

General

Contents

▸ **Sections**

▾ **Results**

- ☑ Deformation
- ☑ Displacement
- ☑ Displacement Vector
- ☑ Displacement Component 1
- ☑ Displacement Component 2
- ☑ Displacement Component 3
- ☑ Von Mises Stress
- ☑ Principal Stress Directions
- ☑ Stress Component 11
- ☑ Stress Component 22
- ☑ Stress Component 33
- ☑ Stress Component 12
- ☑ Stress Component 13
- ☑ Stress Component 23
- ☑ Factor of Safety
- ☑ Compression - Tension

OK   Cancel

Figure 2–83

2. Click **Browse** and select an output folder and the file name for the report.

3. In the *Results* section, activate the results shown in Figure 2–84 and deactivate the rest.

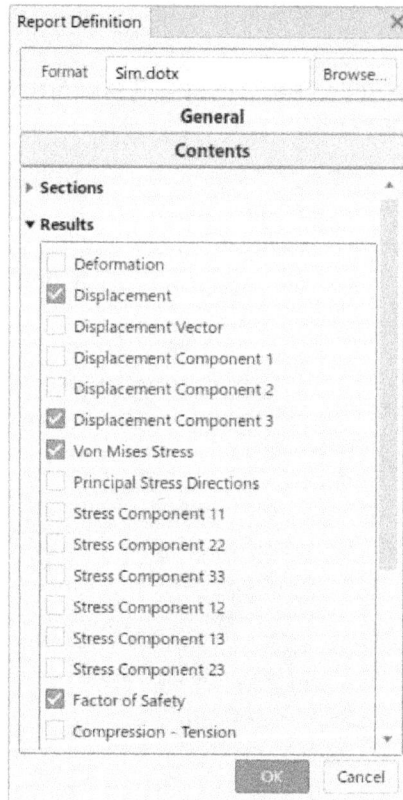

Figure 2–84

4. Click **OK**. The report opens in MS Word, as shown in Figure 2–85.

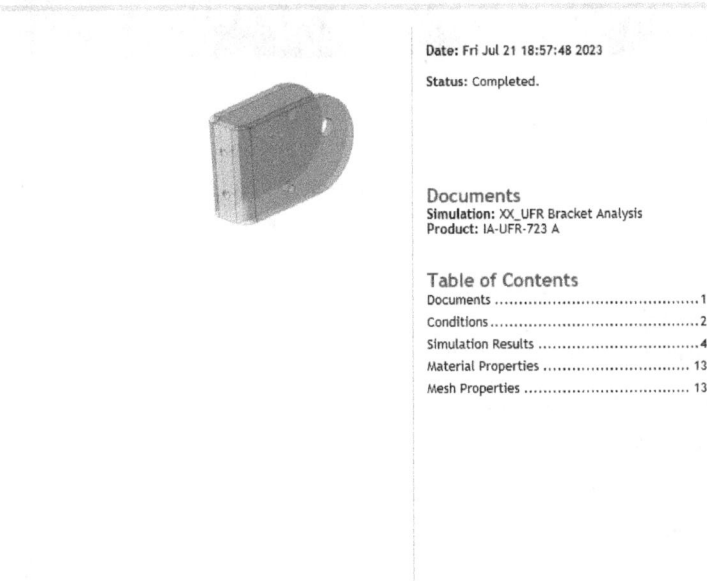

Date: Fri Jul 21 18:57:48 2023

Status: Completed.

Documents
Simulation: XX_UFR Bracket Analysis
Product: IA-UFR-723 A

Table of Contents

Figure 2–85

5. Scroll down and examine the contents of the analysis report.

Task 17: Save and close the model.

1. Click (Result Visualization) in the Action Bar to return to the model view.
2. Optionally, save the analysis document and the redesigned part for future reference.
3. Close all windows.

End of practice

Practice 2b
Static Stress Analysis of a Hanger

Practice Objectives

- Apply the material.
- Mesh the model.
- Apply loads and restraints.
- Compute the analysis.
- Display and animate deformation and displacements.
- Display Von Mises stress and principal stress.
- Locate maximum stresses.
- Perform cut plane analysis.
- Create analysis report.

In this practice, you will set up and run a static stress analysis on a hanger part shown in Figure 2-86.

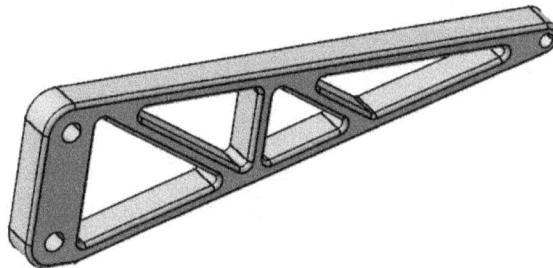

Figure 2-86

Task 1: Open the part.

1.   Import with your initials and open **Hanger_02.3dxml**.

2. Set the model display as ⬚ (Shading with Sharp and Smooth Edges). The part displays as shown in Figure 2–87.

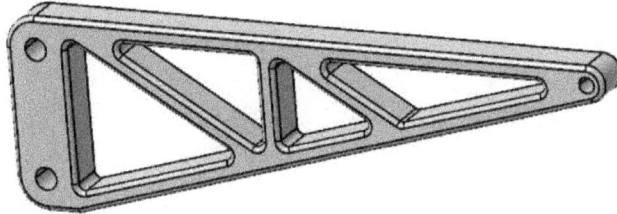

Figure 2–87

3. Select **Preferences>Common Preferences>Parameters, Measures, and Units>Units** and set the units as follows:

- *Length:* **Millimeter (mm)**
- *Force:* **Newton (N)**
- *Moment:* **Newton x Meter (Nxm)**
- *Pressure:* **Megapascal (MPa)**
- *Stress: **Megapascal (MPa)***

Task 2: Create the material.

In this task, you will create the material definition for the hanger part.

1. Click the outer ring of the Compass, and in the list of *My Apps,* select the **Material Definition** app.

2. In the *Core Material* dialog box, enter **<Your Initials>_Steel** for the *Title* and click **OK**, as shown in Figure 2–88.

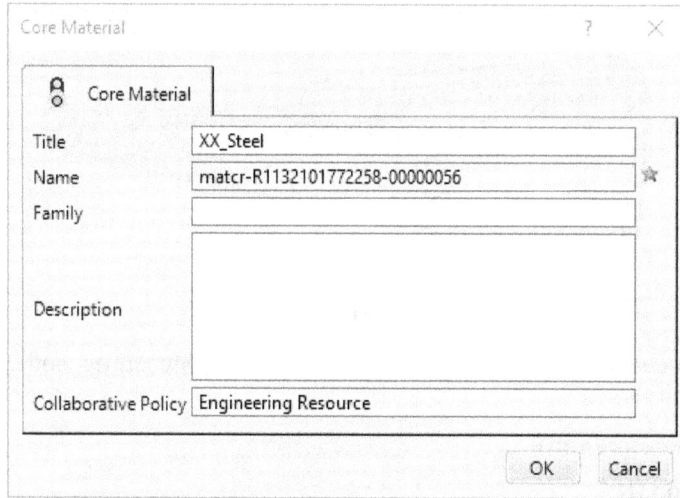

Figure 2–88

3. The *Material Editor* window opens. Select **Steel** in the tree, and in the Action Bar, click
    (Add Domain).

4. In the *Add Domain* dialog box, select **Simulation Domain** and click **OK**, as shown in Figure 2–89.

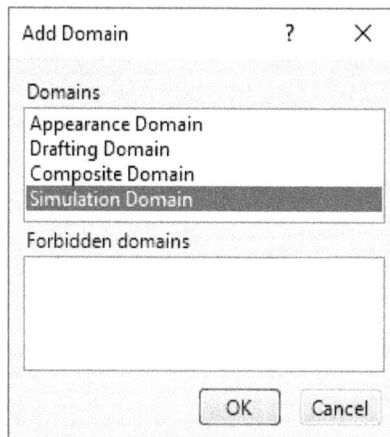

Figure 2–89

5. In the *Material Simulation Domain* dialog box, enter **<*Your Initials*>_Steel Simulation Domain** for the *Title* and click **OK**, as shown in Figure 2–90.

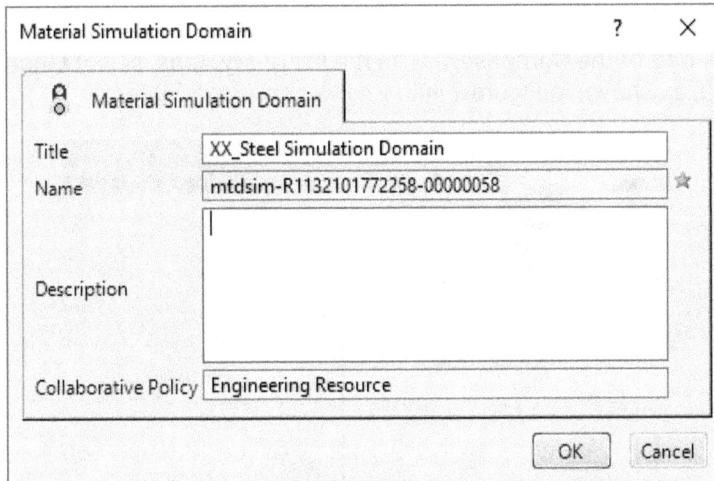

Figure 2–90

6. Double-click **Steel Simulation Domain** in the tree. Enter the following mechanical properties, as shown in Figure 2–91:

- *Density:* **7860 Kg/m3**
- *Proof (Yield) Stress:* **250 MPa**
- *Young's Modulus:* **200000 MPa**
- *Poisson's Ratio:* **0.266**

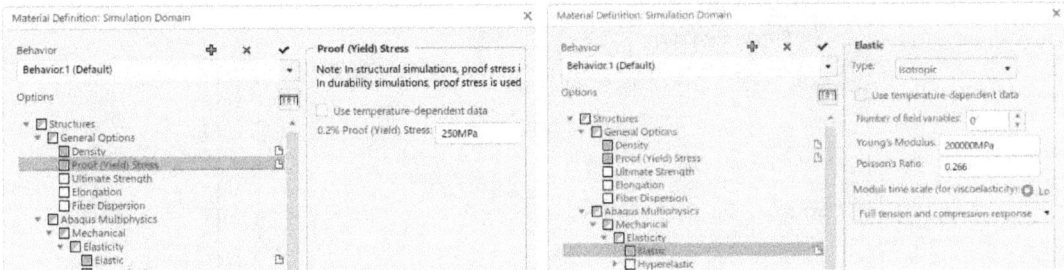

Figure 2–91

7. Click **OK** to complete. Save the material to the 3DEXPERIENCE database, but do not close the *Material Editor* window to keep the material definition in session.

Task 3: Launch the Linear Structural Validation app.

1. Activate the *Hanger* window.

2. Click the outer ring of the Compass, and in the list of *My Apps,* select **Linear Structural Validation** app, as shown in Figure 2−92.

Figure 2−92

3. In the *Physics Simulation* dialog box, enter **<*Your Initials>*_Hanger Simulation** for the *Title* and click **OK**, as shown in Figure 2−93.

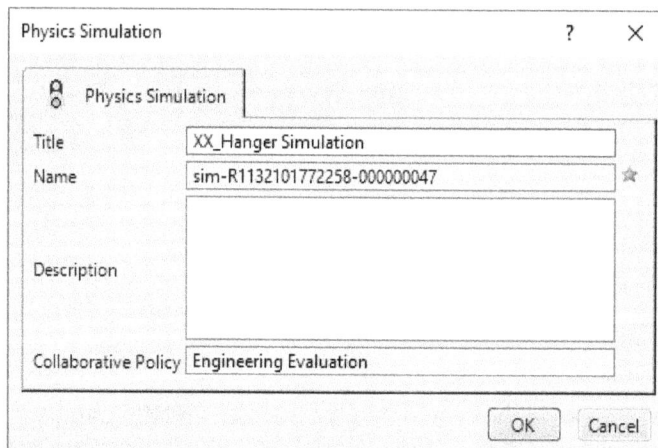

Figure 2−93

4. In the *Simulation Initialization* dialog box that opens, select **Structural** for *Analysis* type, and click **OK**, as shown in Figure 2–94.

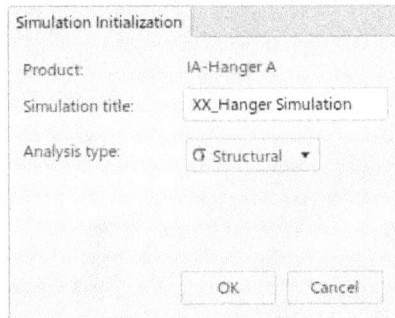

Figure 2–94

5. 3DEXPERIENCE opens a new window, named *Hanger Simulation*.

Task 4: Apply the material.

You can apply the material for the analysis either by searching and selecting from the 3DEXPERIENCE database, or by picking a material already open in 3DEXPERIENCE session.

In this task, you will apply the material you created in Task 2.

1. In the *Setup* section of the Action Bar, click (Material Palette). In the drop-down menu in the top left corner of the *Material Palette* dialog box, select **In-Session**. The *Material Palette* dialog box opens as shown in Figure 2–95.

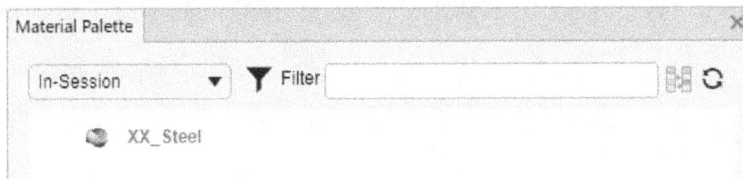

Figure 2–95

2. Drag and drop the **Steel** from the Material Palette onto the part body. Click (Close) in the context toolbar to confirm the operation.

3. Close the *Material Palette* dialog box.

Task 5: Mesh the part.

In this task, you will mesh the hanger part using default meshing specification, such as element size and number of elements per hole.

1. In the *Mesh* section of the Action Bar, select (Generate Mesh). The mesh for the part is generated and displayed, as shown in Figure 2–96.

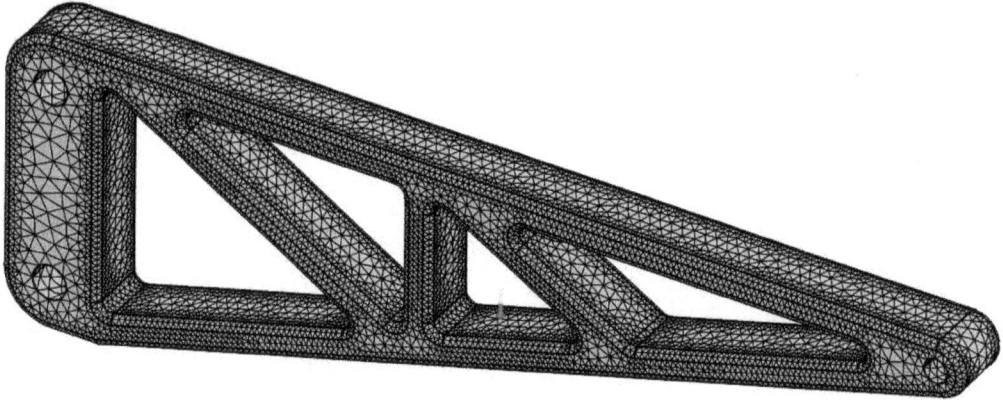

Figure 2–96

2. Select (Hide/Show Mesh) to hide the mesh.

Task 6: Apply Boundary Conditions.

In this task, you will apply the **Clamp** boundary condition to the two holes on one end of the hanger. This models the hanger being rigidly bolted to the adjoining structure.

In the *Linear Structural Validation* app, loads and boundary conditions can be applied either by using the simulation Assistant, or by selecting relevant icons in the Action Bar. In this practice, you will use the Action Bar.

1. Select (Clamp) in the *Boundary Conditions* section of the Action Bar. The *Clamp* dialog box opens, as shown in Figure 2–97.

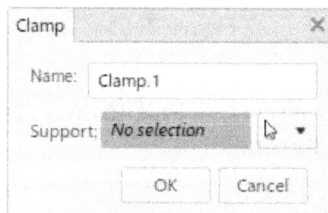

Figure 2–97

2.   Select the inside surfaces of the two holes, as shown in Figure 2−98.

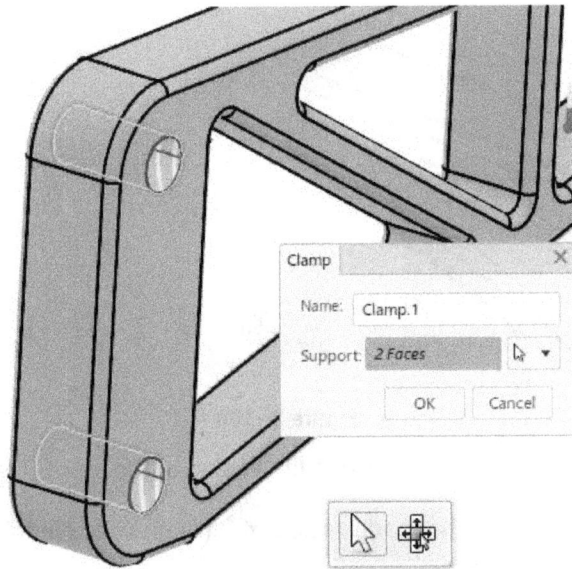

Figure 2−98

3.   Click **OK** to complete.

Task 7: Apply Loads.

In this task, you will apply a **1000N** vertical force to the hole on the other end of the hanger.

1.   Select (Force) in the *Loads* section of the Action Bar. The *Force* dialog box opens, as shown in Figure 2−99.

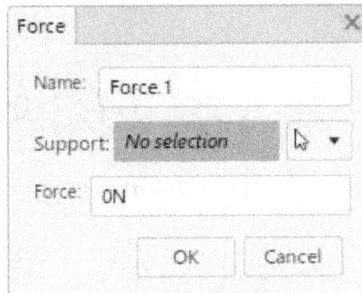

Figure 2−99

2. Select the inside surface of the hole. The model displays as shown in Figure 2–100.

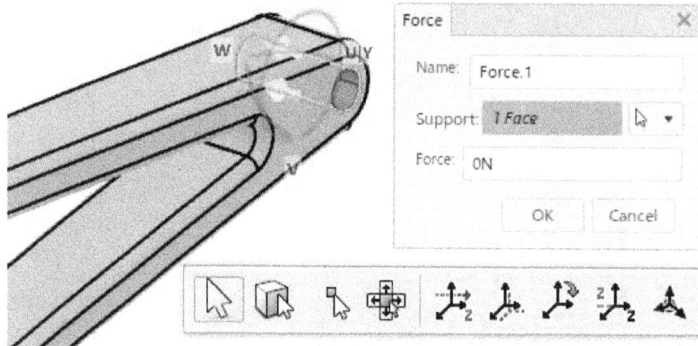

Figure 2–100

3. The force direction is always aligned with the **W** axis of the robot. To align the **W** axis of the robot with the **Z** direction in the model, select ⚒ (Align Triad Handle with the Global Axis System) in the context toolbar.

4. Enter **-1000N** as the force magnitude, as shown in Figure 2–101.

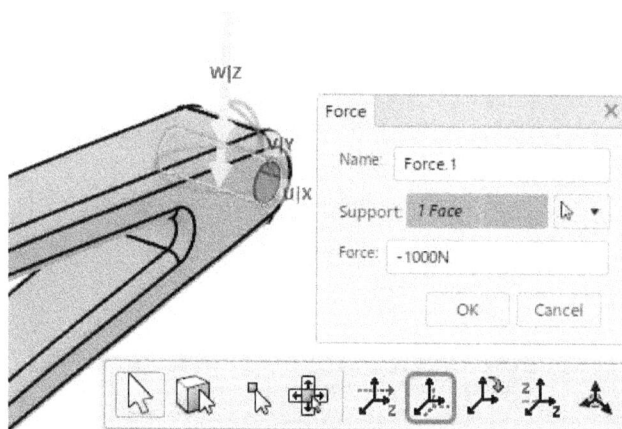

Figure 2–101

5. Click **OK** to complete. The model displays as shown in Figure 2–102.

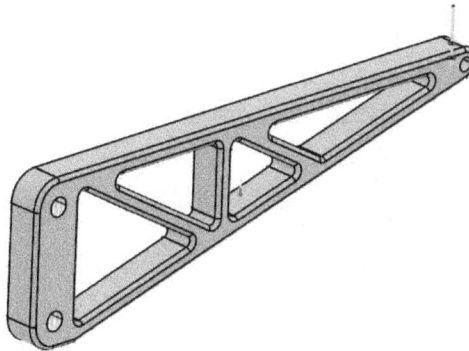

Figure 2–102

Task 8: Run the analysis.

1. Select (Simulate) in the *Results* section of the Action Bar.

2. Click **OK** to close the *Simulate* dialog box when it displays.

3. Wait until computation completes, and the *Simulation Status* dialog box displays the message "Static Stress Simulation completed". The computation for this model should take under **60sec**.

4. Close the *Simulation Status* dialog box.

Task 9: Display and animate the displacements.

Once the computation completes, 3DEXPERIENCE displays the *Von Mises stress* result plot. In this task, you will display and animate the model displacements.

1. Locate the *Plot* drop-down menu on the screen, and select **Displacement**, as shown in Figure 2–103.

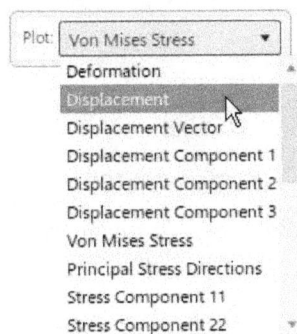

Figure 2–103

2. The displacement magnitude result plot is displayed, as shown in Figure 2–104.

   - Note that the maximum displacement under the 1000N load is **0.221mm**.

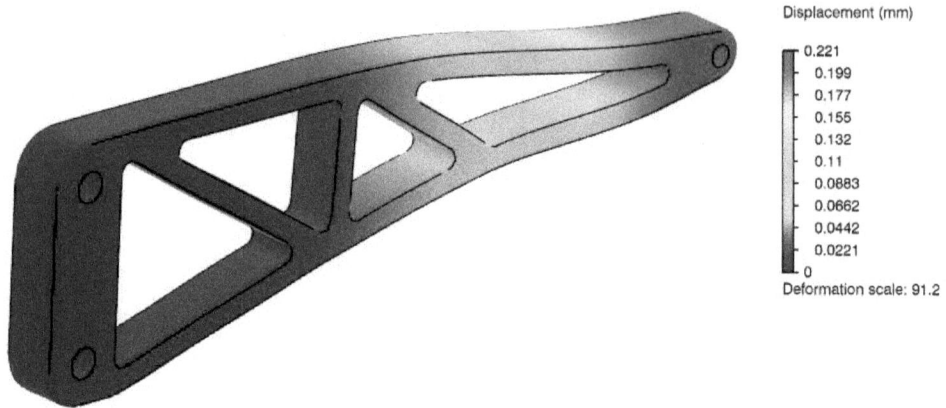

Figure 2–104

3. In the Action Bar, select ⬛▷ (Play Animation). The model deformation is now animated, and the Action Bar displays animation controls, as shown in Figure 2–105.

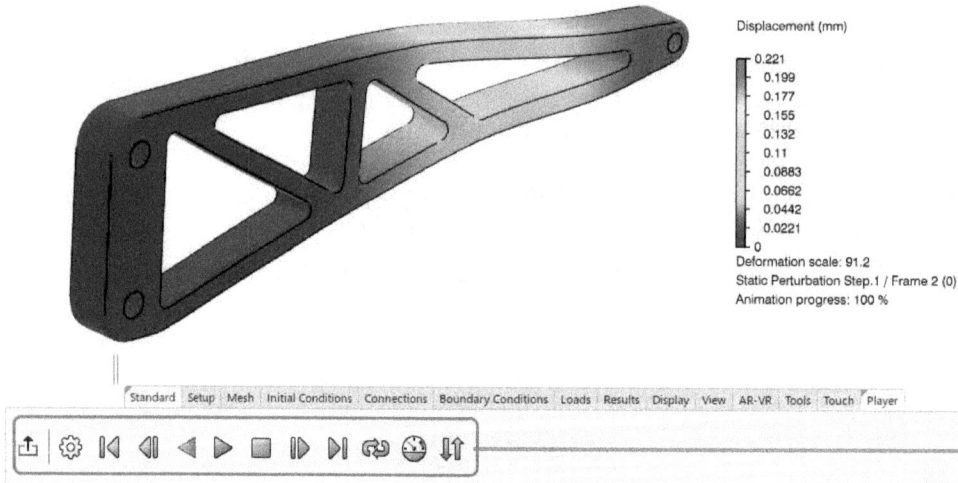

Figure 2–105

4. Using Animation controls, pause and restart the animation, as well as step through the animation frame-by-frame.

5. Click ⬆ (Exit) exit the animation.

Task 10: Display Von Mises Stress.

Von Mises stress is a value used to determine if the material will yield and is mostly used for ductile materials such as metals. The hanger is made of Steel, which is a ductile metal, therefore *Von Mises stress* would be an appropriate criterion to predict the hanger's failure.

1. In the **Plot** drop-down menu, select **Von Mises Stress**. The stress image displays as shown in Figure 2–106.

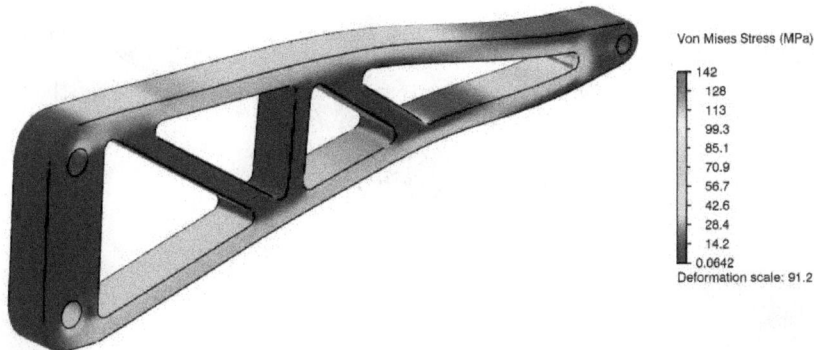

Von Mises Stress (MPa)

| 142 |
| 128 |
| 113 |
| 99.3 |
| 85.1 |
| 70.9 |
| 56.7 |
| 42.6 |
| 28.4 |
| 14.2 |
| 0.0642 |

Deformation scale: 91.2

Figure 2–106

2. Rotate and visually examine the stress plot. Note that the maximum *Von Mises stress* is occurring in the triangular pocket near the loaded hole. You will later use the **Show Min/Max Values** tool to precisely locate the area of maximum stress.

    *   Note that the maximum *Von Mises stress* in the model is approximately **142MPa**, which is well below the material's *Yield (Proof) Stress* of **250MPa**. Therefore, the part is predicted to withstand the load without failure.

Task 11: Perform cut plane analysis.

1. In the *Results* section of the Action Bar, select ▢ (View Cut). The model and the context toolbar display, as shown in Figure 2−107.

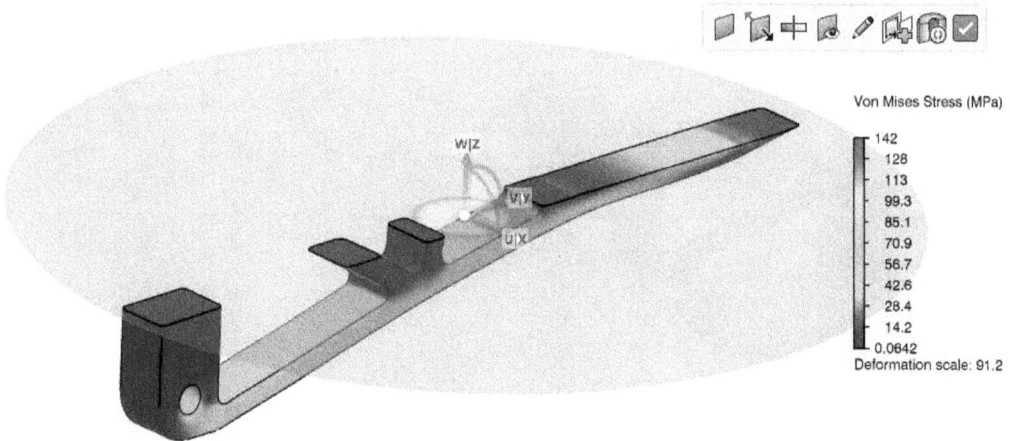

Figure 2−107

2. In the context toolbar, select ▱ (Hide cutting geometry) to hide the cutting plane. The result plot displays as shown in Figure 2−108.

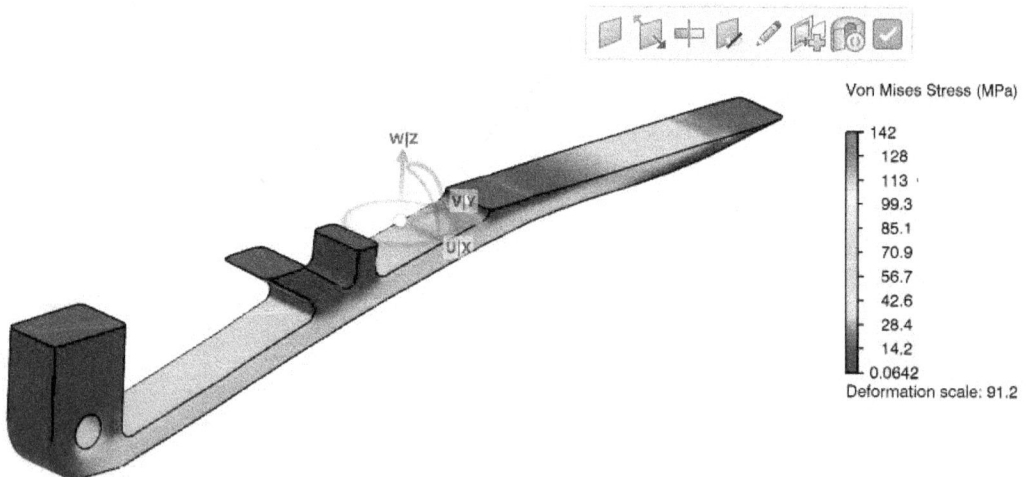

Figure 2−108

3. Select ✎ (Edit cut) in the context toolbar. The *Plot Sectioning* dialog box opens, as shown in Figure 2–109.

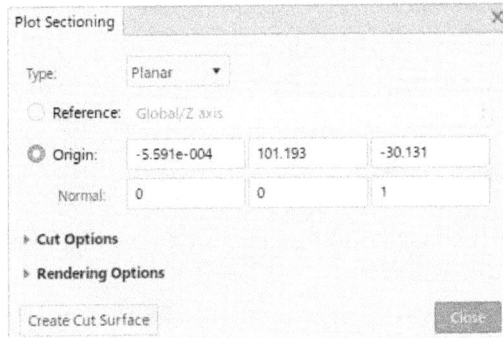

Figure 2–109

4. Enter the origin coordinates and normal directions as shown in Figure 2–110.

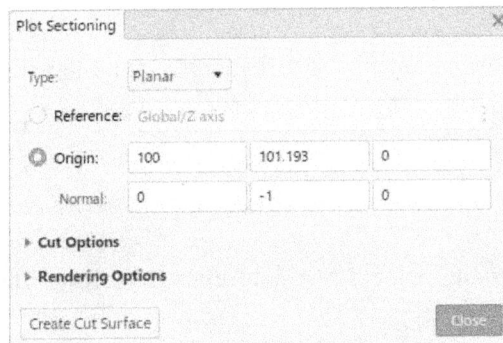

Figure 2–110

5. Click **Close**. The model displays as shown in Figure 2–111.

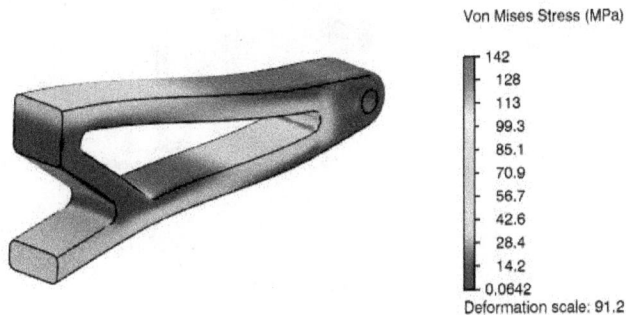

Figure 2–111

6. Click ▥ (View Cut) in the Action Bar to display the robot and the context toolbar again. Drag the **W** axis of the robot to move the cut plane through the model. Examine stress in the cross-sections as you proceed.

7. Click ▥ (Deactivate cut and close) in the context toolbar to exit the view cut mode.

Task 12: Display Principal Stress.

The *Von Mises stress* is a scalar value, and, as such, it does not differentiate between tension and compression. It is always positive.

In some cases, it is the tensile stress that causes material failure, not the compressive stress. This includes working with brittle materials that are less strong in tension than in compression, as well as dealing with metal fatigue, where it is the tensile normal stress that causes the crack initiation.

To visualize the tensile and compressive stresses, we need to look at the principal stress, not just the *Von Mises stress*.

The principal stresses are the so-called stress invariants, and there are three at each infinitesimal point in the model: S_1, S_2, and S_3. S_1 is the maximum normal stress at the point, and it typically is the tensile stress. S_3 is the minimum normal stress at a point, and it typically is the compressive stress. S_2 is the stress in between, and is seldom used in material strength estimations.

1. In the *Plot* drop-down menu, select **Principal Stress Directions**. The result image displays as shown in Figure 2−112.

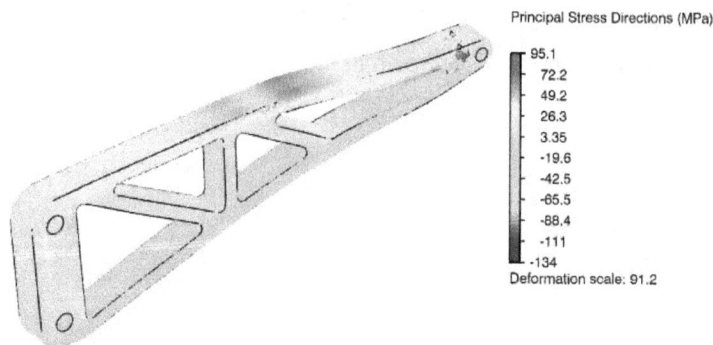

Principal Stress Directions (MPa)

95.1
72.2
49.2
26.3
3.35
-19.6
-42.5
-65.5
-88.4
-111
-134
Deformation scale: 91.2

Figure 2−112

2. The results are represented as vectors at each mesh node. If the mesh is dense, it might be difficult visually to discern the magnitude and directions of the principal stress. In the next step, you will decrease the density of the arrows.

3. Select the result plot and click ✐ (Plot options) in the context toolbar, as shown in Figure 2–113.

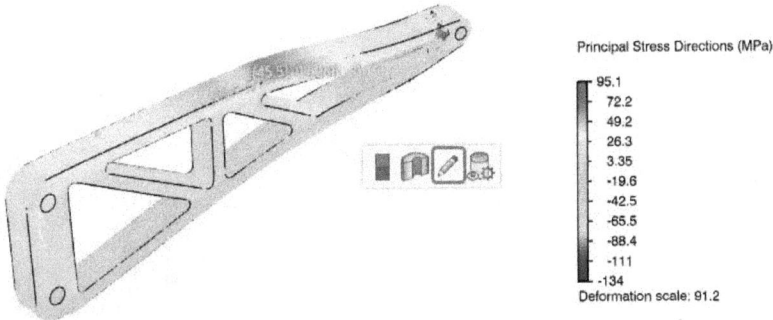

Principal Stress Directions (MPa)

```
  95.1
  72.2
  49.2
  26.3
  3.35
 -19.6
 -42.5
 -65.5
 -88.4
 -111
 -134
```
Deformation scale: 91.2

Figure 2–113

4. In the *Symbol Plot* dialog box, set the *Symbol density* to **20**, as shown in Figure 2–114.

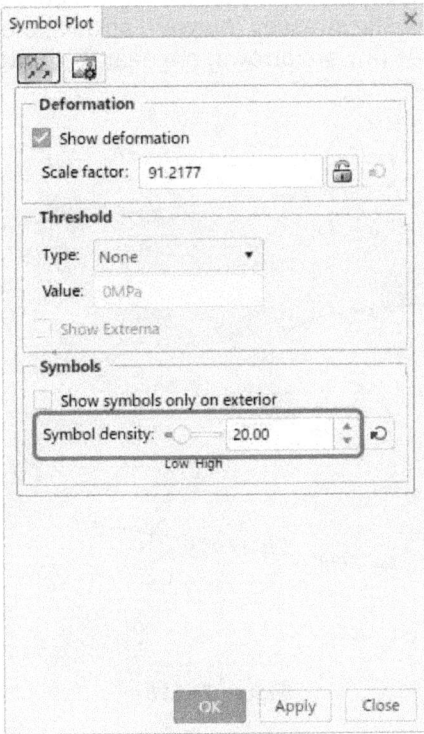

Figure 2–114

5. Click **OK**. The result plot displays, as shown in Figure 2–115. Each arrow in the plot displays the direction and the magnitude of the principal stress, with the outward arrows indicating tension, and inward arrows indicating compression.

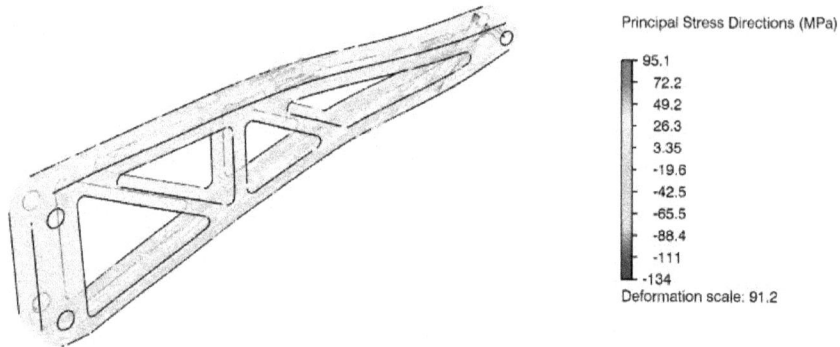

Principal Stress Directions (MPa)

95.1
72.2
49.2
26.3
3.35
-19.6
-42.5
-65.5
-88.4
-111
-134
Deformation scale: 91.2

Figure 2–115

6. Select the **Front View** and zoom-in on the area near the loaded hole, as shown in Figure 2–116. Note that tensile stresses (outward arrows) are near the top of the pocket, while compressive stresses (inward arrows) are near the bottom.

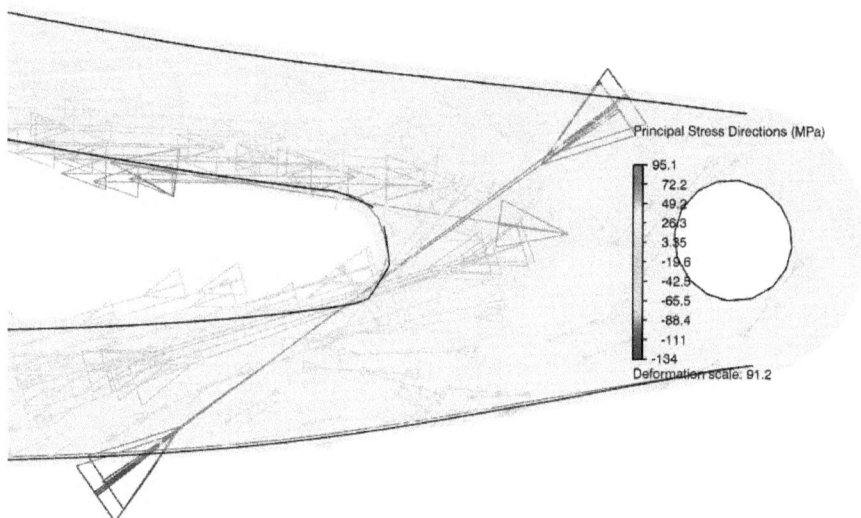

Principal Stress Directions (MPa)

95.1
72.2
49.2
26.3
3.35
-19.6
-42.5
-65.5
-88.4
-111
-134
Deformation scale: 91.2

Figure 2–116

Task 13: Locate areas of maximum tensile stress.

1. In the *Results* section of the Action Bar, select ▮ (Show Min/Max Values). In the context toolbar, select ▢ (Show only Max value), as shown in Figure 2–117.

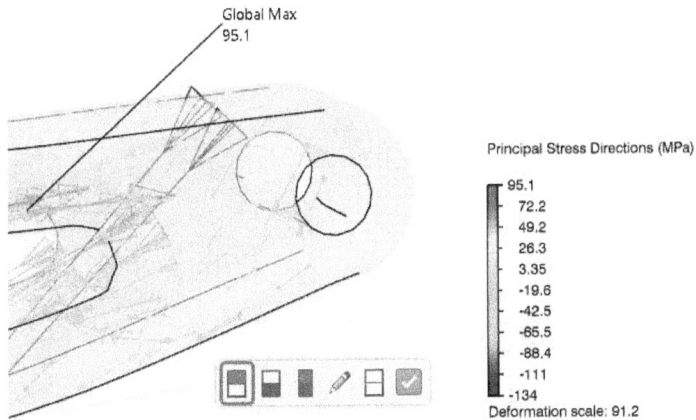

Figure 2–117

2. Click ☑ in the context toolbar. The result plot displays as shown in Figure 2–118.

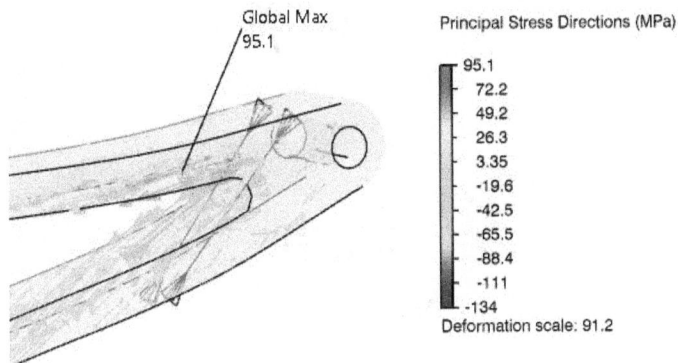

Figure 2–118

3. Rotate the model to locate the area that is indicated with the label, which is the fillet in the pocket nearest to the loaded hole, as shown in Figure 2−119.

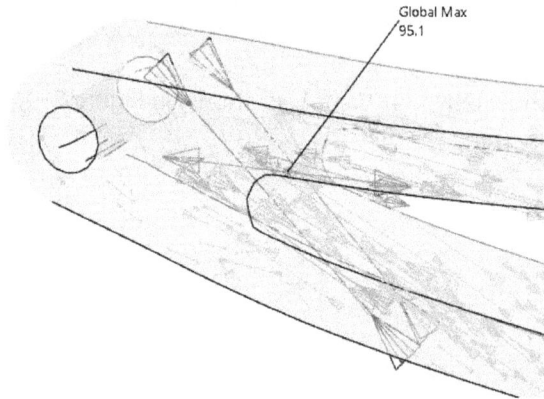

Global Max
95.1

Figure 2−119

Task 14: Create the analysis report.

1. In the *Results* section of the Action Bar, select (Report). The *Report Definition* dialog box opens as shown in Figure 2−120.

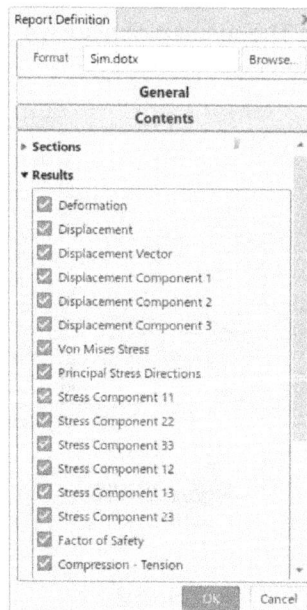

Figure 2−120

2. Click **Browse** and select an output folder and the file name for the report.

3. Select the **General** section. Enter the *Company* name and *Engineer* name, as shown in Figure 2-121.

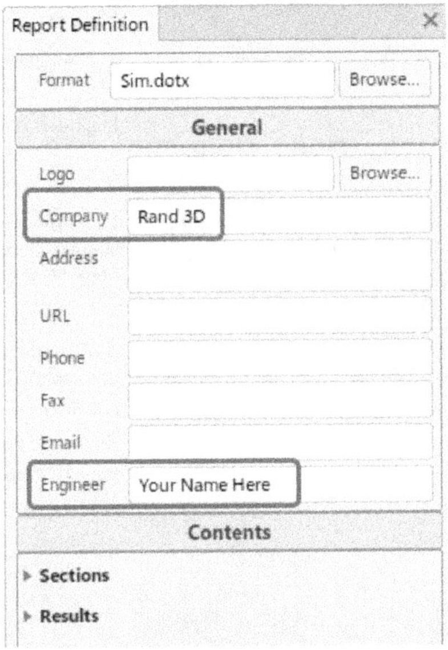

Figure 2-121

4. In the *Results* section, activate the results shown in Figure 2-122 and deactivate the rest.

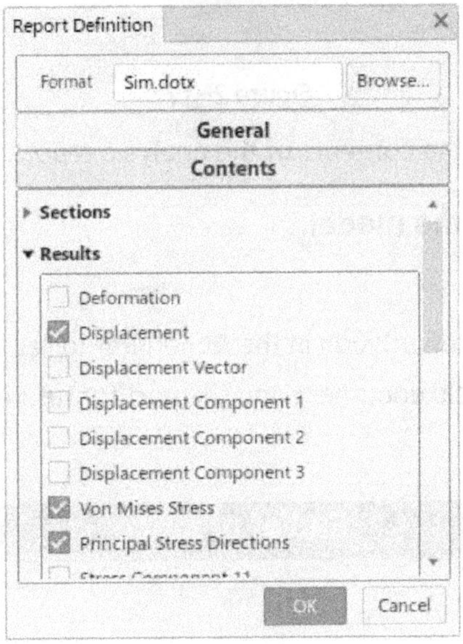

Figure 2-122

5. Click **OK**. The report opens in MS Word, as shown in Figure 2–123.

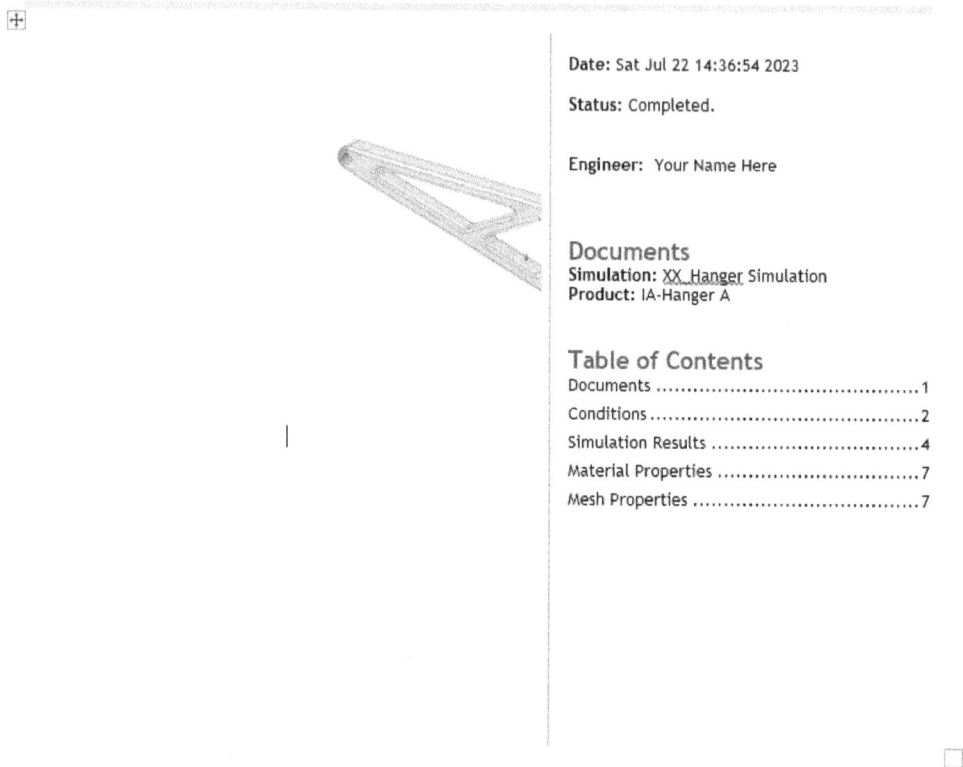

Date: Sat Jul 22 14:36:54 2023

Status: Completed.

Engineer: Your Name Here

Documents
Simulation: XX_Hanger Simulation
Product: IA-Hanger A

Table of Contents

Figure 2–123

6. Scroll down and examine the contents of the analysis report.

Task 15: Save and close the model.

1. Click (Result Visualization) icon in the Action Bar to return to the model view.

2. Optionally, save the analysis document and the part for future reference.

3. Close all windows.

End of practice

Practice 2c
Static Stress Analysis of a Pin

Practice Objectives

- Prepare the model for the analysis.
- Run the analysis.
- Visualize the analysis results.
- Create report.

In this practice, you will set up and run a static stress analysis on a pin model shown in Figure 2-124, with minimum instruction.

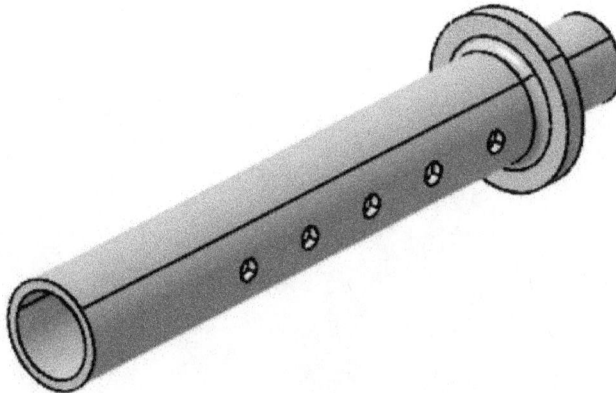

Figure 2-124

Task 1: Prepare the model for the analysis.

1. Import with your initials and open **Pin_02.3dxml**.
2. Launch the **Linear Structural Validation** app.
3. Apply the **Steel** material to the part. Use the material definition created in Practice 2b.
4. Mesh the model with the default meshing parameters.
5. Visually examine the mesh.

6. Clamp the surface shown in Figure 2–125.

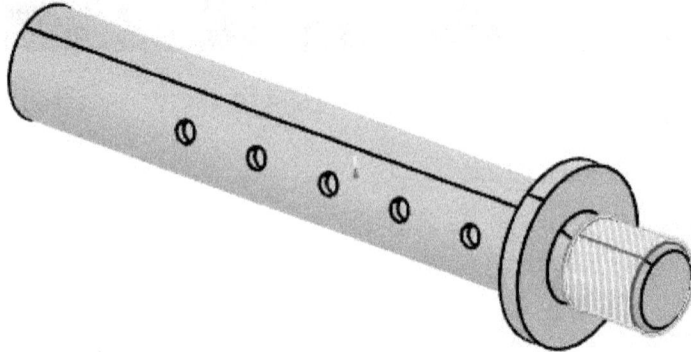

Figure 2–125

7. Apply **1500N** force in +Y direction to the end surface of the pin, as shown in Figure 2–126. Align the robot's **W** axis with the +Y direction using the **zx plane**.

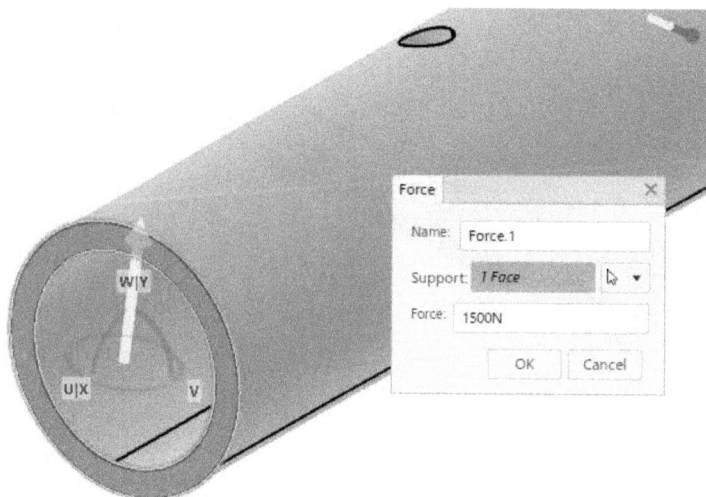

Figure 2–126

Task 2: Run the analysis.

1. Run the analysis and wait until it completes.

Task 3: Visualize and examine the analysis results.

1. Visualize and animate the deformed mesh. Does the part deform according to the applied loads?

2. Display the displacement magnitude color plot. What is the value of the maximum displacement in the model?

3. Display the Von Mises color plot. Does the maximum stress exceed the yield strength of the material?

4. Display the Factor of Safety plot. What is the minimum factor of safety for the part?

   - Factor of Safety value is obtained by dividing the material's yield strength by the maximum stress in the model. Factor of Safety less than 1 indicates failure.

5. Find the location of the maximum stress. Can you think of design changes that would lead to decrease in the stress level in that area?

6. Do the transverse holes cause stress concentration? Should it be a design concern?

7. Close the model without saving.

End of practice

Loads and Boundary Conditions

Loads and boundary conditions represent interactions of your product with its working environment. Selecting the correct boundary conditions for your FEA model is a critical aspect of developing an accurate simulation. Therefore, when you are simulating a product, the loads and boundary conditions placed on it must realistically represent the operating conditions of your product.

In this chapter, you learn about the tools available for applying loads and boundary conditions in a structural simulation.

Learning Objectives

- Understand the rigid body motions.
- Create Clamp, Fixed Displacement, and Applied Translation boundary conditions.
- Create Slider, Hinge, and Ball Joint boundary conditions.
- Use the Planar Symmetry boundary condition.
- Create Pressure and Bearing loads.
- Create Force, Remote Force, and Remote Torque loads.
- Create Gravity and Centrifugal loads.
- Create surface patches to apply loads and boundary conditions.
- Obtain reaction forces in restraints.

3.1 Boundary Conditions

In 3DEXPERIENCE SIMULIA apps, a boundary condition assigns a *prescribed displacement* to one or more geometrical entities in the model. Prescribed displacement means that the displacement of the geometrical entity to which it is applied is enforced throughout the simulation. A prescribed displacement (i.e., restraint) can be of a zero value (which is typically used to simulate all kinds of supports in the analysis model) or of a non-zero value (which is typically used to enforce a specific motion in the model).

Boundary conditions are commonly used to model a true support, such as where a structure is fixed to a rigid foundation or adjoining structure. Another common use is to simulate symmetry conditions.

Although boundary conditions are essential for structural analyses, it is preferable to avoid the use of unnecessary restraints. Since the essence of structural FEA is to calculate displacements (along with the corresponding strains and stresses), the prescribed displacements effectively force an assumed solution onto some of the geometrical entities in the model. Therefore, unnecessary restraints might unnaturally stiffen the model, and, consequently, the stresses might typically err on the low side.

Rigid Body Motions

In static structural analysis, it is necessary to provide sufficient supports to prevent rigid body motions (RBM), which are the movements of parts of the structure that do not produce strain.

An example of a simply supported beam is shown in Figure 3–1.

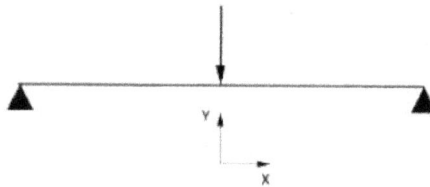

Figure 3–1

When using handbook formulas to calculate deflections and stresses in the beam, the only supports required are those in the vertical Y-direction. Since no loads are applied in the X-direction, a support in that direction is not necessary. However, in FEA, the lack of support in X-direction results in a fatal error, since the beam is unconstrained against moving in the X-direction as a rigid body.

When the FEA solver detects an RBM in the model, the computation is likely to fail. You must add restraints that eliminate all the RBMs, then re-run the simulation.

The number of possible RBMs varies from one model to another. For a single part in 3D, there are six possible RBMs: three translations and three rotations. For an assembly, the number could be much greater, since each part now has six possible RBMs that must be eliminated by connecting the part to the ground (i.e., applying a restraint), or by connecting the part to other parts in the model.

Clamp

The *Clamp* boundary condition renders the surface completely immovable – all translations and rotations are blocked. Usually, a Clamp represents a surface that is welded, bolted, or otherwise connected to the ground or to the adjoining rigid structure.

To apply a Clamp, select ✎ (Clamp) either in the *Assistant* dialog box or in the *Boundary Conditions* section of the Action Bar, and select the surfaces you want to clamp as the **Supports**, as shown in Figure 3–2.

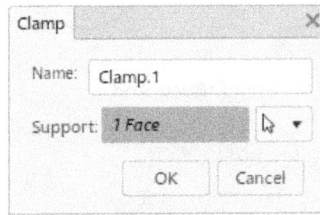

Figure 3–2

Fixed Displacement

The *Fixed Displacement* boundary condition allows the user to restrain a surface from moving in any of the coordinate directions, such as **X**, **Y**, and **Z**.

To apply a Fixed Displacement, select ⚙ (Fixed Displacement) either in the *Assistant* dialog box or in the *Boundary Conditions* section of the Action Bar, then select the surfaces you want to restrain as the **Supports**, and toggle on the directions you want to restrain.

The XYZ directions in the dialog box reference the Robot's axes. You can use the context toolbar to align the Robot's axes as required.

In the example shown in Figure 3-3, the highlighted surface is restrained from motion in **Y** direction.

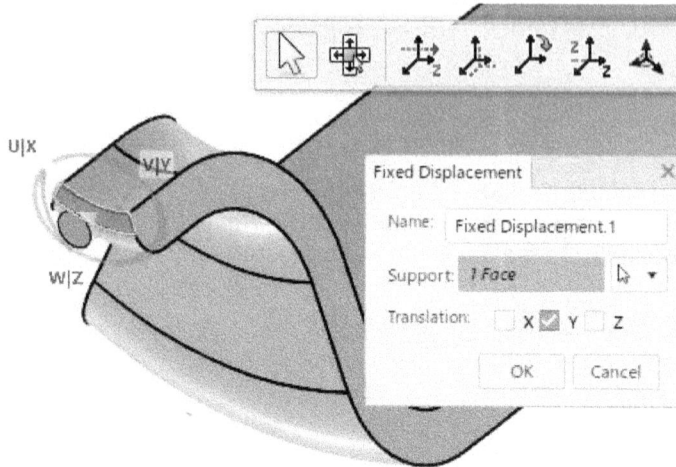

Figure 3-3

Slider

The *Slider* boundary condition restrains displacements in normal to the flat surface direction at every mesh node on that surface. The tangent to the surface directions, however, are not restrained. In result, the surface is allowed to translate within its own plane and rotate about the axis normal to its plane.

In the example show in Figure 3-4, the highlighted surface is free to translate and deform in-plane and to rotate about the normal to plane direction.

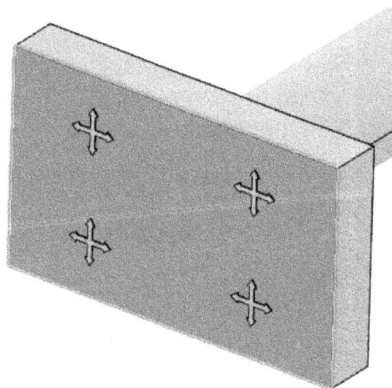

Figure 3-4

To apply a Slider, select ⛰ (Slider) either in the *Assistant* dialog box or in the *Boundary Conditions* section of the Action Bar, and select the **Supports**, as shown in Figure 3−5.

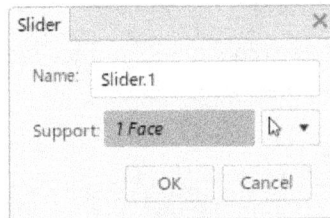

Figure 3−5

Hinge

The *Hinge* boundary condition allows a cylindrical surface to rotate about its own axis, but restrains all other translations and rotations.

In the example show in Figure 3−6, the highlighted surface is free to rotate about its axis; all other rotations and translations are restrained.

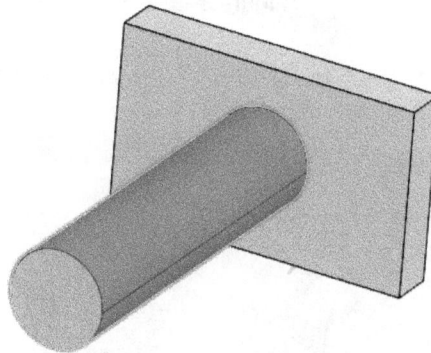

Figure 3−6

To apply a Hinge, select 🔷 (Hinge) either in the *Assistant* dialog box or in the *Boundary Conditions* section of the Action Bar, and select the **Supports**, as shown in Figure 3−7.

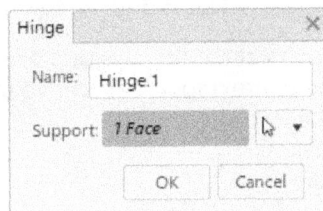

Figure 3−7

Ball Joint

The *Ball Joint* boundary condition allows a surface to rotate about a selected center point. The center of rotation, however, cannot move.

In the example show in Figure 3–8, the highlighted surface is free to rotate about the Robot's origin.

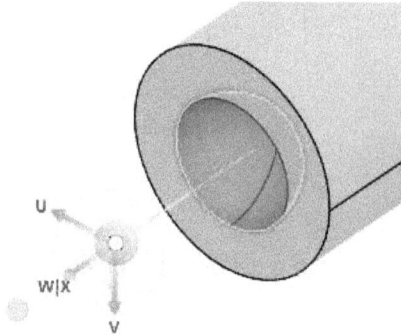

Figure 3–8

To apply a Ball Joint, select ![icon](Ball Joint) (Ball Joint) either in the *Assistant* dialog box or in the Action Bar, and select the **Supports**, as shown in Figure 3–9.

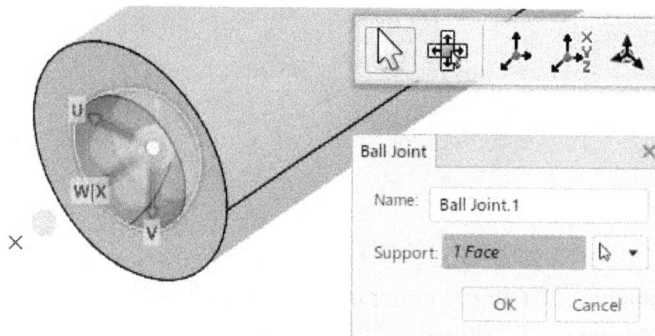

Figure 3–9

The center of rotation is assumed to be at the Robot's origin, which, by default, is located at the CG of the Supports. You can use the context toolbar to move the Robot to a specific point, or to specify the global coordinates of the Robot.

Applied Translation

The *Applied Translation* boundary condition enforces a specific motion on one or more surfaces in your model. I.e., the surface translation is prescribed, and the internal forces and stresses are solved for during the simulation.

To apply a translation, select u (Applied Translation) either in the *Assistant* dialog box or in the Action Bar, and select the surfaces you want to translate, as shown in Figure 3−10.

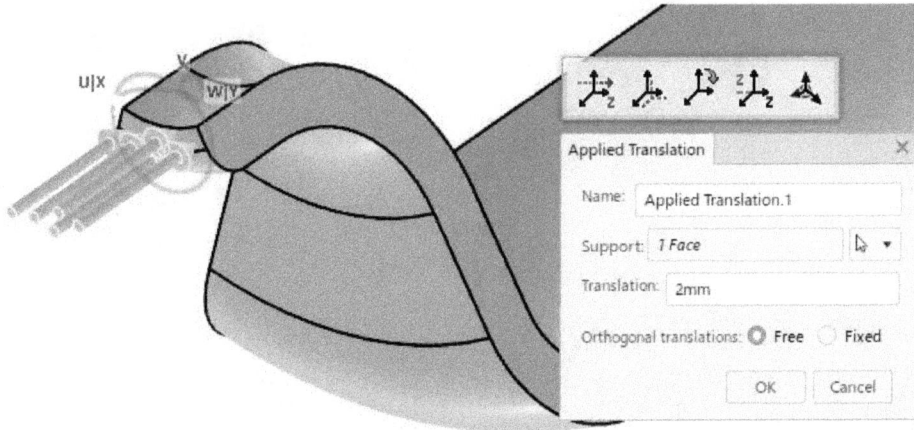

Figure 3−10

The direction of the translation is assumed to be along the W-axis of the Robot. Use the context toolbar to change the Robot's directions, if required.

Planar Symmetry

Using symmetry boundary conditions, you can take advantage of the model's symmetry to reduce the number of finite elements therefore the analysis time. In essence, symmetry conditions enable you to analyze a segment of the model and project the result onto the entire model.

The *Planar Symmetry* boundary condition requires that the model exhibits a *reflective* symmetry about a plane. I.e. the geometry, loads, and restraints on one side of the plane must mirror the geometry, loads, and restraints on the other side of the plane. The model may have one, or two, or even three planes of symmetry.

To apply the symmetry boundary condition, select (Planar Symmetry) either in the *Assistant* dialog box or in the Action Bar, and select the surfaces that lie in the plane of symmetry, as shown in Figure 3−11.

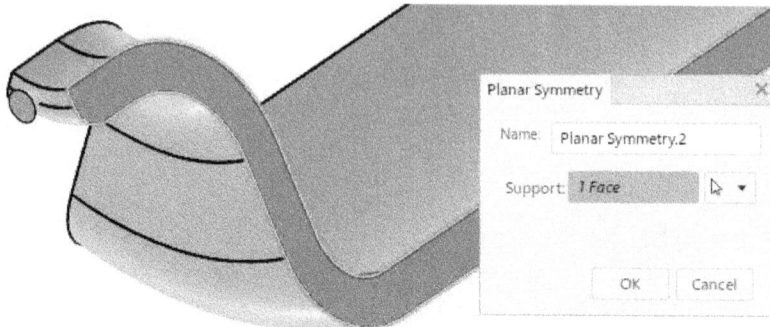

Figure 3−11

3.2 Loads

Unsatisfactory representation of the loading is a common cause of inaccurate analysis results. Therefore, gathering adequate information about the magnitude of the loads is a critical aspect of developing an accurate simulation. It should be noted that, in a linear analysis, the stresses and deformations are directly proportional to the magnitude of the loading. For example, a possible error in loading of 20% leads to a minimum 20% error in stresses and deflections.

Pressure

A *Pressure* load is a distributed surface force that acts in normal to the part surface direction, even if the surface is curved. The positive load direction is toward the part body.

To apply a pressure load, select 𝄃𝄃 (Pressure) either in the *Assistant* dialog box or in the Action Bar to open the *Pressure* dialog box as shown in Figure 3−12. Select the surfaces to which you want to apply the load, enter the pressure magnitude, and click **OK**.

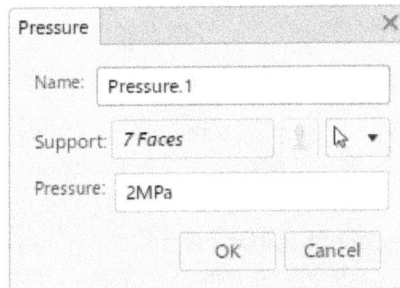

Pressure		×
Name:	Pressure.1	
Support:	7 Faces	
Pressure:	2MPa	
	OK	Cancel

Figure 3−12

Bearing Load

Bearing Load approximates the pressure applied on a cylindrical hole by a rigid pin or shaft passing through that hole.

To apply a bearing load, select ⮂ (Bearing Load) either in the *Assistant* dialog box or in the Action Bar. Select the surfaces to which you want to apply the load, enter the load magnitude, and click **OK**, as shown in Figure 3–13.

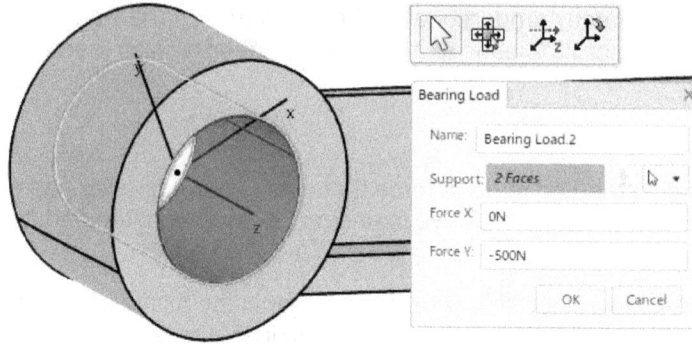

Figure 3–13

Force

A *Force* load applies an equivalent system of tractions on the selected surface, such that the total force on the surface is equal to the specified force magnitude.

To apply a force, select ✎ (Force) either in the *Assistant* dialog box or in the Action Bar. In the *Force* dialog box that opens, select the surfaces to which you want to apply the load and enter the force's magnitude, as shown in Figure 3–14.

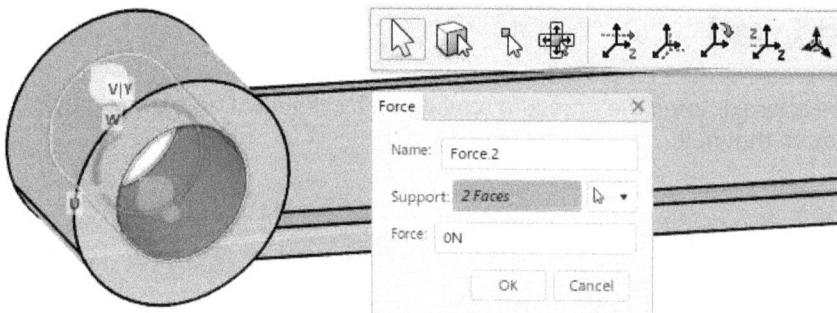

Figure 3–14

The direction of the load is always aligned with the **W** axis of the Robot. Use the contextual toolbar to change the direction, if required.

Remote Force

A *Remote Force* applies a concentrated force at a point, then transmits this force to the support surface. The transmission is done in equivalent way, so that the total force on the surface is equal to the specified force magnitude at the load application point.

This provides an effective way to represent a force that originates far from the part but is transmitted to the part via other components.

In the example shown in Figure 3–15, the force is applied at a remote point and then transmitted to the inside surface of the boss.

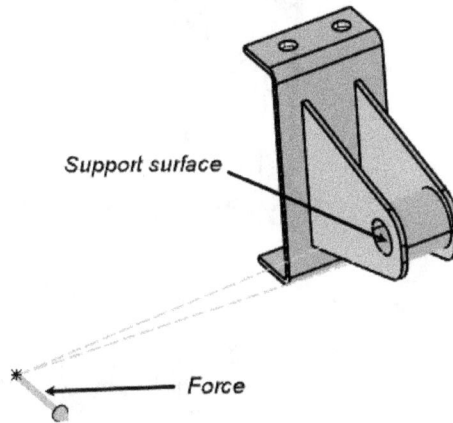

Figure 3–15

To apply a remote force, select ✎ (Remote Force) either in the *Assistant* dialog box or in the Action Bar. In the *Remote Force* dialog box that opens, select the surfaces to which you want to apply the load and enter the force's magnitude, as shown in Figure 3–16.

The force application point is assumed to be at the origin of the Robot, and the force's direction aligned with the **W** axis of the Robot. Use the context toolbar to change the Robot's location and orientation, if required.

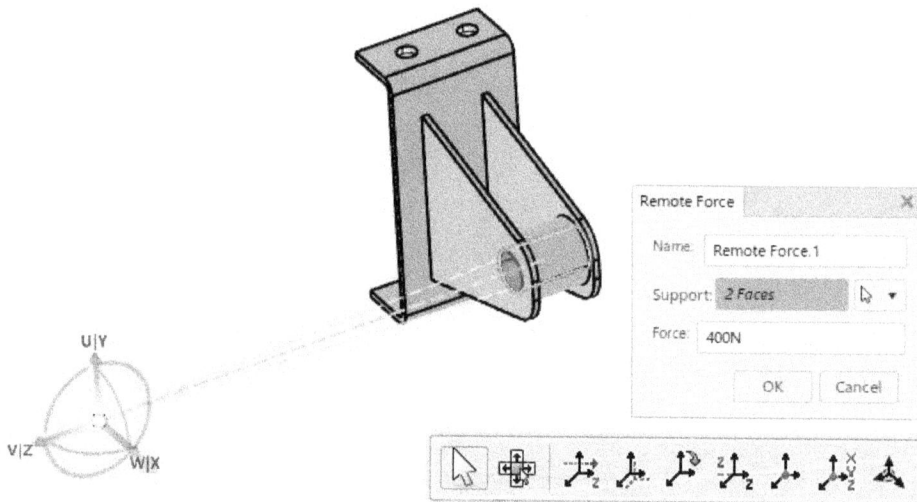

Figure 3–16

Remote Torque

A Torque is a twisting or rotational load. It applies a system of tractions on the supporting surfaces that is equivalent to the magnitude and direction of the given force couple.

To apply a torque load, select ✎ (Remote Torque) either in the *Assistant* dialog box or in the Action Bar. In the *Remote Torque* dialog box that opens, select the entities to which you want to apply the load and enter the torque magnitude, as shown in Figure 3–17.

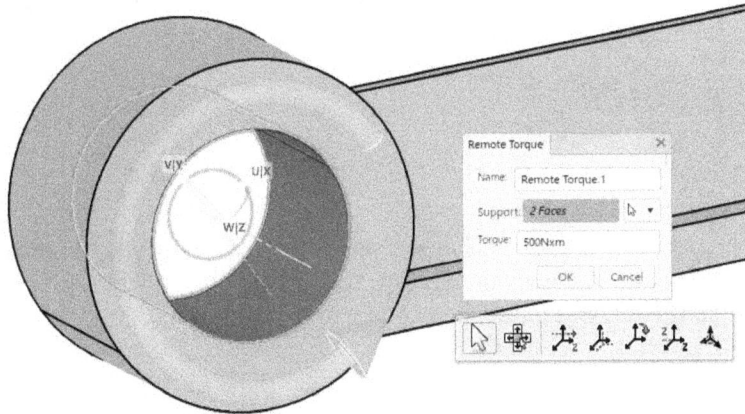

Figure 3-17

The torque is assumed to be acting around the Robot's **W** axis. Use the contextual toolbar to change the orientation of the Robot, if required.

Gravity

A *Gravity* load is a linear body force applied to all the solid bodies in the model, such as due to acceleration or deceleration.

To apply Gravity load, select (Gravity) either in the *Assistant* dialog box or in the Action Bar. In the *Gravity* dialog box, enter the **X**, **Y**, and **Z** components of the acceleration vector, as shown in Figure 3-18.

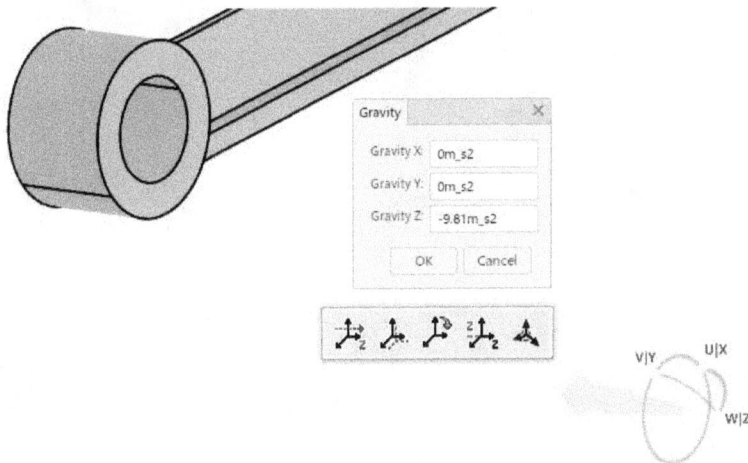

Figure 3-18

The **X**, **Y**, and **Z** directions are assumed to be the Robot's axes. Use the context toolbar to change the orientation of the Robot, if required.

Centrifugal Force

A *Centrifugal Force* simulates the load experienced by rotating bodies.

To apply a Centrifugal Force, select ⟲ (Centrifugal Force) either in the *Assistant* dialog box or in the Action Bar. In the *Centrifugal Force* dialog box that opens, select the *Axis of rotation*, and enter the *Rotational velocity* magnitude, as shown in Figure 3–19.

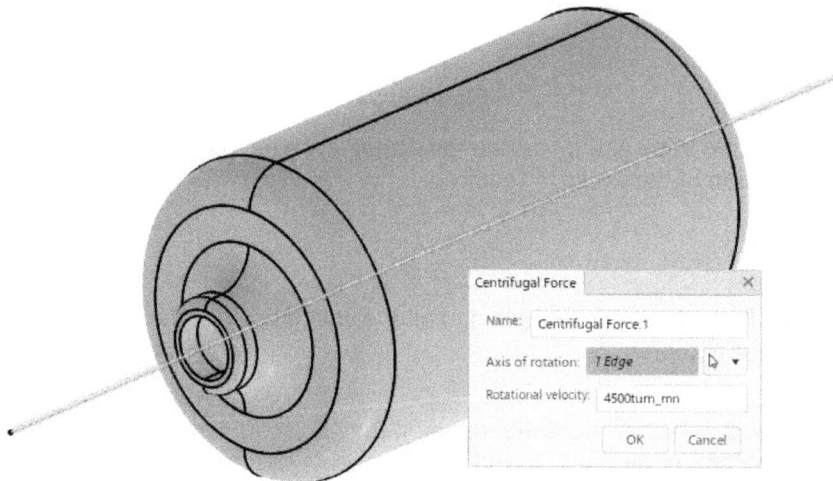

Figure 3–19

3.3 Applying Loads and Restraints on Surface Patches

In some simulations, you might need to apply loads and boundary conditions on the portions of the part surfaces rather than on whole surfaces. For example, for the model shown in Figure 3–20, the restraints must be applied over the weldment area only, which is a thin strip of the part surface going around the entire part. The load also must be applied over a patch on the part surface, as shown.

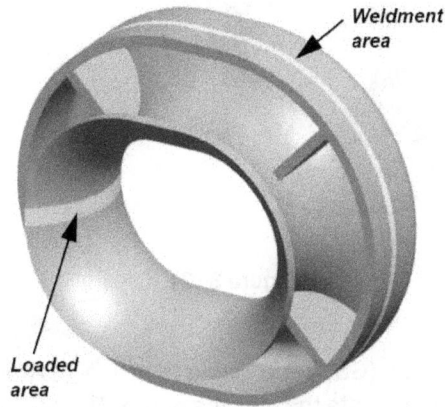

Weldment area

Loaded area

Figure 3–20

Creating geometrical supports for such loads and restraints is a multi-step process, as follows:

- Create a boundary for the surface patch. On a planar surface, use Sketch. On curved surfaces, you can use Projections, Intersections, or other tools as suitable. The boundary of the patch must be a closed contour and must lie on the surface of the part. For example, to simulate clamping action of the bolt head around a hole, the boundary of the area under the bolt head can be sketched, as shown in Figure 3–21.

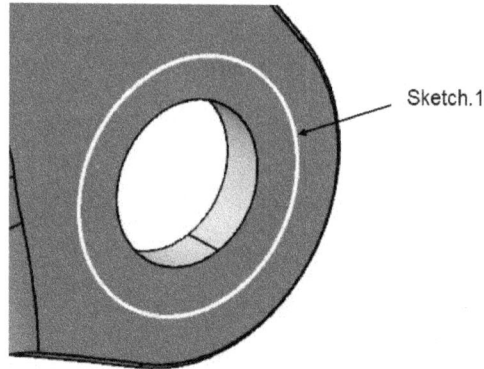

Figure 3–21

- In the *Generative Shape Design* (GSD) app, using the (Extract) tool, extract the solid surface on which you want to create the surface patch. The result, with the **PartBody** hidden, is shown in Figure 3–22.

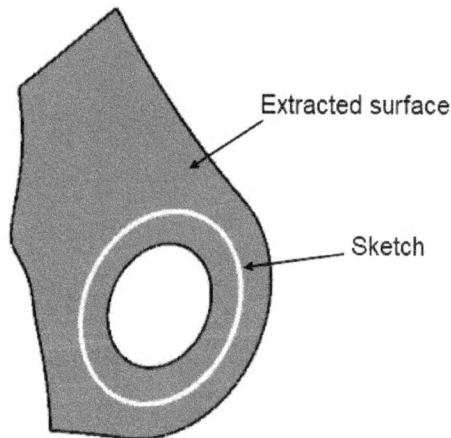

Figure 3–22

- Using the (Split) tool in the *GSD* app, split the extracted surface with the patch's boundary, keeping the side that is inside the patch boundary, as shown in Figure 3-23.

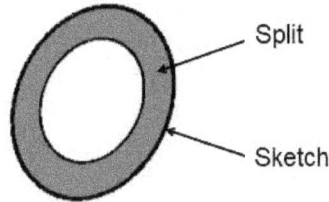

Figure 3-23

- Switch to the *Part Design* app, and unhide and activate the **PartBody**.

- In the *Refine* section of the Action Bar, select (Sew Surface). In the *Sew Surface* dialog box that opens, select the split surface as the **Object to sew** and deactivate the **Simplify geometry** checkbox. Make sure the grey arrow in the preview points toward the solid body, which is the side of the solid to keep. The model displays as shown in Figure 3-24.

  *Note: If **Simplify geometry** option is on, the system will not separate the surface patch from the rest of the solid's surface.*

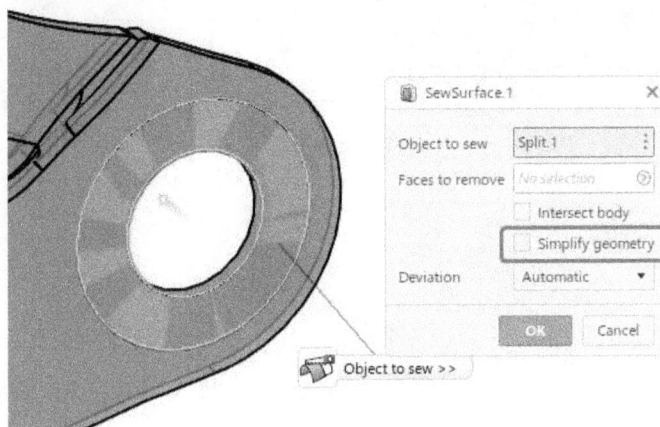

Figure 3-24

- Click **OK** to complete the operation. Hide the split surface and the sketch. The model displays as shown in Figure 3-25. Note that the surface patch area is now separate from the rest of the part surface.

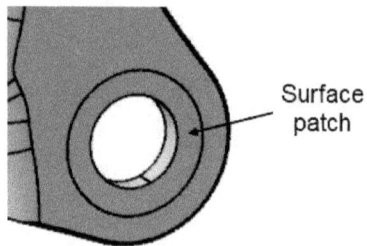

Surface patch

Figure 3-25

Now you can apply a load or a restraint to the created surface patch, as shown in Figure 3-26.

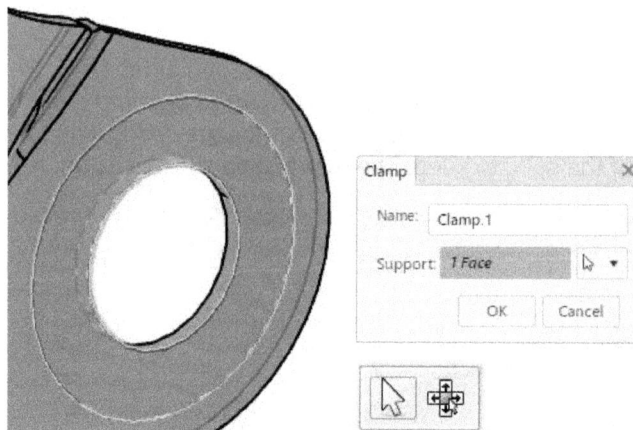

Figure 3-26

3.4 Obtaining Reaction Forces in Restraints

Once the analysis is solved, you can use the **Resultant Sensor** tool to obtain the reactions in a restraint.

- To create a **Resultant Sensor**, select $\overset{\Sigma}{}$ (Resultant Sensor) in the *Results* section of the Action Bar. The *Resultant Sensor* dialog box opens, as shown in Figure 3–27.

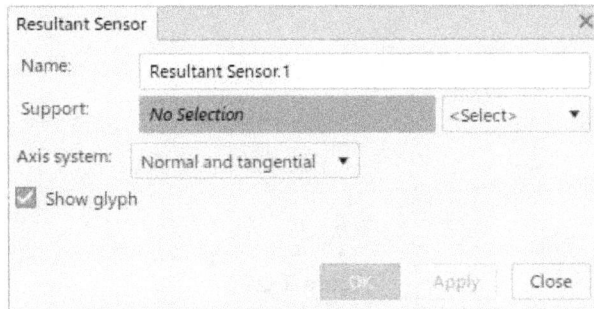

Figure 3–27

- Expand the *<Select>* drop-down menu and select **Restraints**, as shown in Figure 3–28.

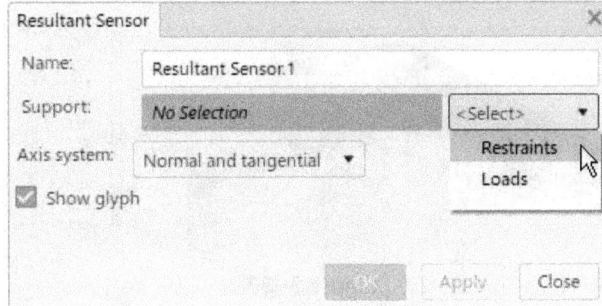

Figure 3–28

- In the *Restraint Selection* dialog box, select a restraint, for example **Clamp.1,** and click **Select**, as shown in Figure 3–29.

Figure 3–29

- The **Resultant Sensor**, both direction and magnitude, displays in the model, as shown in Figure 3–30.

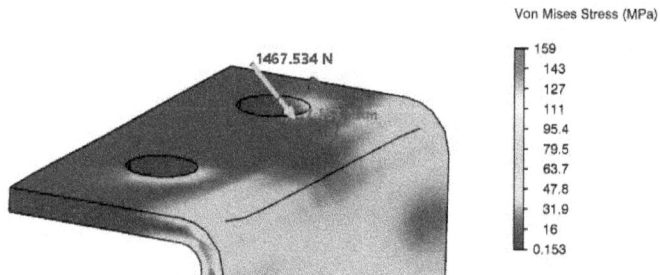

Figure 3–30

Practice 3a
Stress Analysis of a Crank

Practice Objectives

- Apply the material and mesh the model.
- Apply force load in a specific direction.
- Simulate pin and bushing supports with a Hinge boundary condition.
- Display and animate the analysis results.

In this practice, you will set up and run a static stress analysis on a crank part shown in Figure 3-31. The part is restrained by a pin support in the lower boss and by two bushing supports at the ends of the lower rod. This way, the lower beam of the part is not constrained against rotation at its ends, similar to a simply supported beam.

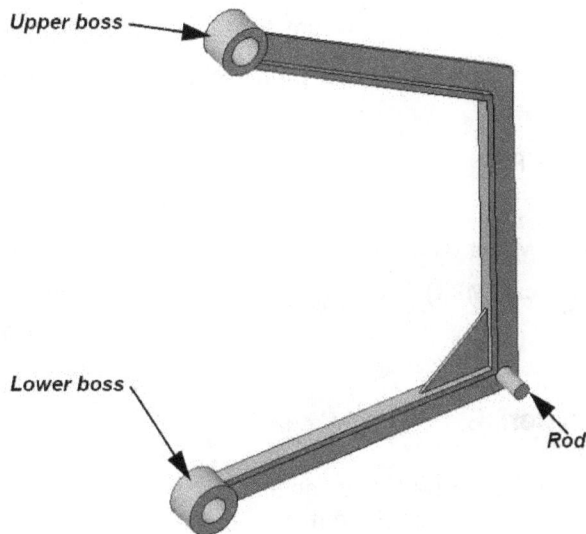

Figure 3-31

Task 1: Open the part.

1. Import with your initials and open **Crank_03.3dxml**.

2. Set the model display as 🛢 (Shading with Sharp and Smooth Edges). The part displays as shown in Figure 3–32.

Figure 3–32

3. Select **Preferences>Common Preferences>Parameters, Measures, and Units>Units** and set the units as follows:

- *Length:* **Millimeter (mm)**
- *Force:* **Newton (N)**
- *Moment:* **Newton x Meter (Nxm)**
- *Pressure:* **Megapascal (MPa)**
- *Stress:* **Megapascal (MPa)**

Task 2: Apply the material.

1. Apply the **Steel** material to the part. You can either use the material definition you created in *Practice 2b* or create a new material. Verify that the applied material has the following properties:

- *Young's Modulus:* **200000 MPa**
- *Poisson's Ratio:* **0.266**
- *Density:* **7860 Kg/m3**
- *Proof (Yield) Stress:* **250 MPa**

Task 3: Launch the Linear Structural Validation app.

1. Activate the *Crank_03* window and launch the **Linear Structural Validation** app.
2. Enter *<Your Initials>***_Crank Simulation** for the *Title* of the Physics Simulation.
3. Select **Structural** for *Analysis type.*

Task 4: Mesh the part.

1. Measure the thickness of the part's profile, as shown in Figure 3-33.

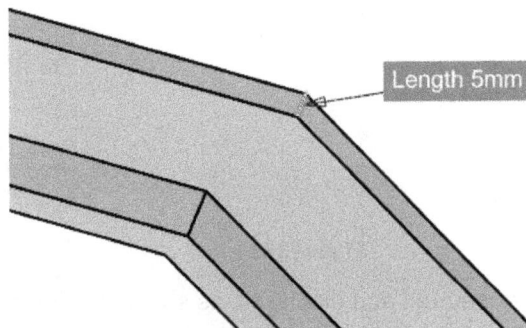

Figure 3-33

2. Select ▤ (Assistant) in the Action Bar. Select the *Setup* section in the *Assistant* dialog box.

3. Select ◈ (Mesh Specifications) in the *Assistant* dialog box, and enter **9mm** as the *Element Size*, as shown in Figure 3–34. Activate the **Generate mesh** option and click **OK** to complete.

   Note: Size **9mm** *is 1.8 times the thickness of the part, which is the recommended ratio for thin-walled parts.*

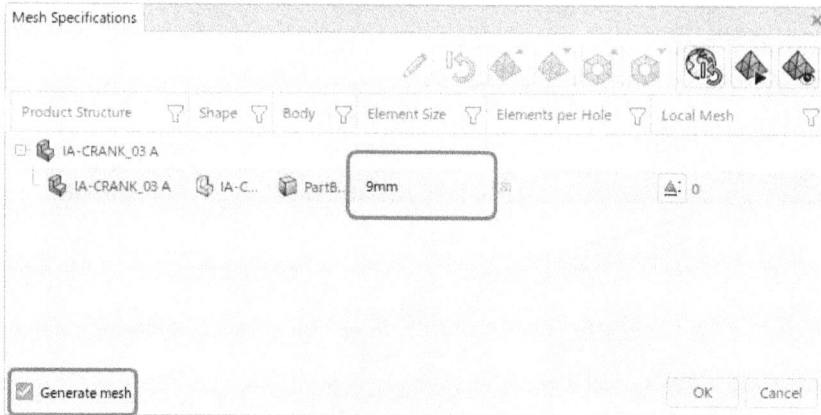

Figure 3–34

4. The mesh for the part is generated and displayed, as shown in Figure 3–35. Rotate the model and examine the mesh in various areas of the part.

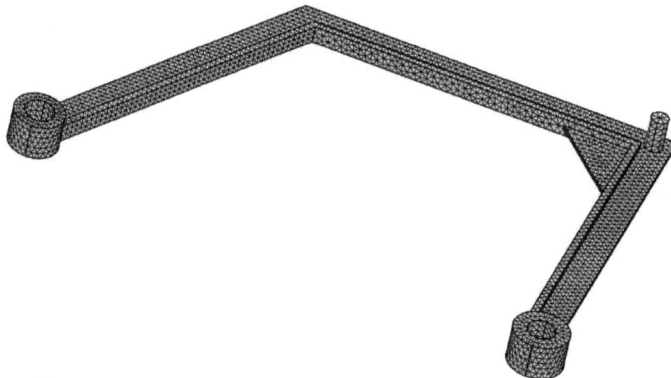

Figure 3–35

5. Select ◈ (Hide/Show Mesh) in the Action Bar to hide the mesh.

Task 5: Apply the load.

In this task, you will apply a **500N** force to the hole in the upper boss, acting in-plane of the crank and in a specific direction. The force direction is specified by a line that you will need to create prior to applying the load.

1. Activate the *Crank_03* window. Double-click the 3D Shape in the tree to activate the **Part Design** app.

2. Create a new geometrical set named **Load Direction**.

3. Using the **Circle/Sphere/Ellipse center** option, create two points (**Point.1** and **Point.2**) at the centers of the circles on both sides of the upper boss, as shown in Figure 3–36.

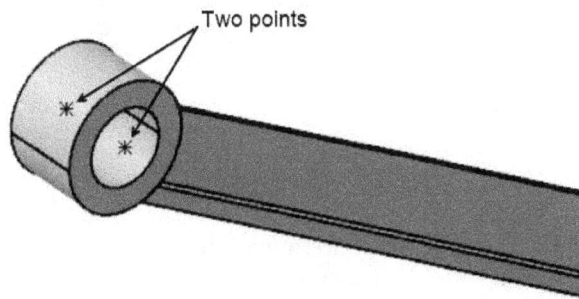

Figure 3–36

4. Using the **Between** option, create the middle point (**Point.3**) between **Point.1** and **Point.2**, as shown in Figure 3–37.

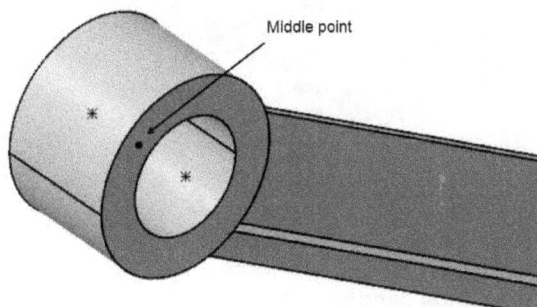

Figure 3–37

5. Using the **Coordinates** option, create the 4th point (**Point.4**) with coordinates (**-100mm, -150mm, 0mm**) and **Point.3** as the **Reference** point, as shown in Figure 3−38.

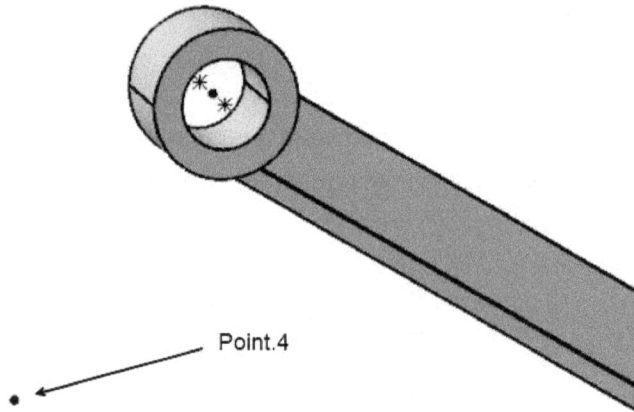

Point.4

Figure 3−38

6. Create a line (**Line.1**) from **Point.3** to **Point.4**, as shown in Figure 3−39.

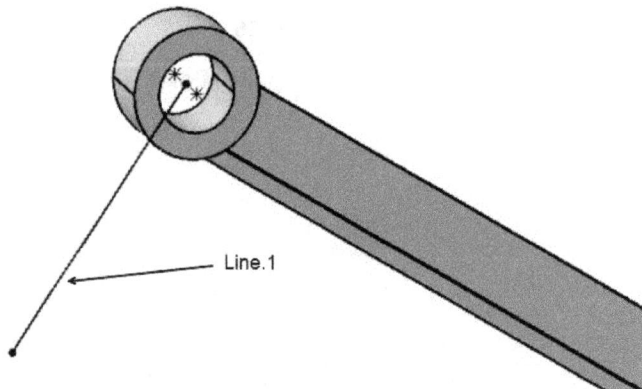

Line.1

Figure 3−39

7. Activate the *Crank Simulation* window.

8. In the *Assistant*, select the *Loads* section and click (Force). Once the *Force* dialog box opens, select the two inside surfaces of the boss as the *Support*, as shown in Figure 3−40.

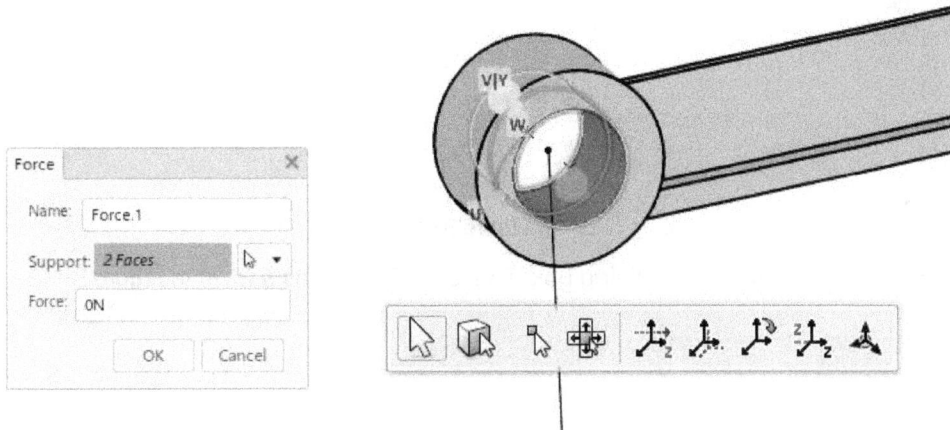

Figure 3−40

9. In the context toolbar, select (Align Triad Handle with a line, plane normal, etc.), then select **Line.1**. This will align the force direction with the line.

10. If necessary, click (Reverse Direction of Triad Handle Z Axis) in the context toolbar, to make sure the force direction preview points down, as shown in Figure 3−41.

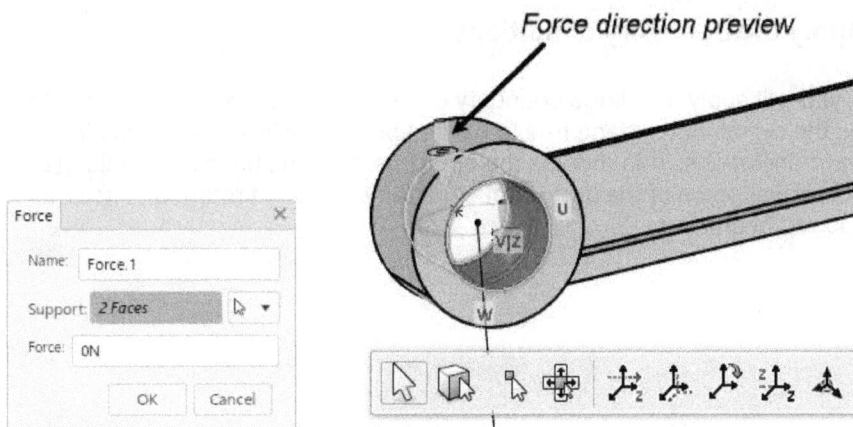

Figure 3−41

11. Enter **500N**, as shown in Figure 3–42.

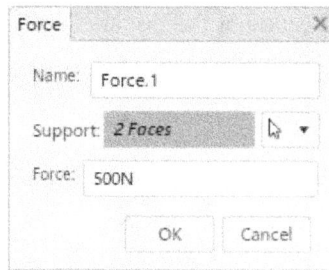

Force		×
Name:	Force.1	
Support:	*2 Faces*	▾
Force:	500N	
	OK	Cancel

Figure 3–42

12. Click **OK** to close the *Force* dialog box. The load displays as shown in Figure 3–43.

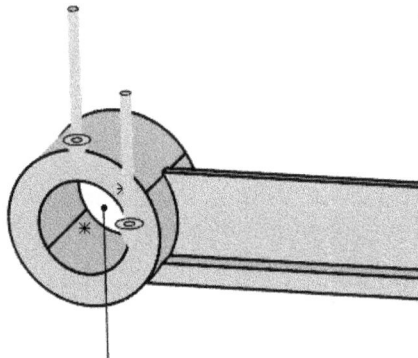

Figure 3–43

Task 6: Apply the boundary conditions.

In this task, you will apply the **Hinge** boundary condition to the lower boss and to the lower rod. Hinge keeps the cylindrical surface free to rotate about its axis, while restraining all other rotations and translations. This models the pin support on the boss and bushing supports on the rod, so the lower beam of the part is not constrained against rotation at its ends, similar to a simply supported beam.

1. In the *Assistant* dialog box, select the **Boundary Conditions** section, and click ✎ (Hinge). The *Hinge* dialog box opens, as shown in Figure 3–44.

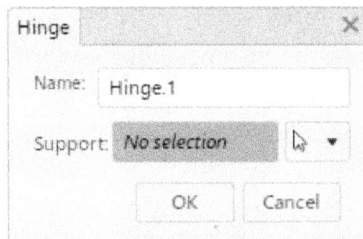

Figure 3–44

2. Select the outside surfaces of the rod, as shown in Figure 3–45.

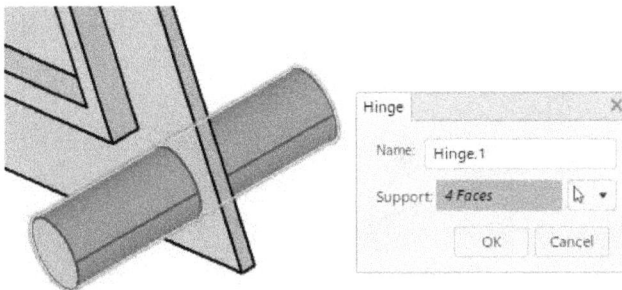

Figure 3–45

3. Click **OK** to close the *Hinge* dialog box.

4. Repeat steps 1 through 3 to apply another **Hinge** boundary condition to the inside surfaces of the lower boss, shown in Figure 3–46.

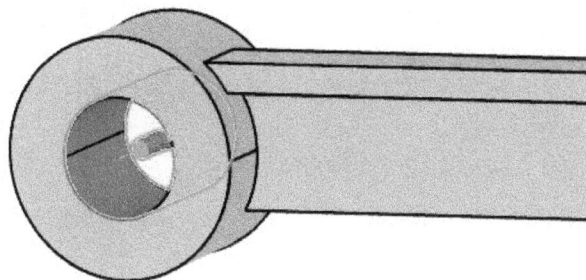

Figure 3–46

Task 7: Run the analysis.

1. Select the *Simulate* section in the *Assistant* dialog box and click ⬱ (Simulate).

2. Once the *Simulate* dialog box opens, accept all the default settings, and click **OK** to start the computation.

3. Wait until computation completes, and the *Simulation Status* dialog box displays the message "Static Stress Simulation completed". The computation for this model should take under **60sec**.

4. Close the *Simulation Status* and the *Assistant* dialog boxes.

Task 8: Display and animate the deformation.

1. In the *Plot* drop-down menu that floats on the screen, select **Deformation**. The deformed model image displays, as shown in Figure 3−47.

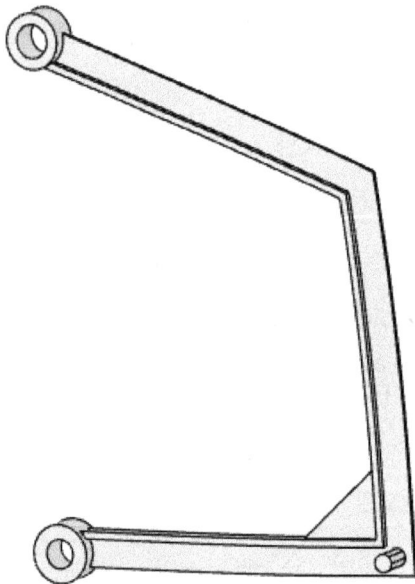

Figure 3−47

2. Double-click the deformed model to open the *Contour Plot* dialog box. Change the *Scale factor* to **30**, as shown in Figure 3−48.

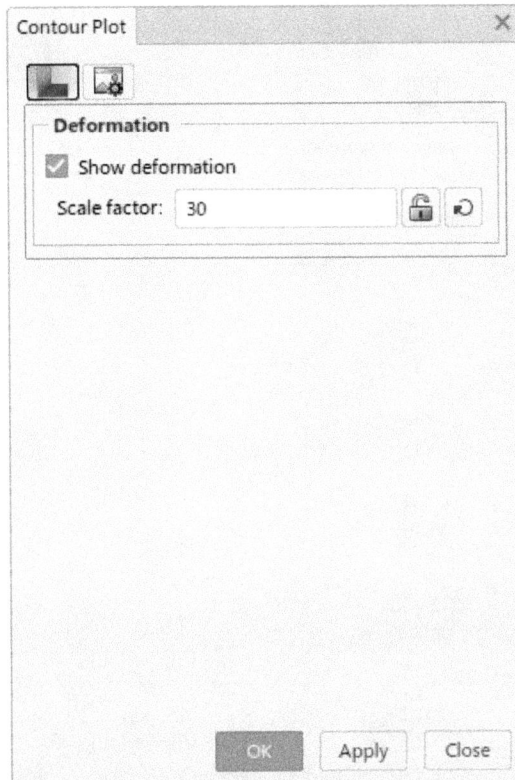

Figure 3−48

3. Activate the (Rendering) section of the *Contour Plot* dialog box, and in the *Visible edges* drop-down menu, select **Mesh**, as shown in Figure 3–49.

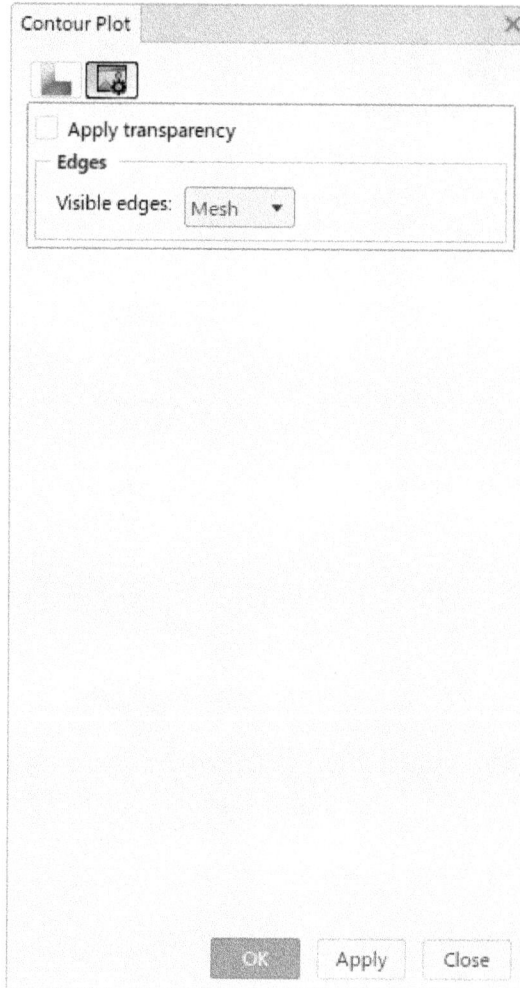

Figure 3–49

4. Click **OK**. The deformed model is now displayed with the mesh, as shown in Figure 3–50.

Figure 3–50

5. Play the animation. Using the Time Control ⊙ animation tool, change the playback **Duration** to approximately **3** seconds, as shown in Figure 3–51.

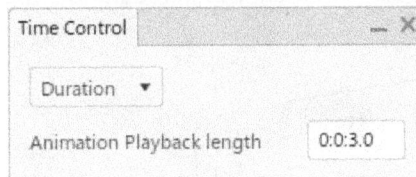

Figure 3–51

6. While playing the animation, zoom in on the rod, as shown in Figure 3–52. Note that the rod's rotation is not restricted, as if it was supported by sleeve bearings or bushings. This is because the *Hinge* boundary condition was applied on the rod's surface.

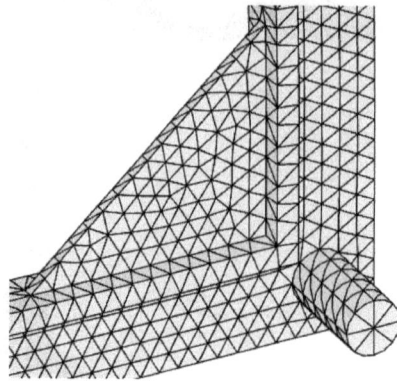

Figure 3–52

7. Zoom in on the lower boss, and note that its rotation is not restricted either, as if it was supported by a rigid pin.

8. Exit the animation.

Task 9: Visualize the displacement magnitude.

1. In the *Plot* drop-down menu, select **Displacement**. The displacement magnitude result plot is displayed, as shown in Figure 3–53.

   • Note that the maximum displacement magnitude under the *500N* load is **6.9mm**.

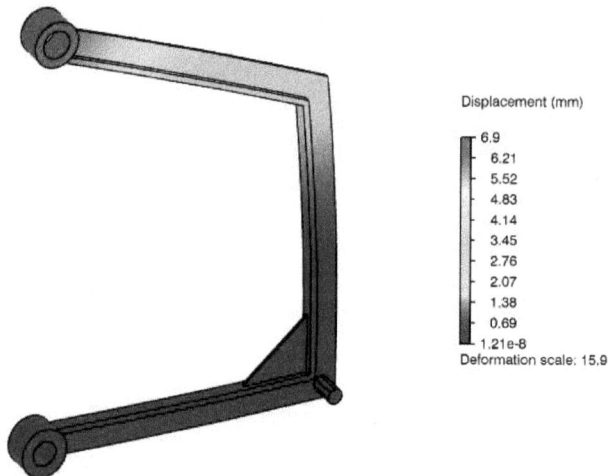

Displacement (mm)

6.9
6.21
5.52
4.83
4.14
3.45
2.76
2.07
1.38
0.69
1.21e-8
Deformation scale: 15.9

Figure 3–53

Task 10: Display Von Mises stress.

1. In the *Plot* drop-down menu, select **Von Mises Stress**. The stress image displays as shown in Figure 3–54.

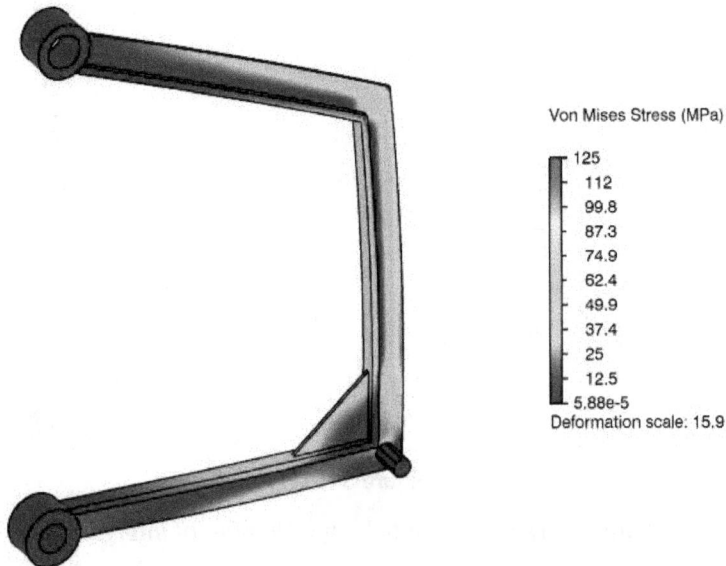

Von Mises Stress (MPa)

125
112
99.8
87.3
74.9
62.4
49.9
37.4
25
12.5
5.88e-5

Deformation scale: 15.9

Figure 3–54

2. Note that the maximum *Von Mises stress* in the model is approximately **125 MPa**, which is well below the material's *Yield Stress* of **250MPa**. Therefore, the part is predicted to withstand the load without failure.

Task 11: Adjust the Legend.

1. Double-click the plot legend to open the *Legend* dialog box, as shown in Figure 3–55.

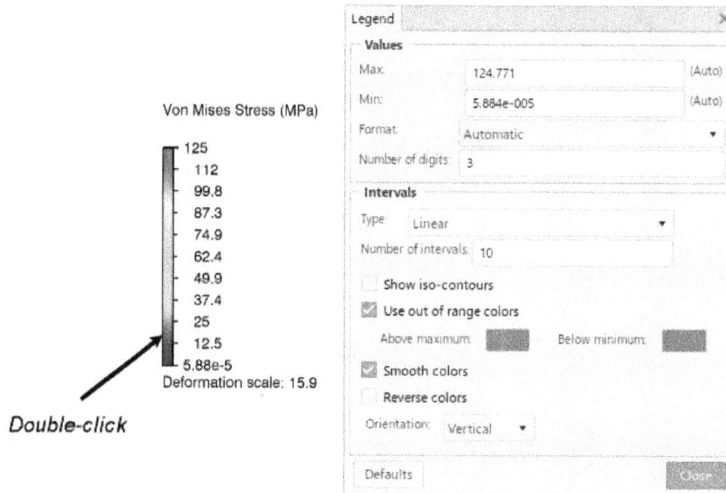

Figure 3–55

2. Deactivate the **Smooth colors** option and change *Number of intervals* to **6**, as shown in Figure 3–56.

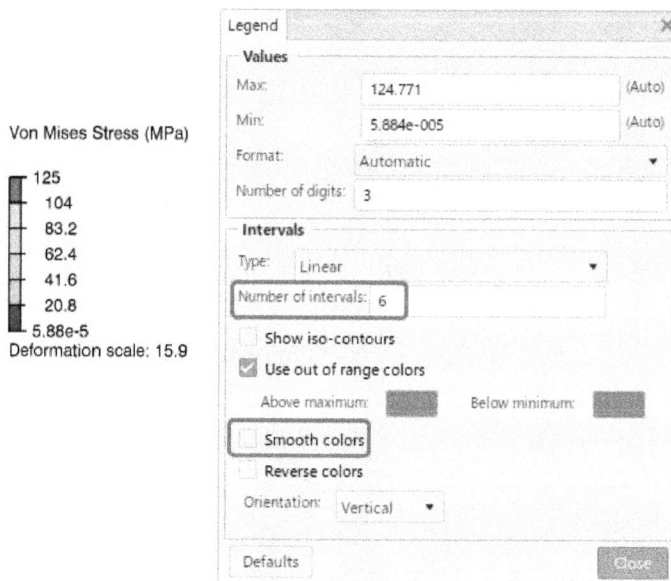

Figure 3–56

3. Click **Close** to close the *Legend* dialog box.

4. Review the stress in various areas of the model. Note that now the color map has six colors and the stress ranges associated with each color are easily identifiable in the image, as shown in Figure 3–57.

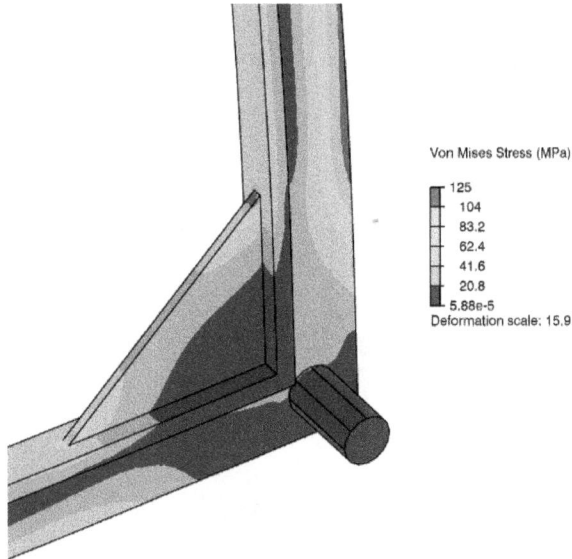

Figure 3–57

Task 12: Locate area of maximum stress.

1. In the *Results* section of the Action Bar, select ▣ (Show Min/Max Values), and in the context toolbar, select ▢ (Show only Max value), as shown in Figure 3–58.

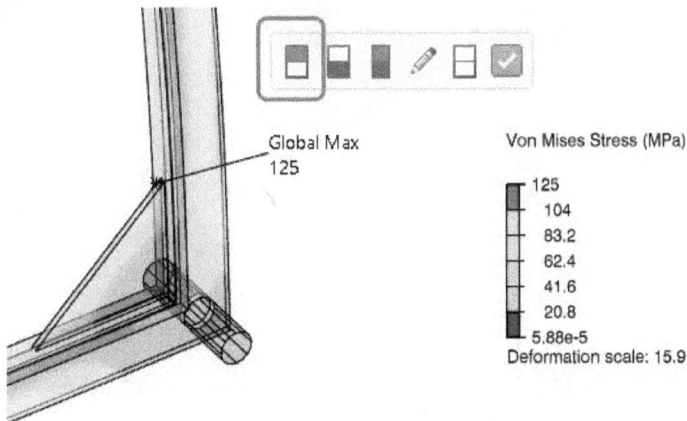

Figure 3–58

2. Move the **Global Max** label with the left mouse button to the location of your liking and click ✅ in the context toolbar to finalize. The result plot displays as shown in Figure 3–59.

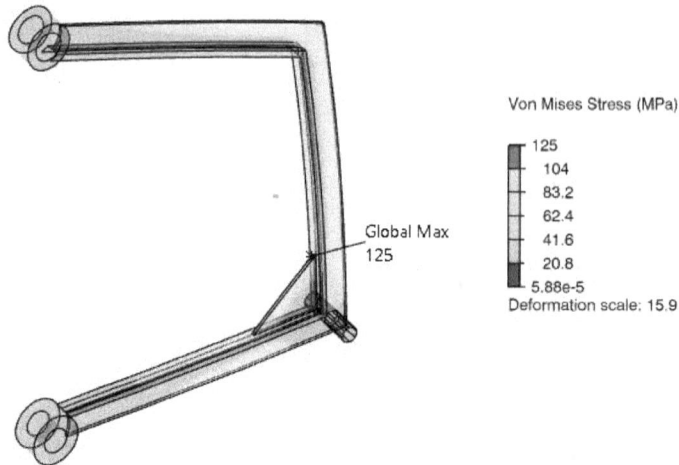

Figure 3–59

Task 13: Capture the image of the maximum stress location.

1. Expand the *Tools* section of the Action Bar to display the 📷 (Capture) icon, as shown in Figure 3–60.

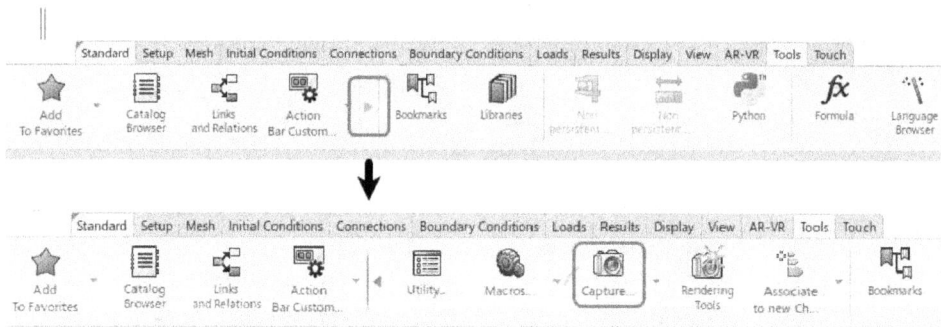

Figure 3–60

2. Select 📷 (Capture). In the *Capture* toolbar that displays, select the **Screen Area** option in the drop-down menu, as shown in Figure 3–61.

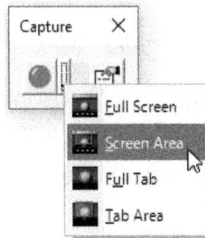

Figure 3-61

3. Click ⬤ (Capture) and drag a "rubber" rectangle around the area of maximum stress, as shown in Figure 3-62.

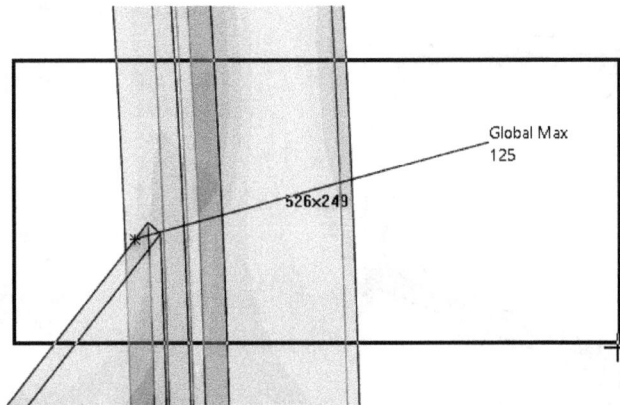

Figure 3-62

4. The *Capture Preview* window opens, as shown in Figure 3-63.

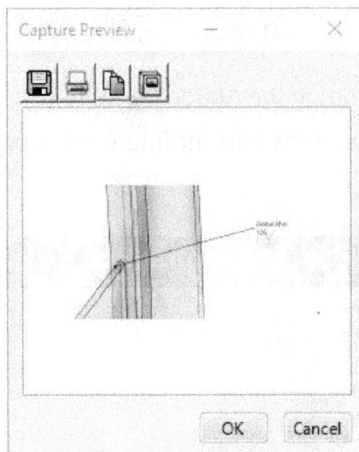

Figure 3-63

5. While the *Capture Preview* window is open, you can use ▣ (Save As) to save the capture to a file, ▣ (Print) to print the capture, or ▣ (Copy) to copy the capture onto the Windows clipboard then paste into another document, such as PowerPoint or Excel.

6. Close the Capture Preview, then the Capture toolbar.

7. Select the result plot, and in the context toolbar, click ▯ (Hide Max or Min values and close), as shown in Figure 3-64, to remove the **Global Max** label from the result plot.

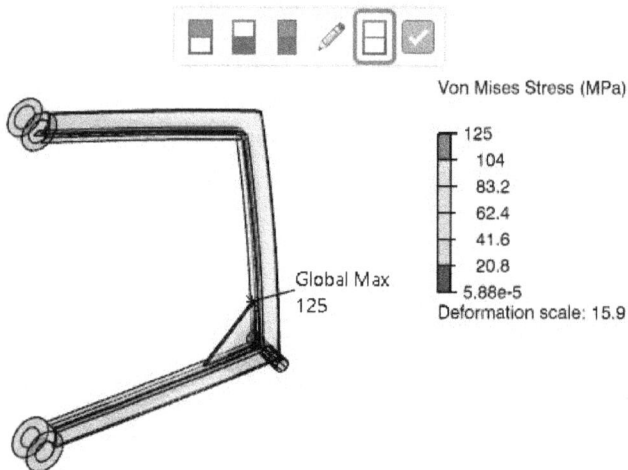

Von Mises Stress (MPa)

125
104
83.2
62.4
41.6
20.8
5.88e-5

Deformation scale: 15.9

Global Max
125

Figure 3-64

Task 14: Save and close the model.

1. Click ▨ (Result Visualization) in the Action Bar to return to the model view.

2. Optionally, save the analysis and the part for future reference.

3. Close all windows.

End of practice

Practice 3b
Bracket Loaded with a Remote Force

Practice Objectives

- Apply the material and mesh the model.
- Apply the remote force.
- Compute the analysis.
- Visualize the analysis results.
- Obtain reaction forces in restraints.

In this practice, you will set up and run a static stress analysis on a bracket, which is a part in the assembly shown in Figure 3–65. The bracket is restrained at the four holes in the top and bottom flanges, and the end of the shaft is loaded with a **400N** force acting in the horizontal direction.

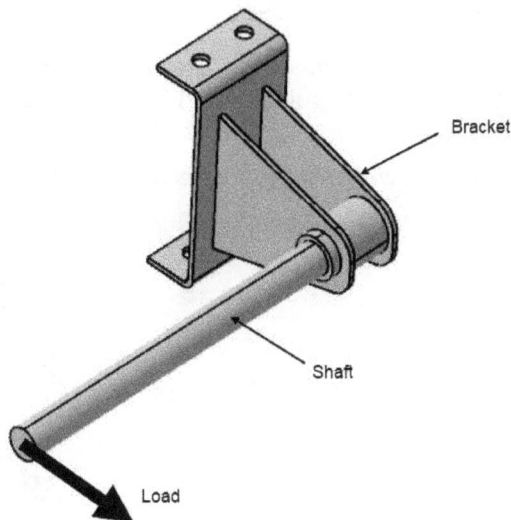

Figure 3–65

Task 1: Open the part.

1. Import with your initials and open **BRACKET_03.3dxml**.

2. Set the model display as 🛢 (Shading with Sharp and Smooth Edges) and change the color of *Point.1* in *Geometrical Set.1* to **black**. The part displays as shown in Figure 3–66.

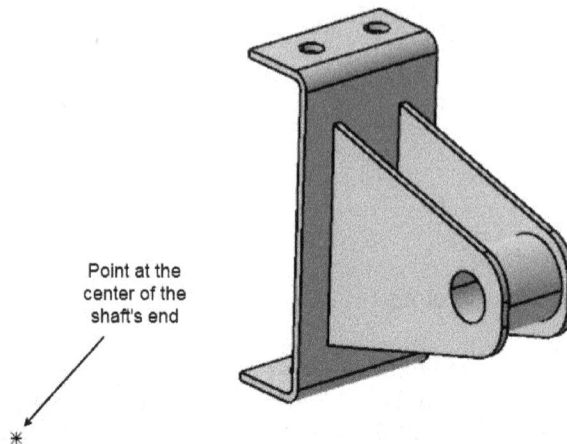

Point at the
center of the
shaft's end

Figure 3–66

*   Note that the shaft part will not be included in the analysis model. Instead, the load on the shaft will be applied at the remote point **Point.1**, which is located at the center of the shaft's end.

3. Select **Preferences>Common Preferences>Parameters, Measures, and Units>Units** and set the units as follows:

    *   *Length:* **Millimeter (mm)**
    *   *Force:* **Newton (N)**
    *   *Moment:* **Newton x Meter (Nxm)**
    *   *Pressure:* **Megapascal (MPa)**
    *   *Stress:* **Megapascal (MPa)**

Task 2: Launch the Linear Structural Validation app.

1. Activate the *BRACKET_03* window and launch the **Linear Structural Validation** app.

2. Enter **<*Your Initials*>_Bracket Simulation** for the *Title* of the Physics Simulation.

3. Select **Structural** for *Analysis type*.

Task 3: Apply the material.

1. Using ⬤ (Material Palette), apply the **Steel** material to the part. You can either use the material definition you created in *Practice 2b* or create a new material. Verify that the applied material has the following properties:

   - *Young's Modulus:* **200000 MPa**
   - *Poisson's Ratio:* **0.266**
   - *Density:* **7860 Kg/m3**
   - *Proof (Yield) Stress:* **250 MPa**

Task 4: Visualize the Mesh.

In this practice, you will use the default mesh specifications.

1. In the *Mesh* section of the Action Bar, select ◆ (Generate Mesh). The mesh for the part is generated and displayed, as shown in Figure 3−67.

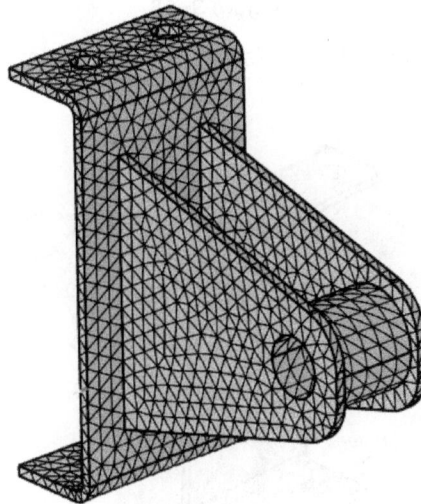

Figure 3−67

2. Select ◆ (Hide/Show Mesh) in the Action Bar to hide the mesh.

Task 5: Apply Boundary Conditions.

In this task, you will apply the **Clamp** boundary condition to the four holes in the bracket. You will create a separate restraint for each hole, in order to facilitate separate reaction force extraction for each hole.

1. Select (Clamp) in the *Boundary Conditions* section of the Action Bar and restrain the inside surface of the 1st hole in the top flange of the bracket, as shown in Figure 3–68.

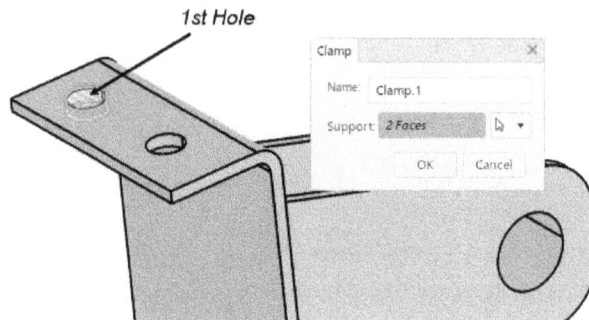

Figure 3–68

2. Repeat step 1 three more times for the remaining three holes, as shown in Figure 3–69.

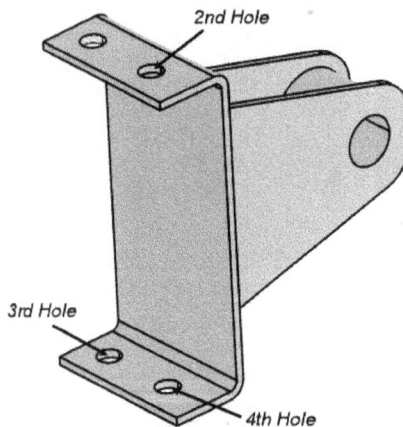

Figure 3–69

Task 6: Apply the Load.

1. Select (Remote Force). Select the inside surface of the boss as the **Supports**, as shown in Figure 3−70.

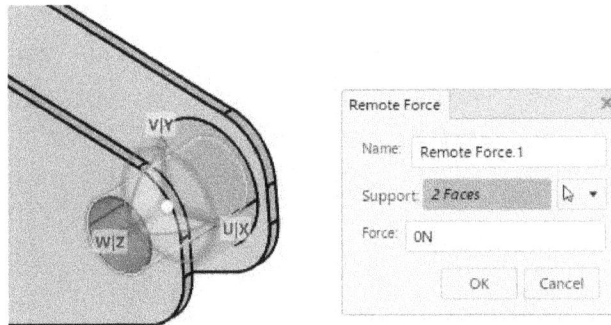

Figure 3−70

2. Select (Locate Handle at a Point) in the context toolbar and select **Point.1** to move the Robot onto **Point.1**, as shown in Figure 3−71. This assumes the force applied at **Point.1**, but then transmitted to the *Support* surfaces.

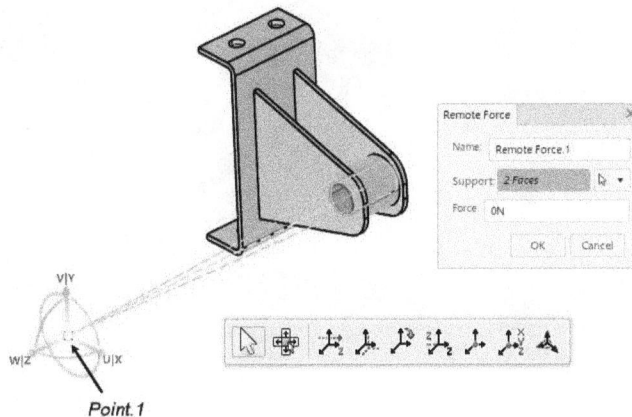

Figure 3−71

3. Select ![triad icon](Align Triad Handle with a line, plane normal, etc.) in the context toolbar and click **yz plane** in the tree to align the **W** axis of the robot, which is the force direction, with the global X-axis, as shown in Figure 3−72.

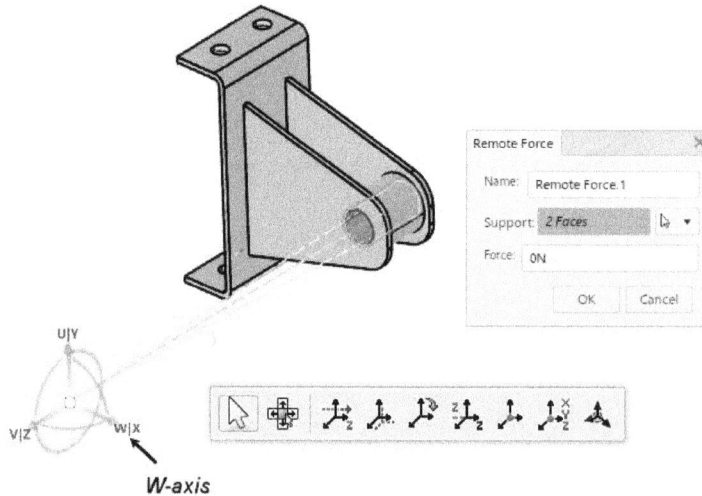

Figure 3−72

4. Enter **400N** as the force's value and click **OK**. The model displays as shown in Figure 3−73.

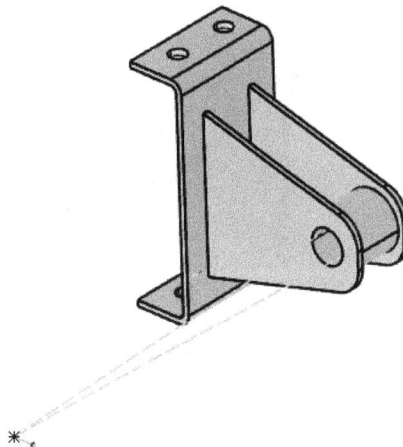

Figure 3−73

Task 7: Run the simulation.

1. Run the simulation and wait until it completes. The computation time should be within 30 seconds.

Task 8: Display and animate the deformed mesh.

1. In the *Plot* drop-down menu, select **Deformation** to display the deformed model. Unhide the **Model** object in the tree to overlay the deformed over the undeformed part, as shown in Figure 3−74.

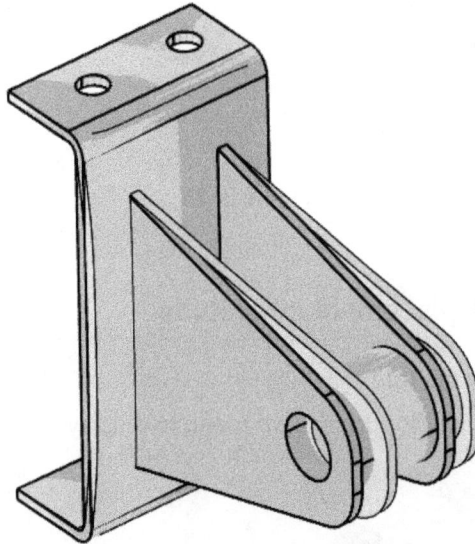

Figure 3−74

2. Double-click the deformed model to open the *Contour Plot* dialog box, and change the *Scale factor* to **150**, as shown in Figure 3−75.

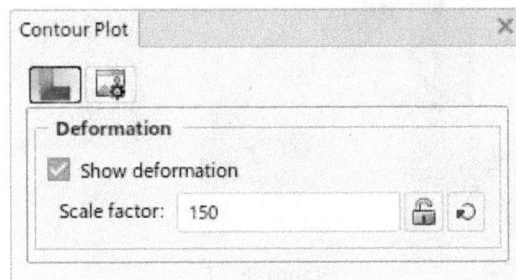

Figure 3−75

3. Animate the deformation. Note that the model deforms according to the applied load, as if the 400N force was indeed applied at the tip of the shaft shown in Figure 3−76. The deformed model at 100% of the animation progress is shown in Figure 3−76.

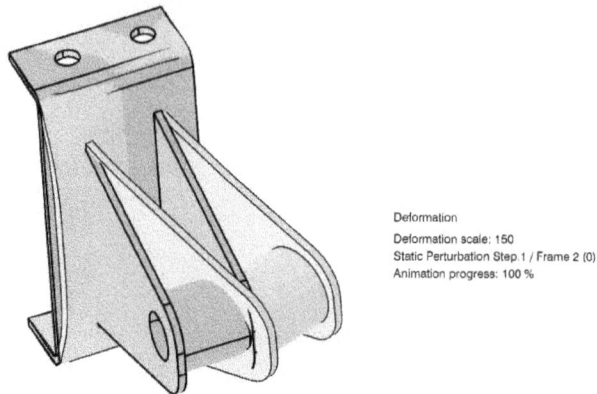

Deformation
Deformation scale: 150
Static Perturbation Step.1 / Frame 2 (0)
Animation progress: 100 %

Figure 3−76

4. Exit the animation.

Task 9: Visualize the displacement magnitude.

1. Hide the **Model** object in the tree.

2. Select **Displacement** in the *Plot* drop-down menu to display the displacement magnitudes, as shown in Figure 3−77.

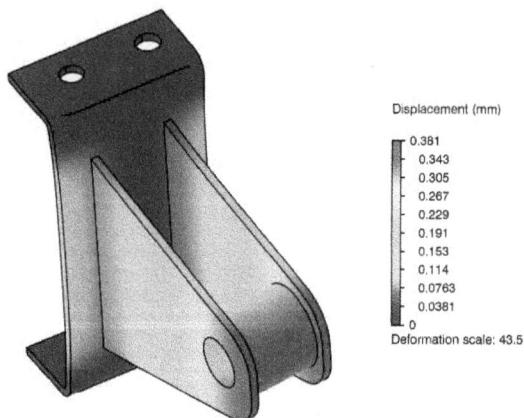

Displacement (mm)

0.381
0.343
0.305
0.267
0.229
0.191
0.153
0.114
0.0763
0.0381
0

Deformation scale: 43.5

Figure 3−77

- Note that the maximum displacement magnitude under the given load is approximately **0.381mm**.

Task 10: Display Von Mises stress

1. Select **Von Mises Stress** in the *Plot* drop-down menu to display the stress image, as shown in Figure 3–78.

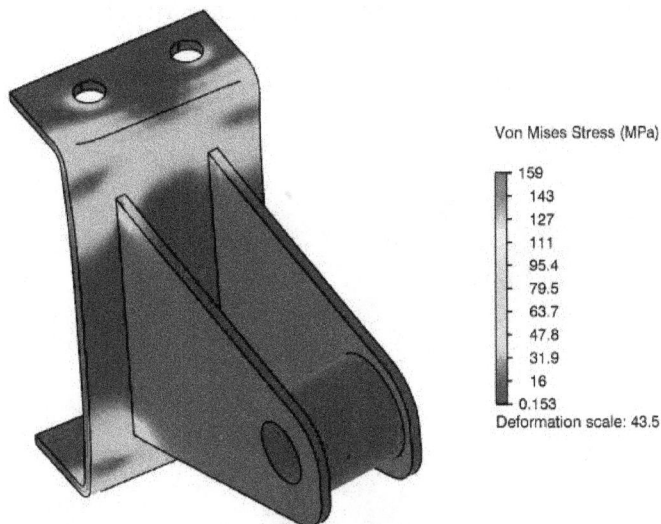

Von Mises Stress (MPa)

159
143
127
111
95.4
79.5
63.7
47.8
31.9
16
0.153
Deformation scale: 43.5

Figure 3–78

2. Note that the maximum *Von Mises stress* (**159 MPa**) is below the material's *Yield Strength* (**250 MPa**), which means that the bracket is not expected to fail under the 400N load.

Task 11: Locate area of maximum stress.

1. In the *Results* section of the Action Bar, select ▉ (Show Min/Max Values), and in the context toolbar, select ▢ (Show only Max value), as shown in Figure 3–79.

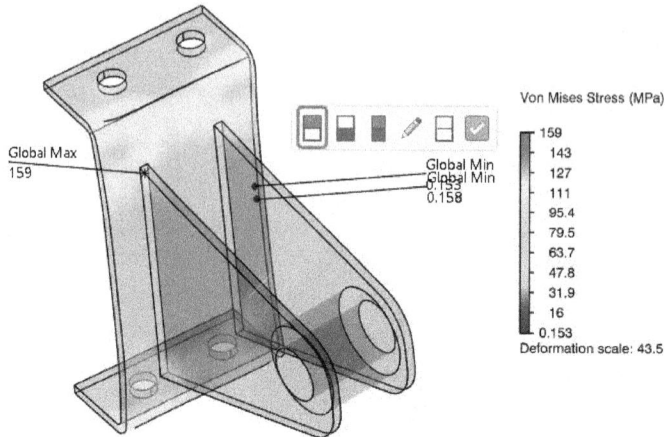

Figure 3–79

2. Move the **Global Max** label with the left mouse button to the location of your liking and click ☑ in the context toolbar to finalize. The result plot displays as shown in Figure 3–80.

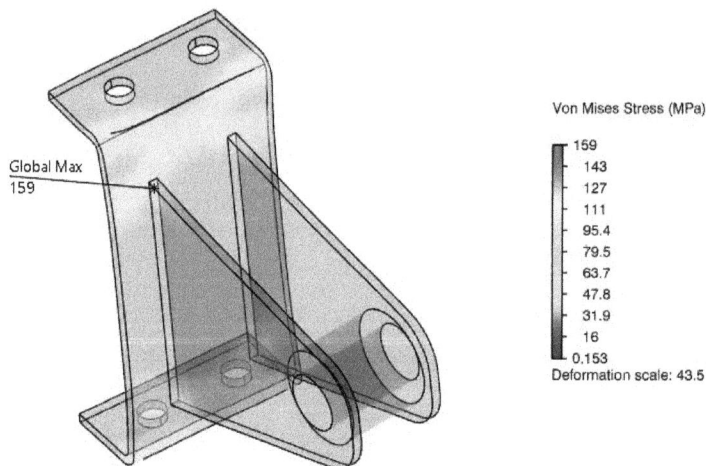

Figure 3–80

3. Select the result plot, and in the context toolbar, click ⬚ (Hide Max or Min values and close) to remove the **Global Max** label from the result plot.

Task 12: Perform cut plane analysis.

1. Double-click the result plot and in the *Contour Plot* dialog box that opens, toggle off the **Show deformation** option, as shown in Figure 3–81.

   - **Note**: This ensures that the cutting plane intersects the result plot on the undeformed, i.e., as in your CAD model, geometry of the part.

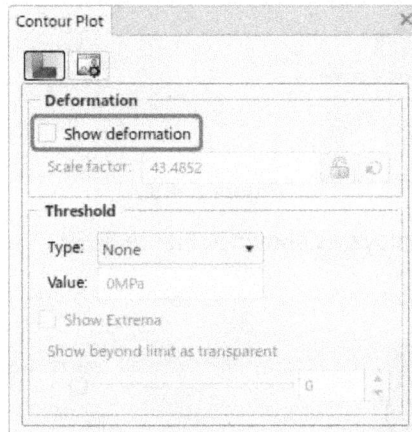

Figure 3–81

2. Select 🗐 (View Cut). In the context toolbar, select 🖊 (Hide cutting geometry) to hide the cutting plane. The result plot displays as shown in Figure 3–82.

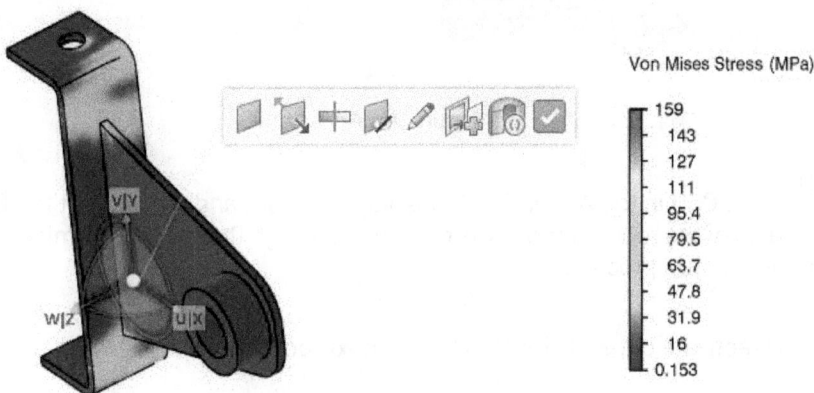

Von Mises Stress (MPa)

159
143
127
111
95.4
79.5
63.7
47.8
31.9
16
0.153

Figure 3–82

3. Select ✐ (Edit cut) in the context toolbar. In the *Plot Sectioning* dialog box that opens, enter the coordinates and the normal direction for the cutting plane, as shown in Figure 3–83.

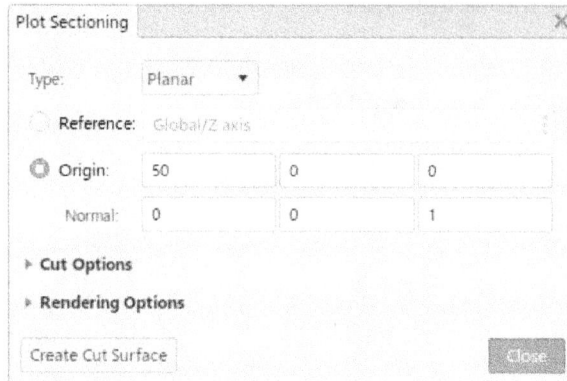

Figure 3–83

4. Click **Close**. The model displays as shown in Figure 3–84.

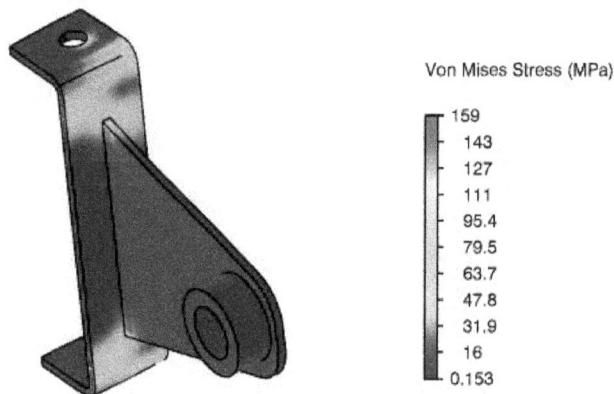

Figure 3–84

5. Click 🔲 (View Cut) in the Action Bar to display the robot and the context toolbar again. Drag the **W** axis of the robot to move the cut plane through the model. Examine stress in the cross-sections as you proceed.

6. Click 🔲 (Deactivate cut and close) in the context toolbar to exit the view cut mode.

Task 13: Obtain Reactions in Restraints.

In this task, you will create **Resultant Sensors** in order to obtain the amounts of force carried by each restraint under the given load on the bracket. This information would help you with proper sizing of the fasteners used for mounting the bracket through the holes.

1. In the *Results* section of the Action Bar, select ⬙ (Resultant Sensor). The *Resultant Sensor* dialog box opens, as shown in Figure 3−85.

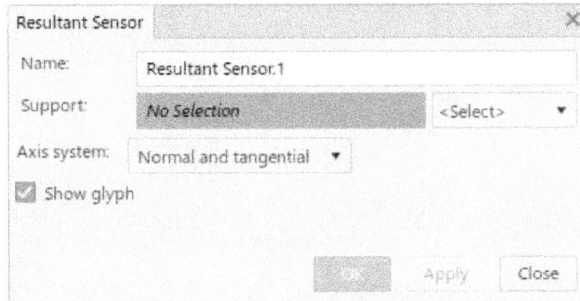

Figure 3−85

2. Expand the *<Select>* drop-down menu and select **Restraints**, as shown in Figure 3−86.

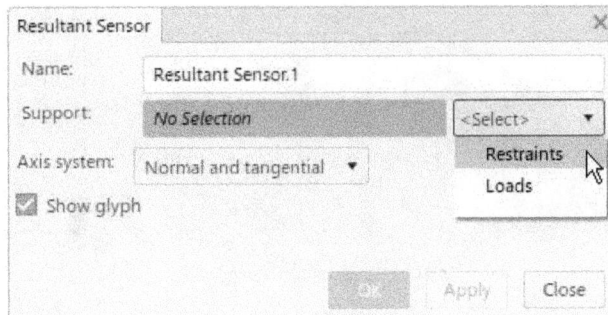

Figure 3−86

3. In the *Restraint Selection* dialog box, select **Clamp.1** and click **Select**, as shown in Figure 3–87.

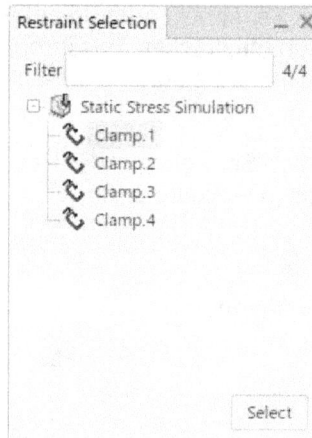

Figure 3–87

4. Click **OK** in the *Resultant Sensor* dialog box. The result plot now displays the reaction force and moment values and directions, as shown in Figure 3–88.

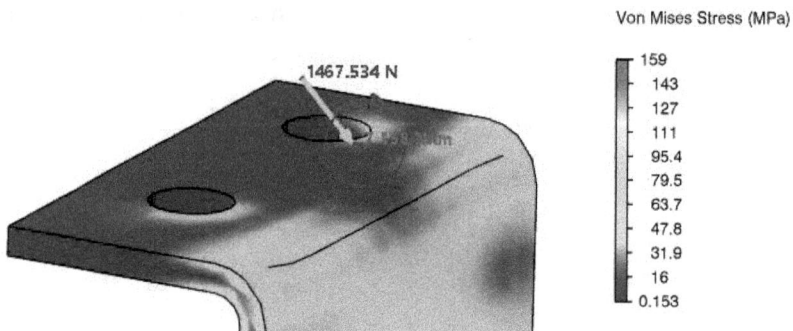

Figure 3–88

5. Repeat steps 1 through 4 for the remaining three holes (**Clamp.2**, **Clamp.3**, **Clamp.4**). The reaction forces for all four holes are now displayed, as shown in Figure 3–89.

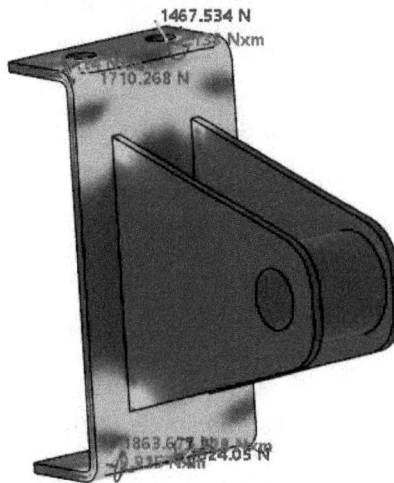

Figure 3–89

Task 14: Save and close the model.

1. Click (Result Visualization) in the Action Bar to return to the model view.
2. Optionally, save the analysis and the part for future reference.
3. Close all windows.

End of practice

Practice 3c
Loads and Restraints on Surface Patches

Practice Objectives

- Create surface patches using the **Sew Surface** tool.
- Apply material and mesh the model.
- Apply symmetry boundary condition.
- Apply loads.
- Compute the analysis.
- Display the results.

In this practice, you will set up and run a static stress analysis on a mooring chock that is used for fastening ships to piers, etc. The model is shown in Figure 3-90. The chock is welded into the hull of the ship over a 1 inch area that is going around the outside surface and loaded by a mooring line over a 2 inch area, as shown in Figure 3-90.

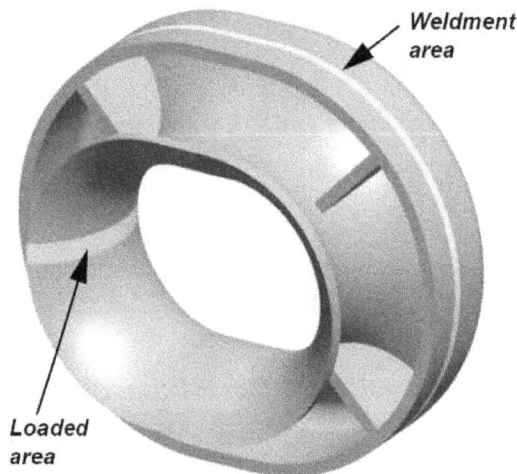

Figure 3-90

You will use the **Sew Surface** tool in the *Part Design* workbench to create the surface patches for applying loads and restraints shown in Figure 3-90.

Task 1: Open the part.

1. Import with your initials and open **Chock_03.3dxml**.

2. Set the model display as ⬚ (Shading with Sharp and Smooth Edges). The part displays as shown in Figure 3−91.

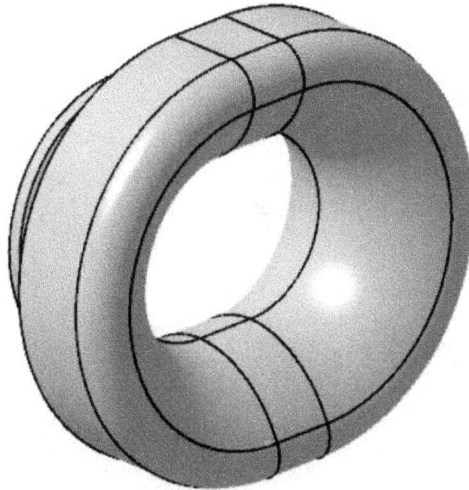

Figure 3−91

3. Set the units as follows:
   - *Length:* **Millimeter (mm)**
   - *Force:* **Newton (N)**
   - *Moment:* **Newton x Meter (Nxm)**
   - *Pressure:* **Megapascal (MPa)**
   - *Stress:* **Megapascal (MPa)**

Task 2: Split the part in half.

The part geometry and the boundary conditions in this model exhibit mirror symmetry, i.e., the geometry, loads, and restraints on the upper half of the chock mirror the geometry, loads, and restraints on the lower half. In this task, you will split the part in half along the symmetry plane and keep the bottom half, to take advantage of symmetry boundary condition later in the analysis.

1. Ensure that **Part Design** is the current app.

2. In the *Transform* section of the Action Pad, select ▦ (Split). The *Split* dialog box opens, as shown in Figure 3–92.

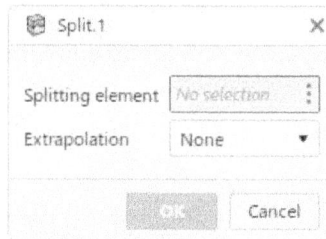

Figure 3–92

3. Select **zx plane** as the *Splitting element*. Ensure that the **grey arrow** points down, opposite to the Y-direction. If not, click on the arrow to flip the direction. The model displays as shown in Figure 3–93.

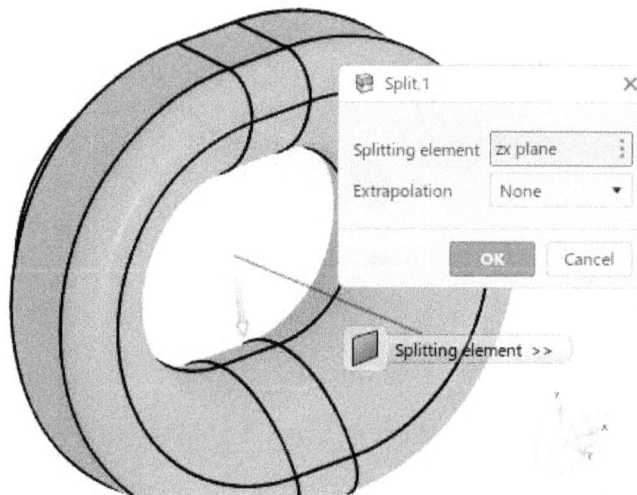

Figure 3–93

4. Click **OK**. The part displays, as shown in Figure 3–94.

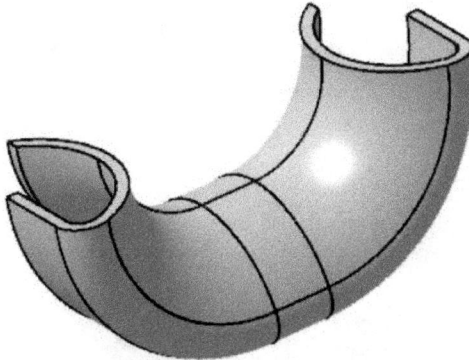

Figure 3–94

Task 3: Create surface patch for the weldment area.

In this task, you will split the part surface in order to separate the welded area from the rest of the solid. The process essentially consists of two steps:

- First, you create a patch of the surface by extracting and splitting the **PartBody**'s surface.
- Second, you sew that patch back onto the **PartBody**, using the **Sew Surface** tool.

1. Switch to the **Generative Shape Design** app.

2. Create a new geometrical set named **GS weldment**.

3. Create two new Planes:

- **Plane.1**: Offset by **88.9mm** (3.5") from **xy plane** toward the positive Z-direction
- **Plane.2**: Offset by **114.3mm** (4.5") from **xy plane** toward the positive Z-direction

4. The model displays as shown in Figure 3–95.

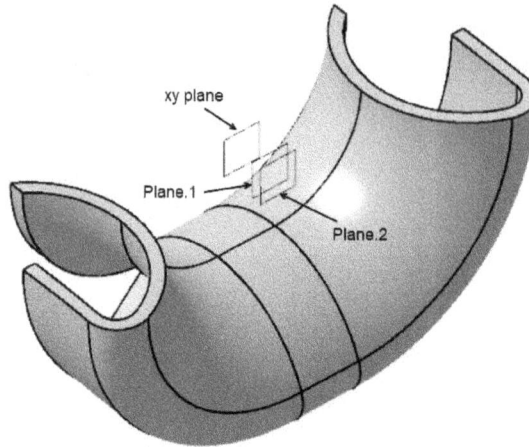

Figure 3–95

5. Extract and join the three outside surfaces. The result, **Join.1**, is shown in Figure 3–96.

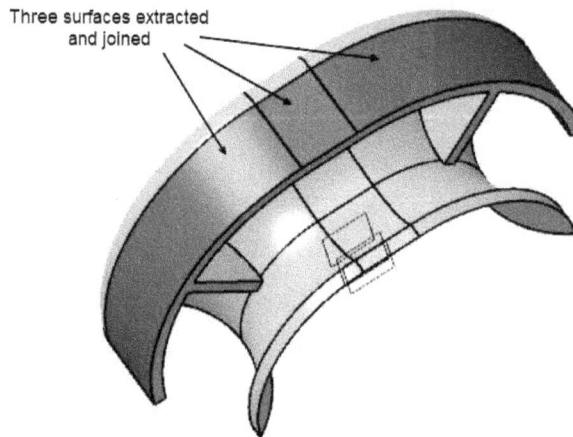

Figure 3–96

6. Split **Join.1** with **Plane.1**, keeping the side toward the positive Z-direction. The result, **Split.1**, is shown in Figure 3–97.

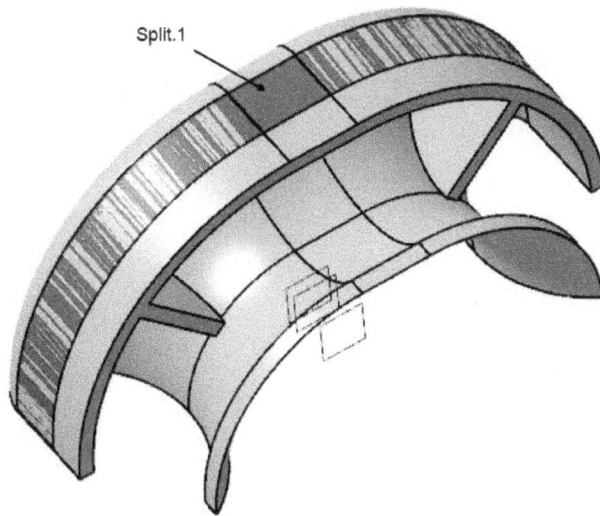

Figure 3-97

7. Split **Split.1** surface with **Plane.2**, keeping the side toward the negative Z-direction. The result, **Split.2**, is shown in Figure 3-98.

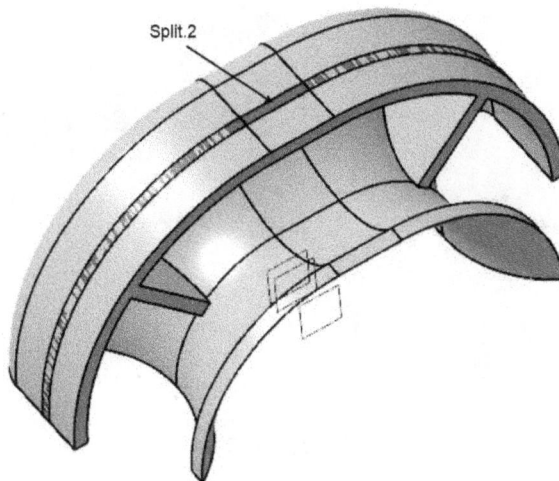

Figure 3-98

8. Switch to the **Part Design** app.

9. Right-click on the **PartBody** and select **Define In Work Object** in the contextual menu.

10. In the *Refine* section of the Action Bar, select ▦ (Sew Surface). The *Sew Surface* dialog box opens, as shown in Figure 3–99.

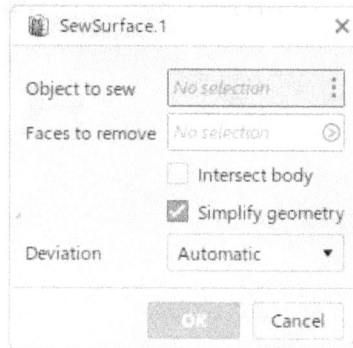

Figure 3–99

11. Select **Split.2** as the *Object to sew* and deactivate the **Simplify geometry** option. Make sure the grey arrow in the preview points toward the solid body. The model displays as shown in Figure 3–100.

- **Note**: If **Simplify geometry** option is activated, the system will not separate the surface patch from the rest of the solid's surface.

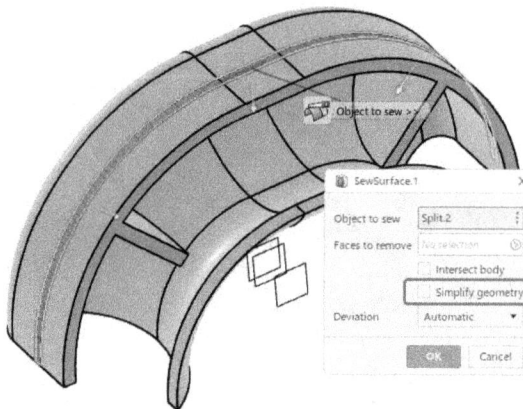

Figure 3–100

12. Click **OK**. Hide the **GS weldment** geometrical set. The model displays as shown in Figure 3–101. Note that the weldment area is now separate from the rest of the part surface.

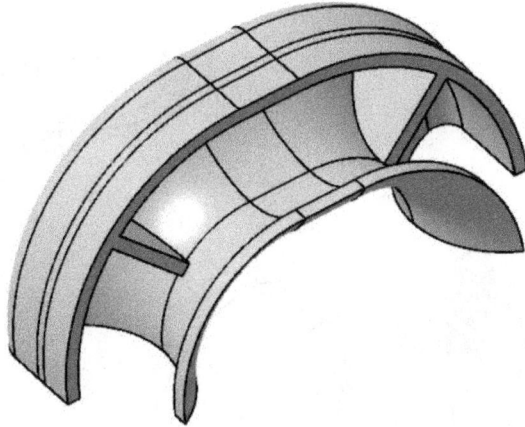

Figure 3–101

Task 4: Create surface patch for the loaded area.

In this task, you will split the part surface again, in order to separate the loaded area from the rest of the solid. The process is very similar to Task 3 above; the only difference will be in how you create the boundary of the surface patch.

1. Switch to the **Generative Shape Design** app.

2. Create a new geometrical set named **GS load**.

3. Create a sketch (**Sketch.1**) on the **yz plane**, with the dimensions as shown in Figure 3–102.

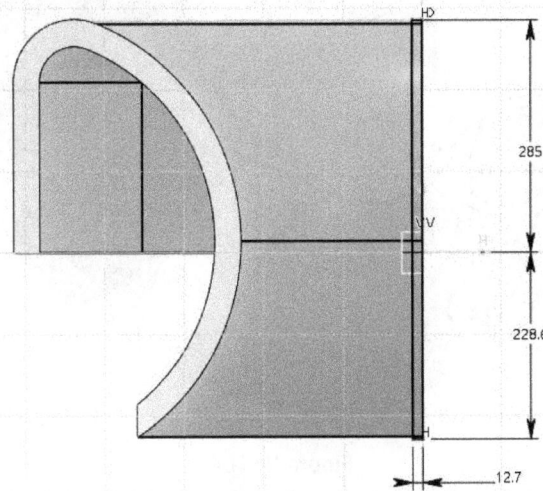

Figure 3–102

4. Exit the **Sketcher** app. The model displays as shown in Figure 3–103.

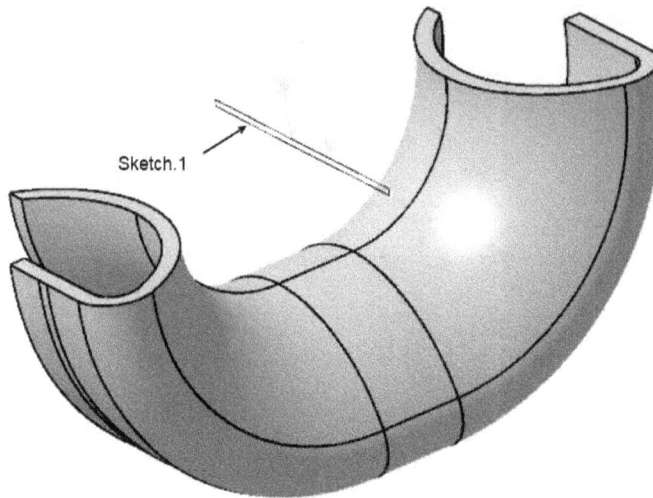

Figure 3–103

5. Extract and join the two inside surfaces that are toward the positive X-direction. The result, **Join.2**, is shown in Figure 3–104.

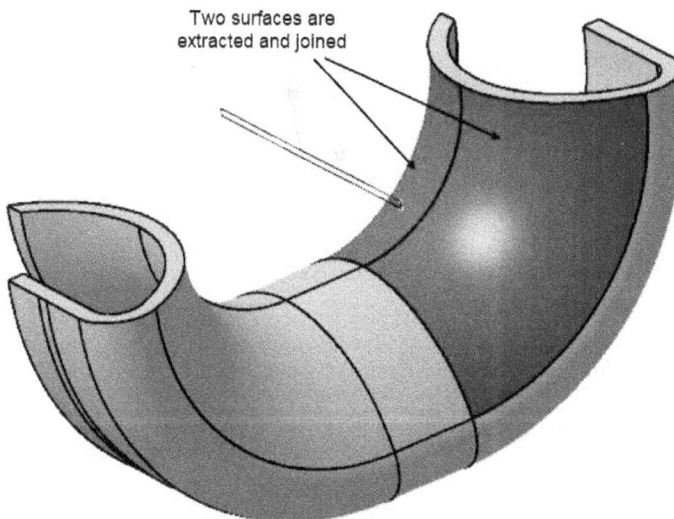

Figure 3–104

- Project **Sketch.1** onto **Join.2**, using the following parameters:
  - *Projection type:* **Along a direction**
  - *Projected:* **Sketch.1**
  - *Support:* **Join.2**
  - *Direction:* **X Axis**

The result, **Project.1**, is shown in Figure 3–105.

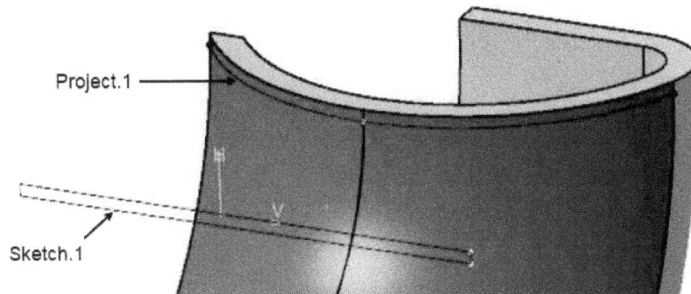

Figure 3–105

6. Split **Join.2** with **Project.1**, keeping the side that is inside **Project.1**. The result, **Split.3**, is shown in Figure 3–106.

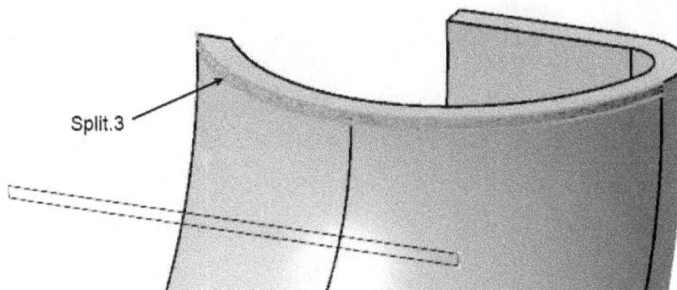

Figure 3–106

7. Switch to the **Part Design** app.
8. Right-click on the **PartBody** and select **Define In Work Object** in the contextual menu.

9. In the *Refine* section of the Action Bar, select ⬛ (Sew Surface). Select **Split.3** as the *Object to sew* and toggle off the **Simplify geometry** option. Make sure the grey arrow in the preview points toward the solid body. The model displays as shown in Figure 3−107.

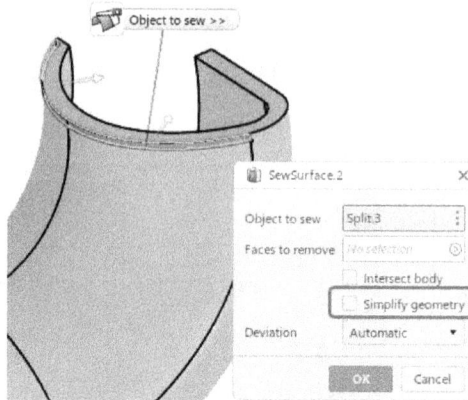

Figure 3−107

10. Click **OK**. Hide the **GS load** geometrical set. The model displays as shown in Figure 3−108. Note that the loaded area is now separate from the rest of the part surface.

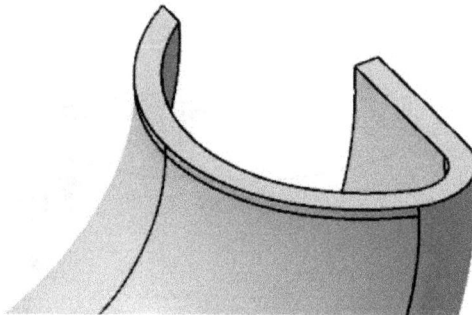

Figure 3−108

Task 5: Apply the material.

1. Apply the **Steel** material to the part. You can either use the material definition you created in *Practice 2b* or create a new material. Verify that the applied material has the following properties:

   - *Young's Modulus:* **200000 MPa**
   - *Poisson's Ratio:* **0.266**
   - *Density:* **7860 Kg/m3**
   - *Proof (Yield) Stress:* **250 MPa**

Task 6: Launch the Linear Structural Validation app

1. Activate the *Chock_03* window and launch the **Linear Structural Validation** app.

2. Enter *<Your Initials>*_**Chock Simulation** for the *Title* of the Physics Simulation.

3. Select **Structural** for *Analysis type*.

Task 7: Mesh the part.

1. Select (Mesh Specifications) in the Action Bar, and enter **22mm** as the *Element Size*, as shown in Figure 3-109. Activate the **Generate mesh** option and click **OK**.

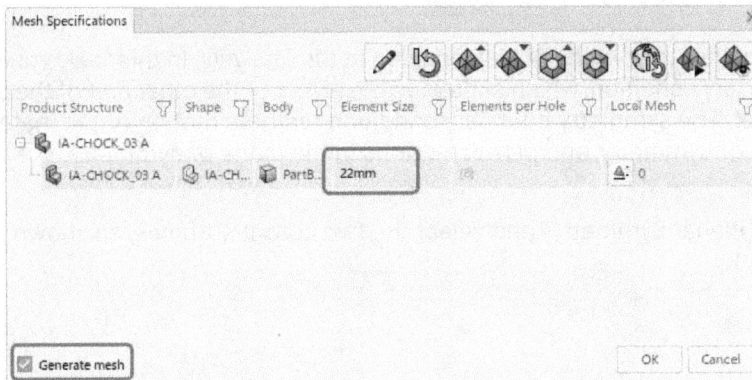

Figure 3-109

2. The part mesh is generated and displayed, as shown in Figure 3–110.

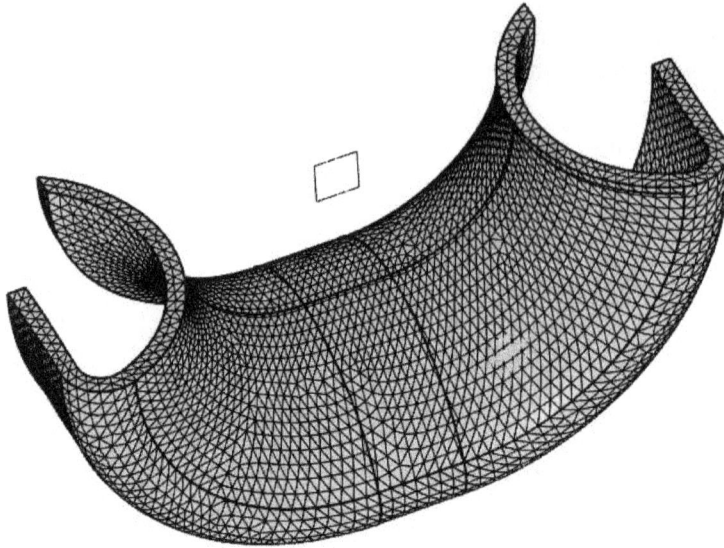

Figure 3–110

3. Click ▲ (Hide/Show Mesh) to hide the mesh.

Task 8: Apply symmetry boundary condition.

Since only one half of the part has been included in the analysis, in this task, you will apply a symmetry boundary condition, which simulates the effect of the other half of the part as if it still was in the model. The symmetry boundary condition restricts motion of the material particles out of the plane of symmetry, and permit motions in the plane of symmetry.

1. Select ▢ (Planar Symmetry) and select the two cutout surfaces, as shown in Figure 3–111.

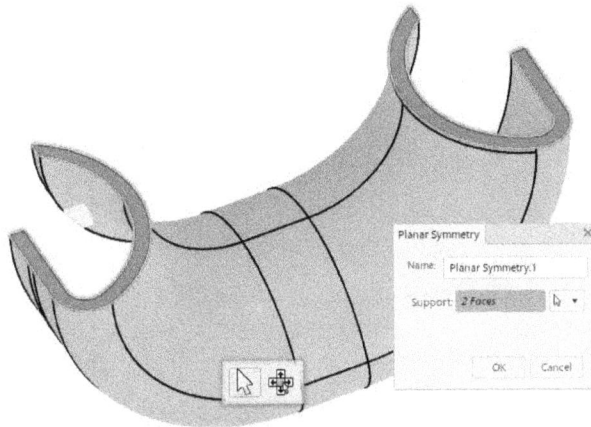

Figure 3–111

2. Click **OK** to complete.

Task 9: Apply weldment restraint.

1. Select 🗝 (Clamp) and restrain the three surfaces of the weldment surface patch, as shown in Figure 3–112.

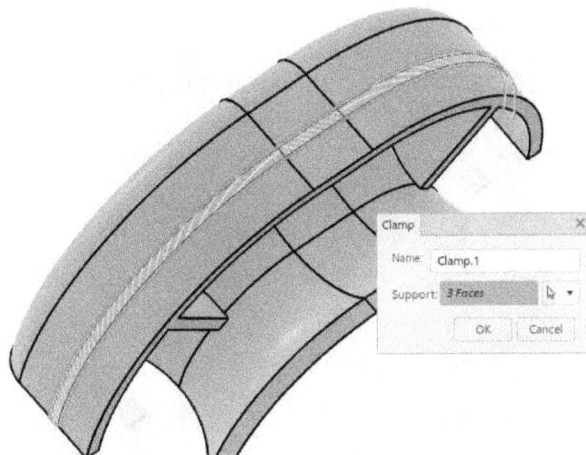

Figure 3–112

Task 10: Apply the load.

The force exerted by the mooring line onto the chock is **80,000 lbs**. Therefore, the amount of force applied to a half of the chock is **80,000 /2 = 40,000 lbs**, which is approximately **178,000N**.

1. Select (Force). Select the loaded surface patch as the **Support**, as shown in Figure 3–113.

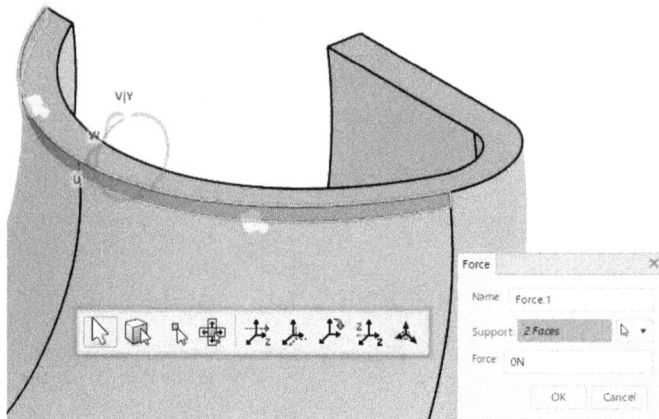

Figure 3–113

2. In the context toolbar, select (Align Triad Handle with a line, plane normal, etc.), then select the **yz plane**. This will align the force direction with the **yz plane** normal.

3. Click (Reverse Direction of Triad Handle Z Axis) in the context toolbar, to ensure the force preview arrows point from the center of the chock and out. Enter **178000N** as the force value. The force preview displays, as shown in Figure 3–114.

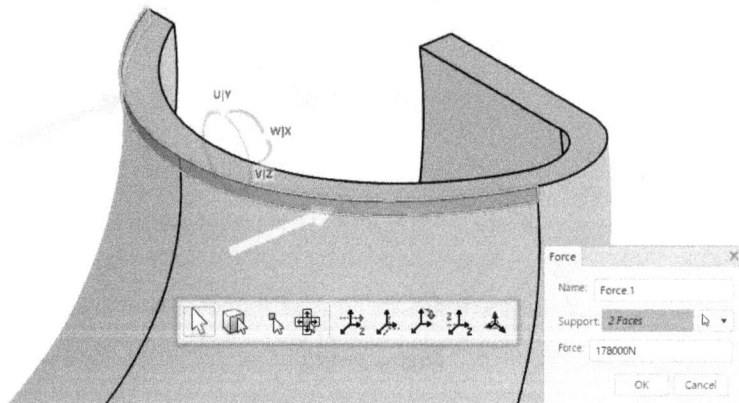

Figure 3–114

4. Click **OK** to complete. The model displays as shown in Figure 3–115.

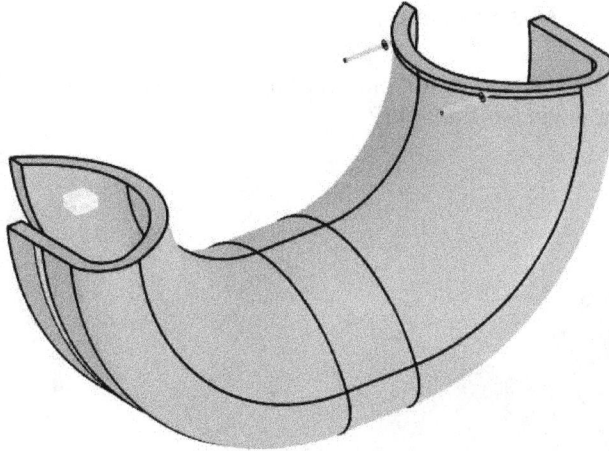

Figure 3–115

Task 11: Run the analysis.

1. Run the simulation with the default computation settings.

2. Wait until the computation completes, which should be within a minute.

Task 12: Display the displacement magnitude.

1. Display the displacement magnitude result plot, overlaid over the CAD model, as shown in Figure 3–116.

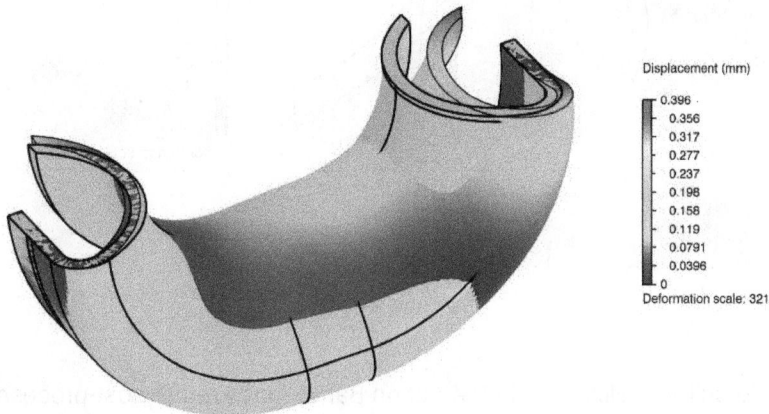

Figure 3–116

2. Start the animation. Check whether the applied boundary conditions behave correctly. Note that the displacements on the plane of symmetry are only in-plane, not out-of-plane.

Task 13: Display Von Mises stress.

1. Display the **Von Mises Stress** result plot. Modify the **Legend**, so it displays 8 colors, and is not smooth, as shown in Figure 3–117.

Von Mises Stress (MPa)

170
149
128
107
85.2
63.9
42.6
21.3
0.0305
Deformation scale: 321

Figure 3–117

2. Verify whether the maximum *Von Mises stress* exceeds the material's yield strength.

3. Display the location of the maximum stress, as shown in Figure 3–118.

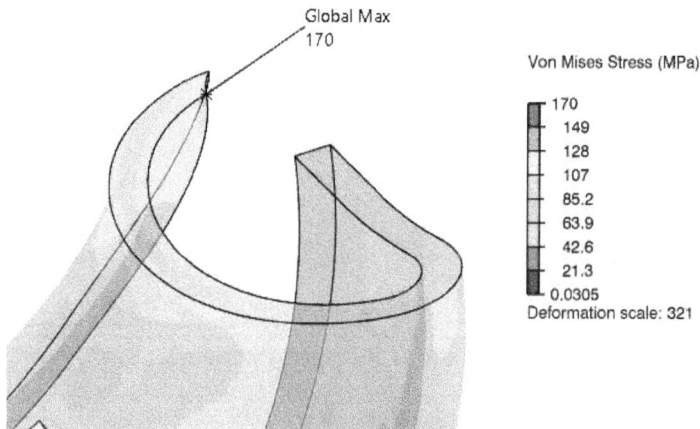

Global Max
170

Von Mises Stress (MPa)

170
149
128
107
85.2
63.9
42.6
21.3
0.0305
Deformation scale: 321

Figure 3–118

4. Click (Result Visualization) in the Action Bar to finish result post-processing and to return to the model view.

Task 14: Save and close the model.

1. Optionally, save the analysis document and the part for future reference.
2. Close all windows.

End of practice

Practice 3d
Stress Analysis of a Pressure Vessel

Practice Objectives

- Apply material and mesh the model.
- Apply symmetry boundary conditions.
- Apply pressure load.
- Run the analysis and display the results.

In this practice, you will set up and run a static stress analysis on a pressure vessel shown in Figure 3-119, with minimum instruction.

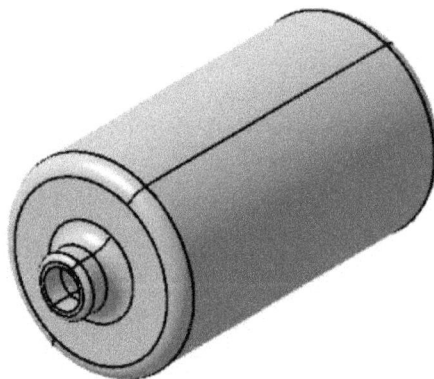

Figure 3-119

Task 1: Prepare the CAD model.

1. Import with your initials and open **Tank_03.3dxml**.

2. From the full model, create the 45 deg segment (i.e., 1/8) of the model, as shown in Figure 3−120.

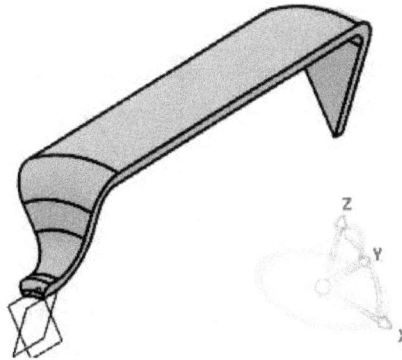

Figure 3−120

3. Apply the **Steel** material to the part.

Task 2: **Prepare the analysis model.**

1. Start the **Linear Structural Validation** app.

2. Generate the mesh with the default specifications.

3. Using ▢ (Planar Symmetry), apply symmetry boundary conditions on both cutout surfaces, as shown in Figure 3−121.

   - **Note:** You must create two Planar Symmetry conditions, one for each of the two cutout surfaces.

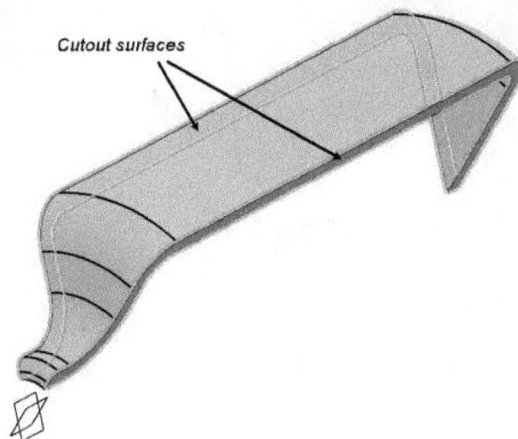

Cutout surfaces

Figure 3−121

4. Using (Fixed Displacement), restrain the end surface of the tank in **Y** direction, as shown in Figure 3–122.

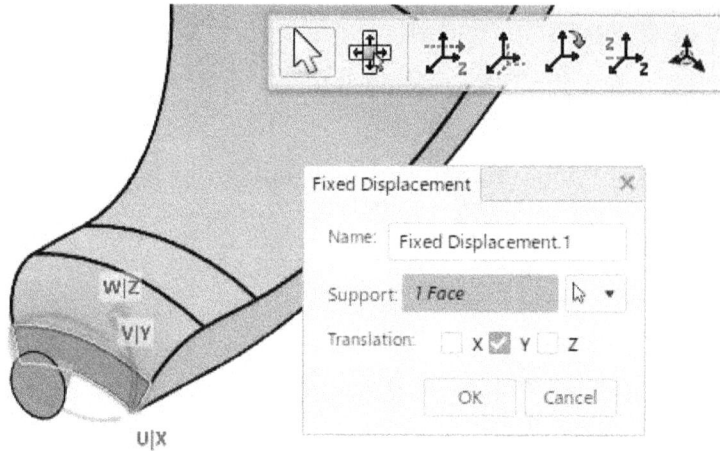

Figure 3–122

5. Apply **800psi (5.516MPa)** pressure to all the inside surfaces of the tank, as shown in Figure 3–123.

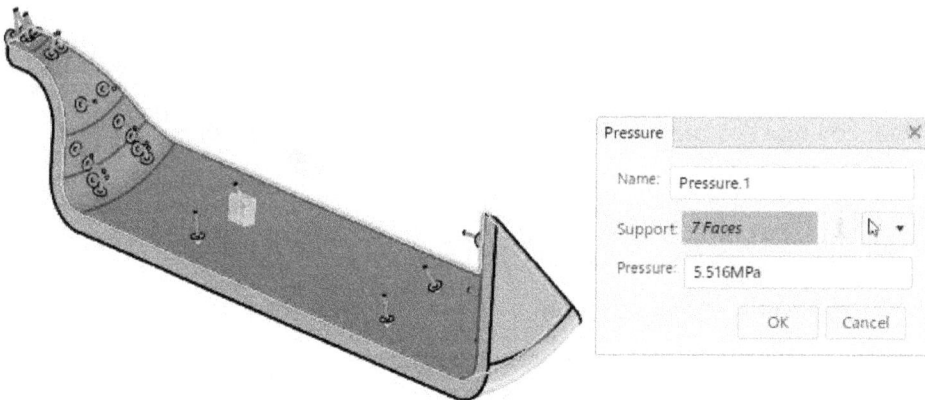

Figure 3–123

Task 3: Run the analysis.

1. Run the analysis and wait until it completes.

Task 4: Visualize the analysis results.

1. Visualize and animate the model deformation. Does the part deform according to the applied loads?

2. Display the displacement magnitude plot. What is the value of the maximum displacement in the model?

3. Display the Von Mises color plot. Does the maximum stress exceed the yield strength of the material?

4. Display the Factor of Safety plot. What is the value of the factor of safety for the part?

   • Factor of Safety value is obtained by dividing the material's yield strength by the maximum stress in the model.

5. Find the location of the maximum stress. Can you think of design changes that would lead to decrease in the stress level in that area?

6. Close the model without saving.

End of practice

Mesh Refinement

Any FEA solution is an approximation, which means it always contains some amount of error. Bringing the FEA approximation error to acceptable levels is a critical aspect of developing an accurate simulation.

In this chapter, you learn about the tools available for the FEA solution refinement in the Linear Structural Validation app.

Learning Objectives

- Understand the discretization error.
- Learn the mesh refinement process.
- Understand the difference between global and local mesh refinement.

4.1 Simulation Accuracy

In structural FEA, the approximation functions are built in such a way that displacement continuity across inter-element boundaries is guaranteed.

The stress contours are then computed based on the relative displacements of the nodes of each element and are not necessarily continuous from one finite element to the next. Essentially, this discontinuity of the stress contour from one element to another is the discretization error. As the size of each element is reduced during the mesh refinement process, the discretization error decreases too.

The amount of stress discontinuity can be used as a measure of error in the solution. 3DEXPERIENCE FEA solver integrates the stress discontinuity error over the volume of each element and calculates the strain energy density error. Then, the ratio of the elemental strain energy density error to the maximum strain energy density in the model is presented in the **Simulation Accuracy** result plot.

Once the simulation is completed, select **Simulation Accuracy** in the *Plot* drop-down menu to display the accuracy plot, as shown in Figure 4−1.

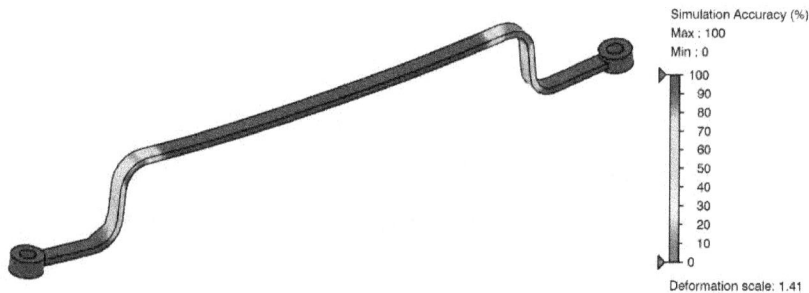

Figure 4−1

The **Simulation Accuracy** image represents a visual map of the discretization error for a given computation. The image provides an insight as to the areas in the model in which the results are relatively accurate, and the areas in which they are not:

- The areas with the greater strain energy density error (red- and yellow-colored finite elements) are the least accurate. The mesh in those areas should be refined.

- The areas with the lower strain energy error (blue-colored finite elements) are relatively accurate.

The image provides qualitative rather than quantitative information to the user. The value of the strain energy density error cannot be directly related to, for instance, error in stress.

While there are no absolutes regarding permissible values for **Simulation Accuracy**, a minimum accuracy of 70% is typically recommended for the general-purpose structural analysis.

4.2 Mesh Refinement Process

Refining the mesh in order to obtain the required analysis accuracy is an iterative process, as shown in Figure 4−2.

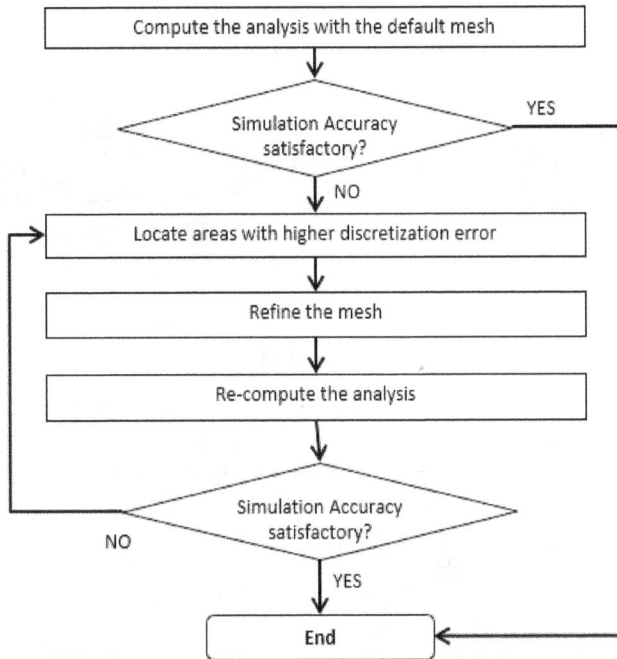

Figure 4−2

The process starts with performing an initial computation, with the default mesh, and checking the Simulation Accuracy.

If the accuracy is too low, the next steps are:

- Using the Simulation Accuracy result plot, locate the areas with the higher discretization error.

- Refine the mesh accordingly.

- Re-compute the analysis and re-check the Simulation Accuracy.

Since it is extremely difficult to predict the mesh size that will yield the desired analysis accuracy, these steps may have to be repeated several times, thus decreasing the error to the acceptable level in iterations.

4.3 Global and Local Mesh Refinement

The mesh in your model could be refined globally or locally. With global mesh refinement, the mesh size is reduced evenly throughout the entire solid, as shown in Figure 4–3.

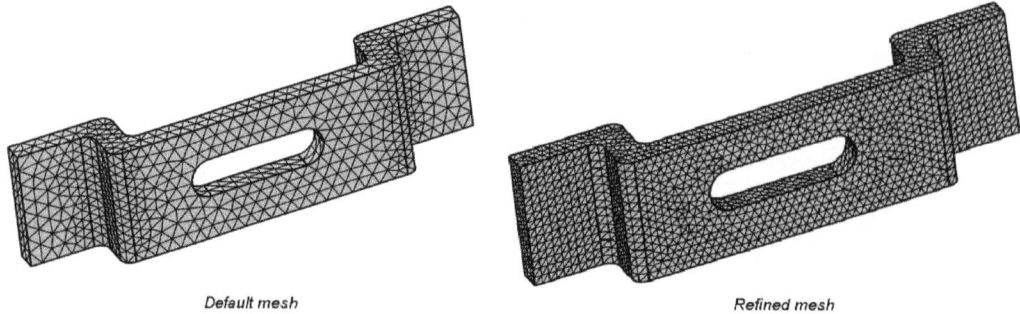

Default mesh   Refined mesh

Figure 4–3

Global mesh refinement is a workable, but uneconomic strategy, since analysis computation time and memory requirements will increase exponentially. With local mesh refinement, the mesh is only made denser in local areas with higher discretization error, as shown in Figure 4–4.

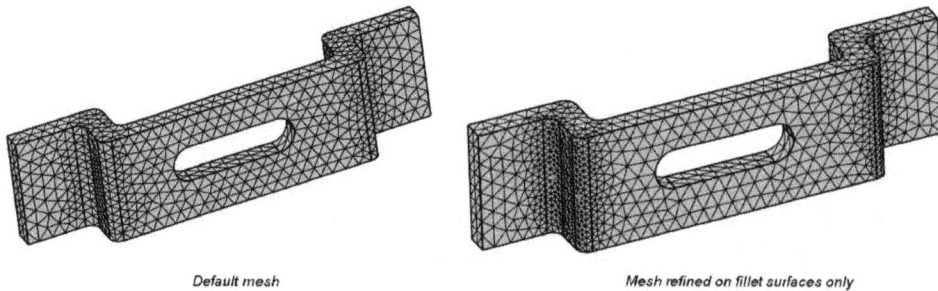

Default mesh   Mesh refined on fillet surfaces only

Figure 4–4

Local mesh refinement is the most efficient strategy that achieves accurate solution with the least expense in terms of computation time and computer memory.

Global Mesh Specification

To adjust global mesh specifications, select ◆ (Mesh Specifications) in the *Assistant* dialog box or in the *Mesh* section of the Action Bar. Once the *Mesh Specifications* dialog box opens, as shown in Figure 4–5, you can modify the global **Element Size** and **Elements per Hole** parameters.

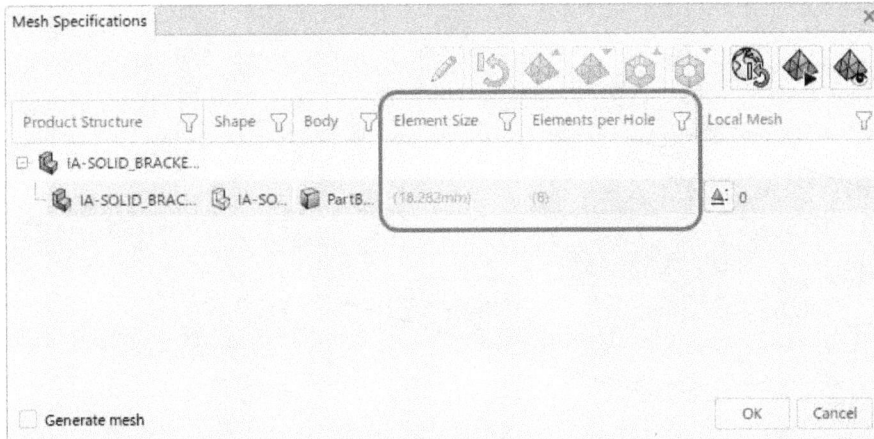

Figure 4–5

Local Mesh Specification

To create local mesh specifications, select ◮ (Local Mesh Specifications) in the *Assistant* dialog box or in the *Mesh* section of the Action Bar. The *Local Mesh Specifications* dialog box opens, as shown in Figure 4–6.

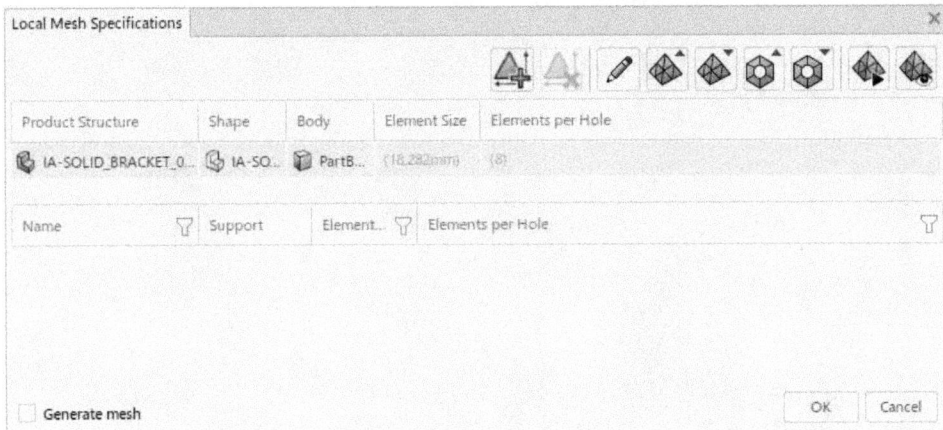

Figure 4–6

Click ![icon](Add Local Mesh Specification), select one or more surfaces in the part, and enter the local **Element Size** and/or **Elements per Hole**, as shown in Figure 4–7.

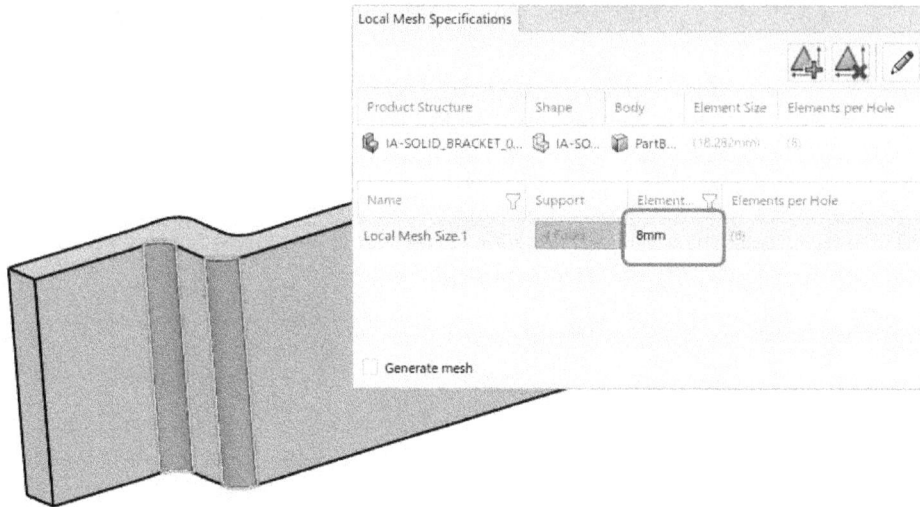

Figure 4–7

Practice 4a
Mesh Refinement

Practice Objectives

- Apply material and mesh the model.
- Apply loads and boundary conditions.
- Run the analysis and display the results.
- Use local mesh refinement to achieve the required analysis accuracy.

In this practice, you will set up and run a static stress analysis on a link part shown in Figure 4–8. You will also refine the mesh in order to achieve analysis accuracy to above 80% Simulation Accuracy.

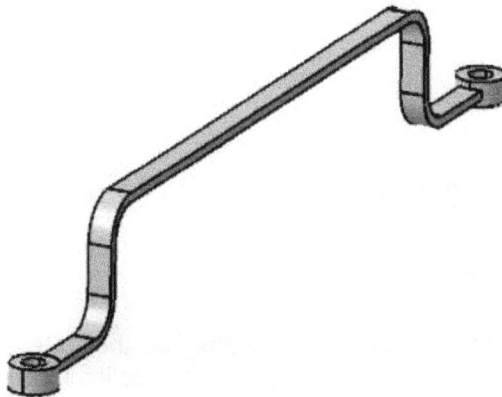

Figure 4–8

Task 1: Open the part.

1. Import with your initials and open **Link_04.3dxml**.

2. Set the model display as ⬡ (Shading with Sharp and Smooth Edges). The part displays as shown in Figure 4−9.

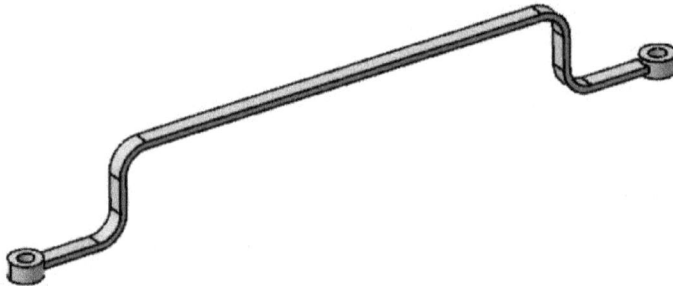

Figure 4−9

3. Set the units as follows:

- *Length:* **Millimeter (mm)**
- *Force:* **Newton (N)**
- *Moment:* **Newton x Meter (Nxm)**
- *Pressure:* **Megapascal (MPa)**
- *Stress:* **Megapascal (MPa)**

Task 2: Apply the material.

1. Apply the **Steel** material to the part. You can either use the material definition you created in *Practice 2b* or create a new material. Verify that the applied material has the following properties:

- *Young's Modulus:* **200000 MPa**
- *Poisson's Ratio:* **0.266**
- *Density:* **7860 Kg/m3**
- *Proof (Yield) Stress:* **250 MPa**

Task 3: Start the Linear Structural Validation app.

1. Activate the *Link_04* window and launch the **Linear Structural Validation** app.

2. Enter *<Your Initials>*_**Link Simulation** for the *Title* of the Physics Simulation.

3. Select **Structural** for *Analysis type*.

Task 4: Mesh the part.

1. Select ◆ (Mesh Specifications), and enter **15mm** as the *Element Size*, as shown in Figure 4–10. Activate the **Generate mesh** option and click **OK**.

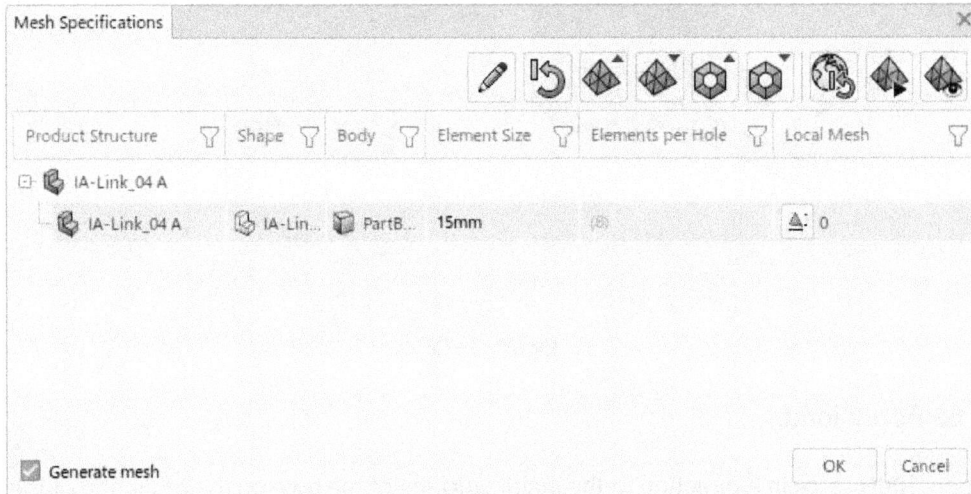

Figure 4–10

2. The part mesh is generated and displayed, as shown in Figure 4–11.

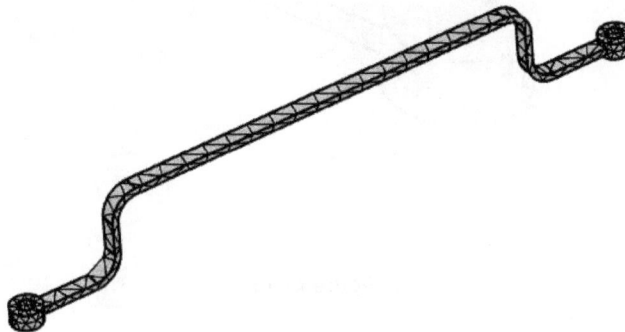

Figure 4–11

3. Select ◆ (Hide/Show Mesh) to hide the mesh.

Task 5: Apply clamp.

1. Clamp the inside surface of the hole on one end, as shown in Figure 4–12.

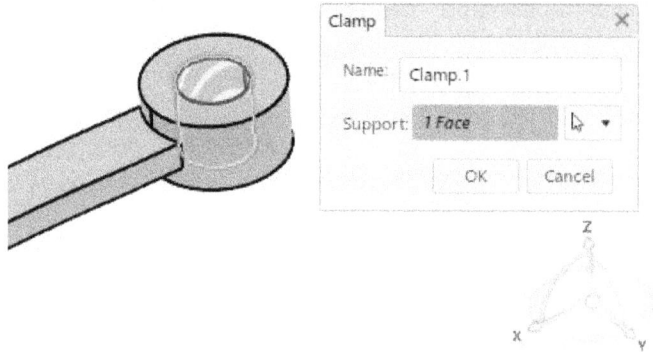

Figure 4–12

Task 6: Apply load.

1. Apply **100N** force in **X** direction to the inside surface of the hole on the other end of the part, as shown in Figure 4–13.

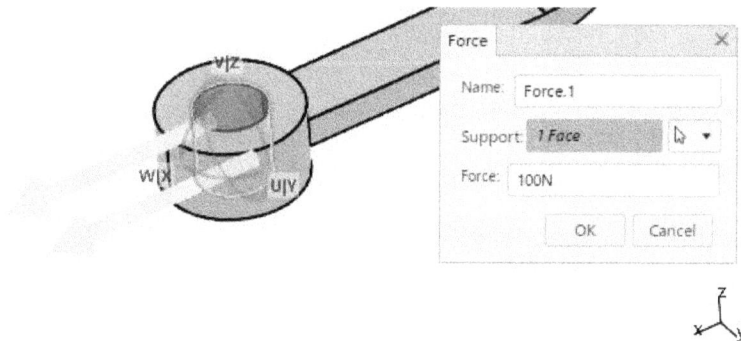

Figure 4–13

Task 7: Run the analysis.

1. Run the analysis and wait until it completes.

Task 8: Display Simulation Accuracy result plot.

1. In the *Plot* drop-down menu, select **Simulation Accuracy**. The *Simulation Accuracy* result plot displays, as shown in Figure 4–14.

Figure 4–14

The result plot displays the ratio of errors in element energy density to the maximum global energy density. The lower accuracy areas are indicated by red and orange colors. In this model, the areas of the lower analysis accuracy are the bends at the ends of the part.

Task 9: Refine the mesh.

In this task, you will refine the mesh in the areas of low accuracy.

1. Click (Result Visualization) in the Action Bar to exit the result visualization mode.

2. In the *Mesh* section of the Action Bar, select (Local Mesh Specifications) and select **Finite Element Model** in the tree. The *Local Mesh Specifications* dialog box displays as shown in Figure 4–15.

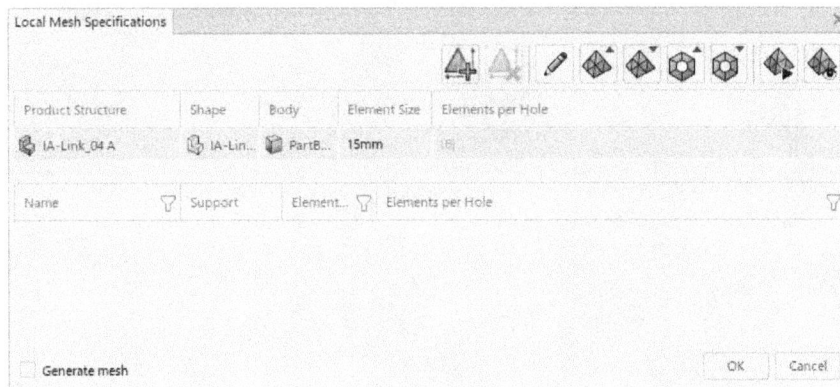

Figure 4–15

3. In the dialog box, select ![icon] (Add Local Mesh Specification), as shown in Figure 4−16.

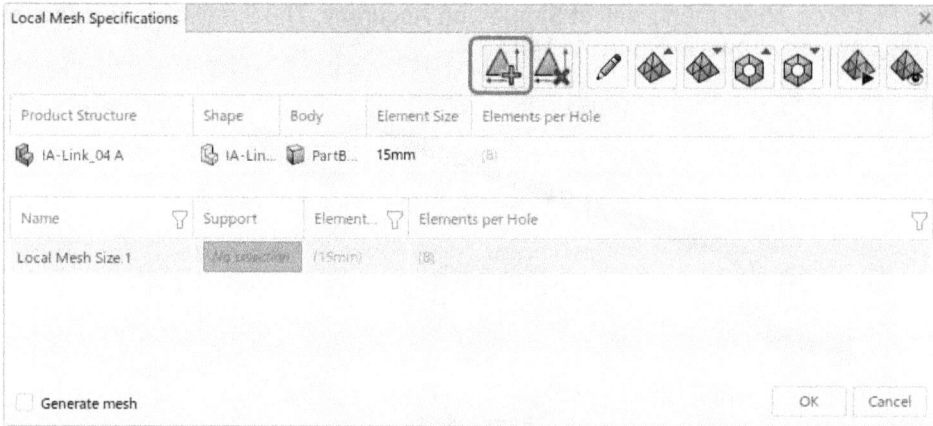

Figure 4−16

4. Select the four surfaces on both upper bends in the part and enter **5mm** as the *Element Size*, as shown in Figure 4−17.

*Note: It is nearly impossible to predict exactly which mesh size would yield the desired analysis accuracy. Therefore, it may require several mesh refinements, gradually moving from larger to even smaller elements, to achieve the desired accuracy. **5mm** size will be your 1st attempt.*

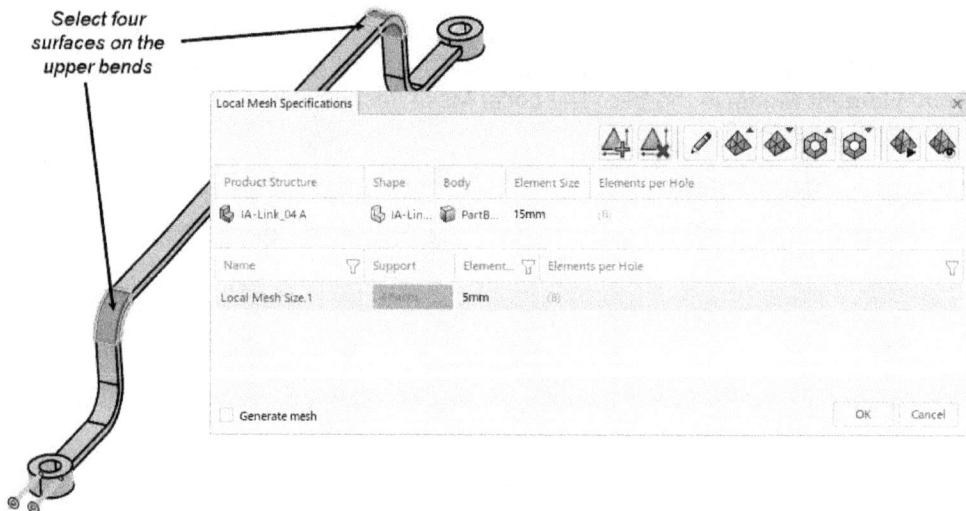

Figure 4−17

5. Generate and display the mesh. Zoom in on one of the bends and note the finer mesh, as shown in Figure 4–18.

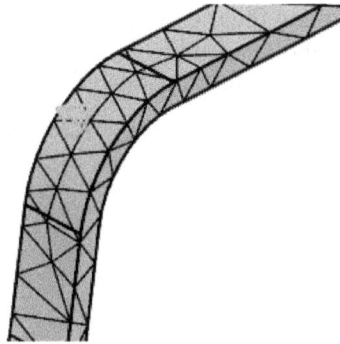

Figure 4–18

6. Hide the mesh.

Task 10: Re-run the analysis.

1. Run the analysis again and wait until it completes.

Task 11: Display Simulation Accuracy result plot.

1. Display the *Simulation Accuracy* result plot, as shown in Figure 4–19.

Figure 4–19

• Note that now there are no red colored areas in the model, which indicates an improvement in accuracy. Still, the bends are colored in light green and yellow, which means the accuracy in those areas is at approximately 30% or less.

Task 12: Refine the mesh.

In this task, you will further refine the mesh. Note that, in general, this process may require several mesh refinement iterations, with the mesh progressively refined to a smaller and smaller size, until the desired accuracy is achieved.

1. Zoom in onto the bend on one end of the part, as shown in Figure 4–20. Note that the elements that display the highest percentage of error are located in the lower bends. Also, the elements in the upper bends, which you refined in Task 9, still exhibit noticeable amount of error.

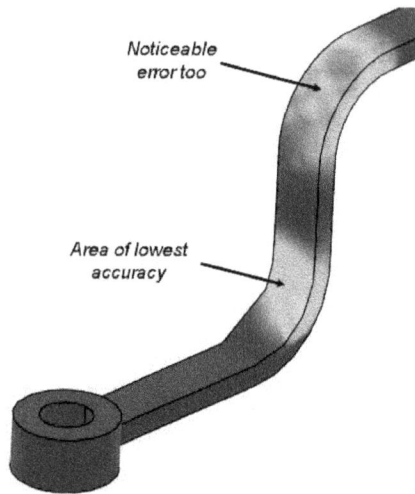

Figure 4–20

2. Click (Result Visualization) in the Action Bar to exit the result visualization mode.

3. Open the *Local Mesh Specifications* dialog box and change the *Element Size* for the upper bends from **5mm** to **2mm**, as shown in Figure 4–21.

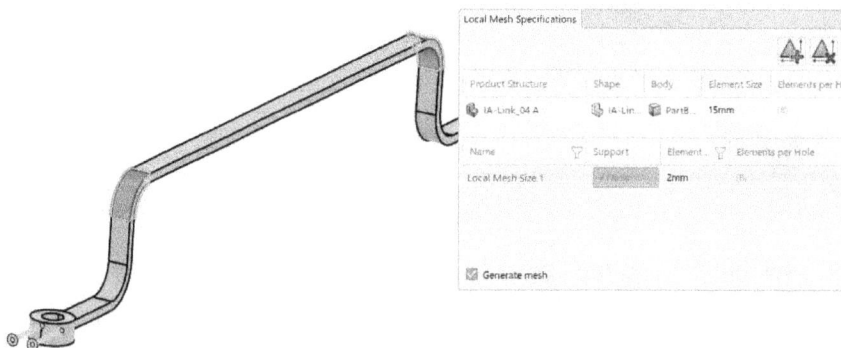

Figure 4–21

4. Select ![icon](Add Local Mesh Specification). Apply **4mm** *Element Size* to the eight surfaces, as shown in Figure 4–22.

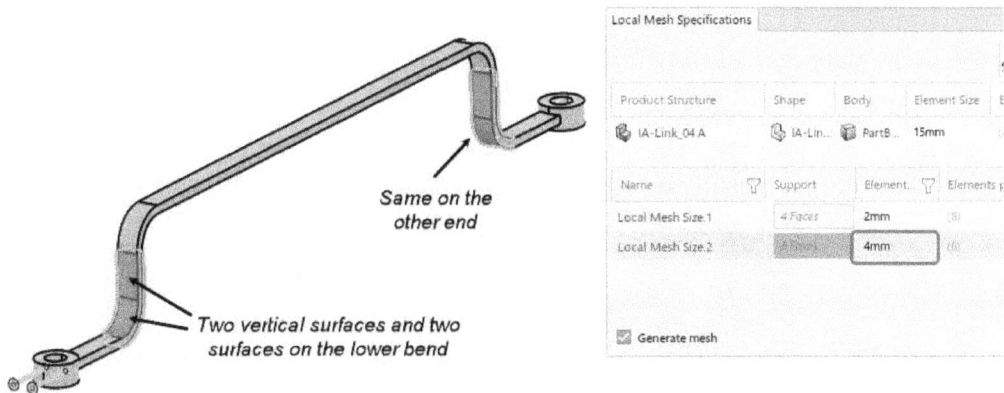

Same on the other end

Two vertical surfaces and two surfaces on the lower bend

Figure 4–22

5. Generate and visualize the refined mesh, as shown in Figure 4–23.

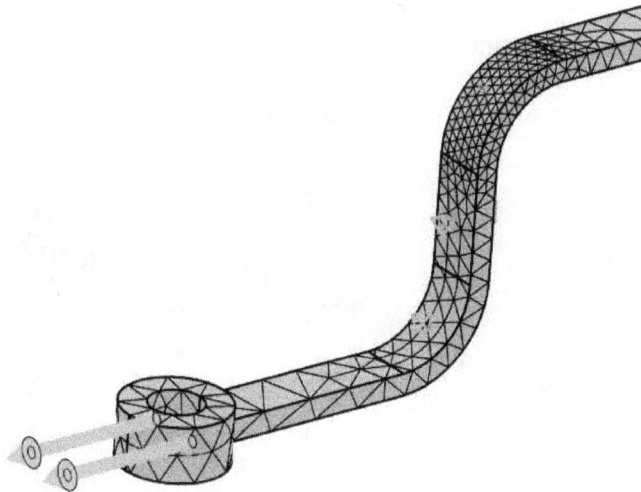

Figure 4–23

6. Hide the mesh.

Task 13: Re-run the analysis.

1. Re-run the analysis.

Task 14: Display Simulation Accuracy result plot.

1. Display the *Simulation Accuracy* result plot, as shown in Figure 4−24.

Figure 4−24

Note that now, the simulation accuracy is better than 86% throughout the entire part. We will consider this accuracy adequate for this simulation.

Task 15: Display the displacement magnitude.

1. Visualize the displacement magnitude image, overlaid over the CAD model, as shown in Figure 4−25.

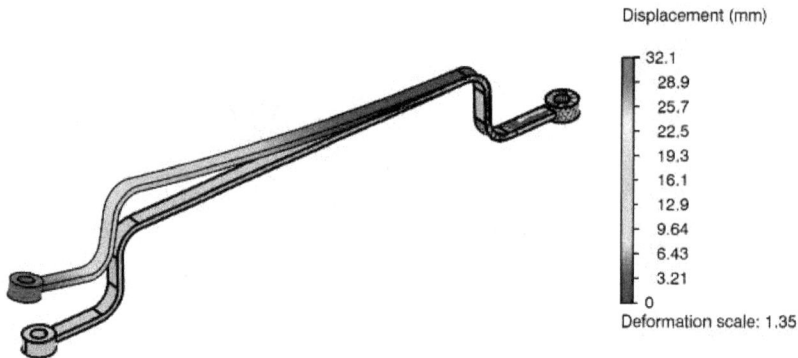

Figure 4−25

2. Animate the displacement magnitude. Check whether the applied loads and restraints behave correctly.

Task 16: Display Von Mises stress.

1. Display the **Von Mises Stress** image, as shown in Figure 4–26. Does the maximum stress exceed the yield strength of the material?

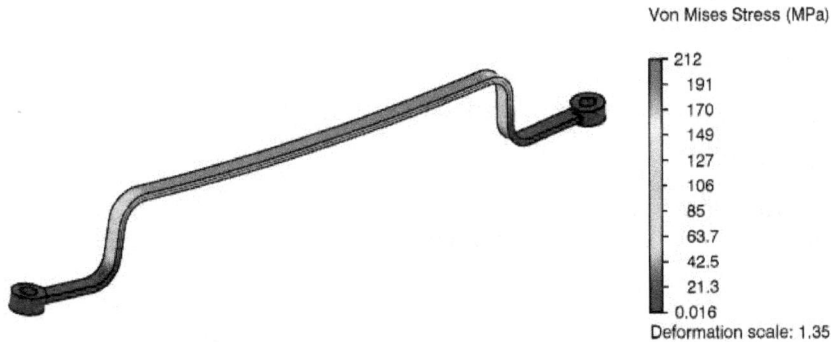

Figure 4–26

2. Locate the maximum stress area, as shown in Figure 4–27. Note that the maximum stress occurs on the inside surface of the upper bend, and this is where you refined the mesh the most.

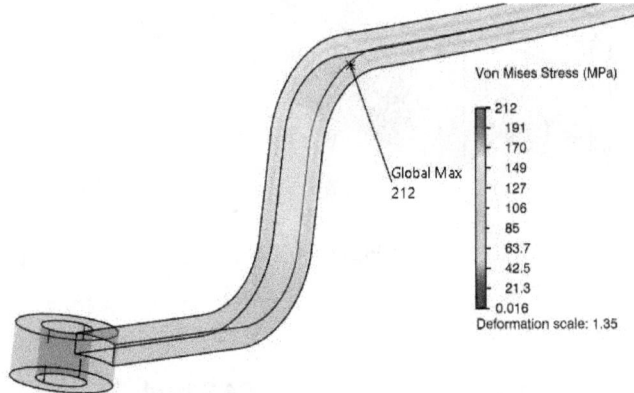

Figure 4–27

3. Click (Result Visualization) in the Action Bar to return to the model view.

Task 17: Save and close the model.

1. Optionally, save the analysis and the part for future reference.

2. Close all windows.

Practice 4b
Solid Bracket with Mesh Refinement

Practice Objectives

- Prepare the model for the analysis.

- Compute the analysis with mesh refinement.

- Display the results.

In this practice, you will set up and run a static stress analysis with mesh refinement on a solid bracket shown in Figure 4-28, with minimum instruction.

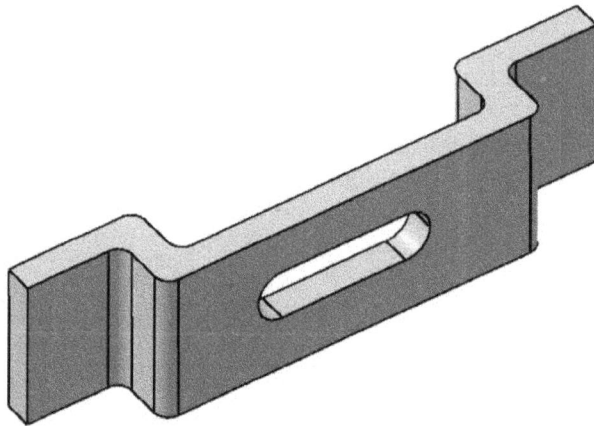

Figure 4-28

Task 1: Open the part.

1. Import with your initials and open **Solid_Bracket_04.3dxml**.
2. Apply the Steel material to the part.

Task 2: Prepare the analysis model.

1.   Start the **LSV** app.
2.   Mesh the model with the default parameters.
3.   Clamp the two surfaces shown in Figure 4–29.

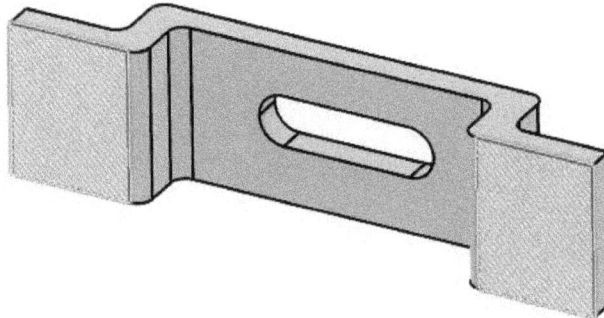

Figure 4–29

4.   Apply **-100,000N** force in Z direction to the surface shown in Figure 4–30.

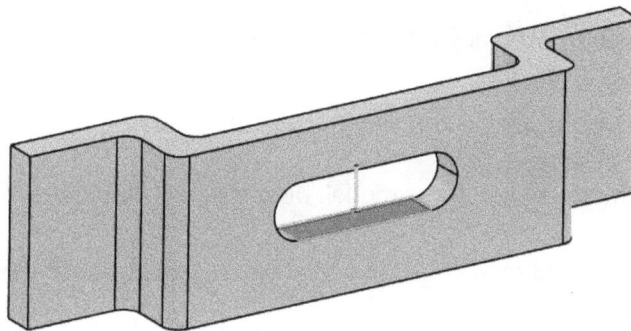

Figure 4–30

Task 3: Run the analysis.

1.   Run the analysis.
2.   Find the Simulation Accuracy with the default mesh size.
3.   Locate the areas of the lowest accuracy.

Task 4: Refine the mesh.

1. Apply **8mm** *Element Size* on the seven surfaces shown in Figure 4–31.

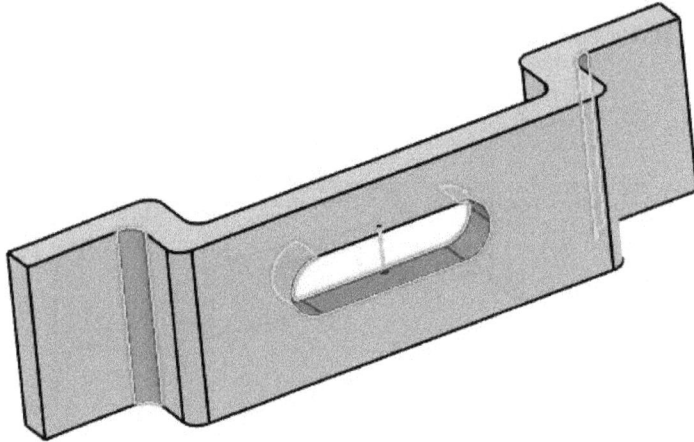

Figure 4–31

2. Re-run the analysis.

3. What is the Simulation Accuracy with the refined mesh?

Task 5: Visualize the analysis results.

1. Visualize and animate the deformed model. Does the part deform according to the applied loads?

2. Display the displacement magnitude color plot. What is the value of the maximum displacement in the model?

3. Display the Von Mises color plot. Does the maximum stress exceed the yield strength of the material?

4. Close the model without saving.

End of practice

Assembly Analysis

In this chapter, you learn how to simulate assemblies.

Learning Objectives

- Understand the assembly analysis process.
- Understand the Bonded and General Contact.
- Understand Rigid, Spring, and Pin connections.
- Visualize the assembly analysis results.

5.1 Assembly Analysis Process

The assembly analysis process in LSV app is shown in Figure 5−1. In general, the process is quite similar to the part analysis, with only two steps being unique to the assembly analysis:

- Specifying contributing parts

- Defining analysis connections

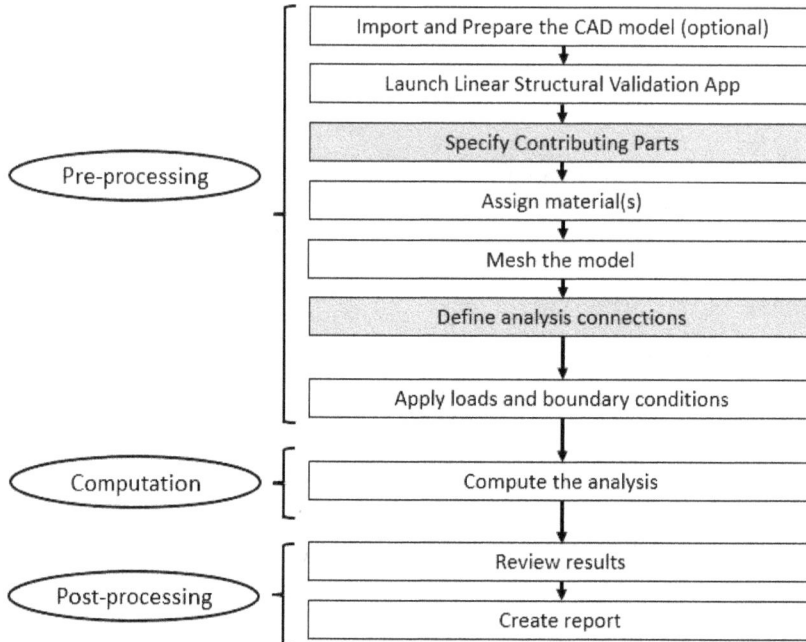

Figure 5−1

Specifying Contributing Parts

In this step, you can specify which parts in the assembly should, and which parts should not participate in the simulation. By default, all parts in the assembly are included in the simulation.

To specify which parts should be excluded from the simulation, select ᵈᴤ (Contributing Parts) in the *Setup* section of the Action Bar. The *Contributing Parts* dialog box opens, as shown in Figure 5–2.

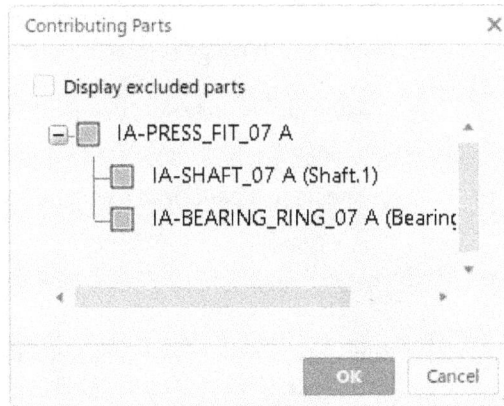

Figure 5–2

Toggle off the parts you want to exclude from the simulation, as shown in Figure 5–3.

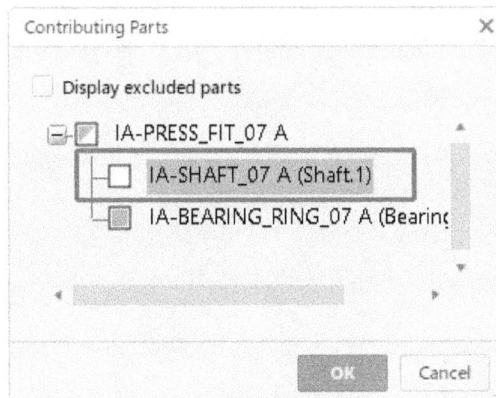

Figure 5–3

Defining Analysis Connections

Initially, the app assumes that all parts in the assembly are *disjoint*, i.e., do not interact with each other when a load is applied. Thus, the parts may interpenetrate, or separate, etc., when they are not supposed to, and the computation is likely to fail due to parts being able to move as rigid bodies.

The user must explicitly define all part interactions by creating analysis *connections*.

The summary of the analysis connections available in LSV app is presented in the following table.

Name	Description
Bonded Contact	Effectively "glues" surfaces together. Neither surface inter-penetration nor separation is permitted.
General Contact	Prevents inter-penetration of the two contacting surfaces, while permitting sliding and/or separation.
Rigid	Creates an infinitely rigid connection between two parts.
Spring	Connects two parts with a linear elastic spring.
Pin	Models "pin-in-a-hole" connection, e.g., in a hinged joint.
Bolt	Connects two parts with a specified bolt tension applied along the bolt axis. Discussed in detail in chapter 6.

5.2 Bonded Contact

Bonded Contact permanently attaches a surface of one part to a surface of another part. From the FEA standpoint, this is equivalent to merging two meshes together. Bonded Contact is suitable to simulate parts that are arc-welded, or bonded, or fusion-welded, etc.

Bonded Contact can be defined either manually or automatically.

To define bonded contact automatically, use the 🔍 (Bonded Contact Detection) tool, as shown in Figure 5–4.

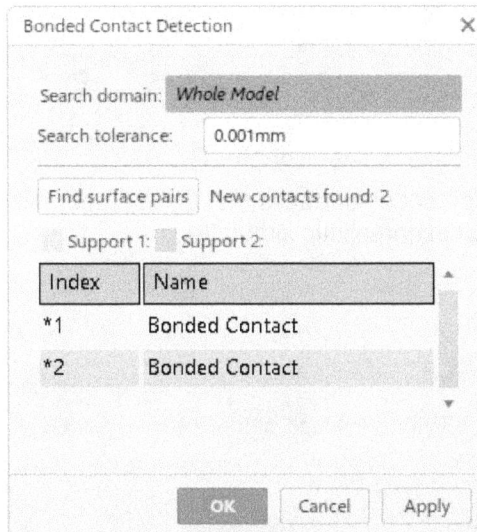

Figure 5–4

The tool searches all surfaces in the model and creates surface pairs that satisfy the proximity conditions. By default, the **Whole Model** is included in the search. Alternatively, use the *Search domain* field to limit search to specific parts.

Once the search completes, the detected surface pairs can be reviewed and/or deleted if required.

To define bonded contact manually, use the ![icon](Bonded Contact) tool, as shown in Figure 5–5. Manually select the surfaces to be bonded.

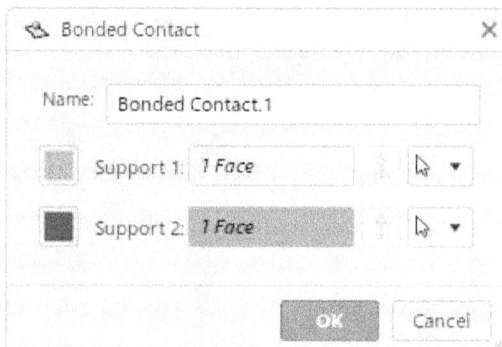

Figure 5–5

Note that defining bonded contact on surfaces that do not meet the proximity requirement (0.001mm or less) may result in unrealistic simulations.

5.3 General Contact

In a *General Contact* connection, the parts are free to move apart and/or slide along each other under the applied loading, but they cannot interpenetrate. The parts are initially permitted to be at a clearance but might come into contact during the analysis. Only compressive normal stresses are transmitted through the contacting surfaces (i.e., the surfaces cannot *pull* each other).

General Contact is the most realistic model for simulating parts that must remain separate from each other during the analysis, yet do not interpenetrate. From the FEA standpoint, the contact connection represents a boundary condition that changes during the loading. For example, when a chain roller is pressed against a sprocket, the line contact changes to an area contact.

In the example shown in Figure 5–6, there is a gap between the plate and block initially (configuration 1 in Figure 5–6). Once the load has been applied, the plate bends freely, until it comes into contact with the block, as shown in configuration 2 in Figure 5–6. If the load is further increased, the area of contact shifts from the edge of the plate to the edge of the block (configuration 3 in Figure 5–6). Therefore, the contact area and location change depending on the amount of load applied.

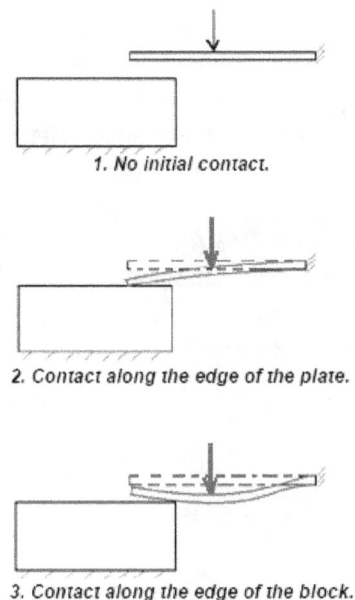

1. No initial contact.

2. Contact along the edge of the plate.

3. Contact along the edge of the block.

Figure 5–6

General Contact in the LSV app models small-sliding, frictionless interactions between the parts.

General Contact domain includes all parts and surfaces in the simulation; there is no need to manually specify surface pairs. To define general contact, select ⚬ (General Contact) in the *Connections* section of the Action Bar, or in the *Contact* section of the *Assistant* dialog box. The *General Contact* dialog box opens, as shown in Figure 5−7.

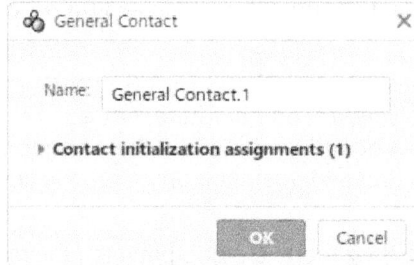

Figure 5−7

A Contact Initialization specifies how the app treats overclosures, i.e., interferences, of the surfaces at the beginning of the analysis.

The Default Contact Initialization considers such overclosures as unintentional, possibly due to slight inaccuracies in part positioning or geometry. To eliminate those unintentional overclosures without modifying the assembly, the app offsets, strain-free, the mesh nodes at the beginning of simulation to create zero gap between the surfaces.

If surface overclosures are intentional, as in press-fit assemblies, the contact initialization can specify such overclosures as interference fits. For an interference fit, the app computes the contact stresses required to eliminate the overclosure.

To define a Contact Initialization, select ⚬ (Contact Initialization) in the *Connections* section of the Action Bar. The *Contact Initialization* dialog box opens, as shown in Figure 5−8.

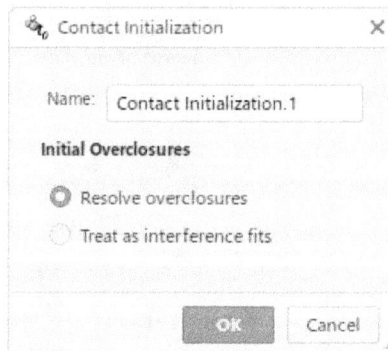

Figure 5−8

The default option is **Resolve overclosures**, which is a strain-free adjustment of the mesh nodes. If overclosures in your model are intentional, select **Treat as interference fits** and click **OK**.

To use a specific contact initialization in the analysis, right-click the **Support** line in the *General Contact* dialog box, and select **Edit**, as shown in Figure 5−9.

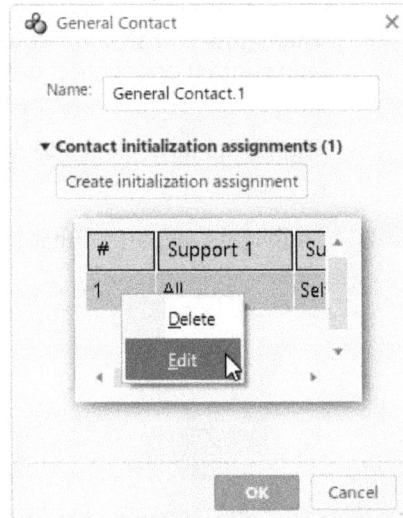

Figure 5−9

Then select the contact initialization you wish to use in the drop-down menu, as shown in Figure 5−10.

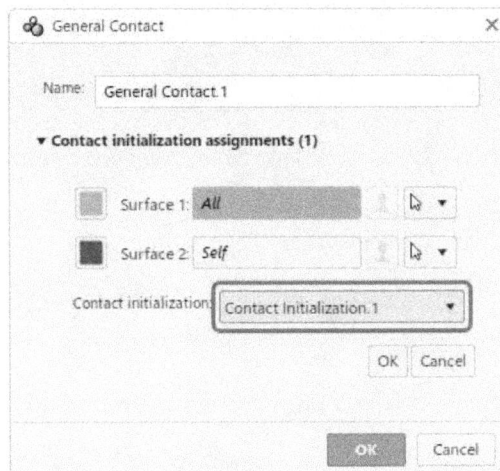

Figure 5−10

5.4 Contact Diagnostics

The contact diagnostics tools are in the *Connections* section of the Action Bar. The summary is presented in the following table.

Name	Description
Show Disconnected Bodies	Highlights all parts that are touching, but do not have any contact connection defined between them
Show Contacting Bodies	Highlights all surfaces that are in contact
Show Intersecting Bodies	Highlights all parts that intersect each other

5.5 Rigid Connection

Rigid Connection joins two parts using a virtual rigid beam, as shown in Figure 5–11.

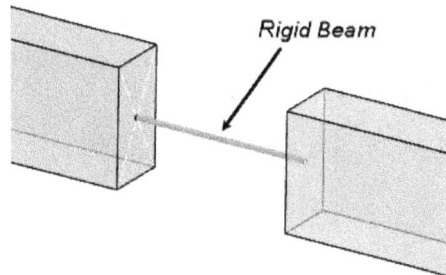

Figure 5–11

A Rigid connection effectively "locks" the connected parts together. While the parts can move and deform under the loading, the distance and angle between the connected surfaces won't change.

To create a Rigid connection, select ⬛ (Rigid) in the *Connections* section of the Action Bar or of the *Assistant* dialog box, and select the **Supports**, as shown in Figure 5–12.

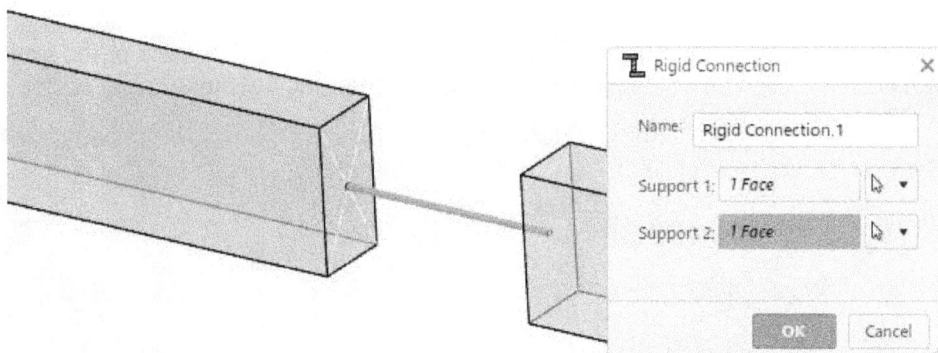

Figure 5–12

5.6 Spring Connection

Spring Connection joins two parts using a virtual linear spring, as shown in Figure 5−13.

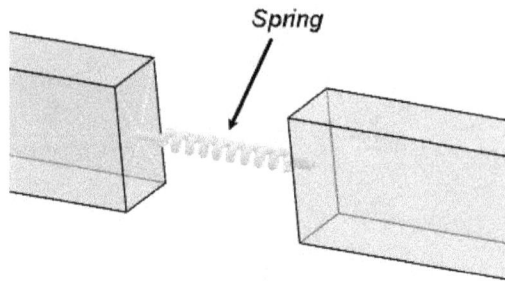

Spring

Figure 5−13

A Spring connection creates an elastic link between the parts. When a spring is compressed or stretched from its resting position, it exerts an opposing force proportional to its change in length. The exerted force value equals the change in length multiplied by the spring's stiffness.

Spring connections are used to model actual physical springs, as well as idealizations for various 1D components such as rods, links, etc.

To create a *Spring* connection, select (Spring) in the *Connections* section of the Action Bar or of the *Assistant* dialog box, select the **Supports,** and enter the **Stiffness** value, as shown in Figure 5−14.

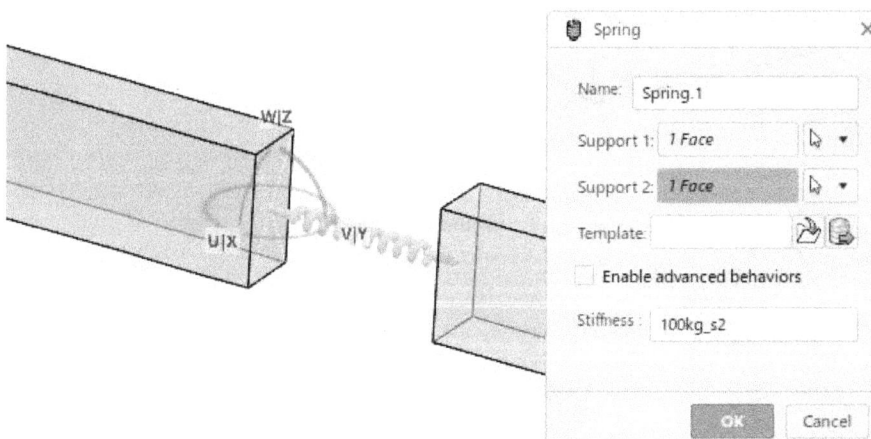

Figure 5−14

If no geometrical entity is selected for **Support 2**, it creates a grounded spring, as shown in Figure 5-15. A grounded spring connects the part to the ground, which can be used to model elastic boundary conditions in your simulation.

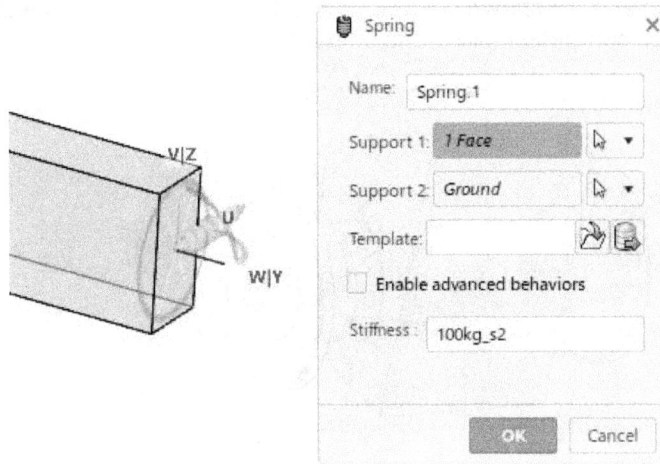

Figure 5-15

5.7 Pin Connection

Pin Connection models a virtual rigid pin that enables rotation of two cylindrical surfaces around their common axis, as shown in Figure 5−16. Examples of pin connections include hinged joints in laptop computers, plies, and actuators.

Pin

Figure 5−16

To create a *Pin* connection, select ⬚ (Pin) in the *Connections* section of the Action Bar or of the *Assistant* dialog box.

Select the first cylindrical surface as **Support 1**, as shown in Figure 5−17.

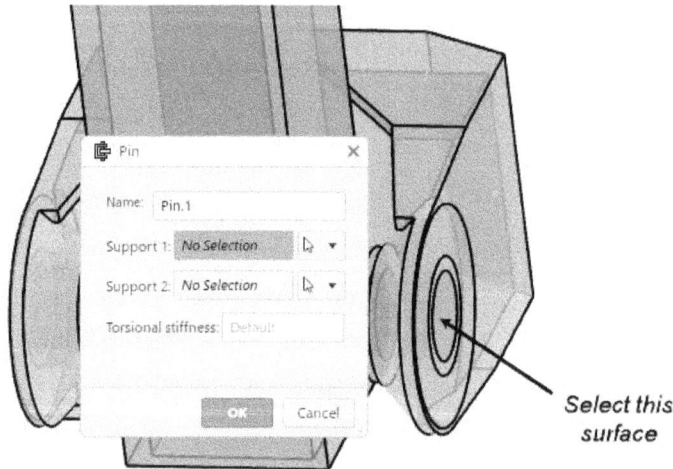

Select this surface

Figure 5−17

The other cylindrical surfaces are auto-selected based on the geometry, as shown in Figure 5–18.

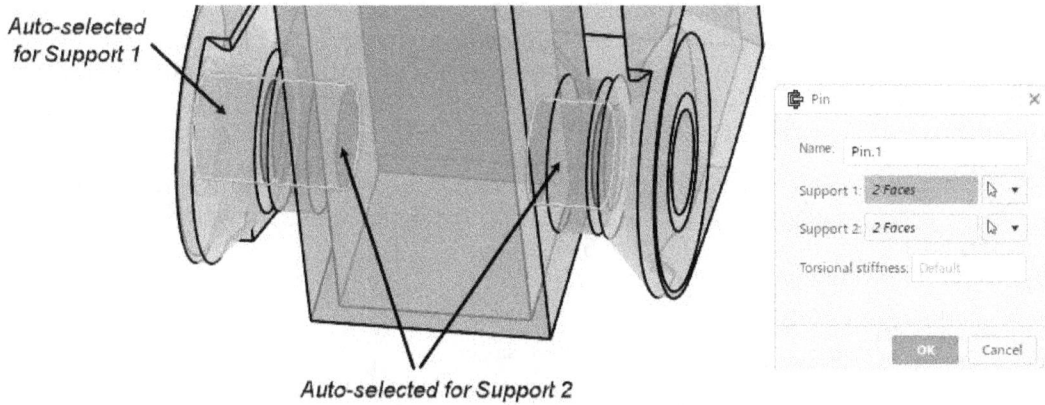

Figure 5–18

By default, the pin has a small torsional stiffness. The default stiffness can be overridden by entering a value for the **Torsional stiffness**.

5.8 Result Visualization

The assembly analysis results are visualized in the same way as for the part analysis, i.e., by selecting an appropriate result type in the *Plot* drop-down menu, such as deformation, displacement, or stress. The results are displayed for all the parts included in the analysis model.

If you want to display the result for a specific part or parts, use the ⊞ (Display Group) tool. In the *Display Groups* dialog box that opens, toggle off the components for which you don't want to display the results, as shown in Figure 5–19.

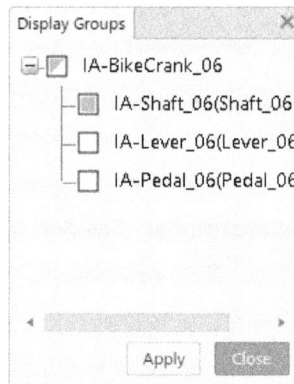

Figure 5–19

Practice 5a
Bicycle Crank Assembly

Practice Objectives

- Apply materials and mesh the model.
- Create analysis connections.
- Apply loads and boundary conditions.
- Compute the analysis.
- Visualize the results.

In this practice, you will set up and run a static stress analysis on a crank assembly for a children's bicycle shown in Figure 5–20. The shaft is made of steel, while the crank and the pedal are made of aluminum alloy. The assembly is loaded by a vertical force on the pedal.

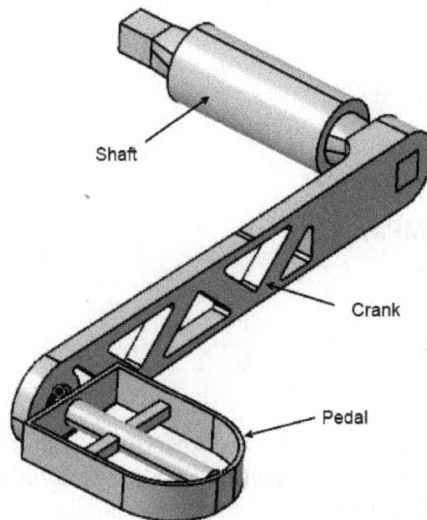

Shaft

Crank

Pedal

Figure 5–20

Task 1: Open the assembly.

1. Import with your initials and open **BikeCrank_06.3dxml**.

2. Set the model display as 🛢 (Shading with Sharp and Smooth Edges). The assembly displays as shown in Figure 5–21.

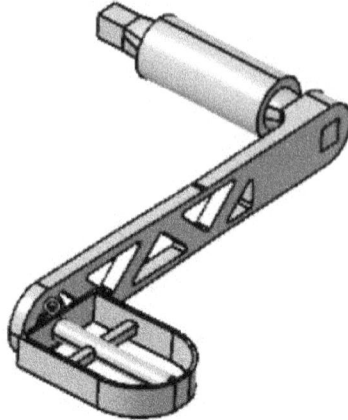

Figure 5–21

3. Set the units as follows:

- *Length:* **Millimeter (mm)**
- *Force:* **Newton (N)**
- *Moment:* **Newton x Meter (Nxm)**
- *Pressure:* **Megapascal (MPa)**
- *Stress:* **Megapascal (MPa)**

Task 2: Apply the materials.

1. Using the 🔵 (Material Browser) tool in the *Assembly Design* app, apply the materials to the assembly parts as follows. You can either use the material definitions you created in Practice 2b and Practice 2b or create new material definitions.

- *Shaft_06:* **Steel**
    - *Density:* **7860 Kg/m3**
    - *Proof (Yield) Stress:* **250 MPa**
    - *Young's Modulus:* **200000 MPa**
    - *Poisson's Ratio:* **0.266**

- *Lever_06, Pedal_06:* **Aluminum**
    - *Density:* **2710 Kg/m3**
    - *Proof (Yield) Stress:* **95 MPa**
    - *Young's Modulus:* **70000 MPa**
    - *Poisson's Ratio:* **0.346**

Task 3: Launch the Linear Structural Validation app.

1. Activate the *BikeCrank_06* window and ensure that the root product is active. Launch the **Linear Structural Validation** app.
2. Enter ***<Your Initials>_Bike Crank Simulation*** for the *Title* of the Physics Simulation.
3. Select **Structural** for *Analysis type*.

Task 4: Mesh the model.

In this task, you will mesh the assembly using the default mesh specifications.

1. Select (Mesh Specifications) in the Action Bar to open the *Mesh Specifications* dialog box, as shown in Figure 5–22. Note that each part in the assembly has its own mesh specification.

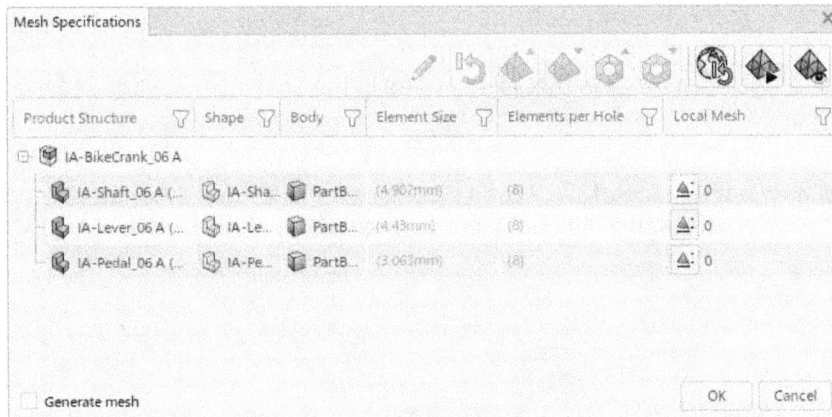

Figure 5–22

2. Close the Mesh Specifications dialog box.

3. Select ◈ (Generate Mesh) in the Action Bar. The mesh is generated and displayed, as shown in Figure 5-23.

Figure 5-23

4. Select ◈ (Hide/Show Mesh) in the Action Bar to hide the mesh.

Task 5: Create analysis connections.

In this simulation, you will assume that all the parts in the assembly are bonded over their mated surfaces.

1. In the *Connections* section of the Action Bar, select ◈ (Bonded Contact Detection). The *Bonded Contact Detection* dialog box opens, as shown in Figure 5-24.

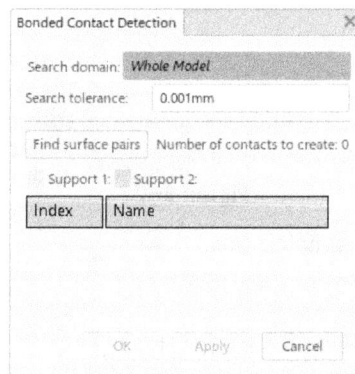

Figure 5-24

2. Click **Find surface pairs**. The system detects five bonded contacts within the search tolerance and lists them in the dialog box, as shown in Figure 5–25.

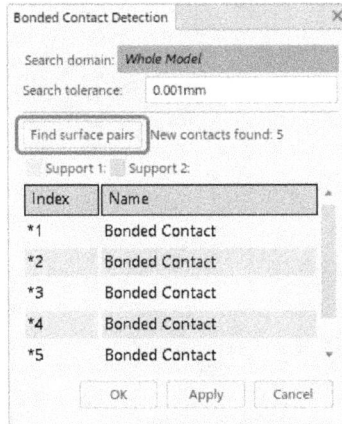

Figure 5–25

3. Select the first **Bonded Contact** in the list. The surfaces are highlighted in the model, as shown in Figure 5–26.

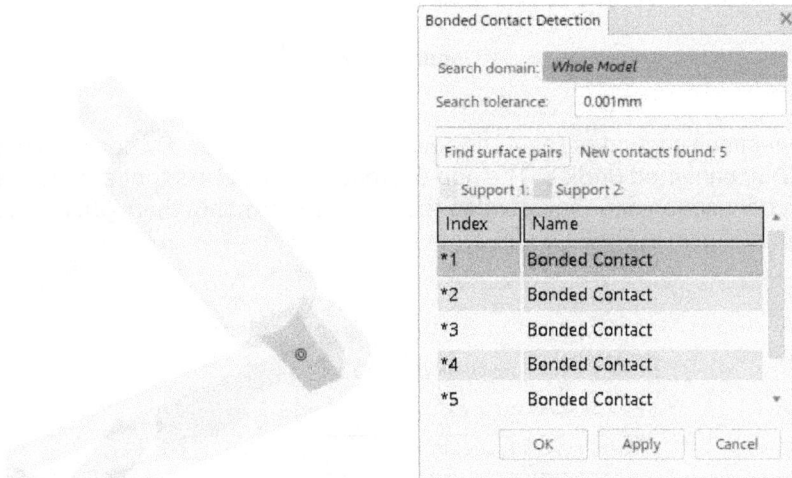

Figure 5–26

4. Select the remaining four **Bonded Contacts** to review them. Click **OK** to close the *Bonded Contact Detection* dialog box when done.

5. The created Bonded Contacts are not displayed in the tree. However, you can use the **Feature Manager** tool ( ) to manage and edit Bonded Contacts at any time, as shown in Figure 5–27.

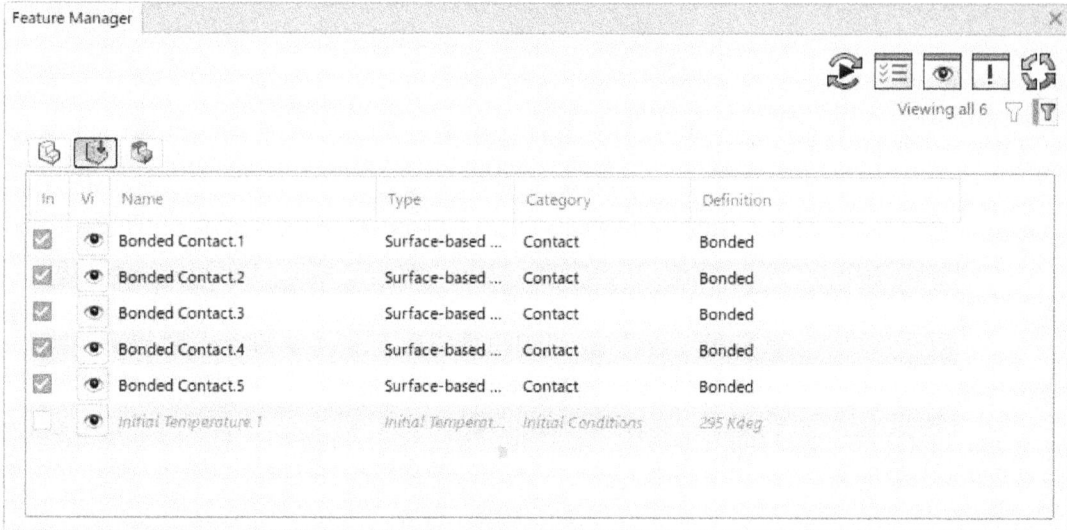

Figure 5–27

6. In the *Connections* section of the Action Bar, select (Show Disconnected Bodies) and click **Find Disconnected Bodies**. The app searches for the parts that are touching but have no contact connection defined between them, and reports that there are no such parts in the model, as shown in Figure 5–28.

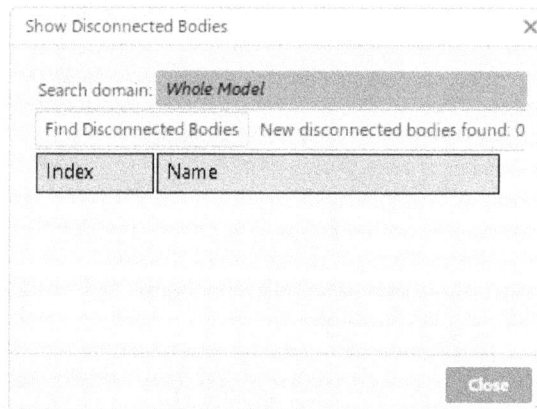

Figure 5–28

Task 6: Apply the load.

1. Select ✎ (Force) and apply **-80N** downward force (-Z direction) to the top surface of the pedal, as shown in Figure 5–29.

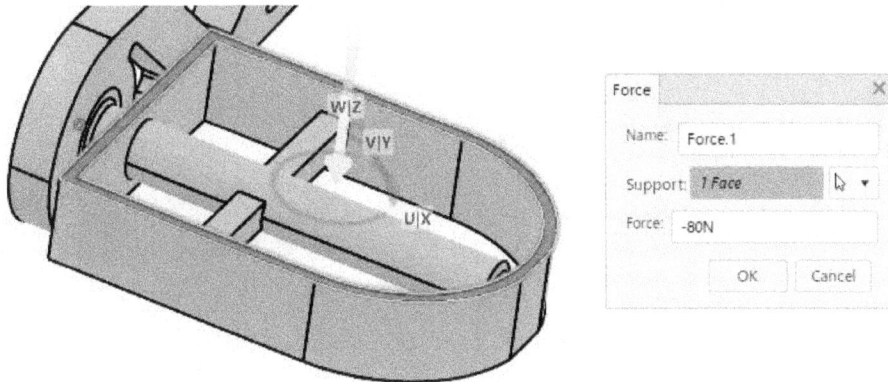

Figure 5–29

Task 7: Apply the boundary conditions.

1. Apply the ▨ (Hinge) to the outside diameter of the shaft, as shown in Figure 5–30.

    *   Note: This simulates a bushing-type support on this section of the shaft.

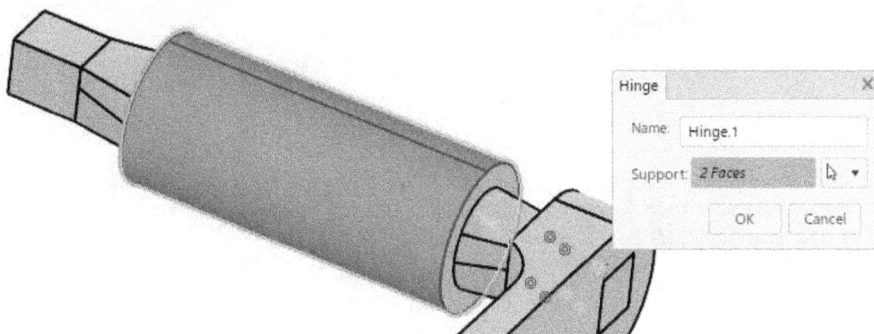

Figure 5–30

2. Apply the ✎ (Clamp) to the four surfaces, all around, on the square end of the shaft, as shown in Figure 5–31.

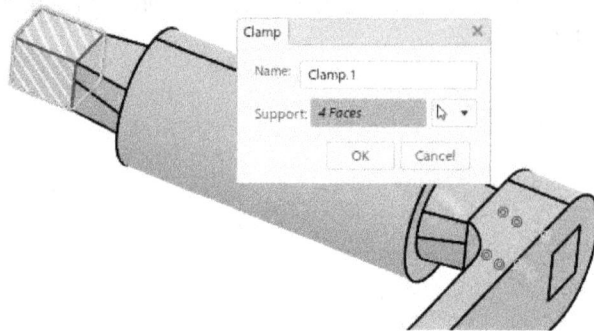

Figure 5–31

3. The model displays as shown in Figure 5–32.

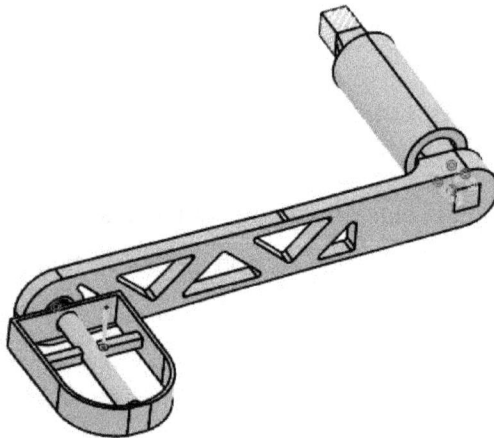

Figure 5–32

Task 8: Run the analysis.

1. Select ⟳ (Simulate) in the *Results* section of the Action Bar.

2. Click **OK** to close the *Simulate* dialog box when it displays.

3. Wait until computation completes, and the *Simulation Status* dialog box displays the message, "Static Stress Simulation completed". The computation for this model should take under **60sec**.

4. Close the *Simulation Status* dialog box.

Task 9: Display and animate the displacement magnitude.

1. Select **Displacement** in the *Plot* drop-down menu to visualize the displacement magnitude. Unhide the CAD model to overlay it over the result plot, and animate, as shown in Figure 5–33. Does the model deform according to the applied loads and restraints?

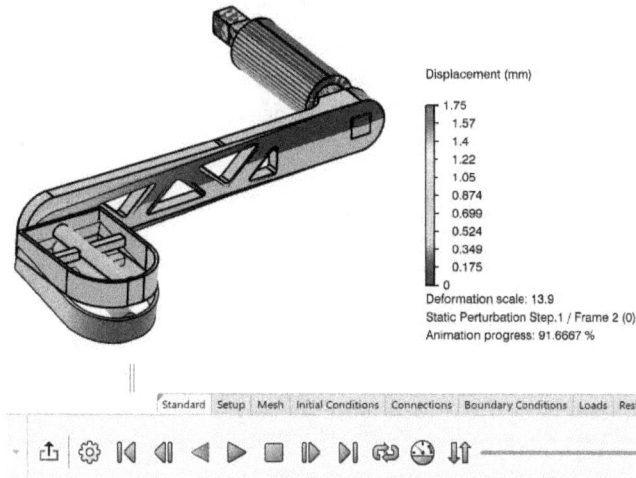

Figure 5–33

Task 10: Display Von Mises Stress in the shaft part.

1. Select **Von Mises Stress** in the *Plot* drop-down menu. The stress plot for the entire assembly displays as shown in Figure 5–34.

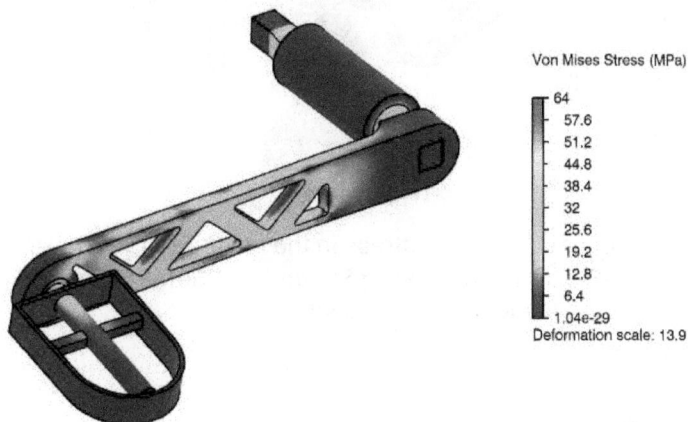

Figure 5–34

2. Select ⬚ (Display Group) in the *Results* section of the Action Bar. In the *Display Groups* dialog box that opens, deactivate the Lever_06 and Pedal_06 parts, as shown in Figure 5–35.

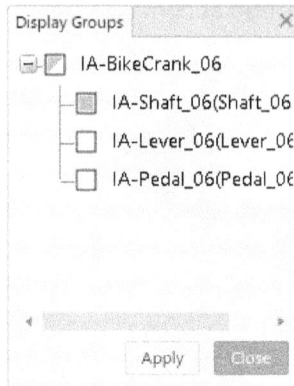

Figure 5–35

3. Click **Apply** and **Close**. Now the stress result is only displayed for the shaft part, as shown in Figure 5–36.

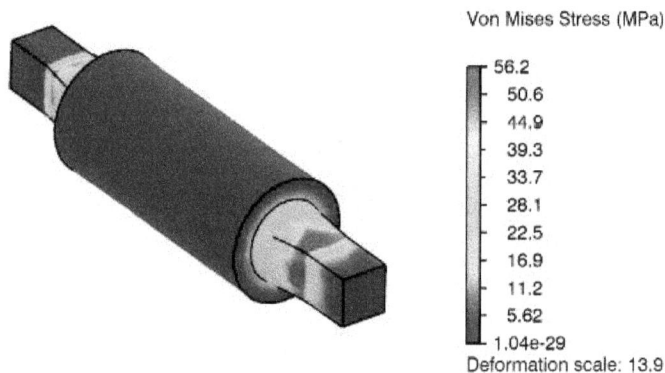

Von Mises Stress (MPa)

- 56.2
- 50.6
- 44.9
- 39.3
- 33.7
- 28.1
- 22.5
- 16.9
- 11.2
- 5.62
- 1.04e-29

Deformation scale: 13.9

Figure 5–36

- Note that the maximum Von Mises stress in the shaft part is approximately **56.2 MPa**, which is below the **Steel** material's *Yield Strength* of **250MPa**. Therefore, the shaft is predicted to withstand the load without failure.

4. Using the ▮ (Show Min/Max Values) tool, locate the area of maximum stress in the shaft, as shown in Figure 5–37. Note that the maximum stress occurs where the shaft fits into the lever part.

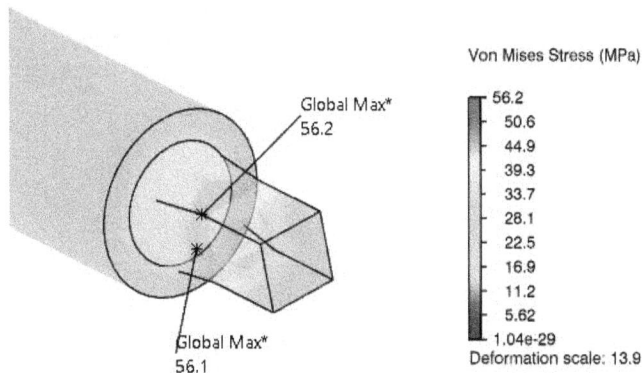

Von Mises Stress (MPa)

| 56.2 |
| 50.6 |
| 44.9 |
| 39.3 |
| 33.7 |
| 28.1 |
| 22.5 |
| 16.9 |
| 11.2 |
| 5.62 |
| 1.04e-29 |

Deformation scale: 13.9

Global Max*
56.2

Global Max*
56.1

Figure 5–37

5. Using the ▮ (Show Min/Max Values) tool, remove the maximum stress label from the result plot.

Task 11: Display Von Mises Stress in the Lever part.

1. Select ▦ (Display Group) in the Action Bar. Activate **Lever_06** and deactivate **Shaft_06** and **Pedal_06** parts, as shown in Figure 5–38.

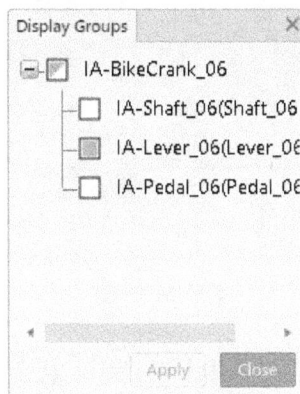

Display Groups　　　　　　　　×

- ☑ IA-BikeCrank_06
  - ☐ IA-Shaft_06(Shaft_06
  - ☑ IA-Lever_06(Lever_06
  - ☐ IA-Pedal_06(Pedal_06

Apply　　Close

Figure 5–38

2. Click **Apply** and **Close**. The stress result is only displayed for the lever part, as shown in Figure 5–39.

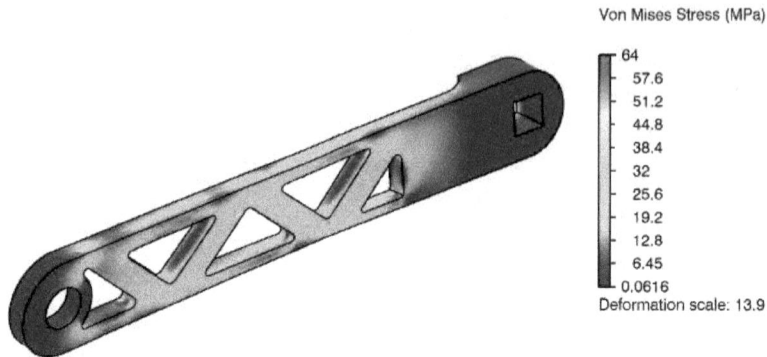

Figure 5–39

- Note that the maximum Von Mises stress in the lever part is approximately **64 MPa**, which is below the Aluminum material's *Yield Strength* of **95MPa**. Therefore, the crank is predicted to withstand the load without failure.

3. Using the ▪ (Show Min/Max Values) tool, locate the area of maximum stress in the lever, as shown in Figure 5–40. Note that the maximum stress occurs in one of the triangular pockets.

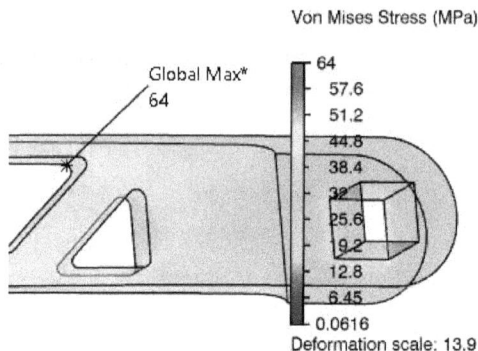

Figure 5–40

Task 12: Display Von Mises stress in the pedal part.

1. Using the instruction in Task 10, display and examine the **Von Mises Stress** in the pedal part.

Task 13: Save and close the model.

1. Click (Result Visualization) in the Action Bar to return to the model view.
2. Optionally, save the analysis and the assembly for future reference.
3. Close all windows.

Practice 5b
Pin-Jointed Assembly

Practice Objectives

- Apply materials and mesh the model.
- Create Bonded Contact analysis connection.
- Create General Contact analysis connection.
- Apply loads and boundary conditions.
- Compute the analysis.
- Visualize the results.

In this practice, you will set up a contact analysis on a pin-jointed assembly model. The assembly that you will analyze consists of three parts; the exploded view is shown in Figure 5-41.

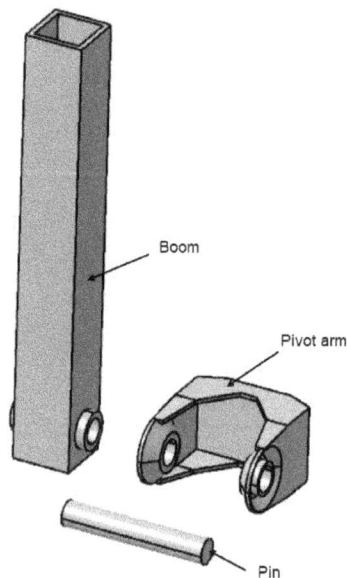

Figure 5-41

The pin is press-fit into the pivot arm holes. Therefore, the pin is fully fixed to the pivot arm. However, the boom is assembled on the pin with a small clearance, to be able to rotate around the pin when the boom is moving.

Task 1: Open the assembly.

1. Import with your initials and open **PIN_JOINT_07.3dxml**.

2. Set the model display as ⬡ (Shading with Sharp and Smooth Edges). The assembly displays as shown in Figure 5-42.

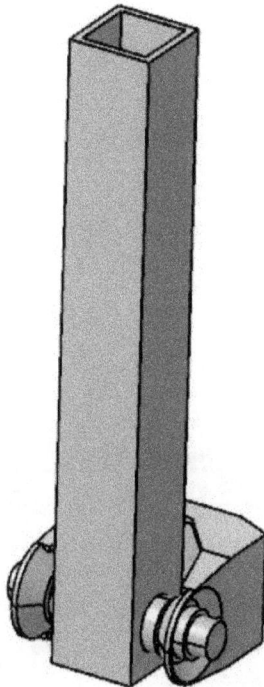

Figure 5-42

3. Set the units as follows:
    - *Length:* **Millimeter (mm)**
    - *Force:* **Newton (N)**
    - *Moment:* **Newton x Meter (Nxm)**
    - *Pressure:* **Megapascal (MPa)**
    - *Stress:* **Megapascal (MPa)**

Task 2: Apply the material.

1. Using the ⬤ (Material Browser) tool in the *Assembly Design* app, apply the **Steel** material to all parts in the assembly, as shown in Figure 5–43. You can either use the material definition you created in Practice 2b or create a new material definition. Verify that the material properties are as follows:

   - *Density:* **7860 Kg/m3**
   - *Proof (Yield) Stress:* **250 MPa**
   - *Young's Modulus:* **200000 MPa**
   - *Poisson's Ratio:* **0.266**

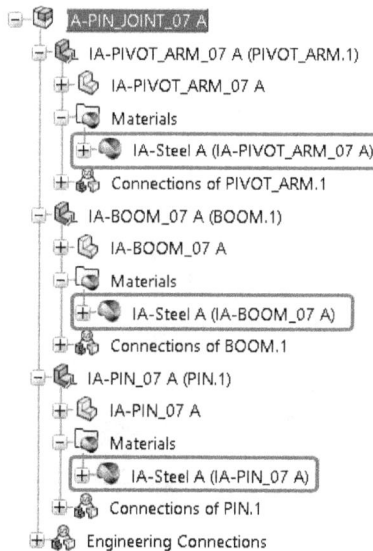

Figure 5–43

Task 3: Start the Linear Structural Validation app.

1. Ensure that the root product **PIN_JOINT_07** is active. Launch the Linear Structural Validation app.

2. Enter **<*Your Initials*>_Pin Joint Simulation** for the *Title* of the Physics Simulation.

3. Select **Structural** for *Analysis type*.

Task 4: Mesh the model.

For better stress accuracy in contact analysis, the mesh on the contact surfaces should be refined. This can be accomplished by using local mesh specifications.

1. In the *Mesh* section of the Action Bar, select ⬛ (Local Mesh Specifications) and select the outer surface of the Pin. Enter **5mm** as the *Element Size*, as shown in Figure 5–44.

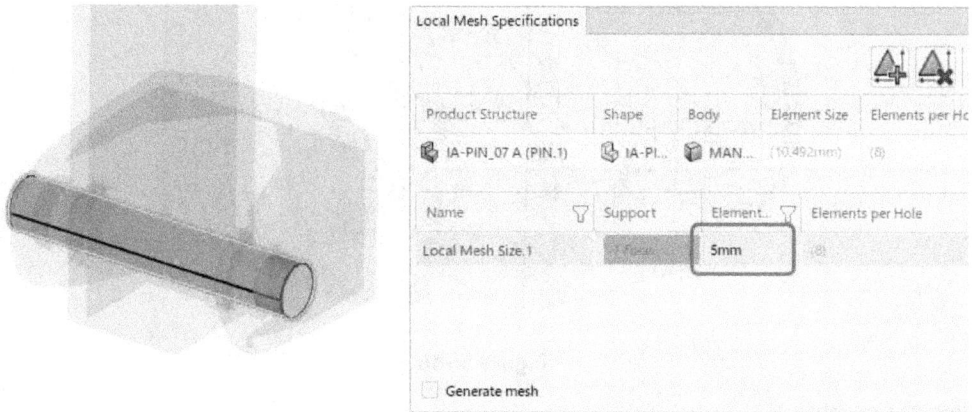

Figure 5–44

2. Click **OK** to close the *Local Mesh Specifications* dialog box.

3. Repeat step 1, now for the two inside surfaces of the holes in the Boom, as shown in Figure 5–45.

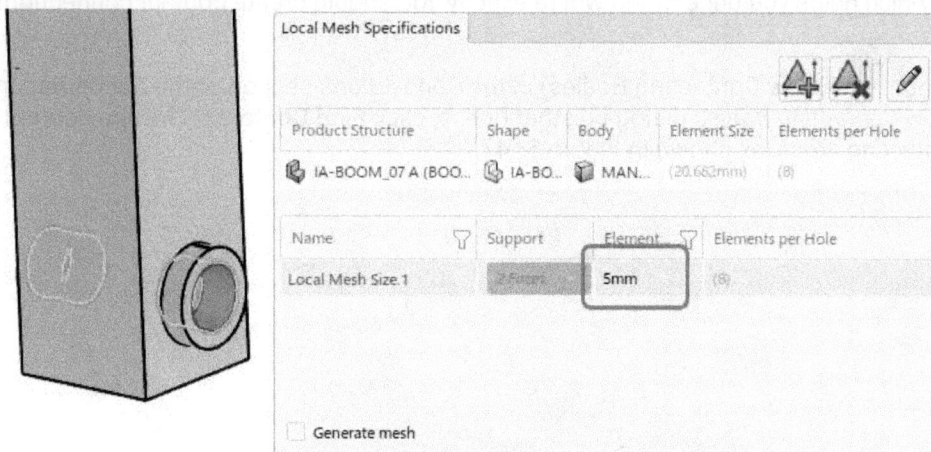

Figure 5–45

4. Generate and display the mesh, as shown in Figure 5−46. Note the smaller elements on the surfaces with the *Local Mesh Specification*.

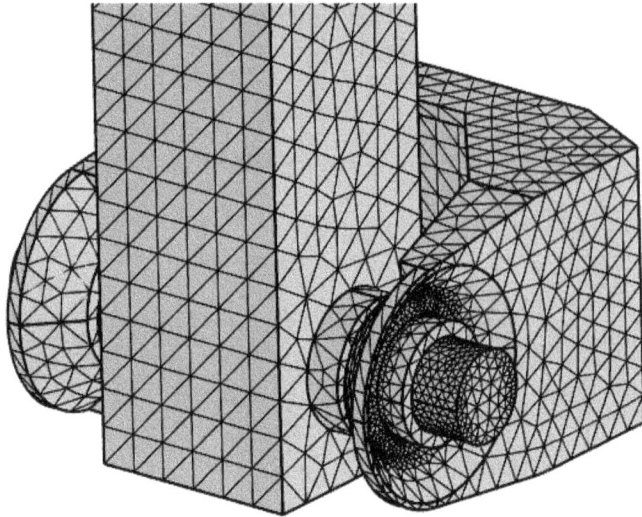

Figure 5−46

5. Hide the mesh.

Task 5: Display contacting parts.

The ⬚ (Show Contacting Bodies) tool searches and displays all mated surfaces in your model, which helps you understand where exactly you should create contact connections.

1. Select ⬚ (Show Contacting Bodies) in the *Connections* section of the Action Bar. In the *Show Contacting Bodies* dialog box that opens, click **Find Contacts**. The app detects two contacting areas, as shown in Figure 5−47.

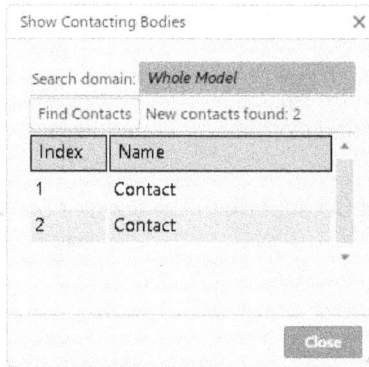

Figure 5–47

2. Select the first contact in the list. The contact areas between the pin and the boom are highlighted, as shown in Figure 5–48.

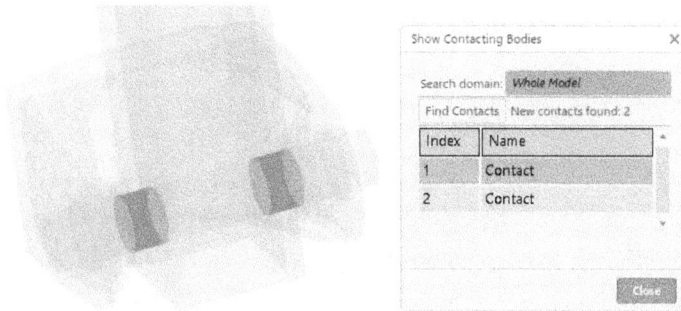

Figure 5–48

3. Select the second contact in the list. The contact areas between the pin and the pivot arm are highlighted, as shown in Figure 5–49.

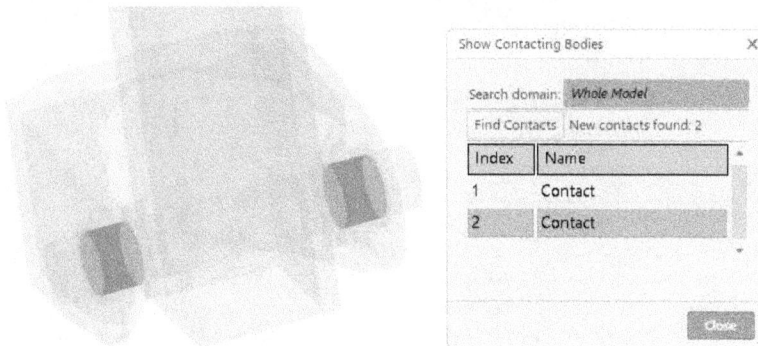

Figure 5–49

4. Close the *Show Contacting Bodies* dialog box.

Task 6: Create Bonded Contact connection.

The pin is press-fit into the pivot arm holes. Therefore, the pin is fully fixed to the pivot arm, which can be simulated by a Bonded Contact between the pin and the pivot arm.

1. Select ⚲ (Bonded Contact Detection). In the *Bonded Contact Detection* dialog box that opens, click Find surface pairs. The system detects two bonded contacts, as shown in Figure 5–50.

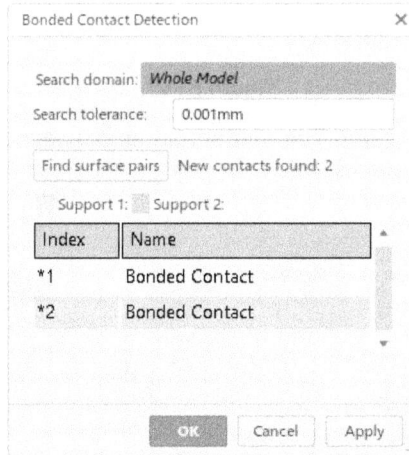

Figure 5–50

2. Select the first bonded contact in the list. The outside surface of the pin and the inside surfaces of the hole in the boom are highlighted, as shown in Figure 5–51.

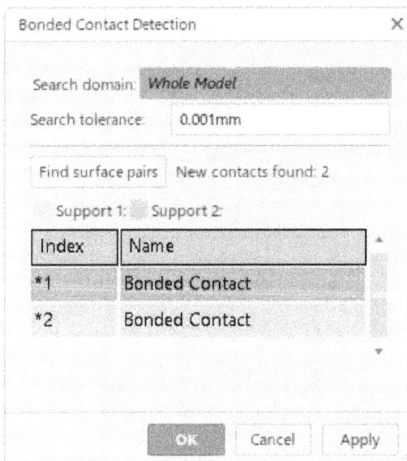

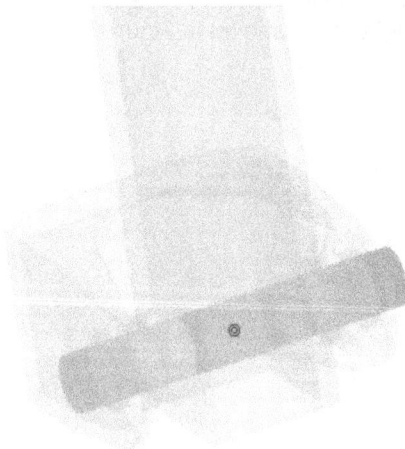

Figure 5–51

3. The boom, however, should not be bonded to the pin. Right-click the first bonded connection and select **Remove Selected,** as shown in Figure 5–52.

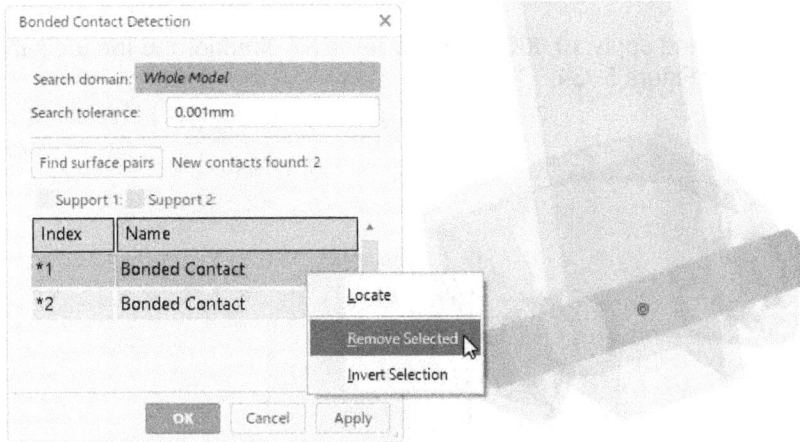

Figure 5–52

4. Click **OK** to complete.

Task 7: Create General Contact connection.

The boom is assembled on the pin in such a way that it can rotate around the pin when the boom is moving. At the same time, when a load is applied to the boom, the pin bends ever slightly, and no longer contacts the holes in the boom over their entire surface areas. This behavior can be simulated by General Contact connection.

The General Contact automatically considers all surfaces that are already in contact or may come into contact under the applied loads. There is no need to select any particular parts or surfaces for the General Contact.

1. Select (General Contact). The *General Contact* dialog box opens, as shown in Figure 5–53.

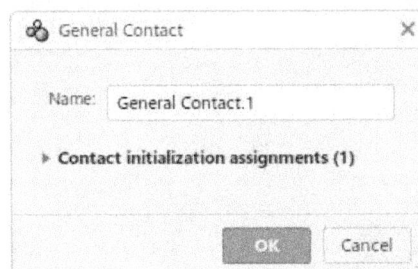

Figure 5–53

2. Click **OK** to complete.

Task 8: Apply the load.

1. Select ✐ (Force) and apply **10,000N** upward force (-Y direction) to the top surface of the boom, as shown in Figure 5-54.

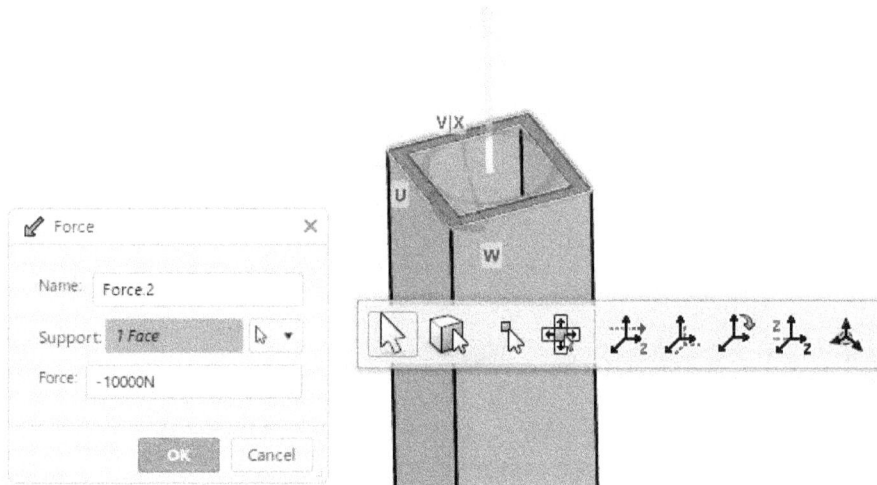

Figure 5-54

Task 9: Apply boundary conditions.

1. Select ⚓ (Fixed Displacement) and restrain the **X-** and **Z-** directions on the end surface of the boom, as shown in Figure 5-55. Ensure that you leave the **Y-** direction free; this is the direction of the load.

Note: This boundary condition is required to eliminate the rigid body rotation and sliding motions of the boom about the pin. The General Contact connection between the pin and the boom that you defined in Task 7 was frictionless.

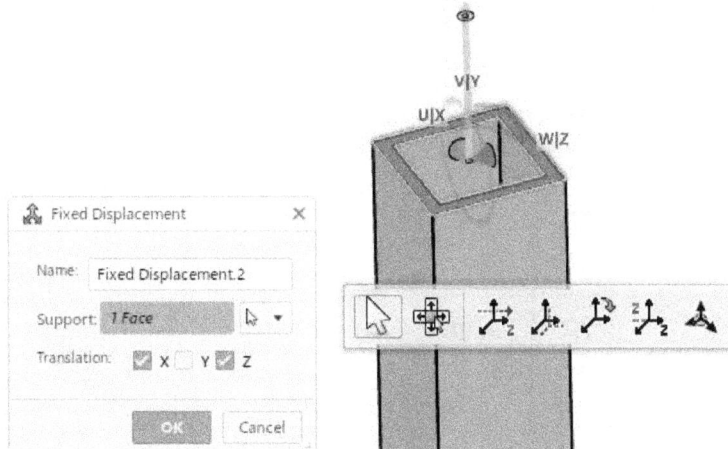

Figure 5-55

2. Apply the 🗗 (Clamp) to the back surface of the pivot arm, as shown in Figure 5-56.

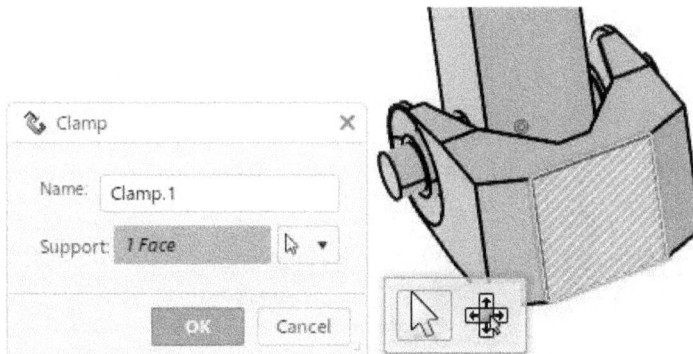

Figure 5-56

Task 10: Run the analysis.

1. Select 🗗 (Simulate) in the *Results* section of the Action Bar.
2. Click **OK** to close the *Simulate* dialog box when it displays.
3. Wait until computation completes, and the *Simulation Status* dialog box displays the message "Static Stress Simulation completed".
4. Close the *Simulation Status* dialog box.

Task 11: Display and animate the displacements.

1. Select **Displacement** in the *Plot* drop-down menu to visualize the displacement magnitude. Unhide the CAD model to overlay it over the result plot, and animate, as shown in Figure 5–57. Does the model deform according to the applied loads and restraints?

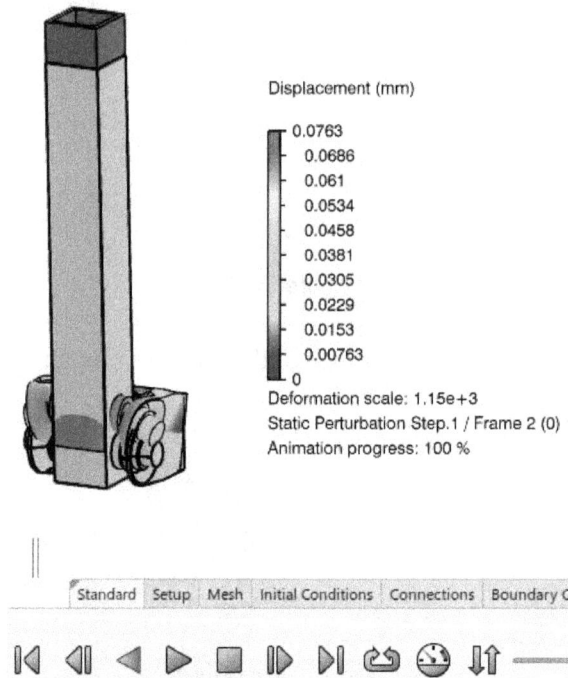

Displacement (mm)

	0.0763
	0.0686
	0.061
	0.0534
	0.0458
	0.0381
	0.0305
	0.0229
	0.0153
	0.00763
	0

Deformation scale: 1.15e+3
Static Perturbation Step.1 / Frame 2 (0)
Animation progress: 100 %

Standard Setup Mesh Initial Conditions Connections Boundary C

Figure 5–57

Task 12: Display the Von Mises stress.

1. Hide the CAD model and select **Von Mises Stress** in the Plot drop-down menu. The stress result displays as shown in Figure 5–58.

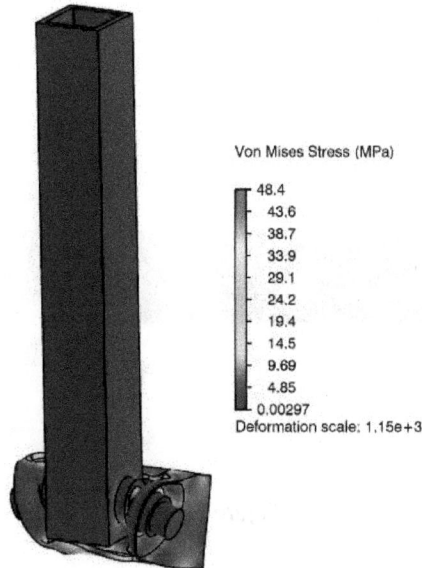

Figure 5–58

2. Double-click the color map and set the *Max* value to **30**, as shown in Figure 5–59.

   Note: The maximum stress in this model occurs in the pivot arm part near the clamp, while the stress level in the pin and the boom is much lower. Modifying the Max value helps to reveal stress image in the pin and boom parts.

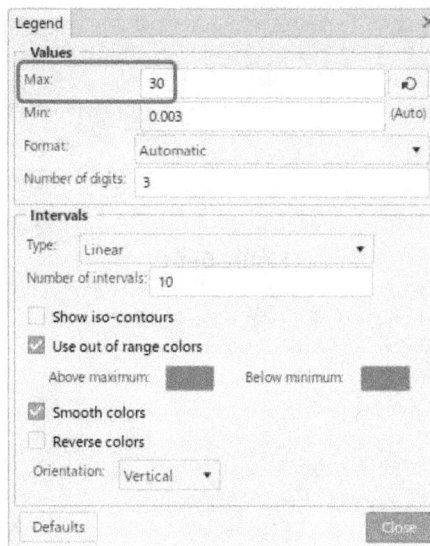

Figure 5–59

3. Select ⬛ (Back) view. The result displays as shown in Figure 5–60.

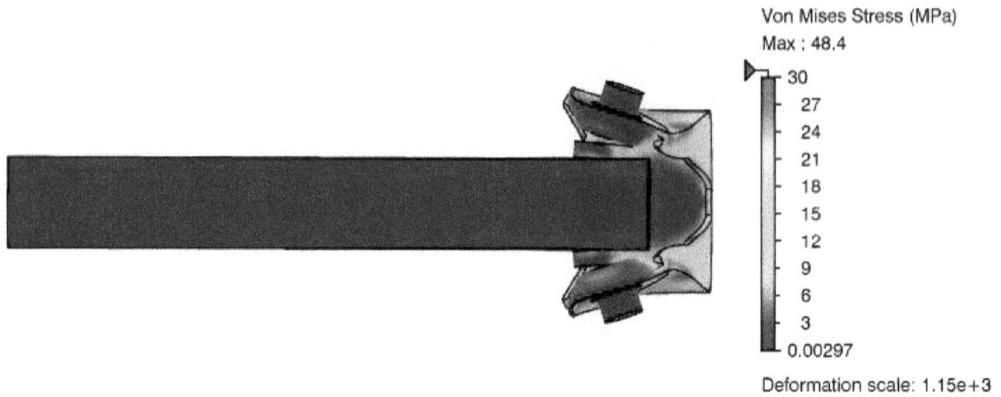

Von Mises Stress (MPa)
Max : 48.4

30
27
24
21
18
15
12
9
6
3
0.00297

Deformation scale: 1.15e+3

Figure 5–60

4. Select ⬛ (View Cut). The result and the context toolbar display, as shown in Figure 5–61.

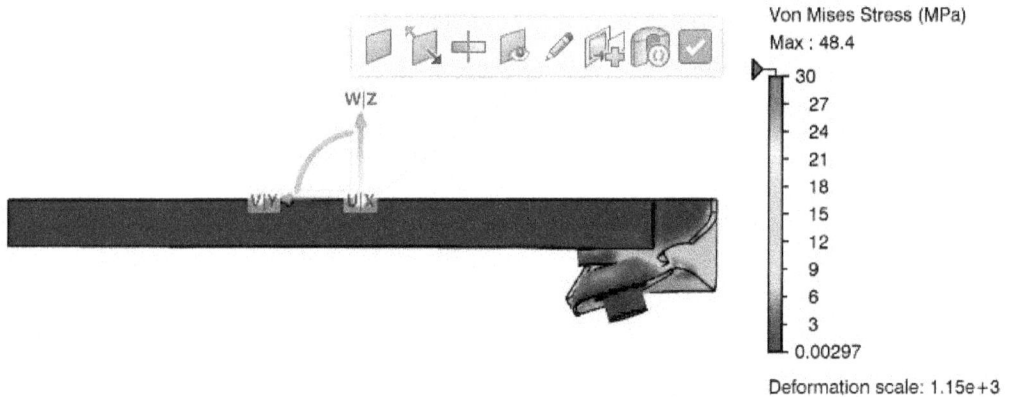

Von Mises Stress (MPa)
Max : 48.4

30
27
24
21
18
15
12
9
6
3
0.00297

Deformation scale: 1.15e+3

Figure 5–61

5. In the context toolbar, select ✏ (Hide cutting geometry) and ✏ (Edit cut). In the *Plot Sectioning* dialog box, enter the origin coordinates and normal directions as shown in Figure 5−62.

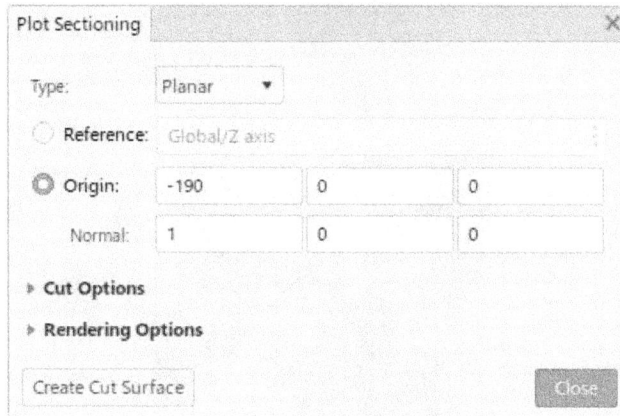

Plot Sectioning			×
Type:	Planar ▾		
○ Reference:	Global/Z axis		
◉ Origin:	-190	0	0
Normal:	1	0	0
▸ Cut Options			
▸ Rendering Options			
Create Cut Surface			Close

Figure 5−62

6. Click **OK** to close the *Plot Sectioning* dialog box.

7. Select 🗐 (View Cut) again. Using 🔲 (Reverse Cut) icon in the context toolbar, ensure that the front of the model is clipped out. Click ✅ (**OK**) to finalize the section. The result plot displays as shown in Figure 5−63.

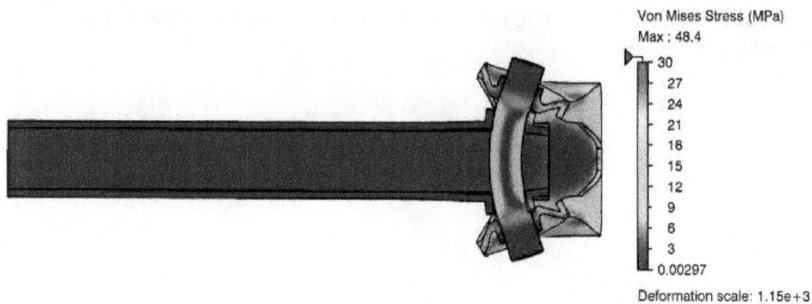

Von Mises Stress (MPa)
Max : 48.4

30
27
24
21
18
15
12
9
6
3
0.00297

Deformation scale: 1.15e+3

Figure 5−63

8. Zoom in on the area around the pin, as shown on Figure 5–64. Note the well-pronounced bending stress pattern in the pin.

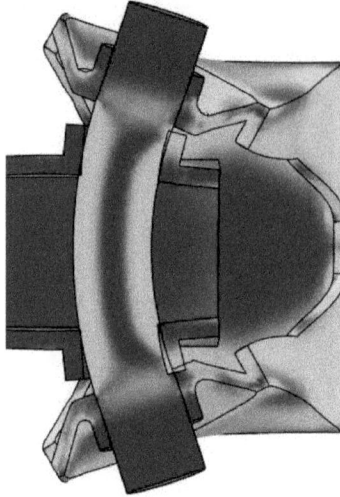

Figure 5–64

9. Select ⬚ (View Cut) and click ⬚ (Deactivate cut and close) in the context toolbar to exit the view cut mode.

Task 13: Display the contact pressure.

1. Select **Contact Pressure** in the *Plot* drop-down menu. The contact pressure result displays as shown in Figure 5–65.

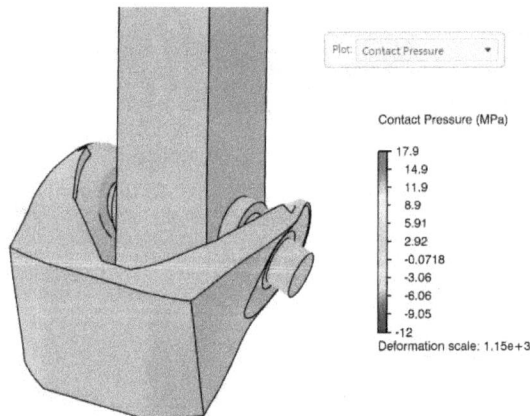

Figure 5–65

2. Using the ⬚ (Display Group) tool, display the contact pressure result for the **PIN_07** part alone, as shown in Figure 5–66. Note that the maximum contact pressure **17.9MPa** occurs near the edges of the hole in the boom part, as it should be.

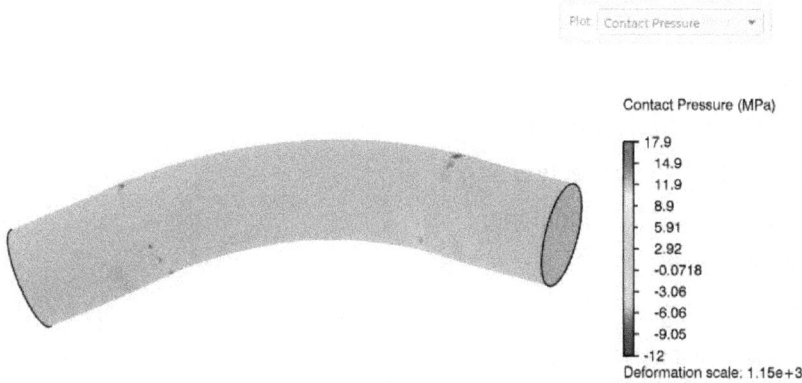

Plot Contact Pressure ▾

Contact Pressure (MPa)

17.9
14.9
11.9
8.9
5.91
2.92
-0.0718
-3.06
-6.06
-9.05
-12
Deformation scale: 1.15e+3

Figure 5–66

Task 14: Save and close the model.

1. Click 🗗 (Result Visualization) in the Action Bar to return to the model view.
2. Optionally, save the analysis and the assembly for future reference.
3. Close all windows.

Practice 5c
Press-Fit Analysis

Practice Objectives

- Simplify the model.
- Apply materials and create the mesh.
- Create General Contact connection.
- Apply loads and boundary conditions.
- Compute the analysis.
- Visualize results.

In this practice, you will set up a press-fit contact analysis on a shaft and a ball bearing assembly model. The area of interest is the contact between the shaft and the inner ring of the bearing.

The exploded view of the assembly that you will analyze is shown in Figure 5-67.

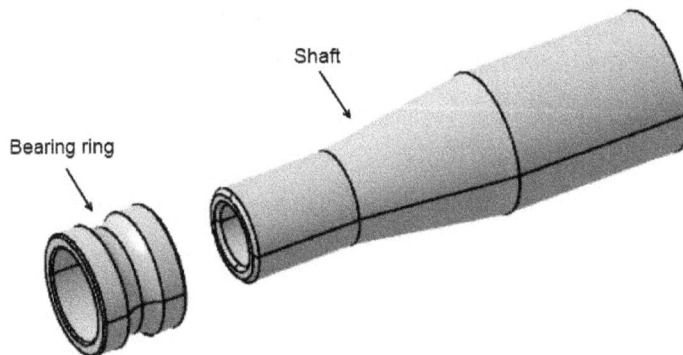

Figure 5-67

The bearing ring is press-fit onto the shaft. The outer diameter (OD) of the shaft is **20mm**, and the inner diameter (ID) of the ring is **19.96mm**. The objective is to determine deformation and stress in the parts due to the press-fit.

Task 1: Open the assembly.

1. Import with your initials and open **PRESS_FIT_07.3dxml**.

2. Set the model display as 🛢 (Shading with Sharp and Smooth Edges). The assembly displays as shown in Figure 5–68.

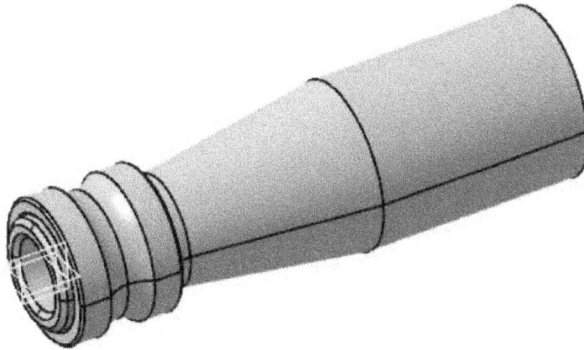

Figure 5–68

3. Set the units as follows:

    - *Length:* **Millimeter (mm)**
    - *Force:* **Newton (N)**
    - *Moment:* **Newton x Meter (Nxm)**
    - *Pressure:* **Megapascal (MPa)**
    - *Stress:* **Megapascal (MPa)**

Task 2: Apply the materials.

1. Using the 🔵 (Material Browser) tool in the *Assembly Design* app, apply the **Steel** material to the **BEARING_RING_07** part and **Aluminium** material to the **SHAFT_07** part. You can either use the material definitions you created earlier in the class or create new material definitions. Verify that the material properties are as follows:

    - **Aluminum**
        - *Density:* **2710 kg_m3**
        - *Proof (Yield) Stress:* **95 MPa**
        - *Young's Modulus:* **70000 MPa**
        - *Poisson's Ratio:* **0.346**

- **Steel**
  - *Density:* **7860 Kg/m3**
  - *Proof (Yield) Stress:* **250 MPa**
  - *Young's Modulus:* **200000 MPa**
  - *Poisson's Ratio:* **0.266**

Task 3: Simplify the model.

In this task, you will simplify the model in order to reduce the analysis runtime. Since the model is symmetric, you will analyze a quarter of the assembly.

1. Hide the **BEARING_RING_07** part.

2. Double-click on the **SHAFT_07** 3D Shape to activate the **Part Design** app.

3. In the *Essentials* section of the Action Bar, select (Split). The *Split* dialog box opens, as shown in Figure 5–69.

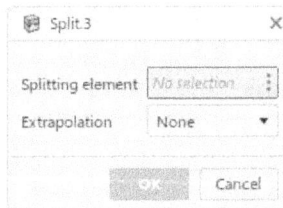

Figure 5–69

4. Select the **xy plane** as the *Splitting Element*. Make sure that the **grey arrow**, which indicates the side to keep, points toward the **+Z** direction, as shown in Figure 5–70. If it does not, click on the **grey arrow** to flip.

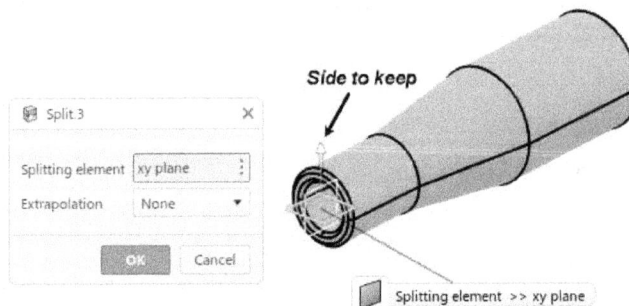

Figure 5–70

5. Click **OK**. The shaft part is cut in half, as shown in Figure 5–71.

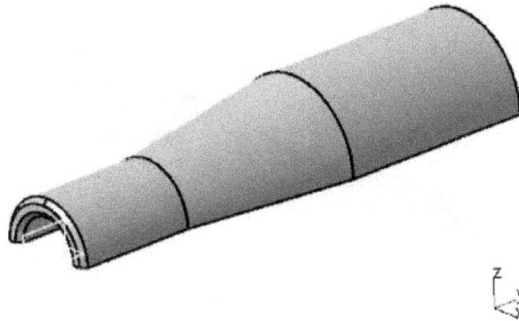

Figure 5–71

6. Select ⬚ (Split) and split the part again, now using the **yz plane** as the *Splitting Element*, keeping the side that is toward the **-X** direction, as shown in Figure 5–72.

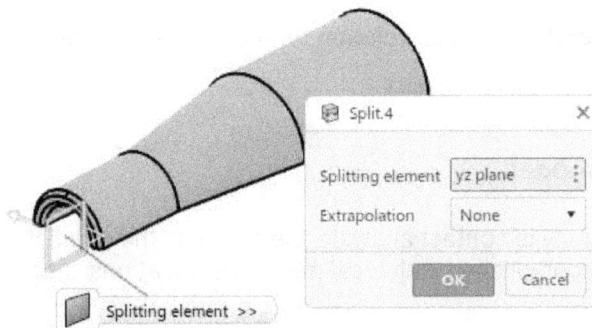

Figure 5–72

7. Click **OK**. The part displays as shown in Figure 5–73.

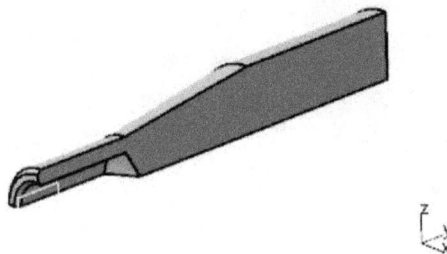

Figure 5–73

8. Double-click the **PRESS_FIT_07** assembly in the tree to switch back to the **Assembly Design** app.

---

9. Using the previous steps as a guideline, split the bearing ring twice to obtain ¼ of the model. The ¼ of the assembly should display as shown in Figure 5−74.

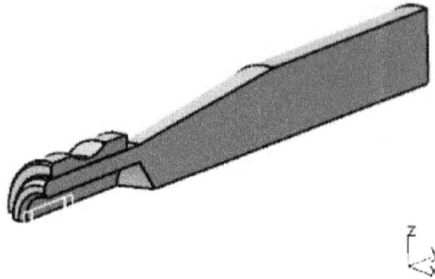

Figure 5−74

Task 4: Start the Linear Structural Validation app.

1. Ensure that the root product **PRESS_FIT_07** is active. Launch the **Linear Structural Validation** app.

2. Enter *<Your Initials>*_**Press Fit Simulation** for the *Title* of the Physics Simulation.

3. Select **Structural** for *Analysis type*.

Task 5: Mesh the model.

For better stress accuracy in contact analysis, the mesh on the contact surfaces should be refined. This can be accomplished with local mesh specifications.

1. In the *Mesh* section of the Action Bar, select ⬛ (Local Mesh Specifications).

2. Hide the ring part, select the outer surface of the shaft under the bearing ring and enter **0.8mm** as the *Element Size*, as shown in Figure 5−75.

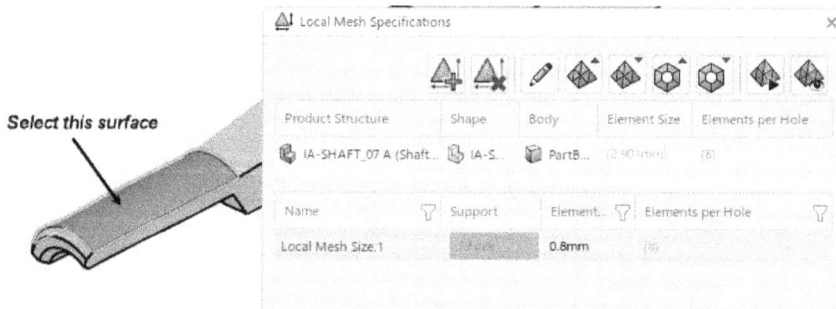

Figure 5−75

3. Click **Close**.

4. Using steps 1 through 3 as a guideline, apply **0.8mm** local element size to the inside surface of the bearing ring, as shown in Figure 5-76.

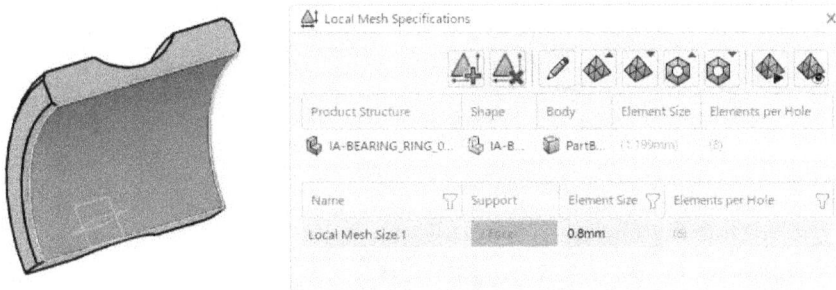

Figure 5-76

5. Generate and display the mesh. Zoom in on the mesh near the contacting surfaces and note the finer mesh in the area, as shown in Figure 5-77.

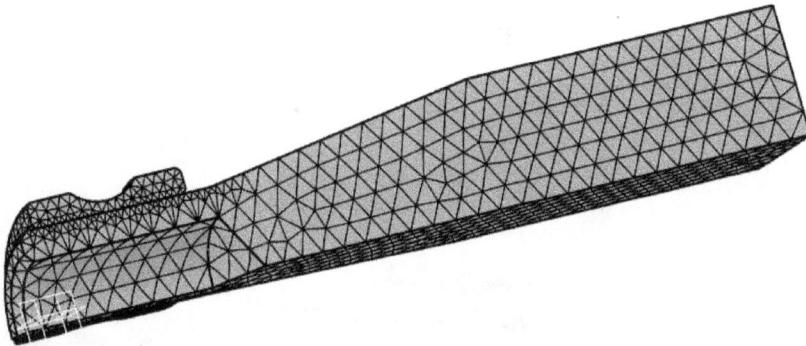

Figure 5-77

6. Hide the mesh.

Task 6: Create Contact Initialization.

By default, LSV app treats all interferences of contacting surfaces as unintentional, possibly due to slight inaccuracies in part positioning or geometry. To eliminate those unintentional overclosures, the app offsets the mesh nodes at the beginning of simulation to create zero gap between the surfaces.

In this model, the interference is intentional. The *Contact Initialization* lets you treat the overclosure as an interference fit. For an interference fit, the app computes the contact stresses required to eliminate the overclosure.

1. In the *Connections* section of the Action Bar, select ⚙ (Contact Initialization). The *Contact Initialization* dialog box opens, as shown in Figure 5–78.

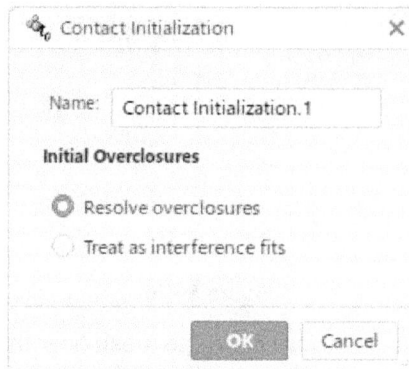

Figure 5–78

2. Activate the **Treat as interference fits** option, as shown in Figure 5–79.

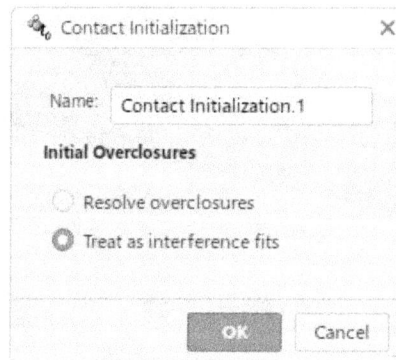

Figure 5–79

3. Click **OK**.

Task 7: Create General Contact connection.

1. Select ![icon](General Contact). In the *General Contact* dialog box that opens, expand the *Contact initialization assignments* section, as shown in Figure 5−80.

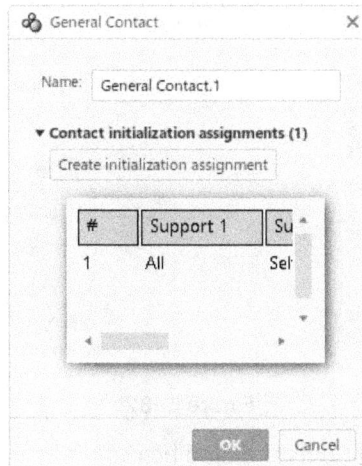

Figure 5−80

2. Right-click the first line in the list and select **Edit**, as shown in Figure 5−81.

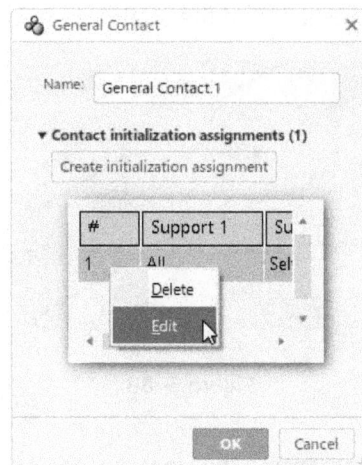

Figure 5−81

3. In the *Contact Initialization* drop-down menu, select **Contact Initialization.1**, as shown in Figure 5–82.

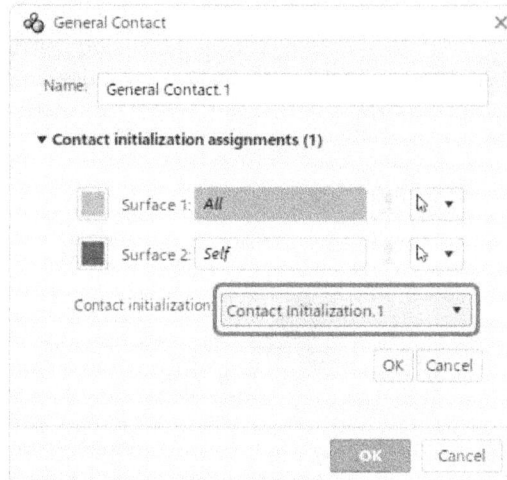

Figure 5–82

4. Click **OK** to close the *General Contact* dialog box.

Task 8: Apply boundary conditions.

1. Apply the (Clamp) to the back end of the shaft, as shown in Figure 5–83.

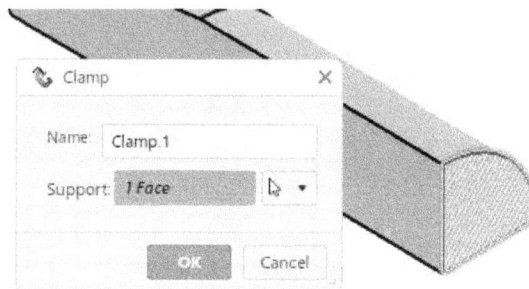

Figure 5–83

2. Apply the (Fixed Displacement) to the front surface of the bearing ring. Restrain the **Y** direction, as shown in Figure 5–84.

   Note: This boundary condition is necessary to eliminate sliding of the bearing ring along the shaft, because the General Contact connection is frictionless.

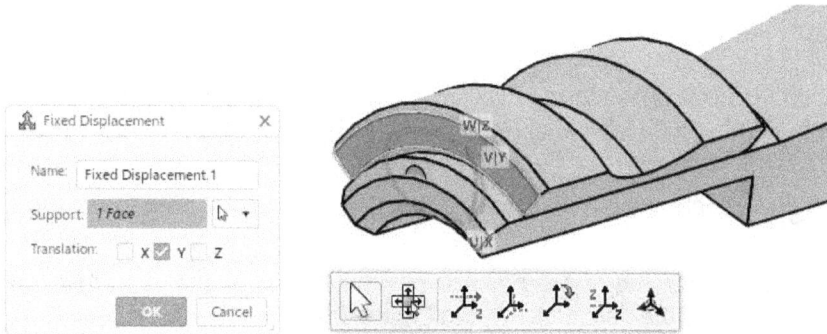

Figure 5–84

3. Apply the ⬚ (Planar Symmetry) to the two cutout surfaces on the YZ plane, as shown in Figure 5–85.

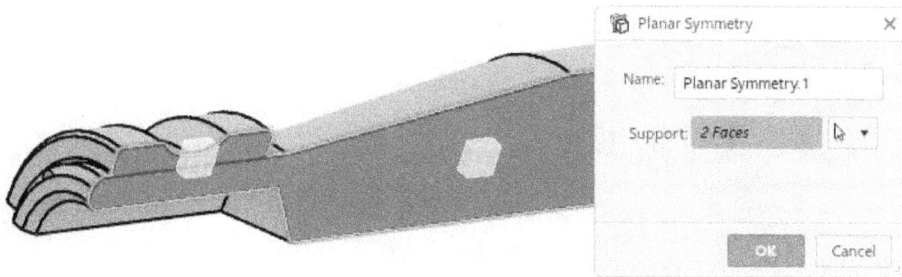

Figure 5–85

4. Apply the ⬚ (Planar Symmetry) to the two cutout surfaces on the XY plane, as shown in Figure 5–86.

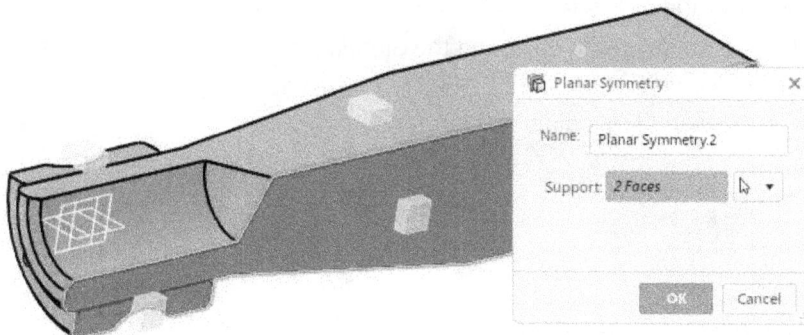

Figure 5–86

Task 9: Apply loads.

The intent of this simulation is to study deformations and stresses caused by the press-fit condition, with no other loads applied. However, the app requires a load to be present in the model to run a simulation.

In this task, you will apply a very small load to the model, just to be able to run the simulation.

1. In the *Loads* section of the Action Bar, select ⚡ (Pressure) and apply **1Pa** pressure to the ball race surfaces of the ring, as shown in Figure 5−87.

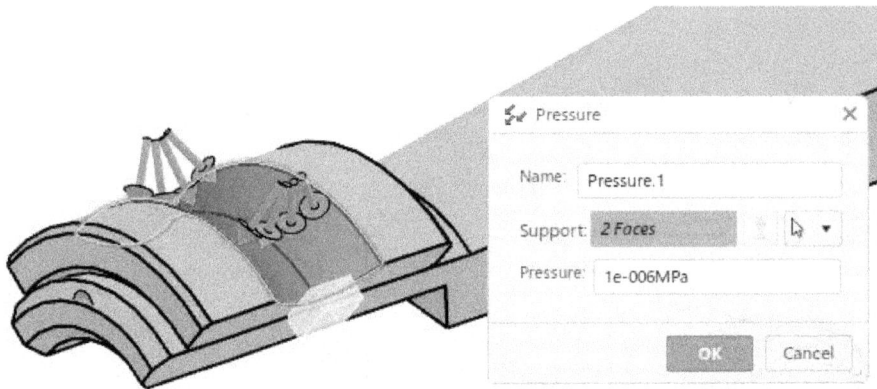

Figure 5−87

Task 10: Run the analysis.

1. Select 🔄 (Simulate) in the *Results* section of the Action Bar.
2. Click **OK** to close the *Simulate* dialog box when it displays.
3. Wait until computation completes, and the *Simulation Status* dialog box displays the message "Static Stress Simulation completed".
4. Close the *Simulation Status* dialog box.

Task 11: Display the deformation.

1. Select **Deformation** in the *Plot* drop-down menu to visualize the model deformation, as shown in Figure 5–88. Note that the deformation image displays a substantial gap between the ring and the shaft, which is because, by default, the app exaggerates the displayed deformation.

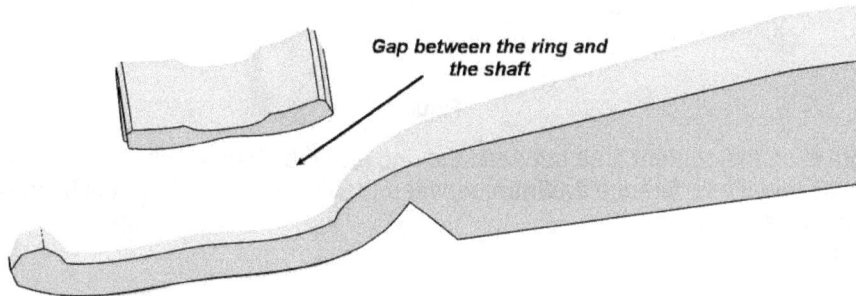

Gap between the ring and the shaft

Figure 5–88

2. Double-click the deformed model image. In the *Contour Plot* dialog box that opens, set

   Scale factor to **1** and select 🔒 (Lock scale factor) to lock it in other results plots you will display later, as shown in Figure 5–89.

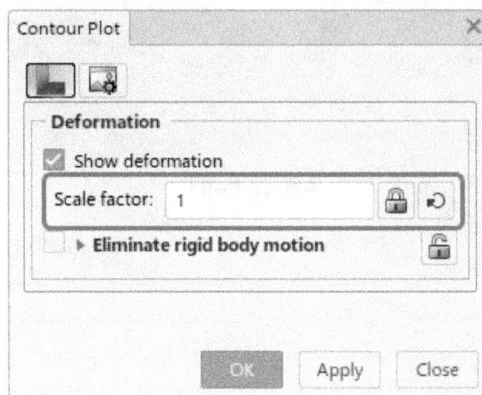

Figure 5–89

3. Click **OK**. The deformed model displays as shown in Figure 5-90. Note that now there is no gap between the ring and the shaft, as it should be.

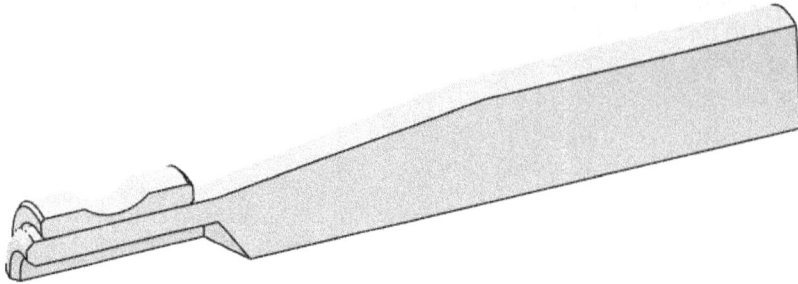

Figure 5-90

4. Zoom in on the contact area between the ring and the shaft, as shown in Figure 5-91. Note that the initial interference **0.02mm** between the ring and the shaft has been removed during the simulation.

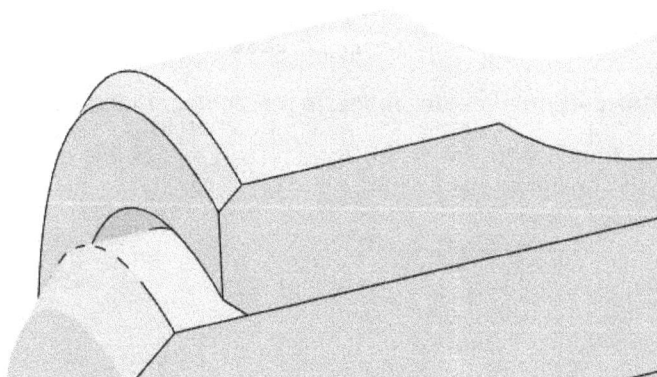

Figure 5-91

Task 12: Determine the radial displacement.

1. Select **Displacement Component 3** in the *Plot* drop-down menu to visualize displacements in the **Z-** direction, as shown in Figure 5–92.

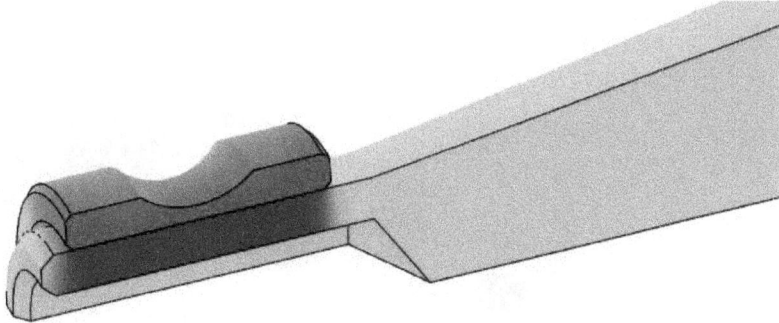

Figure 5–92

2. Select ⬚ (Front) view. Move the mouse pointer over the bottom of the ball race, as shown in Figure 5–93. Note that the **Z-** displacement at the bottom of the ball race is approximately **0.0094mm**.

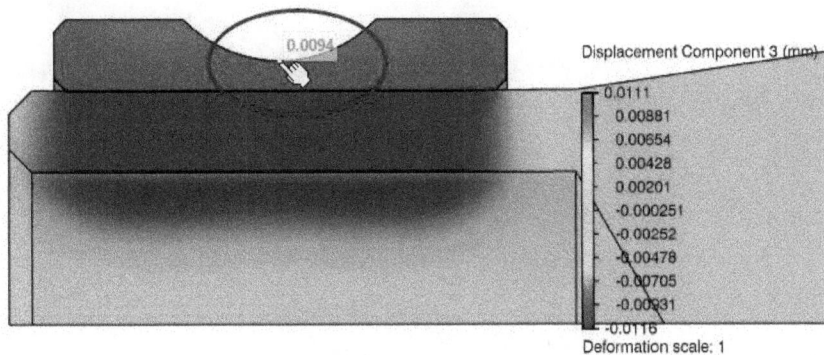

Figure 5–93

The **Z-** direction at this location corresponds to the radial direction on the shaft and the ring. Therefore, the increase in the OD of the ball race in the inner ring after assembling the bearing on the shaft is estimated to be **2x0.0094 = 0.0188mm**, and the reduction of clearance between the inner and the outer rings of the bearing is estimated to be **0.0094mm**.

Task 13: Display Von Mises stress in the bearing ring.

1. Select **Von Mises Stress** in the *Plot* drop-down menu. The stress plot displays as shown in Figure 5–94.

Figure 5–94

2. Select ⊞ (Display Group) in the *Results* section of the Action Bar. In the *Display Groups* dialog box that opens, deactivate the **SHAFT_07** part, as shown in Figure 5–95.

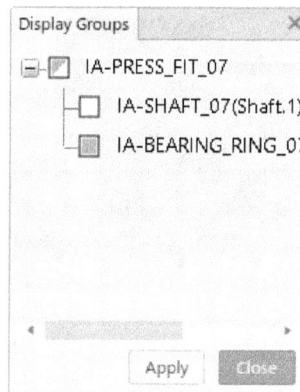

Figure 5–95

3. Click **Apply** and **Close** in the *Display Groups* dialog box. Now the stress result is only displayed for the bearing ring, as shown in Figure 5–96.

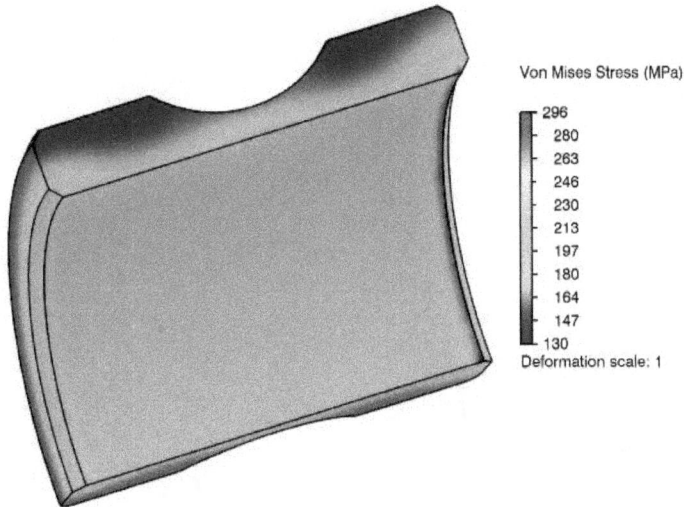

Von Mises Stress (MPa)

```
296
280
263
246
230
213
197
180
164
147
130
```
Deformation scale: 1

Figure 5–96

4. Rotate the model and examine the stress result. Note that the maximum stress occurs on the outer extremities of the ring.

Task 14: Save and close the model.

1. Click (Result Visualization) in the Action Bar to return to the model view.
2. Optionally, save the analysis and the assembly for future reference.
3. Close all windows.

Fasteners

Many structural failures of mechanical assemblies and systems are found in joints rather than continuous material. Mechanical joints typically involve the use of bolts, screws, nuts, and other fasteners. Therefore, proper modeling of fasteners is important for accurate estimates of the strength of assembly joints.

In this chapter, you learn how to model fastened connections between assembly components.

Learning Objectives

- Understand the various fastener modeling methods.
- Use the Rigid connection to simulate fasteners.
- Understand the Bolt connection.
- Use the Bolt Replication tool.
- Check fastener strength.
- Use the General Contact connection.

6.1 Fastener Modeling Methods in FEA

There is no singular commonly accepted method for fastener modeling in FEA. Instead, several techniques have been developed, based on the analysis accuracy and level of detail requirements.

The current commonly accepted fastener models in FEA fall into the following four categories, from the simplest to the most complex:

Model Class 1:

- The clamped parts are modeled as two separate bodies.
- No bolt is in the model.
- Bolt preload is ignored.
- Bolt loads (tensile and shearing) are read out from the model.
- With these bolt loads, the bolt is evaluated using hand calculations.

Model Class 2:

- The clamped parts are modeled as two contacting bodies.
- The bolt is idealized using a beam or a spring element connected to the bolt head and nut contact areas.
- Bolt preload is modeled with a pre-tension element.
- Bolt loads (tensile and shearing) are read out from the model.
- With these bolt loads, the bolt is evaluated using hand calculations.

Model Class 3:

- The clamped parts are modeled as two contacting bodies.
- The bolt is modeled in a simplified way, as a prismatic body without thread.
- Bolt preload is included.
- Contact below the bolt head and the nut is modeled.
- Nominal stresses in and around the bolt are obtained directly from the analysis.

Model Class 4:

- The bolt and nut geometry are modeled with thread and contacts on all contacting surfaces.
- This model allows a fully detailed view of what happens in the bolt and the connection.

The LSV app enables implementation of the above-listed fastener modeling techniques with the following connection types:

- Rigid Connection

- Bolt Connection

- General Contact

6.2 Rigid Connection

The use of Rigid Connection implements the Class 1 fastener model.

The schematic diagram of the connection is shown in Figure 6–1. The bolt geometry is not present in the model. Instead, the inside surfaces of the fastener holes are connected with rigid beam, as shown in Figure 6-1. Optionally, you may use general contact connection to ensure there is no inter-penetration between the connected parts under the loading.

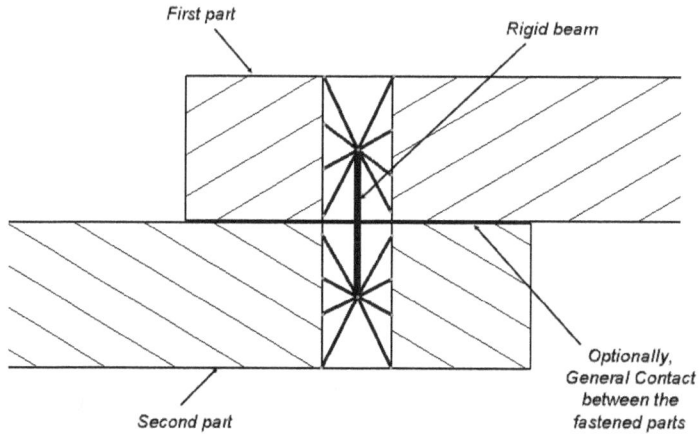

Figure 6–1

To create a Rigid connection, select ⊥ (Rigid) in the *Connections* section of the Action Bar and select the inside surfaces of the two holes, as shown in Figure 6–2.

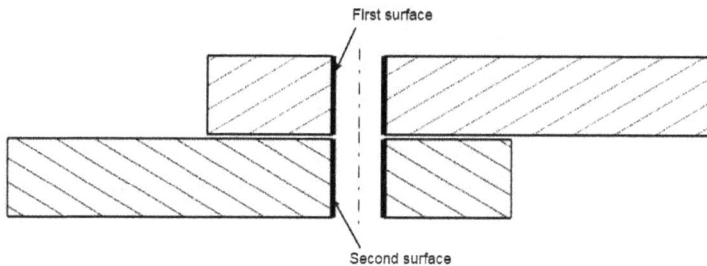

Figure 6–2

6.3 Bolt Connection

The *Bolt* connection implements the fastener model Class 2, i.e., the bolt and the nut are not modeled explicitly.

You can create two types of bolts:

- **Standard**: With a circular head and nut

- **Countersunk**: With a conical head and circular nut

The schematic diagram of the standard and countersunk bolts in through holes is shown in Figure 6−3.

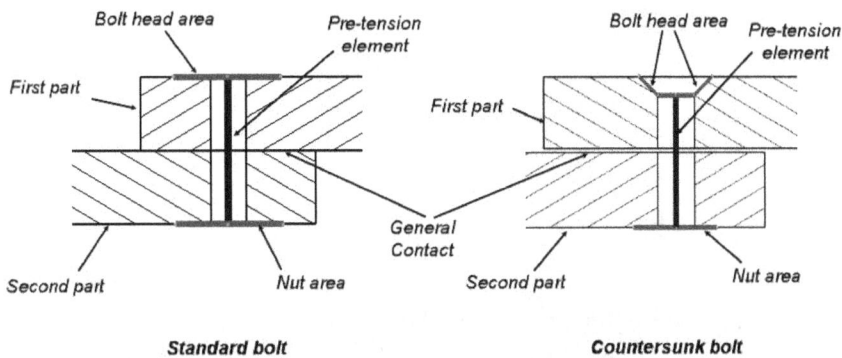

Standard bolt   Countersunk bolt

Figure 6−3

The schematic diagram of the standard and countersunk bolts in blind holes is shown in Figure 6−4.

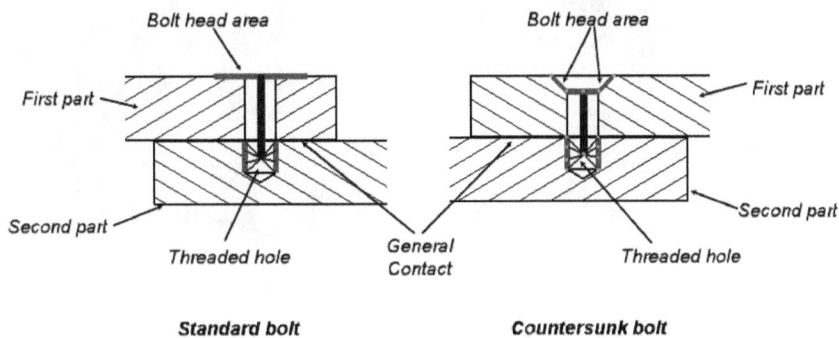

Standard bolt   Countersunk bolt

Figure 6−4

To ensure there is no inter-penetration of the fastened parts when the bolt preload is applied, a general contact connection should be created on the mated surfaces of the two parts, as shown in Figure 6−3 and Figure 6−4.

To create a Bolt connection, select 🔩 (Bolts) in the *Connections* section of the Action Bar. The *Bolt Editor* dialog box opens, as shown in Figure 6–5.

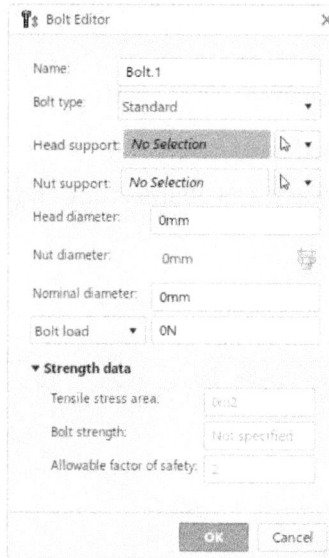

Figure 6–5

Select the **Head support**. For a **Standard** bolt, select the edge of the bolt hole, and for the **Countersunk** bolt, select the conical surface, as shown in Figure 6–6.

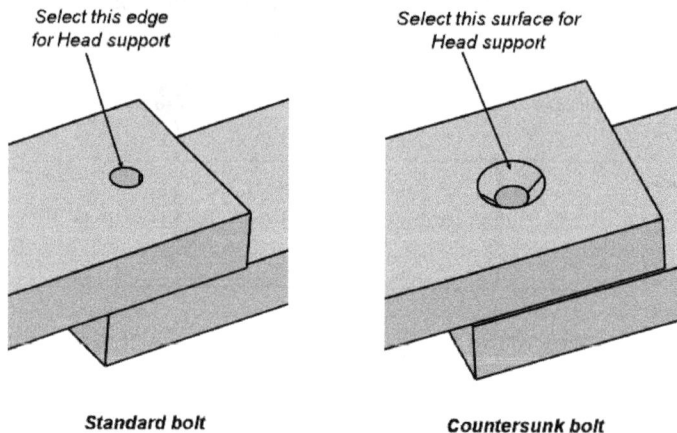

Standard bolt   *Countersunk bolt*

Figure 6–6

The app automatically preselects the **Nut support** edge, as shown in Figure 6–7.

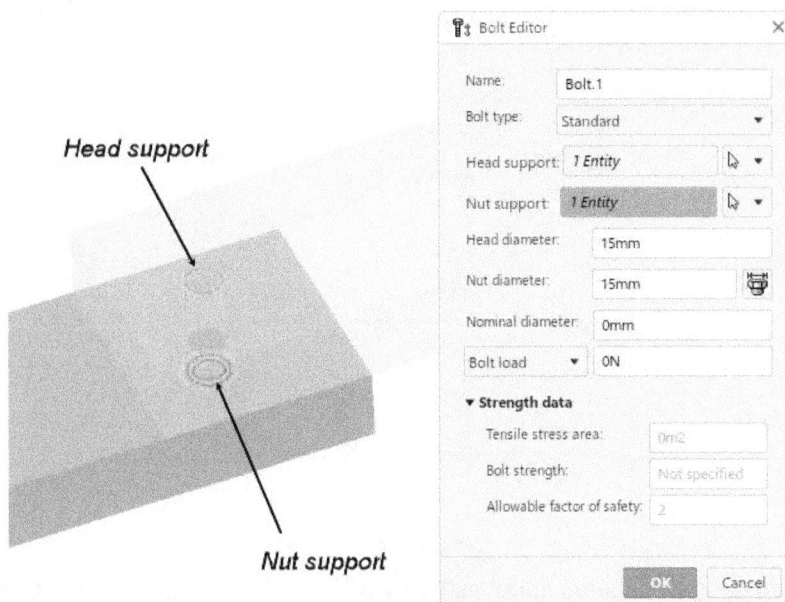

Figure 6–7

If preselected nut support is not correct, right-click the *Nut support* field and select **Remove All** to clear the selection, as shown in Figure 6–8. Then select the correct support:

* For through holes, select either a circular edge or a cylindrical surface.

* For blind holes, select the threaded cylindrical surface.

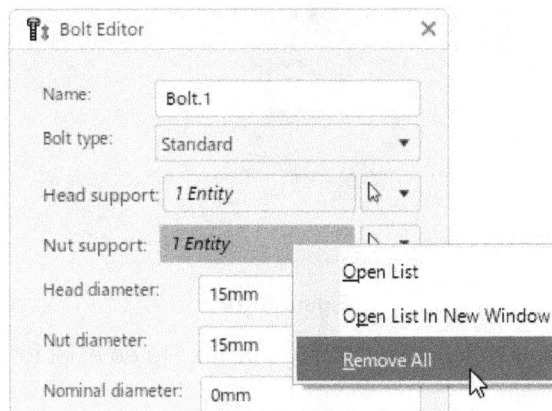

Figure 6–8

Based on the sizes of the selected supports, the app auto-populates the **Head diameter**, the **Nut diameter**, and the **Nominal diameter**, as shown in Figure 6–9. Optionally, enter new values for the head, nut, and bolt diameters.

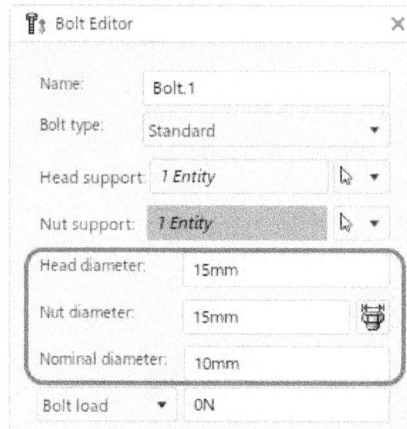

Figure 6–9

The bolt pre-load can be specified either as **Bolt load** or as **Bolt torque**. For the **Bolt torque**, enter the torque value and the **Torque coefficient**, as shown in Figure 6–10.

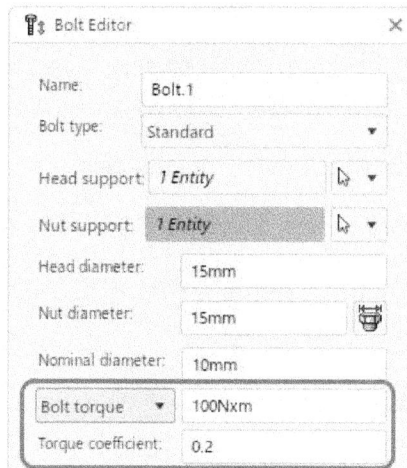

Figure 6–10

The **Torque coefficient** is used to convert the torque load to an axial force load, using the following equation:

$$F = {}^{T}\!/_{KD}$$

Where **F** = resulting axial force (bolt preload), **T** = torque, **D** = nominal bolt diameter, and **K** = torque coefficient.

The **Torque coefficient** depends on the thread geometry, material properties, and the joint lubrication. Its value can be found in standard reference books. The default value is **0.2**.

To enable the factor of safety (SF) calculation, enter the values in the *Strength data* section of the dialog box, as shown in Figure 6–11:

- **Tensile stress area**: Computed by the app, based on the bolt diameter

- **Bolt strength**: Bolt material's Yield (Proof) Stress

- **Allowable factor of safety**: The default value is **2**

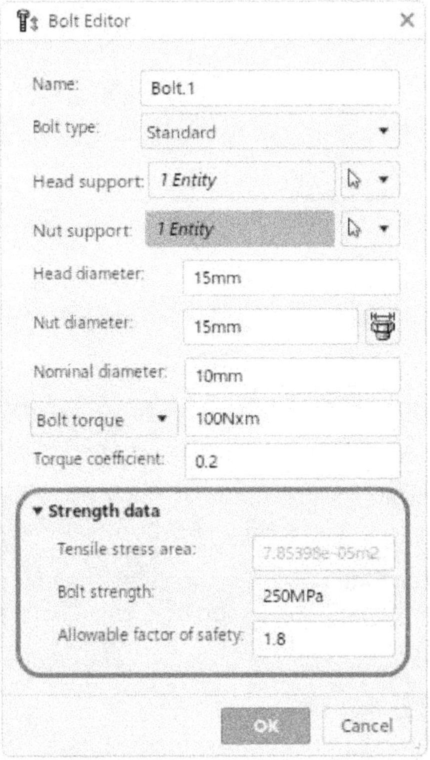

Figure 6–11

6.4 Bolt Replication

Bolt Replication tool enables copying bolt definitions to additional locations in your analysis model. The bolt replicas must connect the same two parts and pass through holes with the same dimensions as the original.

To replicate bolt definitions, select ⬡ (Bolt Replication) in the *Connections* section of the Action Bar. The *Bolt Replication* dialog box opens, as shown in Figure 6–12.

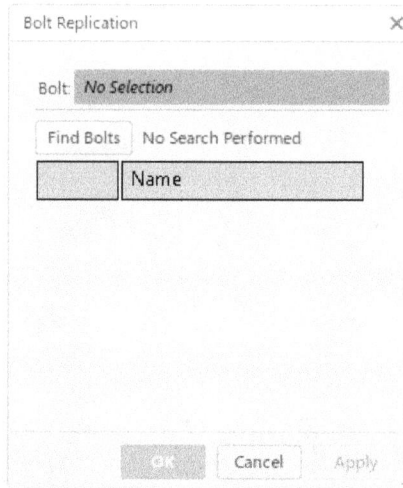

Figure 6–12

Select the original bolt and click **Find bolts**. The app searches for suitable holes in the model and shows the suggested new bolts in the dialog box, as shown in Figure 6–13.

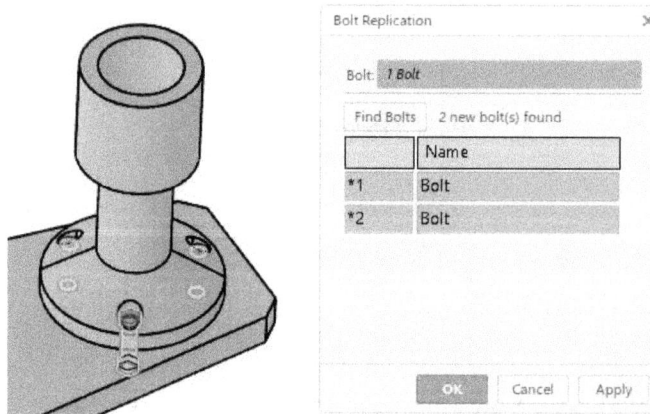

Figure 6–13

You can review the suggested bolt locations by selecting the bolts in the list. To reject a bolt, right-click on it and, from the list, select **Remove Selected**, as shown in Figure 6–14.

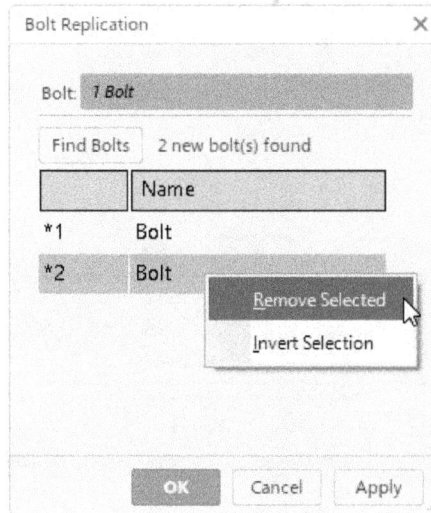

Figure 6–14

Note that the replicated bolts are independent of the original bolt, and you can edit or delete them individually.

6.5 Bolts in the Feature Manager

The *Bolt* connections are displayed in the *Scenario* section of the *Feature Manager*, as shown in Figure 6–15.

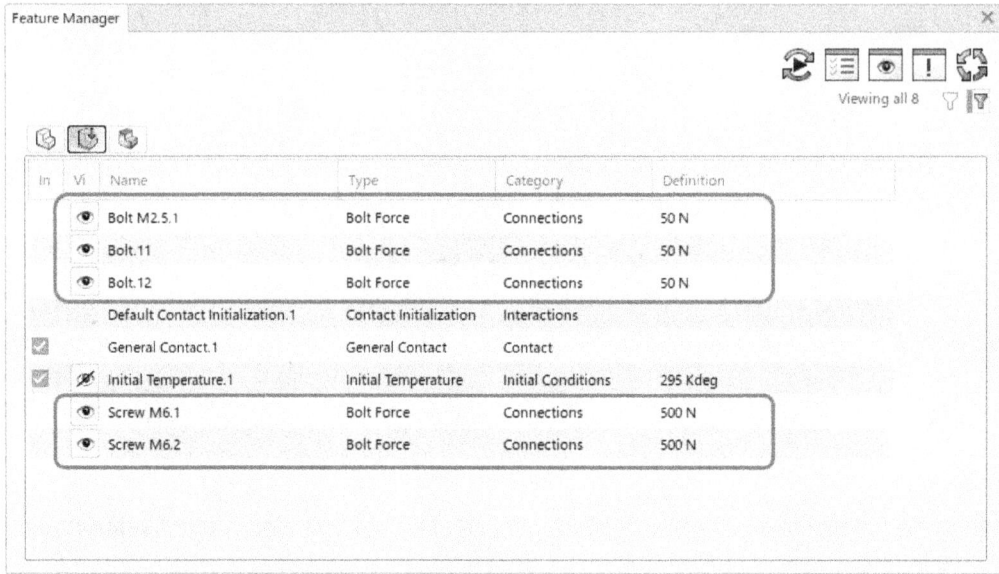

In	Vi	Name	Type	Category	Definition
	👁	Bolt M2.5.1	Bolt Force	Connections	50 N
	👁	Bolt.11	Bolt Force	Connections	50 N
	👁	Bolt.12	Bolt Force	Connections	50 N
		Default Contact Initialization.1	Contact Initialization	Interactions	
☑		General Contact.1	General Contact	Contact	
☑		Initial Temperature.1	Initial Temperature	Initial Conditions	295 Kdeg
	👁	Screw M6.1	Bolt Force	Connections	500 N
	👁	Screw M6.2	Bolt Force	Connections	500 N

Viewing all 8

Figure 6–15

You can **Hide/Show**, **Edit**, or **Delete** a bolt by right-clicking on it and selecting the appropriate action in the contextual menu.

6.6 Virtual Bolt Checker

Virtual Bolt Checker allows you to inspect forces and factors of safety on all bolts in your model.

Select ⬚ (Virtual Bolt Checker) in the *Results* section of the Action Bar. The *Virtual Bolt Checker* dialog box opens, as shown in Figure 6–16.

St	Name	Axial Fo...	Shear F...	Bending ...	Twisting ...	Allowable Fac...	Computed Factor of Safety
✓	Screw M6.1	606.312	301.206	2.71038	1.26889	1.5	1.67253
✓	Screw M6.2	680.574	278.863	1.98518	1.51952	1.5	2.11933
✓	Bolt M2.5.2	50.4774	10.699	0.0420093	0.0221167	1.5	6.63163
✗	Bolt M2.5.3	1.50053	120.871	0.480134	0.0798047	1.5	0.796404
✗	Bolt M2.5.1	402.844	134.137	0.725883	0.061504	1.5	0.450018

Figure 6–16

The state of the bolt is indicated by the **Pass/Fail** icon in the first column. The **Allowable Factor of Safety** indicates the user-specified value entered when creating the bolt. The **Computed Factor of Safety** indicates the actual factor of safety, as computed from the forces in the bolt in the simulation.

6.7 General Contact

General Contact can be used to implement the Class 4 fastener model.

In this case, the bolt, the nut, and the washer if required, must be included in the analysis model, including thread surfaces, as shown in Figure 6-17. The General Contact is then used to simulate interactions between all the parts, including contact between the threads.

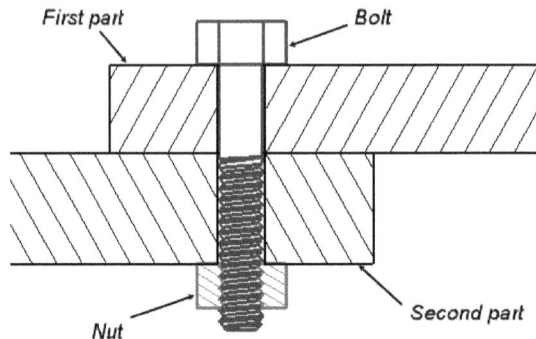

Figure 6-17

This model allows a fully detailed view of what happens in the bolt and the connection. However, be aware that this type of model can be computationally expensive, due to the necessity to adequately refine the mesh in the threads.

Practice 6a
Stress Analysis of a Fastened Assembly

Practice Objectives

- Apply materials.
- Mesh the model.
- Create general contact connection.
- Create rigid connection.
- Create bolt connections.
- Apply loads and boundary conditions.
- Compute the analysis.
- Visualize results.
- Check fastener strength.

In this practice, you will set up and run a static stress analysis on an assembly shown in Figure 6–18.

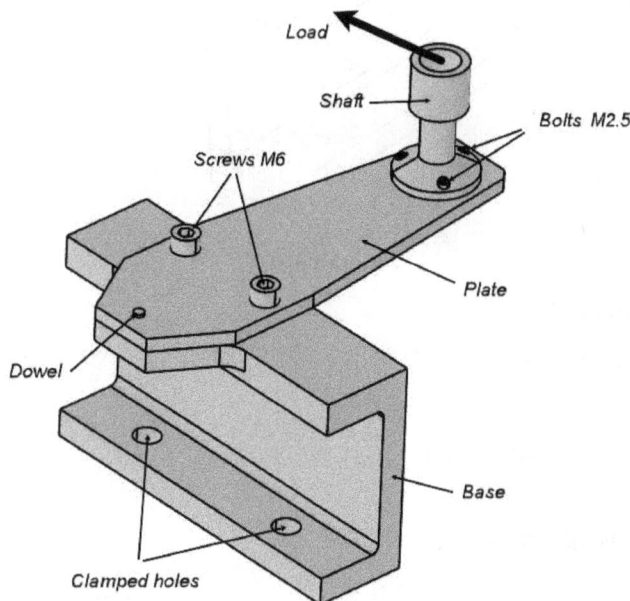

Figure 6–18

The assembly consists of three aluminum parts - the base, the plate, and the shaft. The assembly is clamped at the two bottom holes in the base part and is loaded by a horizontal force on the shaft, as shown in Figure 6a-1. The plate is fastened to the base with two M6 screws. To alleviate shearing forces on the screws, a dowel is also used through the small hole at the end of the plate. The shaft part is fastened to the plate with three M2.5 bolts.

Task 1: Open the assembly.

1. Import with your initials and open **Fasteners_08.3dxml**.

2. Set the model display as 🛢 (Shading with Sharp and Smooth Edges). The assembly displays as shown in Figure 6–19.

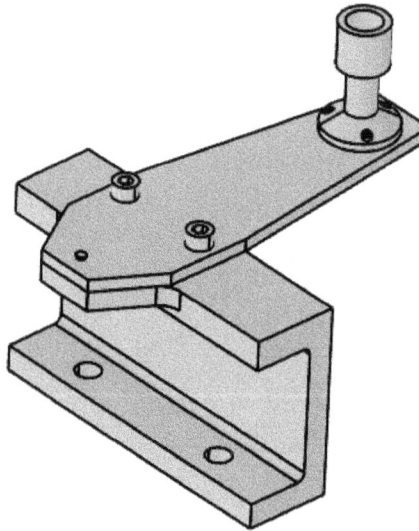

Figure 6–19

3. Set the units as follows:
   - *Length:* **Millimeter (mm)**
   - *Force:* **Newton (N)**
   - *Moment:* **Newton x Meter (Nxm)**
   - *Pressure:* **Megapascal (MPa)**
   - *Stress: Megapascal (MPa)*

Task 2: Apply the materials.

1. Using the ⬤ (Material Browser) tool in the *Assembly Design* app, apply the materials to the assembly parts as follows. You can either use the material definitions you created earlier in the class or create new material definitions.

- *Base_08, Plate_08, Shaft_08:* **Aluminum**
  - *Density:* **2710 kg_m3**
  - *Proof (Yield) Stress:* **95 MPa**
  - *Young's Modulus:* **70000 MPa**
  - *Poisson's Ratio:* **0.346**

- *Screw M6, Screw M2.5, Dowel 4:* **Steel**
  - *Density:* **7860 Kg/m3**
  - *Proof (Yield) Stress:* **250 MPa**
  - *Young's Modulus:* **200000 MPa**
  - *Poisson's Ratio:* **0.266**

Task 3: Launch the Linear Structural Validation app.

1. Ensure that the root product **Fasteners_08** is active and launch the **Linear Structural Validation** app.
2. Enter *<Your Initials>*_**Fasteners Simulation** for the *Title* of the Physics Simulation.
3. Select **Structural** for *Analysis type*.

Task 4: Exclude the screws and the dowel from the simulation.

The intent of this analysis is to obtain deformations and stresses in the base, the plate, and the shaft parts, while modeling the screws and the dowel approximately, using analysis connections. In this step, you will exclude the screw and the dowel bodies from the simulation.

1. Select ⬚ (Contributing Parts) in the *Setup* section of the Action Bar. The *Contributing Parts* dialog box opens, as shown in Figure 6–20.

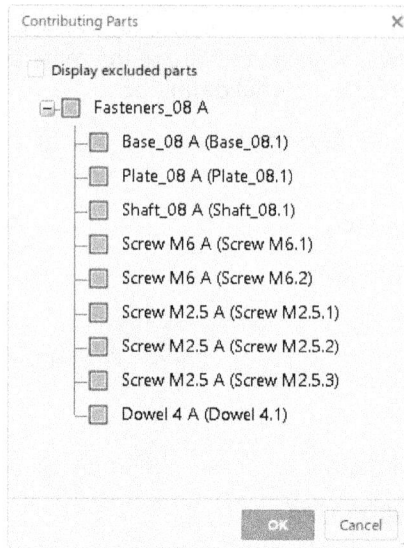

Figure 6–20

2. Toggle off the screws and the dowel, as shown in Figure 6–21.

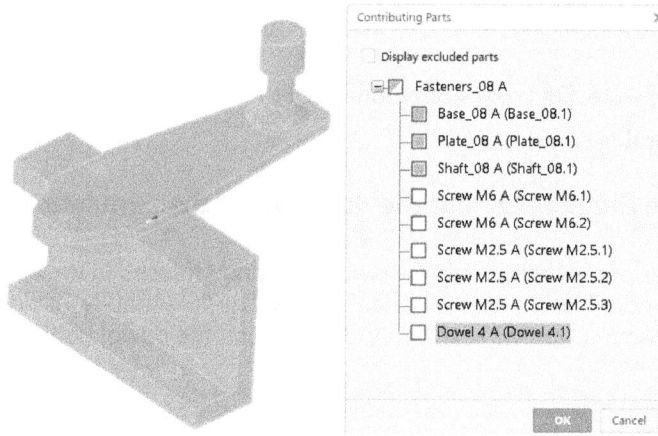

Figure 6–21

3. Click **OK** to complete.

Task 5: Mesh the model.

1. Select ⬥ (Generate Mesh) in the Action Bar. The mesh is generated and displayed, as shown in Figure 6–22. Note that neither the screw nor the dowel bodies have been meshed.

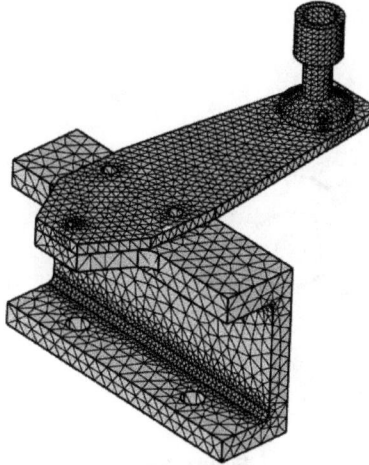

Figure 6–22

2. Select ⬥ (Hide/Show Mesh) to hide the mesh.

Task 6: Create General Contact connection.

1. Select ⬤ (General Contact). The *General Contact* dialog box opens, as shown in Figure 6–23.

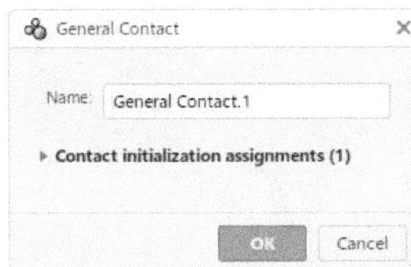

Figure 6–23

2. Click **OK** to complete. This creates a general contact connection between the base and the plate, and the plate and the shaft.

Task 7: Create Rigid connection.

In this task, you will model the dowel with a rigid analysis connection.

1. Select ⫟ (Rigid) in the *Connections* section of the Action Bar. Once the *Rigid Connection* dialog box opens, select the inside surface of the dowel hole in the plate as **Support 1** and the inside surface of the dowel hole in the base as **Support 2**, as shown in Figure 6–24.

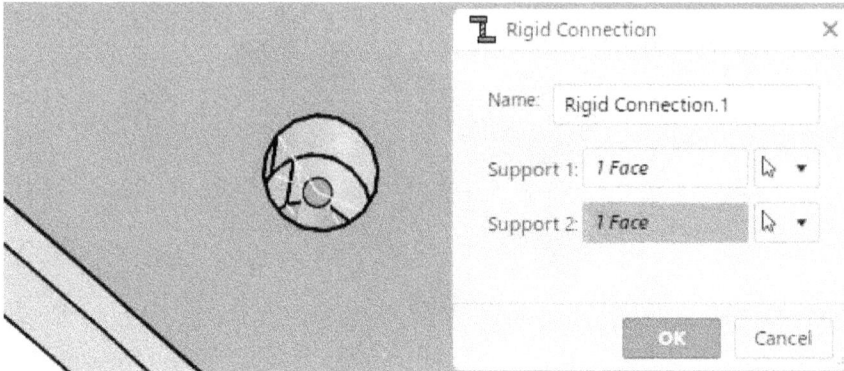

Figure 6–24

2. Click **OK** to complete the connection.

Task 8: Create Bolt connections for the M6 screws.

The two M6 screws in this assembly are tightened to 500N preload, which you will model with a Bolt connection.

1. Select ![bolt icon] (Bolts) in the *Connections* section of the Action Bar. The *Bolt Editor* dialog box opens, as shown in Figure 6–25.

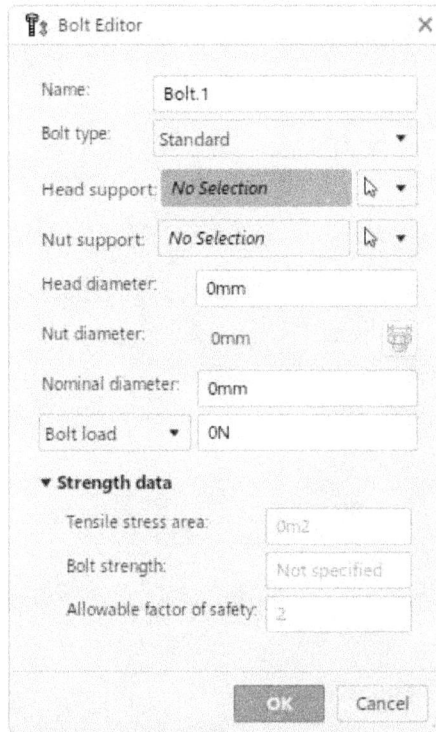

Figure 6–25

2. Enter **Screw M6.1** for the *Name*.

3. Select the top circular edge of the left screw hole in the plate as the *Head support*. The app automatically selects the nut support (indicated by the yellow dashed circle), as shown in Figure 6−26.

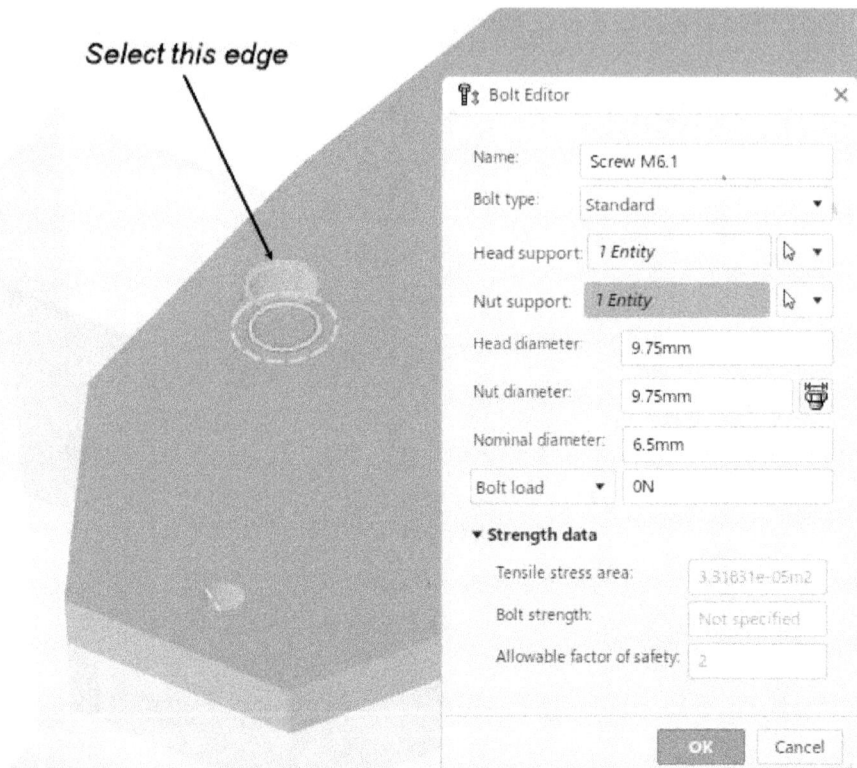

Figure 6−26

4. However, this fastener is a blind screw, and does not have a nut. Right-click on the *Nut support* field, and select **Remove All**, as shown in Figure 6−27.

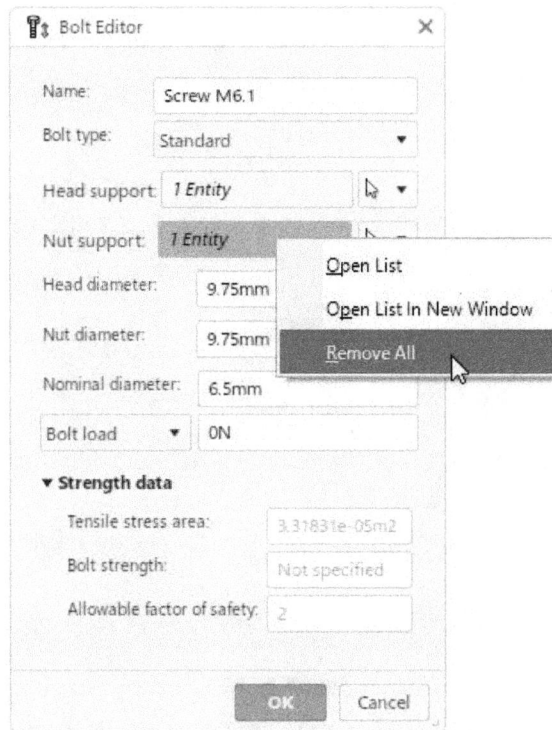

Figure 6−27

5. Select the inside surface of the tapped hole in the Base part for the *Nut support,* as shown in Figure 6−28. The app determines the *Head diameter* as **9.75mm** and the *Nominal diameter* as **6mm** based on the dimensions of the holes, as shown in Figure 6−28.

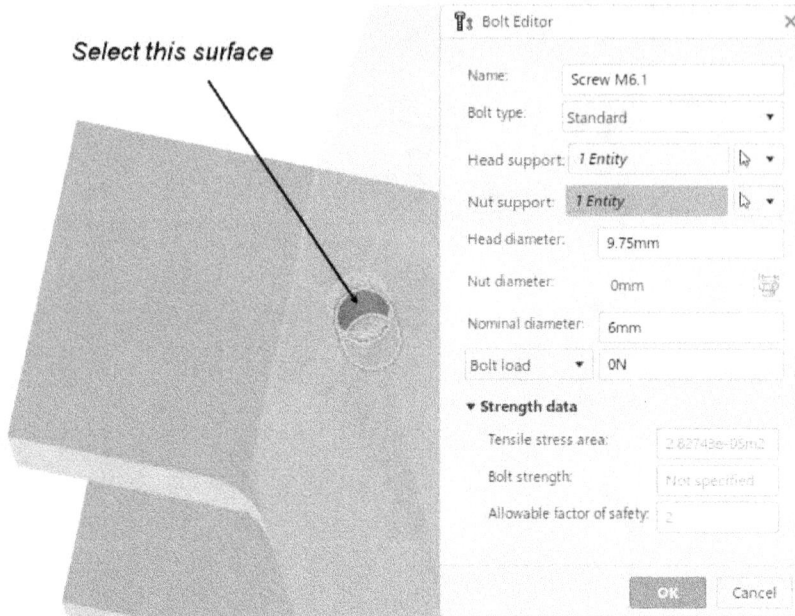

Figure 6−28

6. However, this is a custom-made screw with a head diameter of 10mm. Enter **10mm** for the *Head diameter.*

7. Enter the remaining data as follows:

    *   *Bolt load*: **500N**

    *   *Bolt strength*: **250MPa** (this is the *Proof Stress* for the screw's material)

    *   *Allowable factor of safety*: **1.5** (for this assembly, the default value **2.0** is deemed excessive)

8. The *Bolt Editor* dialog box displays, as shown in Figure 6-29.

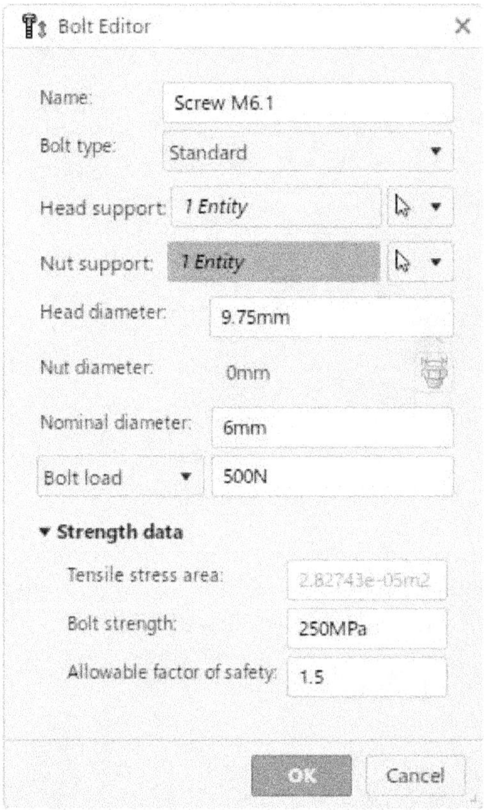

Figure 6-29

9. Click **OK**. The model displays, as shown in Figure 6–30.

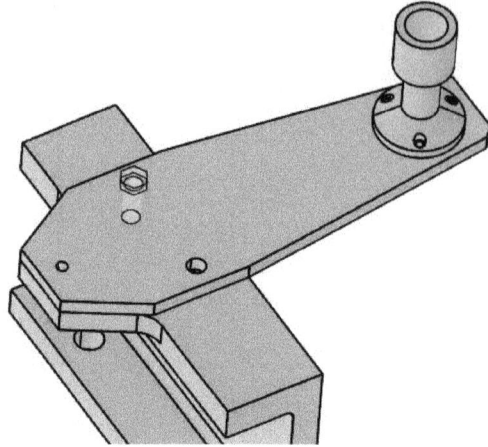

Figure 6–30

10. Select (Bolt Replication) in the *Connections* section of the Action Bar. The *Bolt Replication* dialog box opens, as shown in Figure 6–31.

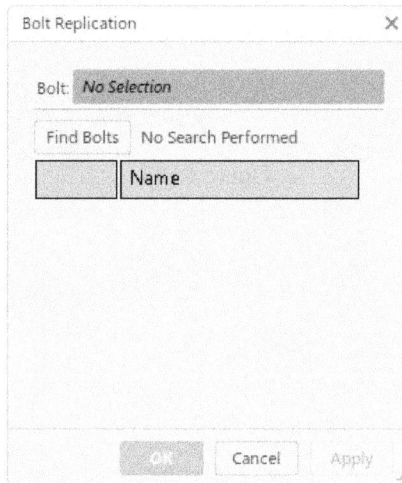

Figure 6–31

11. Select the first bolt and click **Find bolts**. The app finds the location for the second bolt based on the hole dimensions, as shown in Figure 6–32.

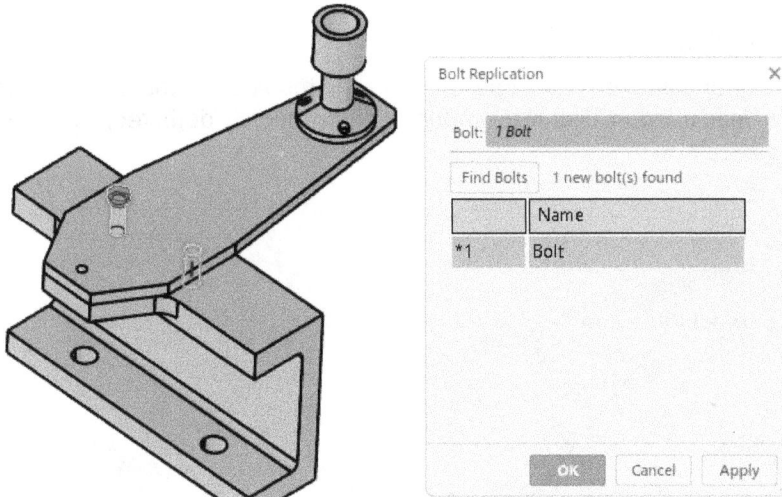

Figure 6–32

12. Click **OK**. The app replicates the first bolt, using the same diameter, bolt load, and other parameters. The model displays, as shown in Figure 6–33.

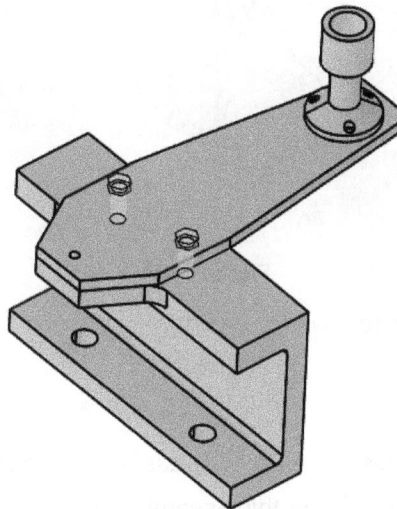

Figure 6–33

13. Select (Feature Manager). In the *Feature Manager* dialog box that opens, right-click the second bolt and select **Edit**. Rename the bolt as **Screw M6.2**.

Task 9: Create Bolt connections for the M2.5 screws.

1. Select ![Bolts icon] (Bolts).

2. In the *Bolt Editor* dialog box that opens, select the top edge of the **M2.5** hole in the shaft part as the *Head support*. The *Nut support* is automatically detected, as shown in Figure 6−34.

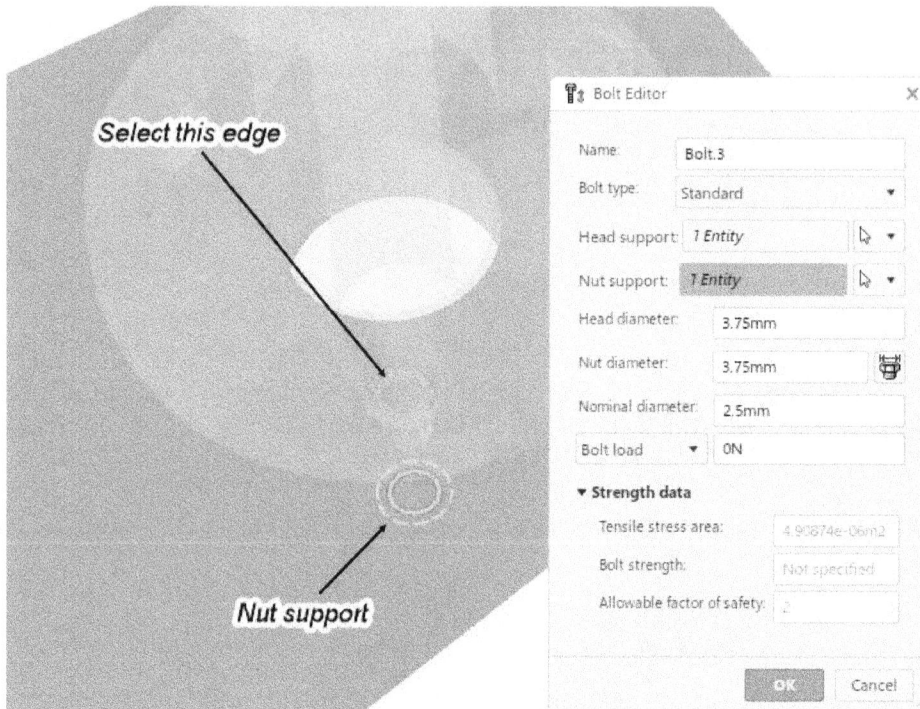

Figure 6−34

3. Enter the remaining data as follows:

    *   *Name*: **Bolt M2.5.1**

    *   *Bolt load*: **50N**

    *   *Bolt strength*: **250MPa** (this is the *Proof Stress* for the bolt's material)

    *   *Allowable factor of safety*: **1.5** (for this assembly, the default value **2.0** is deemed excessive)

4. The *Bolt Editor* dialog box displays, as shown in Figure 6–35.

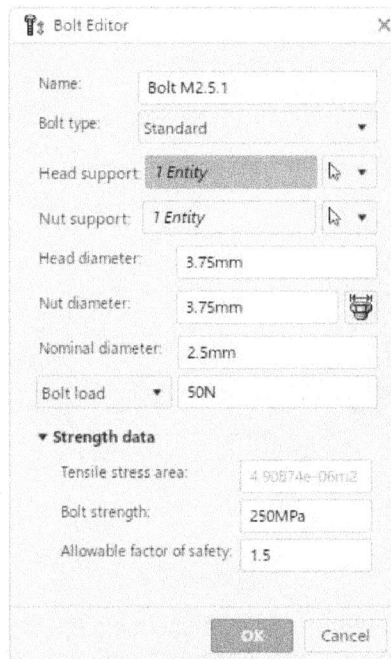

Figure 6–35

5. Click **OK**. The model displays, as shown in Figure 6–36.

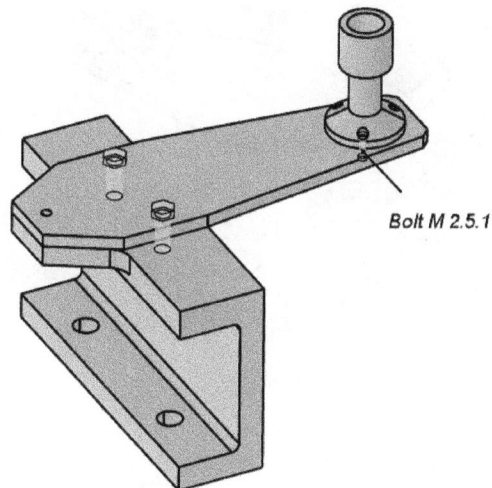

Bolt M 2.5.1

Figure 6–36

6. Select ![icon] (Bolt Replication). Once the *Bolt Replication* dialog box opens, select the first **M2.5** bolt and click **Find bolts**. The app finds the locations for the other two bolts based on the hole dimensions, as shown in Figure 6−37.

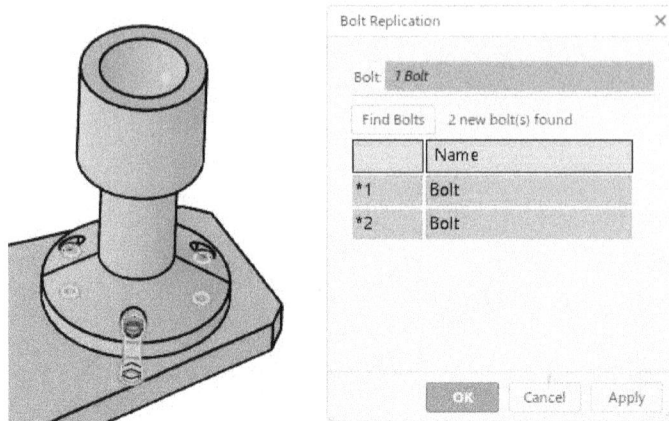

Figure 6−37

7. Click **OK**. The app replicates the first **M2.5** bolt, using the same diameter, bolt load, and other parameters. The model displays, as shown in Figure 6−38.

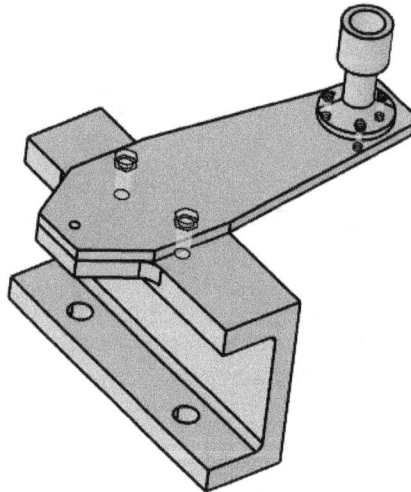

Figure 6−38

8. Select ![icon] (Feature Manager). In the *Feature Manager* dialog box that opens, right-click the second **M2.5** bolt and select **Edit**. Rename the bolt as **Bolt M2.5.2**.

9. Rename the third **M2.5** bolt as **Bolt M2.5.3**.

Task 10: Apply the load.

1. Select 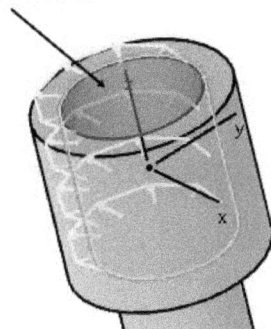 (Bearing Load) and apply **-200N** force in **X** direction to the inside surface of the shaft, as shown in Figure 6−39.

Select this surface

Figure 6−39

Task 11: Apply the boundary conditions.

1. Apply (Clamp) to the two large holes at the bottom of the base part, as shown in Figure 6−40.

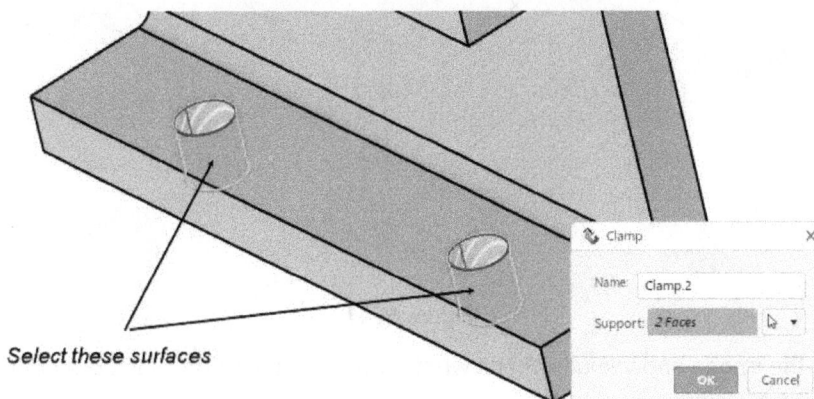

Select these surfaces

Figure 6−40

Task 12: Run the analysis.

1. Select ⟳ (Simulate) in the *Results* section of the Action Bar.
2. Click **OK** to close the *Simulate* dialog box when it displays.
3. Wait until computation completes, and the *Simulation Status* dialog box displays the message "Static Stress Simulation completed".
4. Close the *Simulation Status* dialog box.

Task 13: Display and animate the deformation.

1. Select **Deformation** in the *Plot* drop-down menu to display the model deformation image, as shown in Figure 6–41.

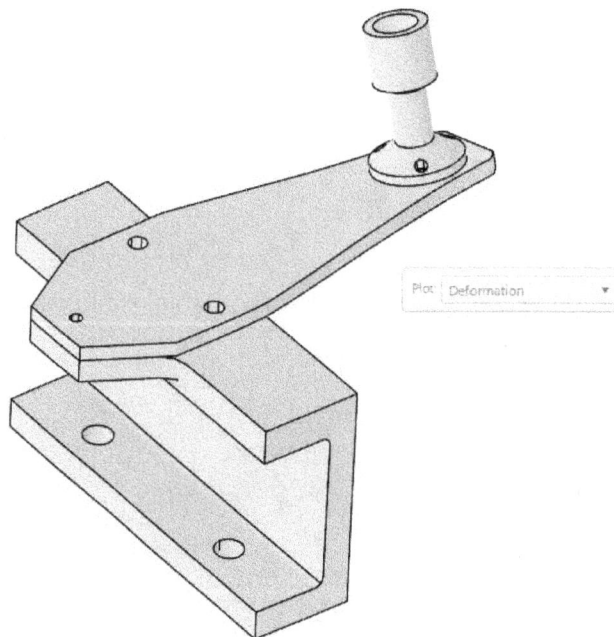

Figure 6–41

2. Animate the image and visually check whether the model deforms according to the applied loads and restraints.

Task 14: Visualize the displacements.

1. Select **Displacement** in the *Plot* drop-down menu to visualize the displacement magnitudes, as shown in Figure 6–42. Note that the tip of the shaft deflects by about **0.694mm**.

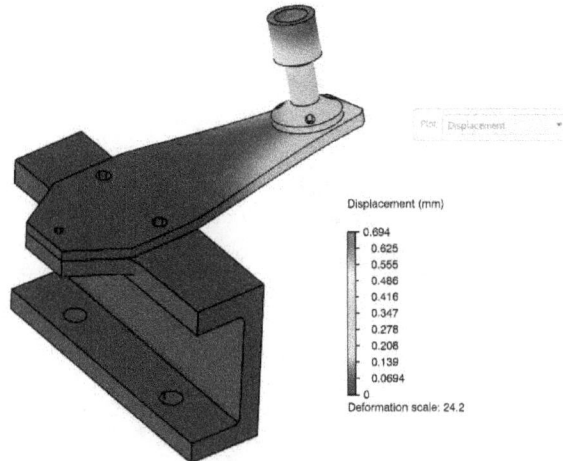

Figure 6–42

Task 15: Display Von Mises stress.

1. Select **Von Mises Stress** in the *Plot* drop-down menu. The stress result for the entire assembly displays as shown in Figure 6–43.

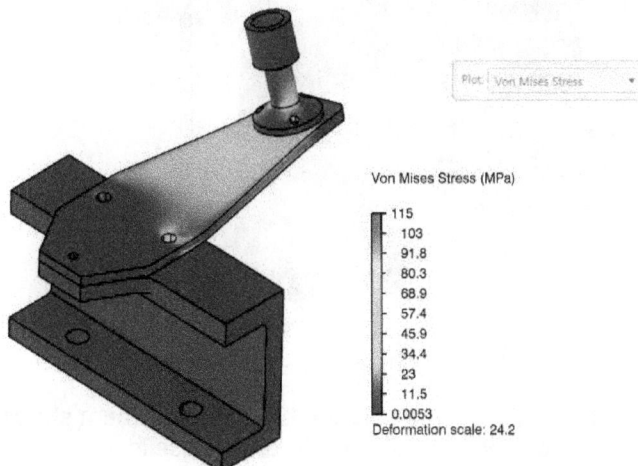

Figure 6–43

2. Select ⊞ (Display Group) in the *Results* section of the Action Bar.

3. In the *Display Groups* dialog box that opens, deactivate the **Plate_08** and **Shaft_08** parts, as shown in Figure 6−44.

Figure 6−44

4. Click **Apply** without closing the *Display Groups* dialog box. Now the stress result is only displayed for the base part, as shown in Figure 6−45.

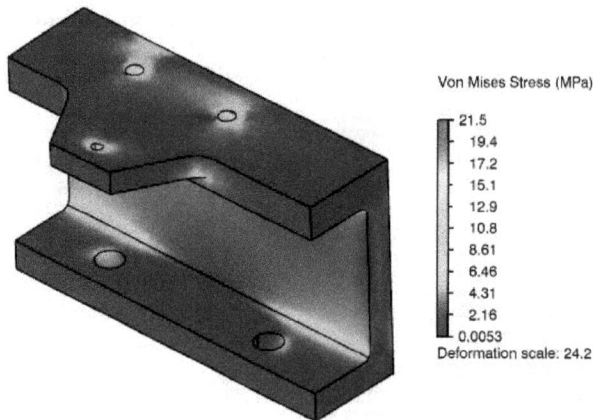

Figure 6−45

5. The **Aluminium** material's *Proof Stress* is **95MPa.** The maximum stress in the part is **21.5MPa**, which is well below **95MPa**. Therefore, the base is predicted to withstand the load without failure.

6. In the *Display Groups* dialog box, deactivate the **Base_08** and activate the **Plate_08** part. Click **Apply** to display *Von Mises stress* in the plate, as shown in Figure 6−46.

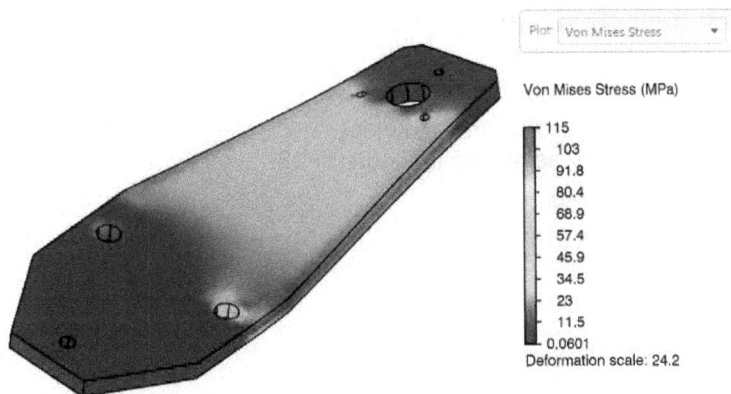

Plot: Von Mises Stress

Von Mises Stress (MPa)

115
103
91.8
80.4
68.9
57.4
45.9
34.5
23
11.5
0.0601
Deformation scale: 24.2

Figure 6-46

- Note that the maximum stress in the plate occurs near the M2.5 screw holes. Also, the maximum stress value **115MPa** exceeds the material's proof stress of 95MPa.

7. In the *Display Groups* dialog box, deactivate the **Plate_08** and activate the **Shaft_08** part. Click **Apply** to display *Von Mises stress* in the shaft, as shown in Figure 6-47.

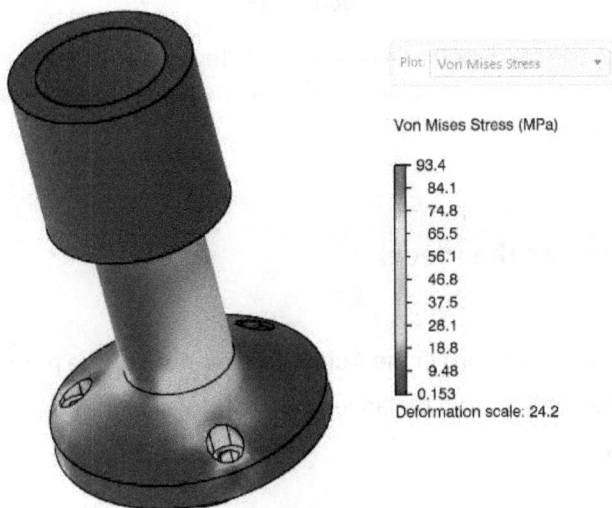

Plot: Von Mises Stress

Von Mises Stress (MPa)

93.4
84.1
74.8
65.5
56.1
46.8
37.5
28.1
18.8
9.48
0.153
Deformation scale: 24.2

Figure 6-47

- Note that the maximum stress in the shaft is approximately **93.4MPa**, which is below the material's proof stress of **95MPa**. Therefore, the shaft part is predicted to withstand the applied load.

8. In the *Display Groups* dialog box, activate all the parts. Click **Apply** and **Close** to display the stress result for the whole assembly.

Task 16: Check the bolt strength.

1. In the *Results* section of the Action Bar, select ⬚ (Virtual Bolt Checker). The *Virtual Bolt Checker* dialog box opens, as shown in Figure 6–48.

St	Name	Axial Fo...	Shear F...	Bending ...	Twisting ...	Allowable Fac...	Computed Factor of Safety
✓	Screw M6.1	606.312	301.206	2.71038	1.26889	1.5	1.67253
✓	Screw M6.2	680.574	278.863	1.98518	1.51952	1.5	2.11933
✓	Bolt M2.5.2	50.4774	10.699	0.0420093	0.0221167	1.5	6.63163
✗	Bolt M2.5.3	1.50053	120.871	0.480134	0.0798047	1.5	0.796404
✗	Bolt M2.5.1	402.844	134.137	0.725883	0.061504	1.5	0.450018

Figure 6–48

- Note that two of the M2.5 bolts have the computed factor of safety well below the allowable **1.5**, therefore are predicted to fail. A possible solution could be to increase the number of bolts, or to use larger bolts.

2. Click **Close**.

Task 17: Save and close the model.

1. Click 📦 (Result Visualization) in the Action Bar to return to the model view.
2. Optionally, save the analysis and the assembly for future reference.
3. Close all windows.

Frequency Analysis

A Frequency analysis helps you determine the natural frequencies and natural modes of vibration for a part or a product. These factors are important for models that are subjected to cyclic or vibrational loads, because resonance occurs at vibrational loads that are at or close to the natural frequencies for the model.

Learning Objectives

- Understand the natural frequency and natural mode of vibration.
- Review the frequency analysis equation.
- Set up a frequency analysis.
- Display the frequency analysis results.

7.1 Natural Frequency

All objects vibrate, when hit, struck, plucked, or otherwise disturbed. When an object vibrates, it tends to do so at a specific frequency or set of frequencies(for example, a guitar string or a tuning fork).

The frequency or frequencies at which an object tends to vibrate when disturbed is called the *characteristic* or *natural frequency* of the object.

Natural frequencies are numbered (1st, 2nd, 3rd, etc.), with the 1st natural frequency being the lowest. The 1st natural frequency is oftentimes called the *fundamental frequency* of an object.

If a dynamic load is applied to a model close to its natural frequency, the model exhibits a larger than normal oscillation. This phenomenon is called *resonance*. Without correct damping, the resonance can become uncontrollable and cause the model to collapse.

Frequency analysis predicts the natural frequencies of your model so that you can determine whether the applied dynamic loads might cause resonance. The results of a modal analysis also help to determine whether a model requires redesign to prevent failure.

7.2 Frequency Analysis Equation

The equation solved in Frequency analysis is the equation of dynamic equilibrium (i.e., Newton's equation) with neither damping nor external loads included. In matrix notation, the equation is written as following:

$$[M] \cdot \ddot{u} + [K] \cdot u = 0 \quad \text{(7.1)}$$

The 1st member in the equation represents the inertia force (i.e., mass times acceleration), while the 2nd member represents the resistance force (i.e., stiffness times displacement).

Note that no external loads are included in the equation. Indeed, the magnitude of the external force that causes the vibration does not affect the vibration frequency. Consider the example of a tuning fork. Whether barely hit or hit hard, the tuning fork emits the same sound tone, i.e., the frequency.

If equation (7.1) is solved for one mass, one degree of freedom system shown in Figure 7–1, the solution produces the well-known equation for the natural frequency ω:

$$\omega = \sqrt{K/M} \quad \text{(7.2)}$$

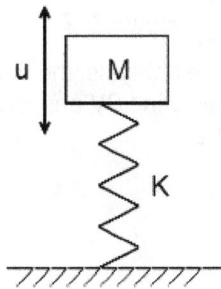

Figure 7–1

It follows from equation (7.2) that when dealing with unwanted resonance, you have two major variables at your disposal – stiffness and mass. To raise the natural frequency, the system should be designed stiffer and lighter. Alternatively, to lower the natural frequency, the system should be designed more flexible and heavier.

7.3 Natural Modes

An object vibrating at a natural frequency creates a physical deformation, or shape, of the object. This shape is called the *natural mode* of vibration.

Using frequency analysis, you can visualize these shapes and the frequency that is associated with them. Two mode shapes are shown in Figure 7–2. By viewing mode shapes, you can determine how a part reacts to different frequencies of vibration.

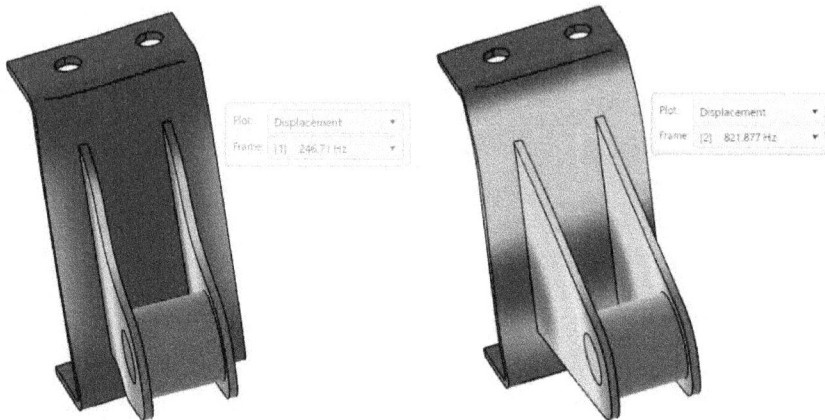

Figure 7–2

Since no external loads are included in the analysis, the displayed natural modes are essentially dimensionless. When mode shapes display in LSV app, only some imaginary magnitudes display, scaled to the maximum value **1.0**.

7.4 Setting Up a Frequency Simulation

To create a frequency simulation, select **Frequency** in the *Simulation Initialization* dialog box when launching the **LSV** app, as shown in Figure 7–3.

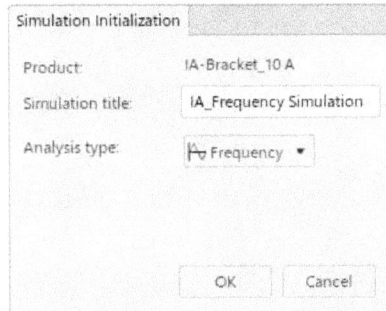

Figure 7–3

The default number of frequencies and modes that the LSV app computes for a frequency

analysis is **10**. To request a different number of frequencies and modes, select 🖊 (Edit Simulation Parameters) in the *Setup* section of the Action Bar and enter the **Number of modes** to compute, as shown in Figure 7–4.

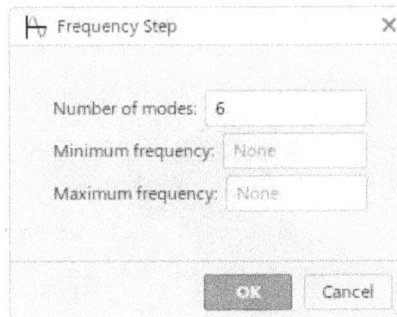

Figure 7–4

Optionally, specify the frequency range by entering the **Minimum frequency** and the **Maximum frequency**.

The rest of the setup, such as meshing, applying boundary conditions, etc., is similar to that in the structural stress analysis. Note that loads are not required.

7.5 Result Visualization

Once the frequency analysis completes, the app displays the **Deformation** result for the first natural frequency, as shown in Figure 7–5.

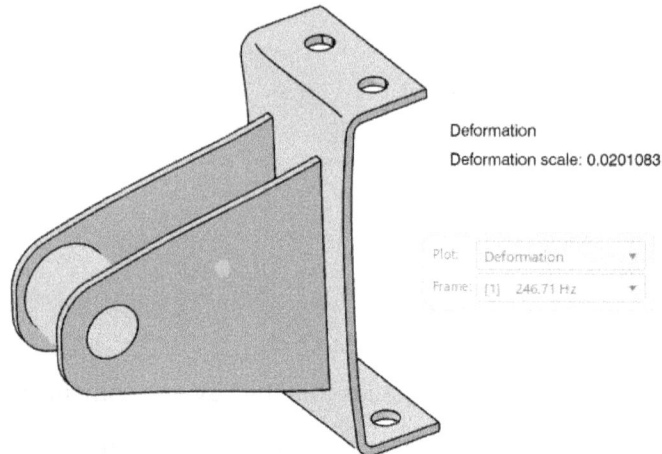

Deformation
Deformation scale: 0.0201083

Plot: Deformation
Frame: [1] 246.71 Hz

Figure 7–5

To display a different type of result, select the appropriate option in the *Plot* drop-down menu, as shown in Figure 7–6.

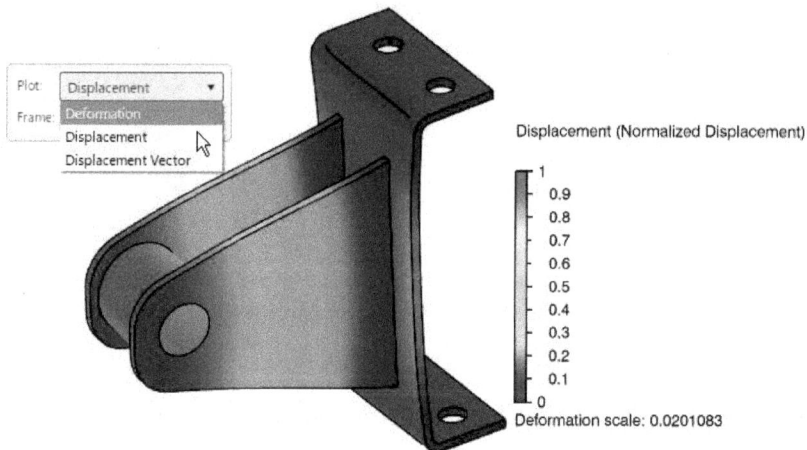

Plot: Displacement
Frame: Deformation
Displacement
Displacement Vector

Displacement (Normalized Displacement)

1
0.9
0.8
0.7
0.6
0.5
0.4
0.3
0.2
0.1
0

Deformation scale: 0.0201083

Figure 7–6

To display the result for a different natural frequency, select the frequency in the *Frame* drop-down menu, as shown in Figure 7–7.

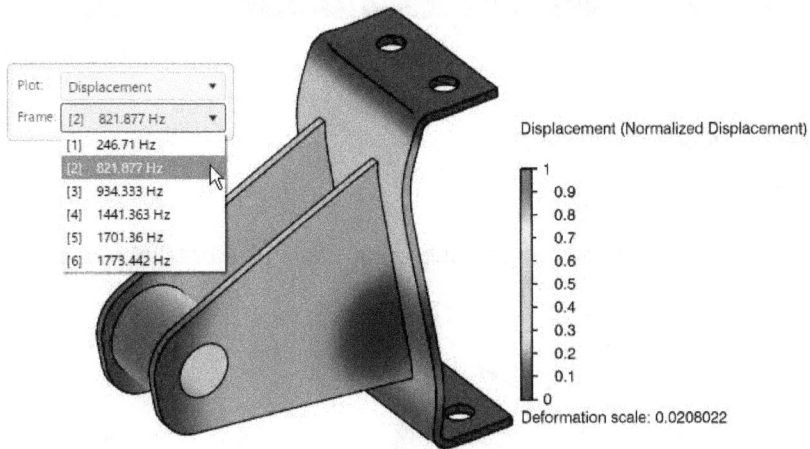

Figure 7–7

Practice 7a
Frequency Analysis of a Bracket

Practice Objectives

- Set up and run a frequency analysis.
- Display the results.

In this practice, you will set up and run a frequency analysis on a bracket model shown in Figure 7−8.

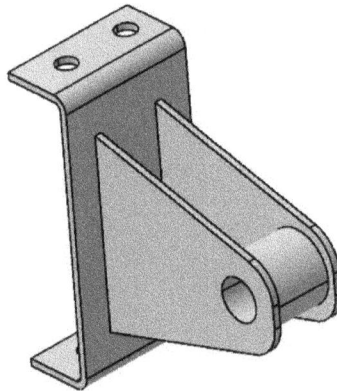

Figure 7−8

Task 1: Open the part.

1. Import with your initials and open **Bracket_10.3dxml**.

2. Set the model display as ▢ (Shading with Sharp and Smooth Edges). The part displays as shown in Figure 7–9.

Figure 7–9

3. Set the units as follows:

- *Length:* **Millimeter (mm)**
- *Force:* **Newton (N)**
- *Pressure:* **Megapascal (MPa)**
- *Stress:* **Megapascal (MPa)**

Task 2: Apply the material.

1. Apply **Steel** to the part. You can either use the material definition you created earlier in the class or create a new material definition. Ensure that the material properties are as follows:

- *Density:* **7860 Kg/m3**
- *Proof (Yield) Stress:* **250 MPa**
- *Young's Modulus:* **200000 MPa**
- *Poisson's Ratio:* **0.266**

Task 3: Launch the Linear Structural Validation app.

1. Launch the **Linear Structural Validation** app.

2. Enter *<Your Initials>_***Frequency Simulation** for the *Title* of the Physics Simulation.

3. Select **Frequency** for *Analysis type* and click **OK**, as shown in Figure 7–10.

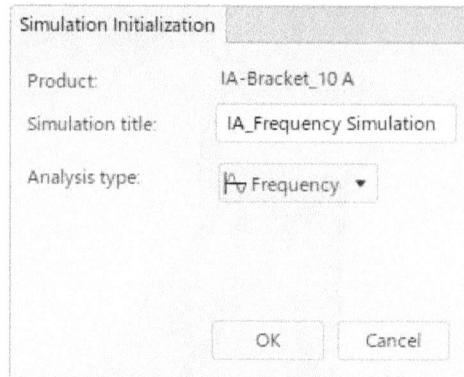

Figure 7–10

Task 4: Mesh the part.

1. Select (Generate Mesh). The mesh is generated and displayed, as shown in Figure 7–11.

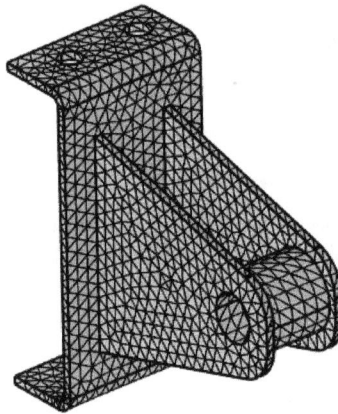

Figure 7–11

2. Select (Hide/Show Mesh) to hide the mesh.

Task 5: Apply the boundary conditions.

1.   Apply ✎ (Clamp) to the inside surfaces of the four holes, as shown in Figure 7-12.

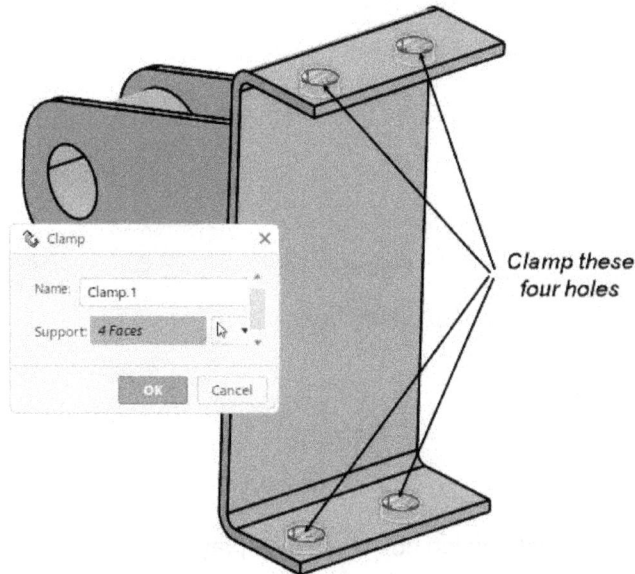

Figure 7-12

Task 6: Select the number of modes to compute.

1.   In the *Setup* section of the Action Bar, select ✎ (Edit Simulation Parameters). The *Frequency Step* dialog box opens, as shown in Figure 7-13.

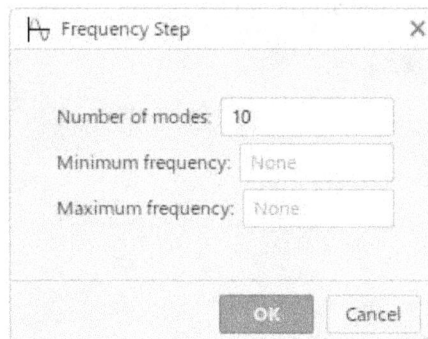

Figure 7-13

2. Enter **6** as the *Number of Modes*. The *Frequency Step* dialog box displays, as shown in Figure 7−14.

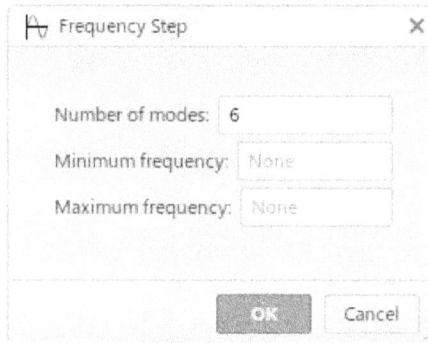

Figure 7−14

3. Click **OK** to close the *Frequency Step* dialog box.

Task 7: Run the analysis.

1. Select (Simulate).

2. Click **OK** to close the *Simulate* dialog box when it displays.

3. Wait until computation completes, and the *Simulation Status* dialog box displays the message "Frequency Simulation completed".

4. Close the *Simulation Status* dialog box.

Task 8: Display and animate the natural modes.

1. Once the computation completes, deformation plot for the 1st natural frequency **246.71Hz** displays, as shown in Figure 7−15.

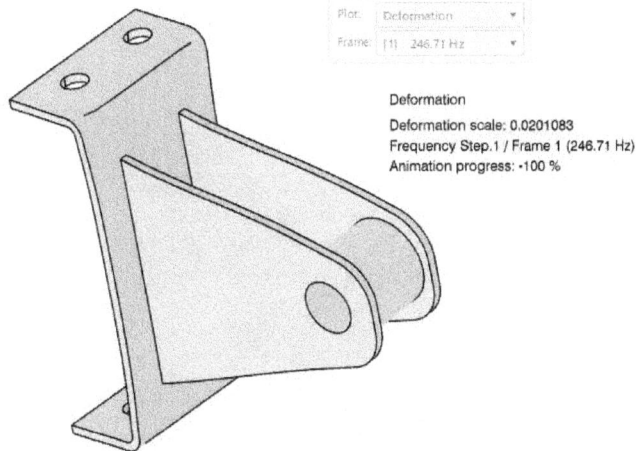

Figure 7-15

2. In the *Results* section of the Action Bar, select (Rendering Settings). Activate the **Show geometry** option, as shown in Figure 7-16, and click **Close**.

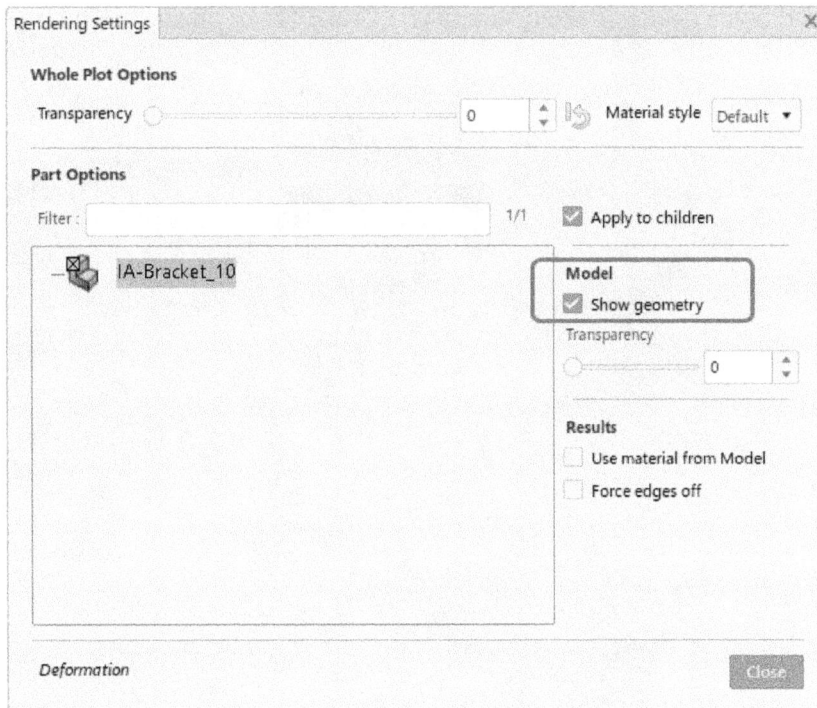

Figure 7-16

3. Animate the deformation. Note that the 1st natural mode of vibration causes bending of the bracket in the horizontal direction, as shown in Figure 7−17.

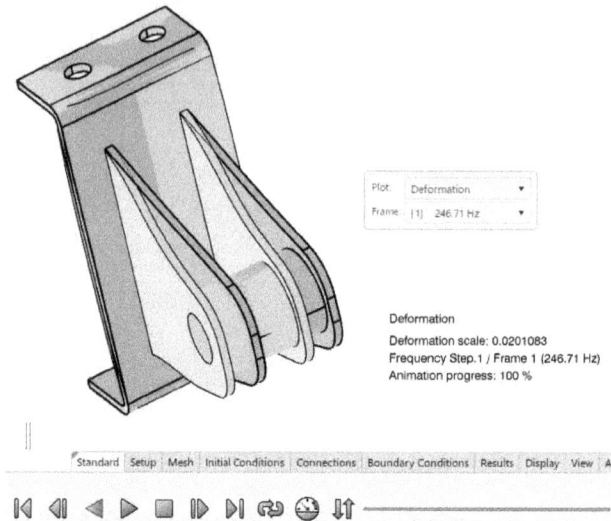

Figure 7−17

4. In the *Plot* drop-down menu, select **Frame [2] 821.877Hz**, as shown in Figure 7−18.

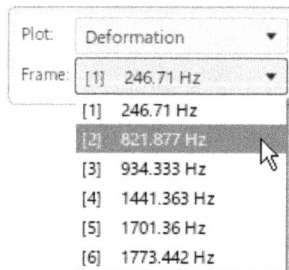

Figure 7−18

5. The deformation image for the 2nd natural mode displays, as shown in Figure 7–19.

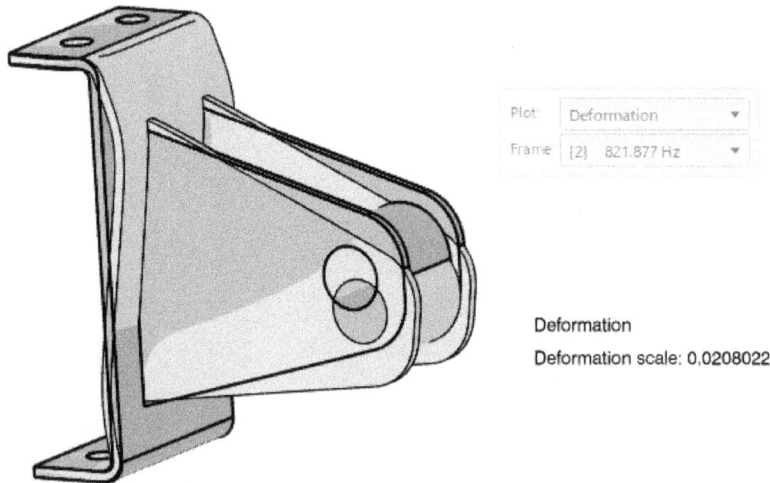

Plot: Deformation ▼
Frame: [2] 821.877 Hz ▼

Deformation
Deformation scale: 0.0208022

Figure 7–19

6. Animate the deformation. Note that the 2nd natural mode of vibration causes bending of the bracket in the vertical direction.

7. Display and animate the remaining modes of vibration. Which mode of vibration causes the twisting deformation of the bracket?

Task 9: Save and close the model.

1. Click [icon] (Result Visualization) to return to the model view.

2. Optionally, save the analysis and the part for future reference.

3. Close all windows.

End of practice

Buckling Analysis

A Buckling analysis calculates the critical buckling load of a structure subjected to predominantly compressive stresses. This is important for slender structures such as columns, posts, masts, etc. that typically exhibit very little deformation prior to buckling.

Learning Objectives

- Understand the concepts of the buckling analysis
- Create a buckling simulation
- Display the buckling analysis results

8.1 Theory of Buckling

Buckling analysis estimates the magnitude of the load at which the loss of structural stability under compressive loads might occur. It is an important analysis for slender structures that are subject to large compressive stresses. For example, these could be structural columns or posts, bridge trusses, submarine hulls, etc.

Buckling might occur at stresses well below the yield stress. This is called *elastic buckling*. Therefore, it is important to analyze such structures for both stress and buckling.

In the example shown in Figure 8–1, a long slender column **AB** of length **L** is constrained at end **A** and loaded with a centrally compressive load **P** at end **B**.

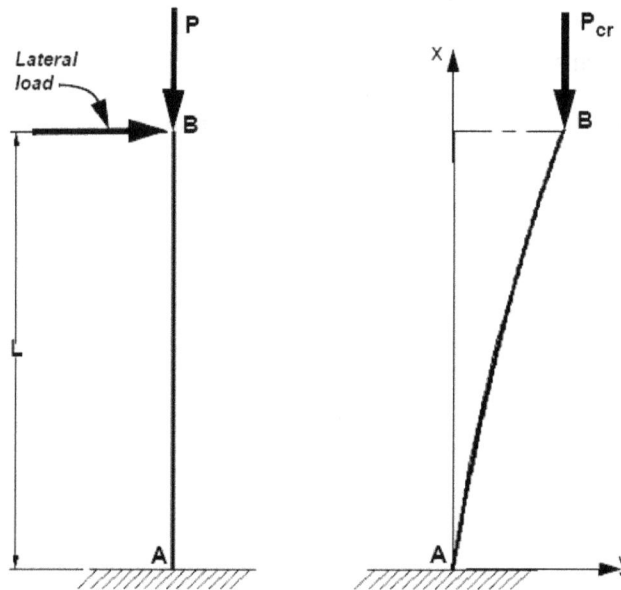

Figure 8–1

When load **P** is small, the compressive column is laterally stable. If end **B** is pushed slightly to one side, the column returns to its straight form as the lateral force is removed. As load **P** gradually increases, the straight form of the column becomes unstable, and the column, if pushed to one side, remains there even if the lateral load is removed. This phenomenon is called *buckling* and the value of the load at which buckling occurs is called the *critical load P_{cr}*.

Buckling analysis calculates the critical load P_{cr} at which loss of structural stability can occur.

Buckling simulation in the LSV app is a linear type of buckling analysis. The linear buckling analysis provides a useful first order approximation of the critical buckling load for designers and generally produces results that are not conservative (i.e., the theory calculates a higher critical load than is actually observed in experiments). Therefore, it is recommended that you use generous safety factors.

8.2 Buckling Load Factor

The main result of the buckling simulation is a load factor called the *Buckling Load Factor* (BLF), as shown in Figure 8−2.

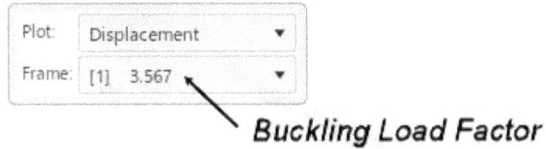

Figure 8−2

To produce a critical buckling load P_{cr} the applied load is multiplied by the BLF:

$$P_{cr} = BLF \times P_{applied}$$

Therefore, the BLF is a safety factor for the structure against buckling. A BLF less than 1.0 indicates that the structure is predicted to buckle under the applied load.

8.3 Buckling Modes

The buckling mode shape indicates how the structure deforms at the onset of buckling, as shown in Figure 8-3.

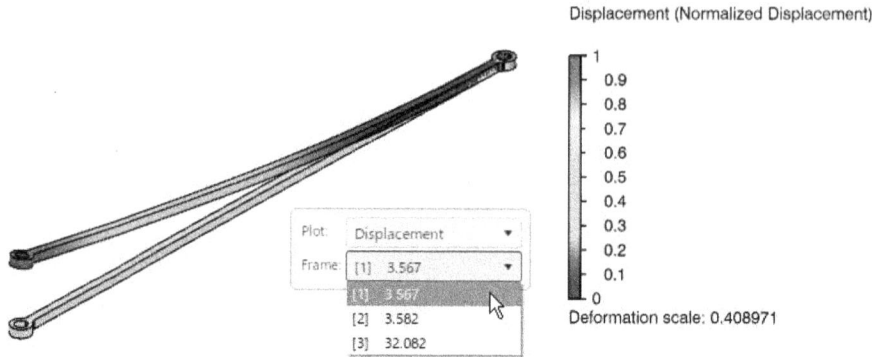

Figure 8-3

The number one mode shape corresponds to the lowest BLF; therefore, it is most likely to be the only one to occur. Therefore, be sure to verify your design for mode 1.

8.4 Setting Up a Buckling Simulation

To create a buckling simulation, select **Buckling** in the *Simulation Initialization* dialog box when launching the LSV app, as show in Figure 8−4.

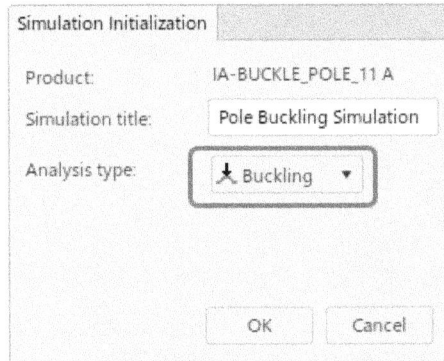

Figure 8−4

To select the number of buckling modes to compute, select ✎ (Edit Simulation Parameters) in the *Setup* section of the Action Bar, as shown in Figure 8−5.

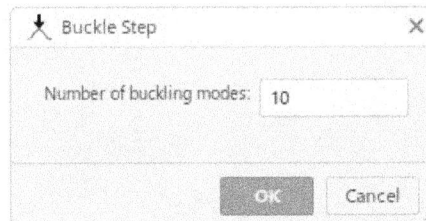

Figure 8−5

The rest of the setup, such as meshing, applying loads and boundary conditions, etc., is similar to that in the structural stress analysis.

8.5 Result Visualization

Once the analysis completes, the app displays the **Deformation** result plot for the first buckling mode, as shown in Figure 8–6.

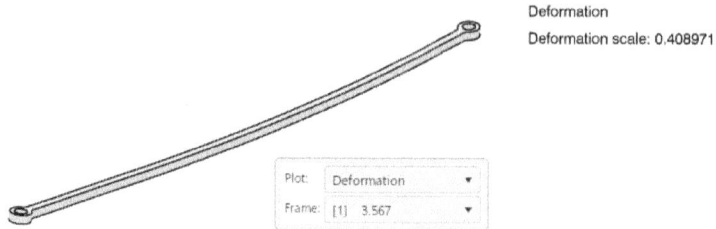

Figure 8–6

To display either the **Displacement** magnitude or **Displacement Vector**, select the appropriate option in the *Plot* drop-down menu, as shown in Figure 8–7.

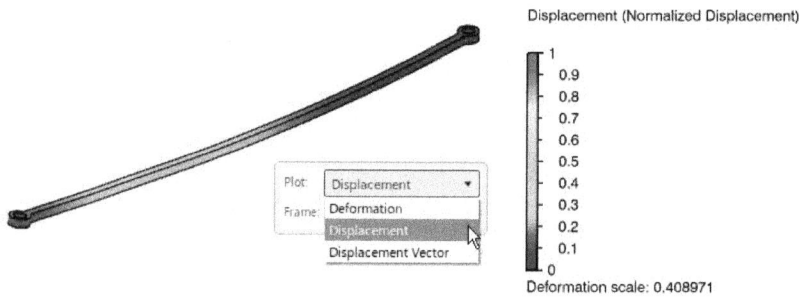

Figure 8–7

To display the result for a different buckling mode, select the mode in the *Frame* drop-down menu, as shown in Figure 8–8.

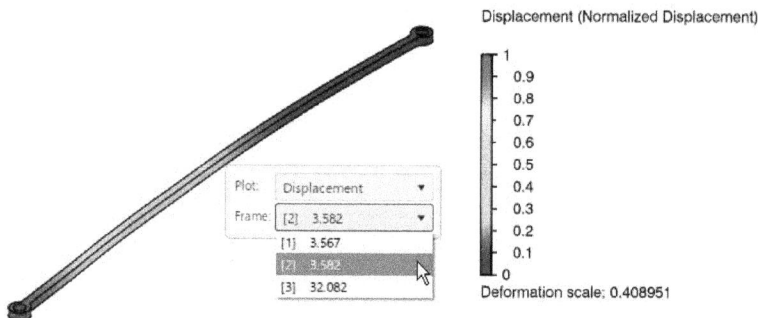

Figure 8–8

Practice 8a
Buckling Analysis of a Pole

Practice Objectives

- Apply material and mesh the model
- Apply loads and boundary conditions
- Set up and run buckling analysis
- Display buckling modes

In this practice, you will set up and run a buckling analysis on a long slender pole shown in Figure 8-9. The pole has a square cross-section (2in x 2in).

Figure 8-9

Task 1: Open the part.

1. Import with your initials and open **BUCKLE_POLE_11.3dxml**.

2. Set the model display as 🛢 (Shading with Sharp and Smooth Edges). The part displays as shown in Figure 8–10.

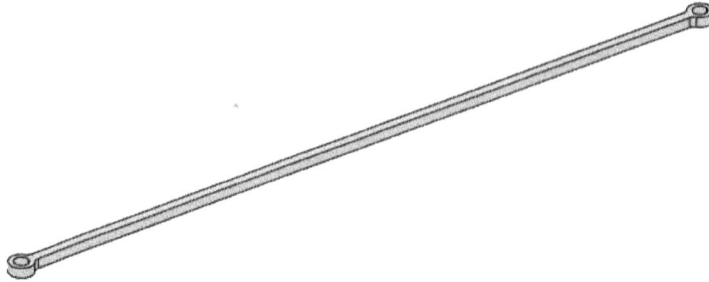

Figure 8–10

3. Set the units as follows:

- *Length:* **Millimeter (mm)**
- *Force:* **Newton (N)**
- *Moment:* **Newton x Meter (Nxm)**
- *Pressure:* **Megapascal (MPa)**
- *Stress:* **Megapascal (MPa)**

Task 2: Apply the material.

1. Apply the **Steel** material to the part. You can either use the material definition you created in an earlier practice or create a new material. Verify that the applied material has the following properties:

- *Young's Modulus:* **200000 MPa**
- *Poisson's Ratio:* **0.266**
- *Density:* **7860 Kg/m3**
- *Proof (Yield) Stress:* **250 MPa**

Task 3: Start the Linear Structural Validation app.

1. Launch the **Linear Structural Validation** app.
2. Enter *<Your Initials>*_**Pole Buckling Simulation** for the *Title* of the Physics Simulation.

3. In the *Simulation Initialization* dialog box, select **Buckling** for *Analysis type* and click **OK**, as shown in Figure 8-11.

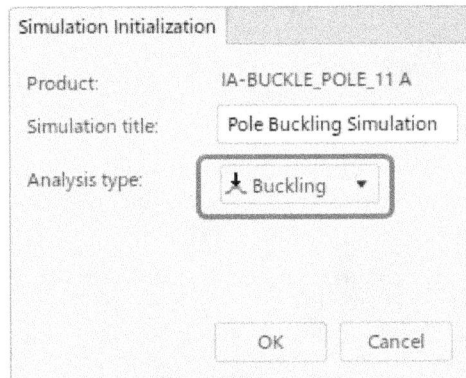

Simulation Initialization	
Product:	IA-BUCKLE_POLE_11 A
Simulation title:	Pole Buckling Simulation
Analysis type:	⚓ Buckling ▼
	OK Cancel

Figure 8-11

Task 4: Mesh the part.

1. Select ⬧ (Generate Mesh). The part mesh is displayed, as shown in Figure 8-12.

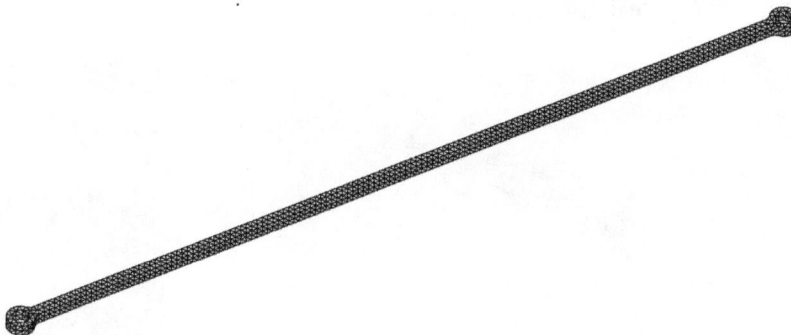

Figure 8-12

2. Select ⬧ (Hide/Show Mesh) to hide the mesh.

Task 5: Apply clamp.

1. Clamp the inside surface of the hole on one end, as shown in Figure 8–13. Select the hole that is toward the **-X** direction.

Figure 8–13

Task 6: Apply load.

1. Apply **5000N** force in **-X** direction to the inside surface of the hole on the other end of the part, as shown in Figure 8–14.

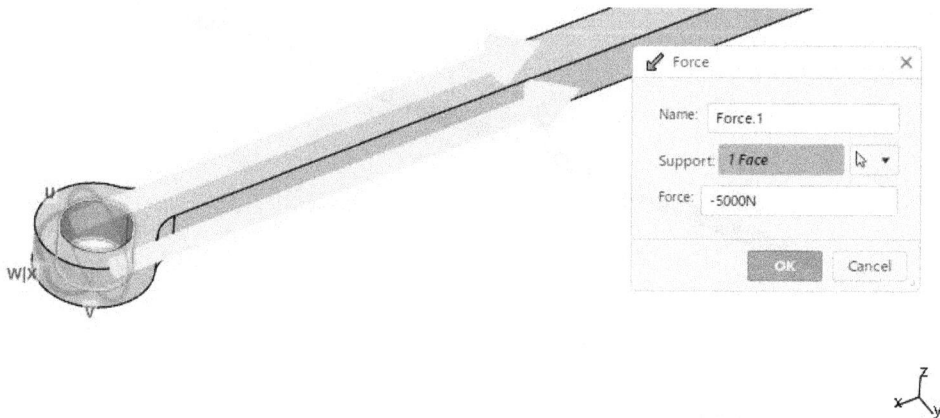

Figure 8–14

Task 7: Select the number of buckling modes to compute.

1. In the *Setup* section of the Action Bar, select ✎ (Edit Simulation Parameters). The *Buckle Step* dialog box opens, as shown in Figure 8–15.

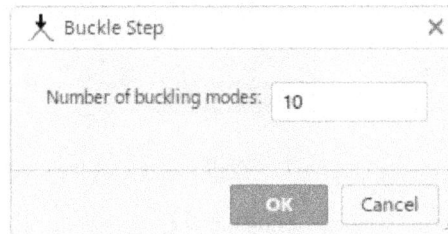

Figure 8–15

2. Enter **3** in the *Number of buckling modes* field, as shown in Figure 8–16.

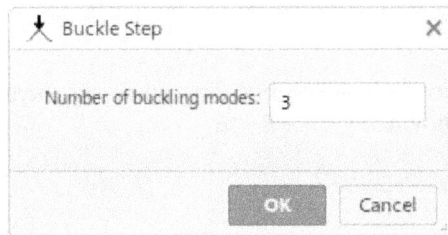

Figure 8–16

3. Click **OK** to close the *Buckle Step* dialog box.

Task 8: Run the analysis.

1. Run the analysis and wait until it completes.

Task 9: Display Buckling Load Factors.

1. Expand the *Frame* drop-down menu to display the *Buckling Load Factors*, as shown in Figure 8–17.

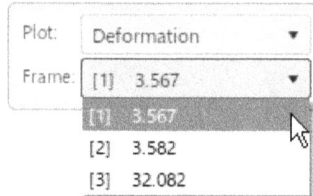

Figure 8–17

2. Note that the lowest buckling load factor is **3.567**. In Task 6, you applied **5000N** compressive load. Therefore, the predicted critical load is **3.567x5,000N = 17,835N**.

Task 10: Display buckling modes.

1. The *Deformation* result plot for the first buckling mode displays automatically when the analysis completes, as shown in Figure 8–18.

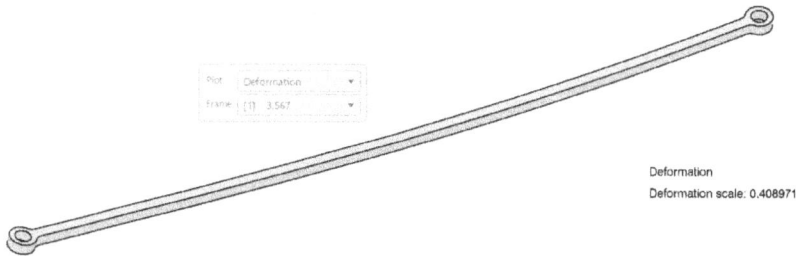

Figure 8–18

2. Select **Displacement** in the *Plot* drop-down menu and unhide the part. The displacement magnitude result plot displays, as shown in Figure 8–19. Note that for the first buckling mode, the pole bends in the **Z**- direction, which means that the pole is predicted to first buckle in this direction.

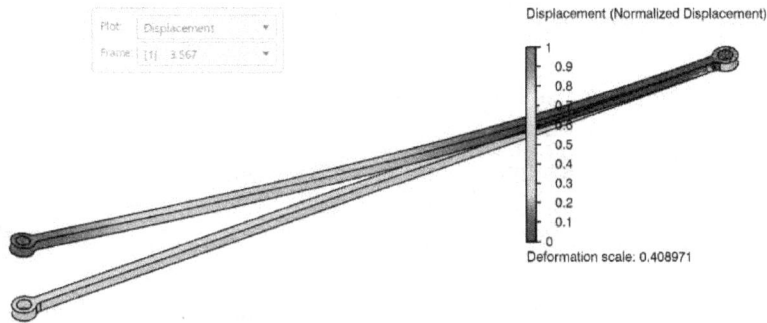

Figure 8–19

3. Using the *Frame* drop-down menu, display buckling mode 2, as shown in Figure 8–20. Note that for the second buckling mode, the pole bends in the **Y-** direction, and the buckling load factor **3.582** is close to that of the first buckling mode **3.567**.

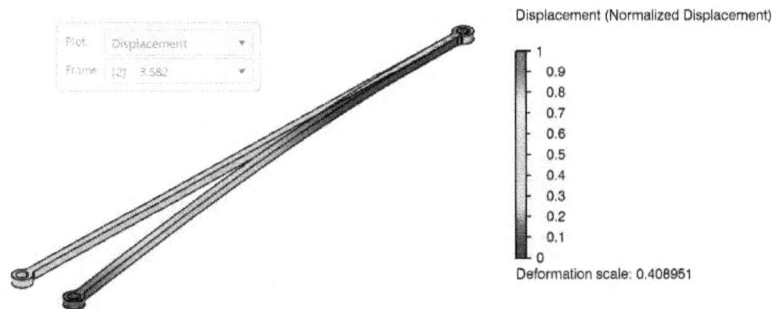

Figure 8–20

4. Display buckling mode 3, as shown in Figure 8–21. The buckling load factor **32.082** for this mode is much greater than for the first and second modes, which means that the pole is unlikely to buckle at the third mode.

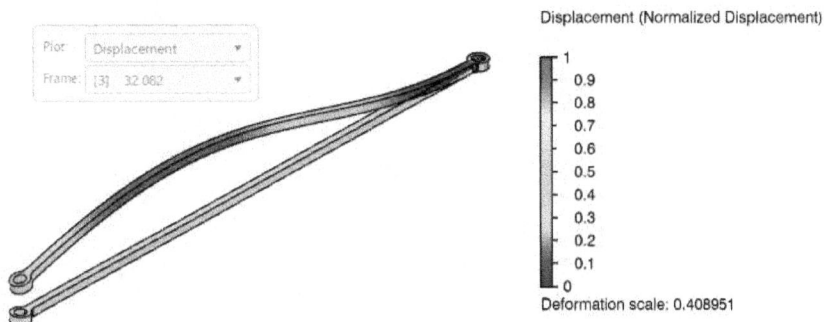

Figure 8–21

Task 11: Evaluate static stress in the pole.

In this task, you will determine whether the stress in the pole might exceed the material's yield stress before the pole starts to buckle.

This could be accomplished by setting up and running a static stress analysis using the LSV app, with the same loads and boundary conditions as in the buckling simulation. However, since the stress state in this model is mostly one-dimensional, you will evaluate the stress using hand calculation.

1. Calculate the stress **S** in the pole under the critical buckling load using the following formula:

$$S = {}^F\!/_A$$

Where **F** = critical buckling load **17,835N** as calculated in task 9,

A = cross-section area of the pole. The cross-section size is **1in = 25.4mm** square.

2. Does the stress exceed the material's yield stress **250MPa**? What is expected to occur first – elastic buckling of the pole? Or yielding of the pole's material before it starts buckling?

Task 12: Save and close the model.

1. Click (Result Visualization) to return to the model view.
2. Optionally, save the analysis and the part for future reference.
3. Close all windows.

End of practice

Practice 8b
Buckling Analysis of a Thin Shell

Practice Objectives

- Set up and run buckling analysis.
- Determine the buckling load factor.
- Display buckling modes.

In this practice, you will set up and run a buckling analysis on the thin cylindrical shell shown in Figure 8-22. The shell is **100mm** in diameter and **2mm** thick.

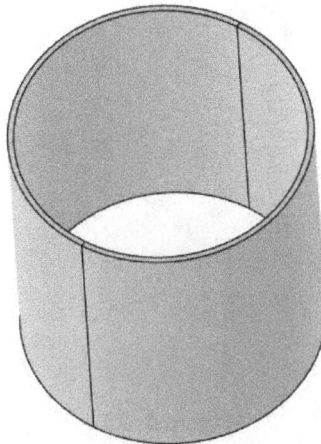

Figure 8-22

Task 1: Open the part and apply material.

1. Import with your initials and open **BUCKLE_SHELL_11.3dxml**.
2. Apply the **Steel** material to the part.

Task 2: Start the Linear Structural Validation app.

1. Launch the **Linear Structural Validation** app.
2. Enter **<Your Initials>_Shell Buckling Simulation** for the *Title* of the Physics Simulation.
3. Select **Buckling** for *Analysis type*.

Task 3: Mesh the part.

1. Mesh the part with the default meshing parameters.

Task 4: Apply loads and boundary conditions.

1. Clamp the bottom annular surface of the cylinder, as shown in Figure 8–23.
2. Apply **100,000 N** force in **-Y** direction to the top annular surface of the cylinder, as shown in Figure 8–23.

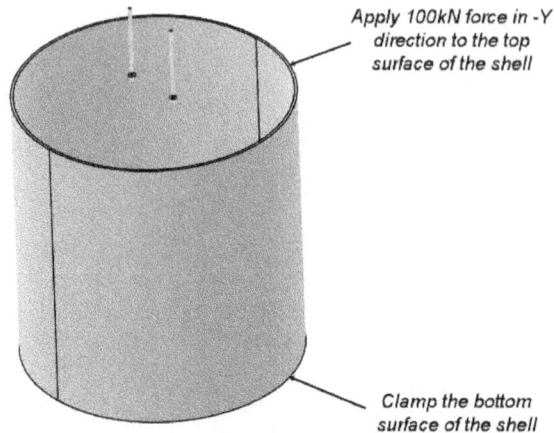

Apply 100kN force in -Y direction to the top surface of the shell

Clamp the bottom surface of the shell

Figure 8–23

Task 5: Select the number of buckling modes to compute.

1. Using the ✏ (Edit Simulation Parameters) tool, set the *Number of buckling modes* to **2**.

Task 6: Run the analysis.

1. Run the analysis and wait until it completes.

Task 7: Obtain Buckling Load Factors.

1. Using the *Frame* drop-down menu, display the **Buckling Load Factors**.
2. Is the part expected to buckle under the given load?

Task 8: Display buckling modes.

1. Using the *Frame* drop-down menu, visualize the buckling modes. Are the first and the second buckling modes similar in shape?

Task 9: Save and close the model.

1. Click (Result Visualization) to return to the model view.
2. Optionally, save the analysis and the part for future reference.
3. Close all windows.

End of practice

Thermal Analysis

A Thermal analysis evaluates the response of your product to various thermal loads. This is important for systems in which you must ensure that the maximum temperature in a part does not exceed the maximum operating temperature, such as in heat exchangers, electronic devices, etc.

Learning Objectives

- Understand the concepts of heat transfer.
- Create a thermal simulation.
- Display the thermal analysis results.

9.1 Modes of Heat Transfer

Thermal analysis measures the effect of heat loads and heat transfer on a product. Heat transfer is the flow of heat through a body in which there is a temperature variance. Heat transfer rates are an important part of engineering analysis in many industries. For example, heat transfer rates have a major role in the design of boilers, turbines, and combustion engines. The designer of these systems often needs to maintain high heat transfer rates while staying inside the material's limits for high temperatures.

There are three modes of heat transfer: conduction, convection, and radiation.

Conduction

Conduction is the transfer of heat through a solid body or a body of stationary fluid (e.g., water or gas), in which temperature variance occurs. The conduction mode of heat transfer occurs in the atomic and molecular structures of a body. An example of conduction in a gas cylinder is shown in Figure 9–1.

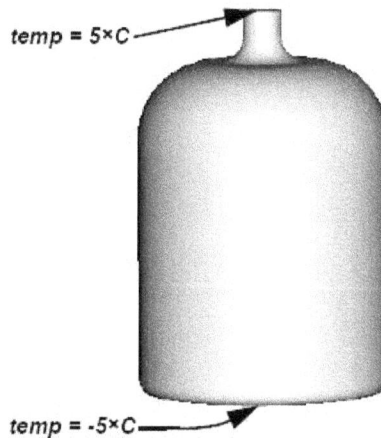

temp = 5×C

temp = -5×C

Figure 9–1

The temperature difference between the top and bottom of the cylinder is assumed to be 10°C. The molecules on the top of the cylinder have higher energies (i.e., they vibrate more freely) because of the higher temperature. Therefore, they collide with neighboring molecules and energy is transferred to these molecules. The process continues from high energy molecules to neighboring molecules from the top of the cylinder to the bottom until equilibrium is reached.

Conduction is the only mode of heat transfer in solid bodies.

Convection

Convection is the transfer of heat from a surface into the surrounding gas or fluid with a lower temperature than the surface. The heat must be conducted through material (e.g., heat exchanger) before it can be carried away by the outside air. There are two types of convection heat transfer: free and forced.

In free convection heat transfer, the moving fluid is free-flowing. For example, if a hot plate is left outside to be cooled on a day with little wind, the air in contact with the hot plate has a lower density than the air above the hot plate. This creates a circulation where warm air moves up and cooler air moves down.

In forced convection heat transfer, the moving fluid is pumped or fanned over a surface. Using the previous example, on a windy day, the primary transfer of heat is through the force of wind, while free convection still exists.

Convection heat transfer is governed by the following equation:

$$\frac{Q}{A} = h\,(T_s - T_a) \tag{9.1}$$

- Where **Q** = amount of transferred heat,

- **A** = surface area,

- T_s = surface temperature (determined during the analysis),

- T_a = reference, or ambient temperature (i.e., temperature of the surrounding gas or fluid), and

- **h** = convection coefficient, also called *film coefficient.*

Radiation

Radiation is the emission of energy from heated surfaces in the form of electromagnetic waves. Heat transfer by radiation does not need a means of transport, such as a solid or a gas.

Radiation heat transfer is governed by the following equation:

$$\frac{Q}{A} = \varepsilon \cdot \sigma \cdot (T_s^4 - T_a^4) \tag{9.2}$$

- Where **Q** = amount of transferred heat,

- **A** = surface area,

- T_s = surface temperature (determined during the analysis),

- T_a = reference, or ambient temperature (i.e., temperature of the surrounding gas or fluid),

- **σ** = Stefan-Boltzmann constant, and

- **ε** = emissivity, which is a property of a surface that determines how quickly it emits the radiative energy (value between 0 and 1).

9.2 Steady State Thermal Analysis

Once the heat loads and boundary conditions have been applied, over time, these thermal conditions create a constant distribution of temperatures throughout the part bodies (i.e., the temperatures and heat flows no longer change with the time duration). This is called thermal equilibrium. The thermal equilibrium is analyzed with a *steady-state thermal analysis*, and this is what is simulated in the LSV app.

However, before the thermal equilibrium is reached, the distribution of temperatures through the parts does change with the duration of time. This could be simulated with a *transient thermal analysis*; however, transient thermal analysis is not supported in the LSV app.

Analogies between Structural and Thermal Analyses

In general, the process of setting up and running a thermal analysis is similar to that of the structural analysis. I.e., you must apply materials, mesh the model, apply loads and boundary conditions, then run the analysis and visualize the results.

The analogies between the Structural and Thermal analysis quantities are presented in the following table.

Structural		Thermal
Stiffness	→	Conductivity
Load	→	Heat
Displacement	→	Temperature
Stress	→	Heat Flux

9.3 Setting Up a Thermal Simulation

To create a thermal simulation, select **Thermal** in the *Simulation Initialization* dialog box when launching the LSV app, as shown in Figure 9-2.

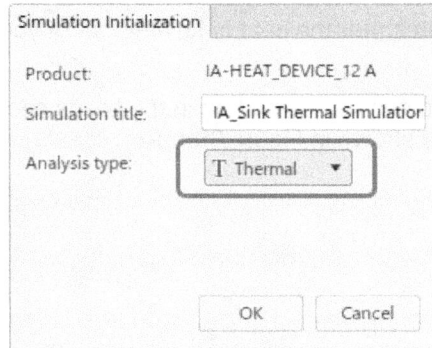

Figure 9-2

Temperature Boundary Condition

The *Temperature* boundary condition can be used to enforce a constant temperature on a surface. Usually, it represents a surface that is connected to a much large component or immersed in a steady temperature field.

To apply a Temperature boundary condition, select ▯ (Temperature) in the *Boundary Conditions* section of the Action Bar. The *Temperature* dialog box opens, as shown in Figure 9-3.

Figure 9-3

Select the *Support*, enter the *Temperature* value and click **OK**.

Heat Flux

The *Heat Flux* thermal load represents a surface of your model that either generates heat energy, or removes heat energy from your model:

- A positive heat flux indicates that the heat is flowing into the model.

- A negative heat flux indicates that the heat is flowing out of your model.

To apply a Heat Flux load, select ✍ (Heat Flux) in the *Loads* section of the Action Bar. The *Heat Flux* dialog box opens, as shown in Figure 9–4.

Figure 9–4

Select the *Support*, enter the heat flux *Magnitude* and click **OK**.

Volumetric Heat Source

The *Volumetric Heat Source* thermal load represents a volume of your model that models either a heat source, or a heat sink. The heat power can be specified in terms of total heat power, or as heat power per unit volume.

To apply a Volumetric Heat Source, select ⬚ (Volumetric Heat Source) in the *Loads* section of the Action Bar. The *Volumetric Heat Source* dialog box opens, as shown in Figure 9−5.

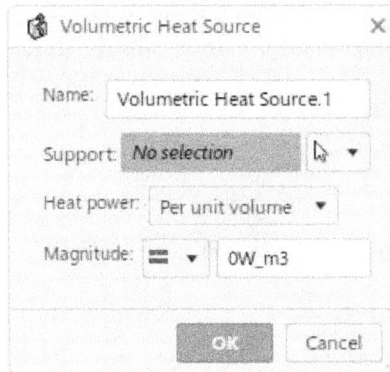

Figure 9−5

Select a part body as the *Support*, specify the *Heat power* either as **Per unit volume** or as **Total**, enter the *Magnitude* value and click **OK**.

Film Condition

Film Condition models convection heat transfer on a surface.

To apply a Film Condition, select ⬚ (Film Condition) in the *Loads* section of the Action Bar. The *Film Condition* dialog box opens, as shown in Figure 9−6.

Figure 9−6

Select the *Support*, enter the *Film Coefficient* (i.e., the convection coefficient) and the *Ref Temperature* (i.e., the ambient temperature) and click **OK**.

Radiation to Ambient

Radiation to Ambient models the radiation heat transfer on a surface.

To apply a Radiation to Ambient, select 🢅 (Radiation to Ambient) in the *Loads* section of the Action Bar. The R*adiation to Ambient* dialog box opens, as shown in Figure 9−7.

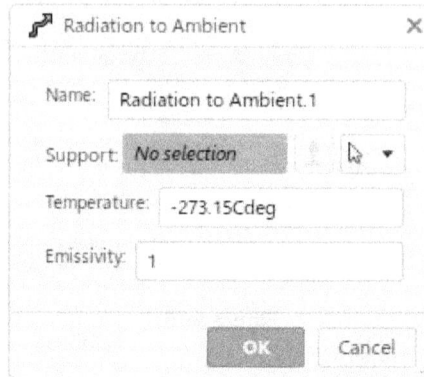

Figure 9−7

Select the *Support* surface, enter the ambient *Temperature* and the *Emissivity* and click **OK**.

Thermal Contact

The Thermal Contact models heat transfer through the contacting surfaces of separate parts, according to the contact's *conductance*:

*   A higher conductance value implies an easier heat transfer between the parts.

*   A zero conductance prevents heat from transferring across the contacting surfaces.

If thermal contact is not defined in a model, temperature changes and heat fluxes in one part will not affect adjacent components.

Thermal contacts can be created either with the 🔍 (Contact Detection) tool, or the

🔍 (Surface-based Contact) tool.

To let the app search for contacts in your model, select ⚲ (Contact Detection) in the *Connections* section of the Action Bar. The *Contact Detection* dialog box opens, as shown in Figure 9–8.

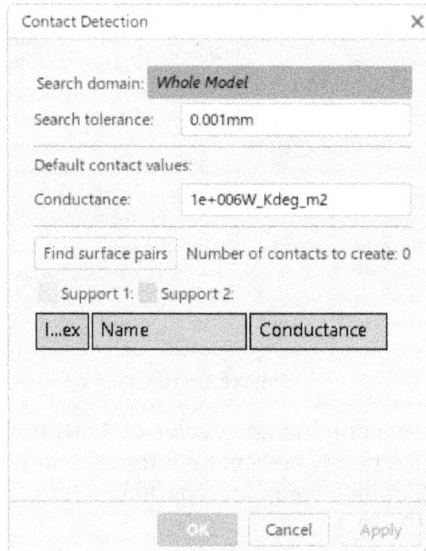

Figure 9–8

Click **Find surface pairs**. The app detects the pairs of contacting surfaces and displays them in the list, as shown in Figure 9–9.

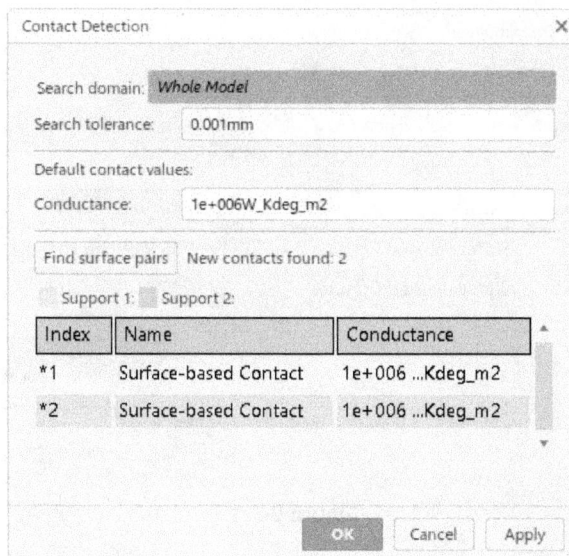

Figure 9–9

Select a contact in the list to highlight the surfaces in the model, as shown in Figure 9–10.

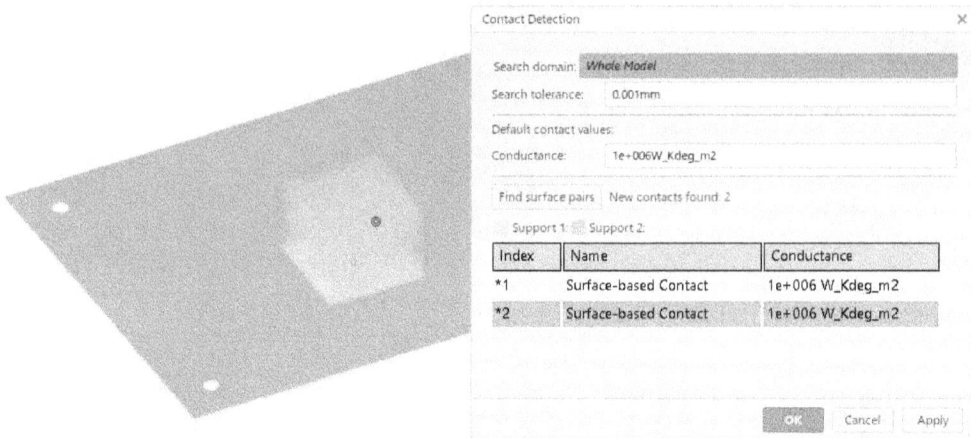

Figure 9–10

By default, a contact is assigned a conductance value of **1e+006 W_Kdeg_m2**. This is a very high conductance, which enables nearly perfect heat transfer through the contacting surfaces. If you wish to modify the conductance value for a particular contact, right-click it in the list and select **Edit**, as shown in Figure 9–11.

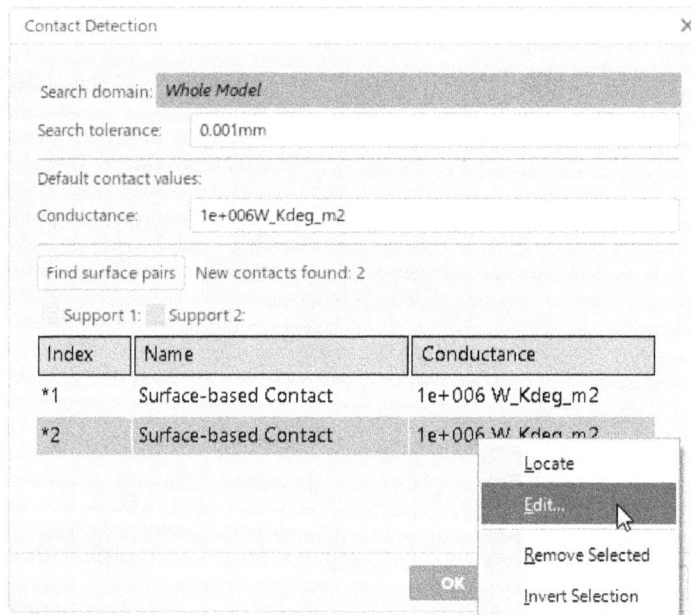

Figure 9–11

Once the *Edit Contact* dialog box opens, enter the new *Conductance* value, as shown in Figure 9–12.

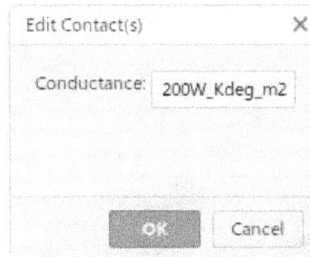

Figure 9–12

To define thermal contacts manually, select 🔍 (Surface-based Contact) in the *Connections* section of the Action Bar. The *Surface-based Contact* dialog box opens, as shown in Figure 9–13.

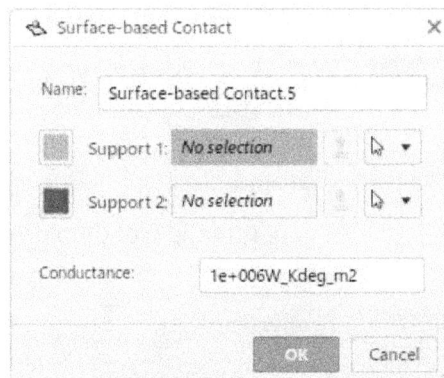

Figure 9–13

Select the contacting surfaces, enter the *Conductance* value, and click **OK**.

Thermal contacts can later be edited independently by double-clicking them in the *Feature Manager*.

9.4 Result Visualization

Once the analysis completes, the app displays the **Temperature** result plot, as shown in Figure 9−14.

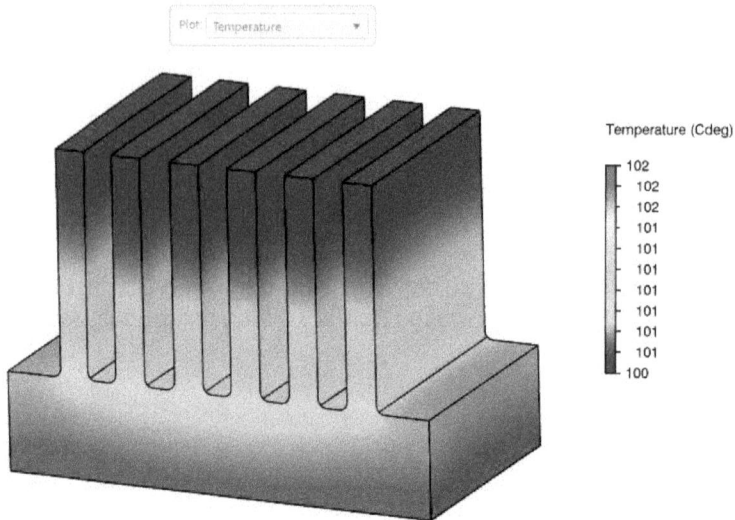

Figure 9−14

To display a different result, select the quantity in the *Plot* drop-down menu, as shown in Figure 9−15.

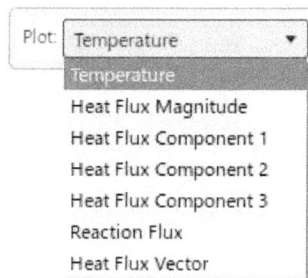

Figure 9−15

Practice 9a
Thermal Analysis of a Heat Sink

Practice Objectives

- Apply thermal boundary conditions.
- Set up and run thermal analysis.
- Display the results of thermal analysis.

In this practice, you will set up and run a thermal steady state analysis on a heat sink shown in Figure 9–16. The heat sink sits on a 10W CPU (heat source) and is cooled by the free convection on the fins. The part is made of aluminum.

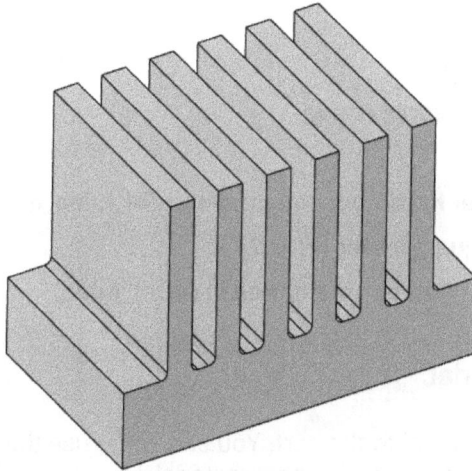

Figure 9–16

Task 1: Open the part.

1. Import with your initials and open **HEAT_DEVICE_12.3dxml**.

2. Set the model display as ⬡ (Shading with Sharp and Smooth Edges). The part displays as shown in Figure 9–17.

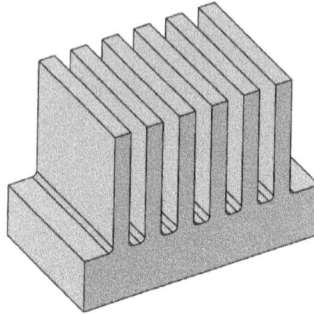

Figure 9–17

3. Set the units as follows:

*   *Length:* **Millimeter (mm)**
*   *Temperature:* **Celsius degree (Cdeg)**
*   *Heat rate:* **Watt (W)**
*   *Heat transfer:* **Watt per Kelvin per square meter (W_Kdeg_m2)**
*   *Heat flux:* **Watt per square meter (W_m2)**
*   *Thermal Conductivity:* **Watt per meter Kelvin (W_m_Kdeg)**

Task 2: Apply the material.

1. Apply the **Aluminium** material to the part. You can either use the material definition you created earlier in the class or create a new material.

2. Double-click the **Material Simulation Domain** in the tree and ensure that the **Thermal Conductivity** for the material is **250 W_m_Kdeg**, as shown in Figure 9–18.

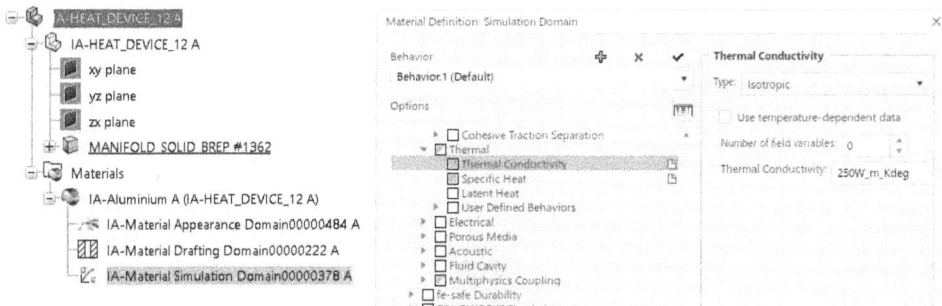

Figure 9–18

Task 3: Start the Linear Structural Validation app.

1. Launch the **Linear Structural Validation** app.

2. Enter **<Your Initials>_Sink Thermal Simulation** for the *Title* of the Physics Simulation.

3. In the *Simulation Initialization* dialog box, select **Thermal** for *Analysis type* and click **OK**, as shown in Figure 9–19.

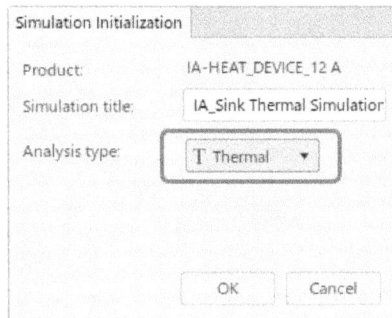

Simulation Initialization

Product:	IA-HEAT_DEVICE_12 A
Simulation title:	IA_Sink Thermal Simulatior
Analysis type:	T Thermal ▼

OK   Cancel

Figure 9–19

Task 4: Mesh the part.

1. Select (Generate Mesh). The part mesh is displayed, as shown in Figure 9–20.

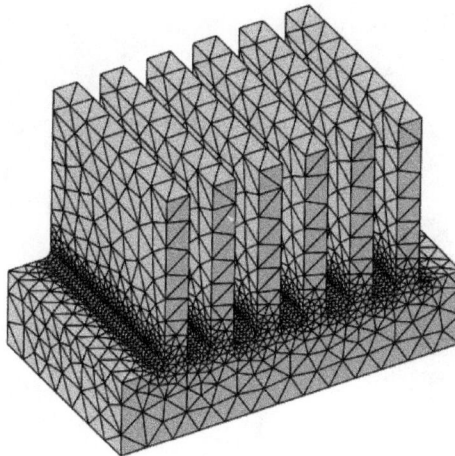

Figure 9–20

2. Select (Hide/Show Mesh) to hide the mesh.

Task 5: Apply the heat load.

The bottom surface of the heat sink is glued to a **10W** CPU, which is the heat source in the model. The area of the bottom surface is **935mm2**, which is **0.000935m2**. Therefore, the magnitude of the heat flux through the surface is **10/0.000935 = 10,695W_m2**.

1. In the *Loads* section of the Action Bar, select (Heat Flux). The *Heat Flux* dialog box opens, as shown in Figure 9–21.

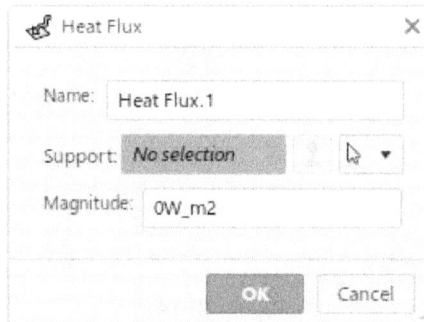

Figure 9–21

2. Select the bottom surface of the sink as the *Support* and enter **10695W_m2** as the *Magnitude*, as shown in Figure 9–22.

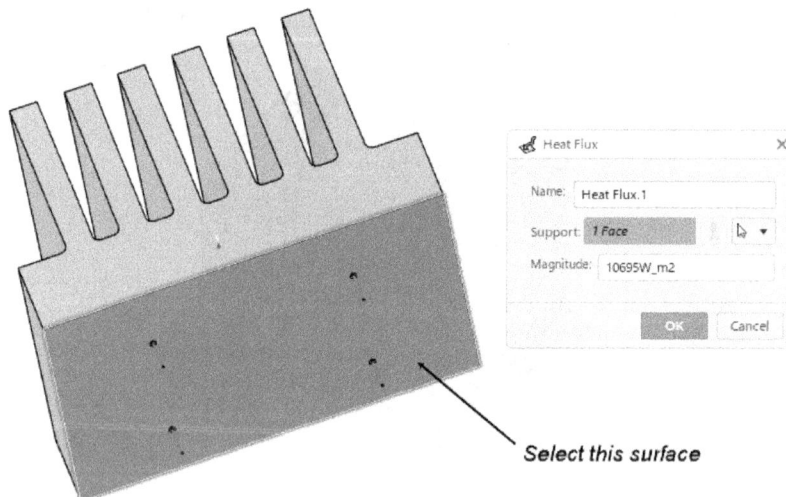

Select this surface

Figure 9–22

3. Click **OK**. The model displays as shown in Figure 9−23.

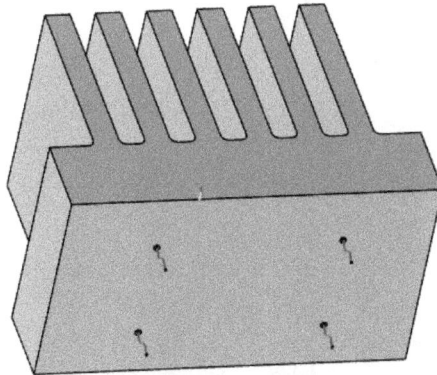

Figure 9−23

Task 6: Apply the convection.

The heat sink is cooled by the free convection through the **20Cdeg** air that surrounds the sink. Typically, the convection heat transfer coefficient for free convection by air varies in the range from **5** to **25W_Kdeg_m2**. For this analysis, you will assume the convection coefficient **15W_Kdeg_m2**.

1. In the *Loads* section of the Action Bar, select (Film Condition). The *Film Condition* dialog box opens, as shown in Figure 9−24.

Figure 9−24

2. Select all the free surfaces of the sink (excluding the bottom surface, 41 surfaces altogether). Enter **15W_Kdeg_m2** as the *Film Coefficient*, and **20Cdeg** as the *Ref Temperature*, as shown in Figure 9–25.

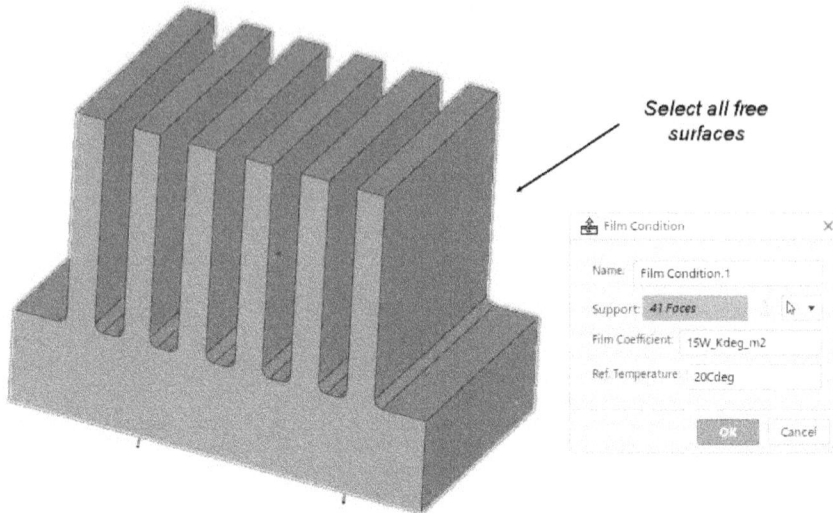

Figure 9–25

3. Click **OK**. The model displays as shown in Figure 9–26.

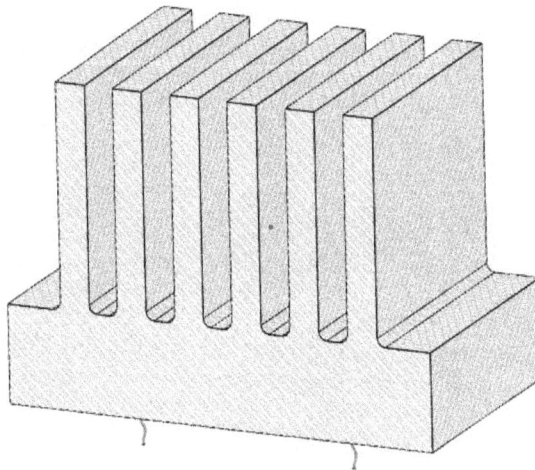

Figure 9–26

Task 7: Run the analysis.

1. Run the analysis and wait until it completes.

Task 8: Display Temperature result plot.

1. Once the analysis completes, the **Temperature** result plot is automatically displayed, as shown in Figure 9–27.

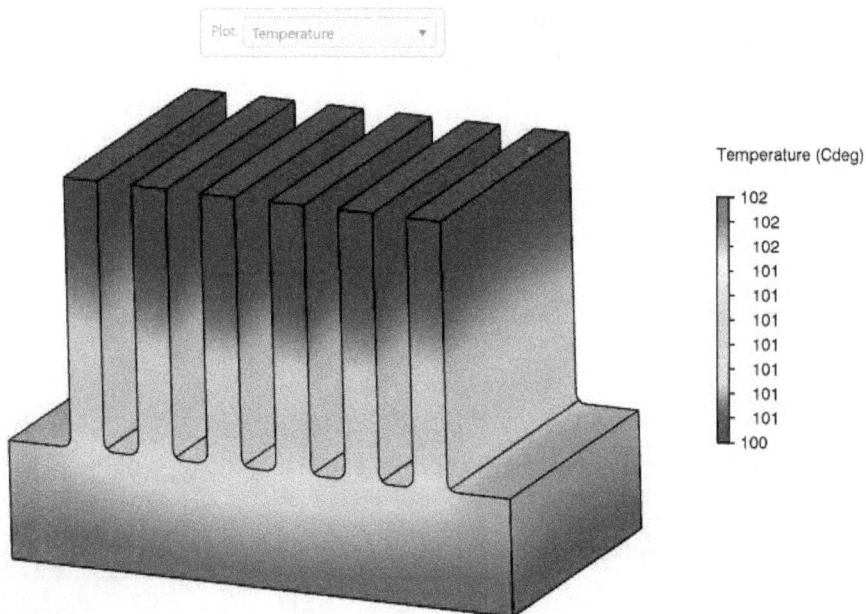

Figure 9–27

Note that the maximum temperature occurs at the bottom of the heat sink, where the heat load is applied. The temperature gradually decreases to the top of the heat sink, due to convection on the fins.

However, the temperature gradient is very small (2C°) from the bottom and to the top of the sink. This indicates that the free air convection is not very effective to cool the CPU. Possible solutions include either a forced convection by means of a fan, or a different design of the heat sink with more fins and a higher fin height.

Task 9: Display Heat Flux.

1. Select **Heat Flux Magnitude** in the *Plot* drop-down menu. The result plot displays, as shown in Figure 9–28.

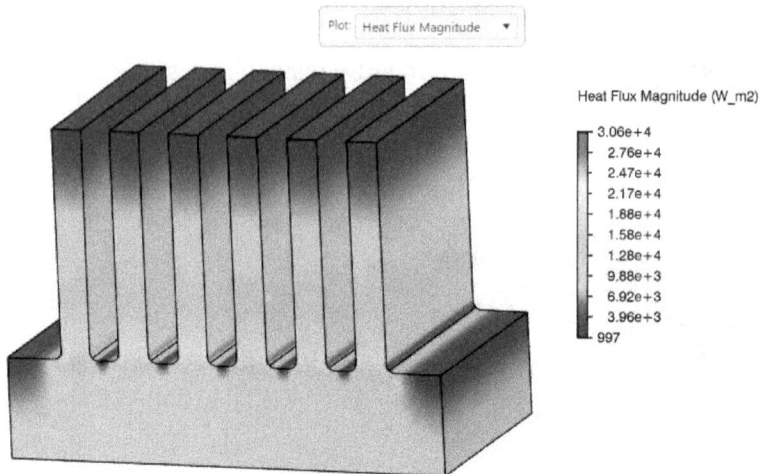

Figure 9–28

Note that the maximum heat flow occurs at the bottoms of the fins. This area acts like a funnel, transferring heat from the heat source at the bottom surface to the tops of the fins.

Task 10: Save and close the model.

1. Click (Result Visualization) to return to the model view.

2. Optionally, save the analysis and the part for future reference.

3. Close all windows.

End of practice

Practice 9b
Thermal Analysis of an Assembly

Practice Objectives

- Apply thermal boundary conditions.
- Apply thermal connections.
- Set up and run thermal analysis.
- Display the results of thermal analysis.

In this practice, you will set up and run a thermal steady state analysis on an electronic assembly shown in Figure 9–29.

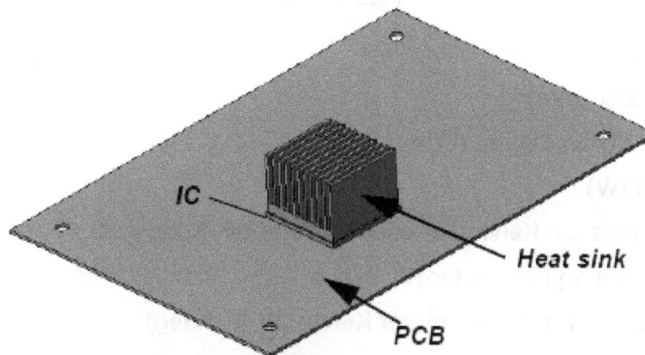

Figure 9–29

The heat source in this simulation is the Integrated Circuit (IC) part, generating 1W of heat. The heat sink is bonded to the IC. The IC is mounted, but not bonded, to the Printed Circuit Board (PCB) part. The generated heat in this design is intended to be dissipated through the means of convection by the heat sink.

Task 1: Open the assembly.

1. Import with your initials and open **PCB_ASM_12.3dxml**.

2. Set the model display as ⬡ (Shading with Sharp and Smooth Edges). The part displays as shown in Figure 9–30.

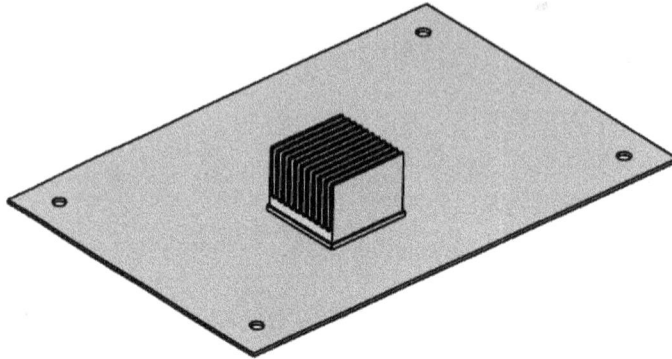

Figure 9–30

3. Set the units as follows:

- *Length:* **Millimeter (mm)**
- *Temperature:* **Celsius degree (Cdeg)**
- *Heat rate:* **Watt (W)**
- Heat *transfer:* **Watt per Kelvin per square meter (W_Kdeg_m2)**
- *Heat flux:* **Watt per square meter (W_m2)**
- *Thermal Conductivity:* **Watt per meter Kelvin (W_m_Kdeg)**

Task 2: Create material definition.

1. Click the outer ring of the Compass and, in the *My Apps* list, select the **Material Definition** app.

2. The Materials in session are displayed in the tree, as shown in Figure 9–31. These are the materials you used in other simulations.

Figure 9–31

3. In the Action Bar, select ![icon] (Create Material). The *Create Material* dialog box opens, as shown in Figure 9–32.

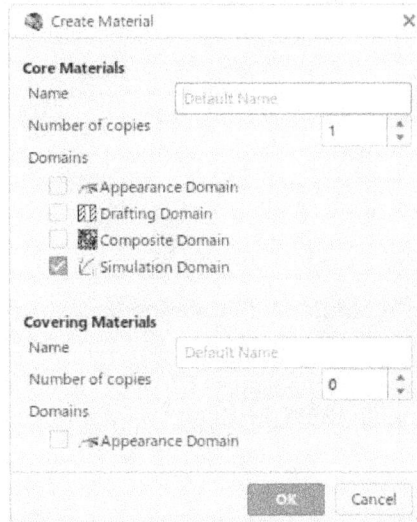

Figure 9–32

4. Enter ***<Your Initials>*_Epoxy** for *Name* and toggle on the **Simulation domain** option, as shown in Figure 9–33.

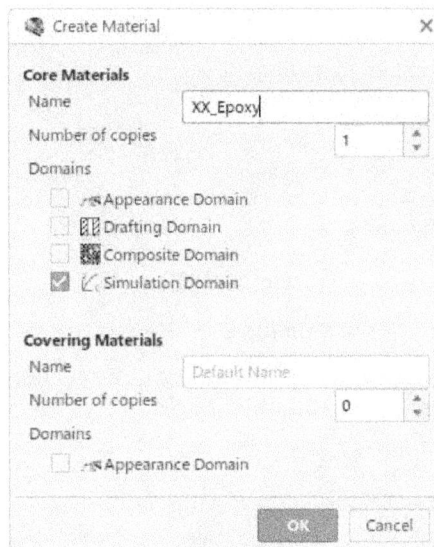

Figure 9–33

5. The new material definition displays in the tree, as shown in Figure 9–34.

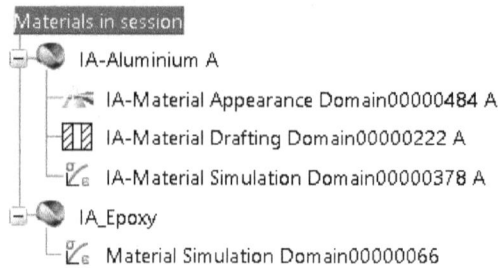

Figure 9–34

6. Double-click the newly created **Material Simulation Domain** in the tree to open the *Simulation Domain* dialog box.

7. Expand the *Structures>Abaqus Multiphysics>Thermal* section and select the **Thermal Conductivity** checkbox. Enter **0.188W_M_Kdeg** for *Thermal Conductivity*, as shown in Figure 9–35.

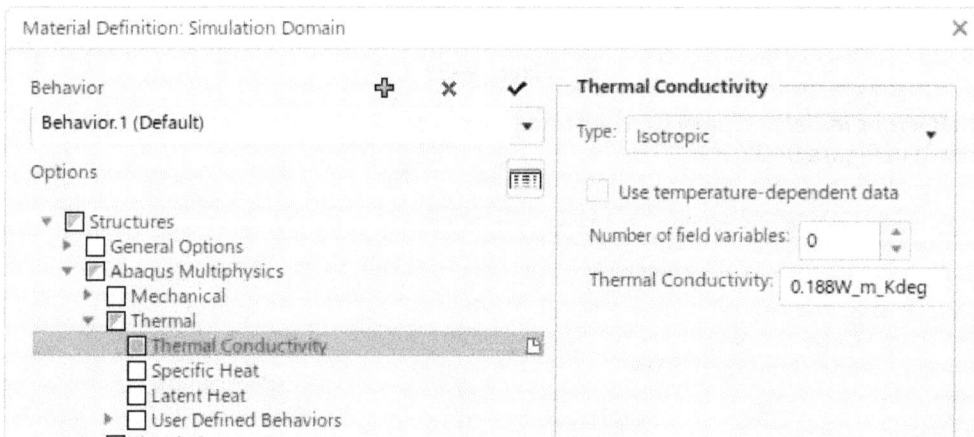

Figure 9–35

8. Click **OK** to complete the material definition.

9. Using Steps 3 through 8 as the guideline, create a material definition for the **<Your Initials>_Nylon** material. Use **0.245W_M_Kdeg** for *Thermal Conductivity*.

10. Do not close the *Material Editor* window.

Task 3: Apply the materials.

1. In the *Material Editor* window, right-click the *Epoxy* material in the tree and select **Apply**, as shown in Figure 9–36.

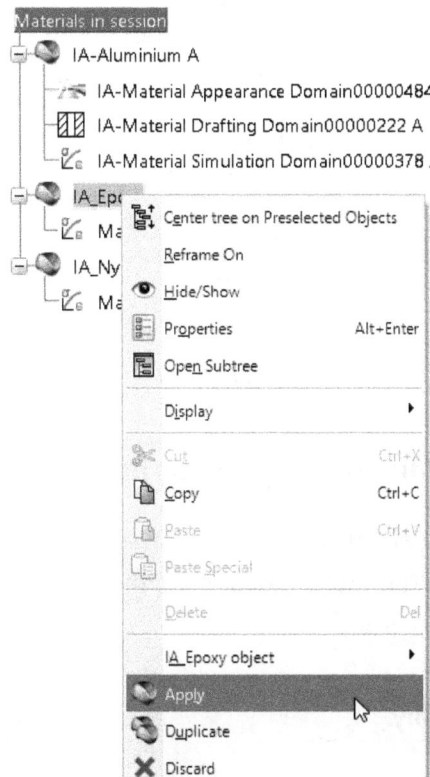

Figure 9–36

2. Activate the **PCB_ASM_12** window, click the **IC** part in the tree and click [checkmark] in the context toolbar to complete.

3. Using Steps 1 and 2 as the guideline, apply **Nylon** material to the **PCB** part.

4. Apply **Aluminum** material to the **HS** part. You can either use the material definition you created earlier in the class or create a new material. Ensure that the **Thermal Conductivity** for Aluminum is **250W_m_Kdeg**.

5. The applied materials display in the assembly's tree, as shown in Figure 9–37.

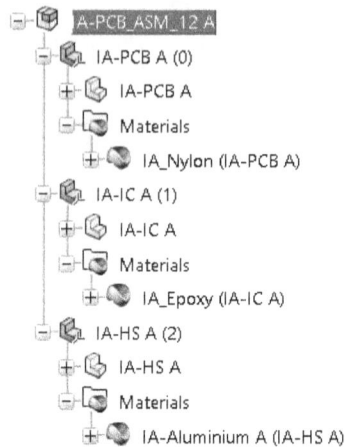

Figure 9–37

Task 4: Start the Linear Structural Validation app.

1. Launch the **Linear Structural Validation** app.

2. Enter **<*Your Initials*>_PCB Thermal Simulation** for the *Title* of the Physics Simulation.

3. Select **Thermal** for *Analysis type*.

Task 5: Mesh the assembly.

1. Select (Generate Mesh). The part mesh is displayed, as shown in Figure 9–38.

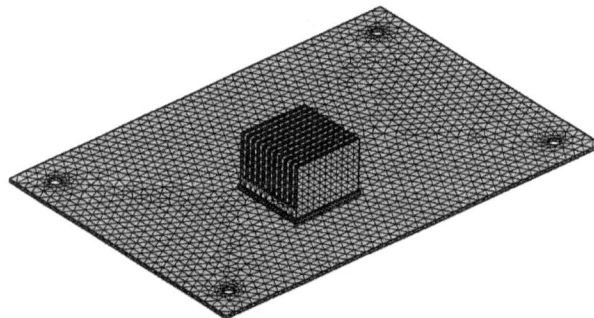

Figure 9–38

2. Select (Hide/Show Mesh) to hide the mesh.

Task 6: Apply the heat load.

The heat in this assembly is generated by the **IC** part, then dissipated by the **HS** part. The amount of heat generated by the IC is **1W**.

1. In the **Loads** section of the Action Bar, select (Volumetric Heat Source). The *Volumetric Heat Source* dialog box opens, as shown in Figure 9–39.

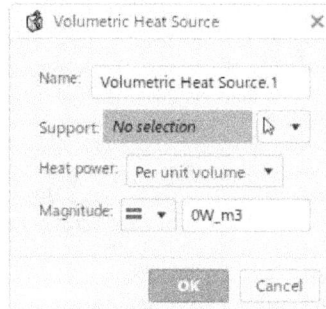

Figure 9–39

2. Select the **IC** part as the *Support*.
3. Select **Total** in the *Heat power* pull-down menu and enter **1W**, as shown in Figure 9b-12.

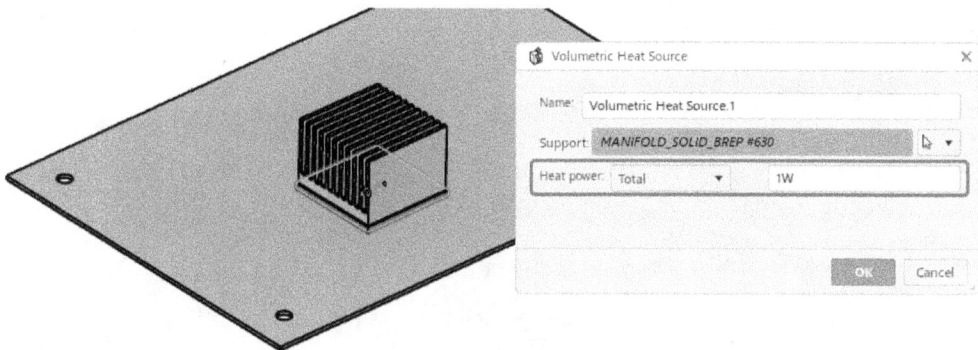

Figure 9b-12

4. Click **OK**.

Task 7: Apply the convection.

1. In the *Loads* section of the Action Bar, select ⬆️ (Film Condition).

2. Select all the surfaces of the sink, except the surface mated with the IC part (44 surfaces altogether). Enter **15W_Kdeg_m2** as the *Film Coefficient*, and **20Cdeg** as the *Ref Temperature*, as shown in Figure 9–40.

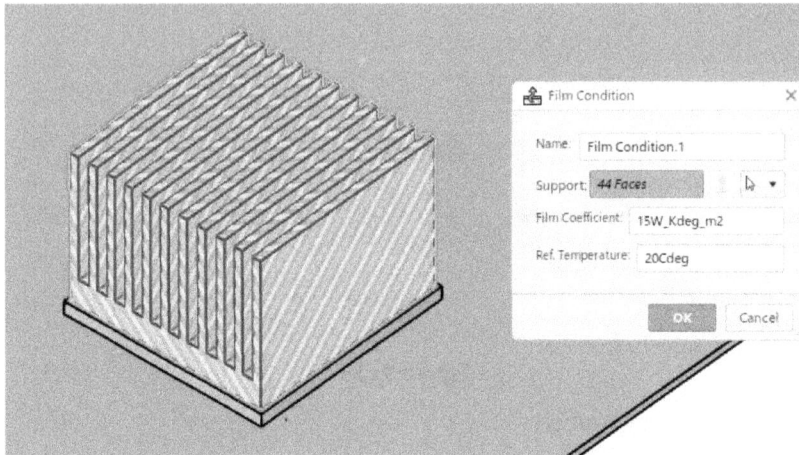

Figure 9–40

3. Click **OK**. The model displays as shown in Figure 9–41.

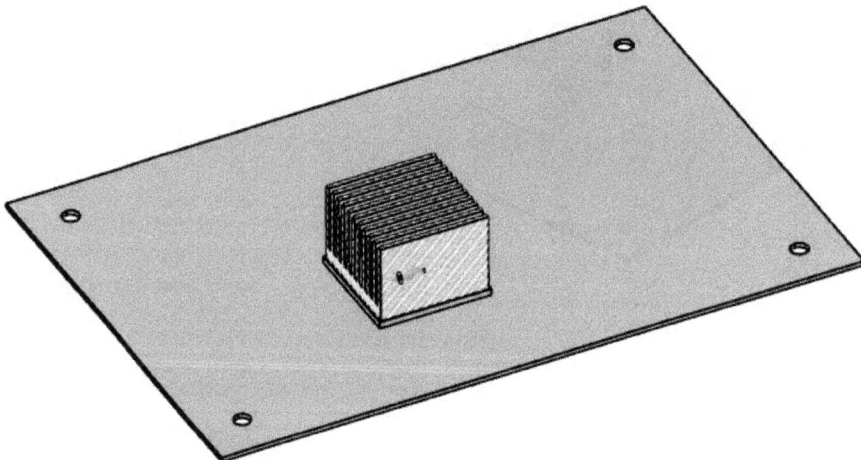

Figure 9–41

4. Using Steps 1 through 3 as the guideline, apply another **Film Condition**, with the same parameters, to the top surface of the **PCB** part, as shown in Figure 9−42.

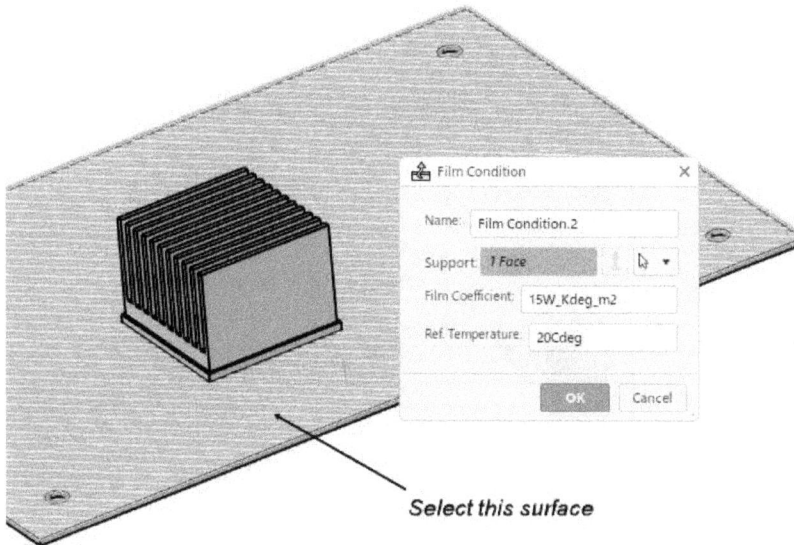

Film Condition

Name: Film Condition.2

Support: 1 Face

Film Coefficient: 15W_Kdeg_m2

Ref. Temperature: 20Cdeg

OK   Cancel

Select this surface

Figure 9−42

5. Using ▦ (Feature Manager), hide the **Volumetric Heat Source** and both **Film Conditions**.

Task 8: Create thermal connections.

Thermal connections define the heat transfer between the contacting parts, according to the contact conductance. The heat sink is glued to the IC part, which enables nearly perfect heat transfer. At the same time, the IC is not bonded to the PCB, which creates lower conductance through the interface between those two parts, due to small air gaps. In this task, you will define contact conductance values for the interfaces between the parts.

1. In the *Connections* section of the Action Bar, select ![] (Contact Detection). The *Contact Detection* dialog box opens, as shown in Figure 9–43.

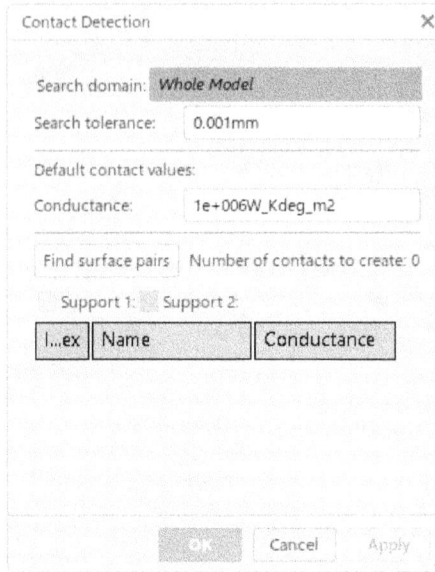

Figure 9–43

2. Click **Find surface pairs**. The app detects two pairs of contacting surfaces, as shown in Figure 9–44.

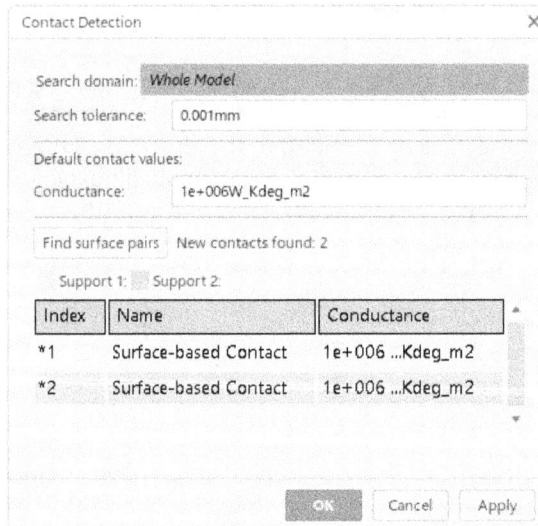

Figure 9–44

3. Select the first contact in the list. The app highlights the contact between the heat sink and the IC, as shown in Figure 9–45. Leave the *Conductance* at the default value **1e+006 W_Kdeg_m2**, which is a very high value, which models a nearly lossless heat transfer between these parts.

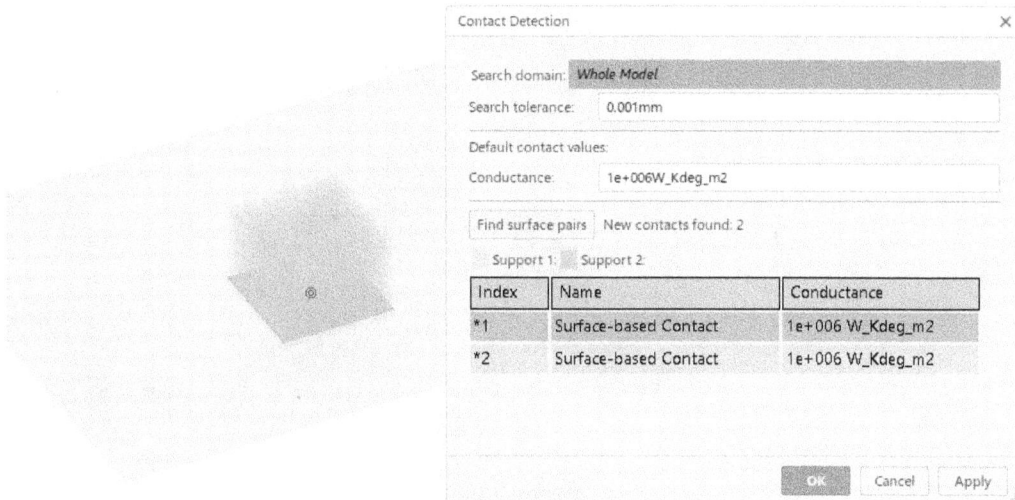

Figure 9–45

4. Select the second contact in the list. The app highlights the contact between the **PCB** and the **IC** parts, as shown in Figure 9–46.

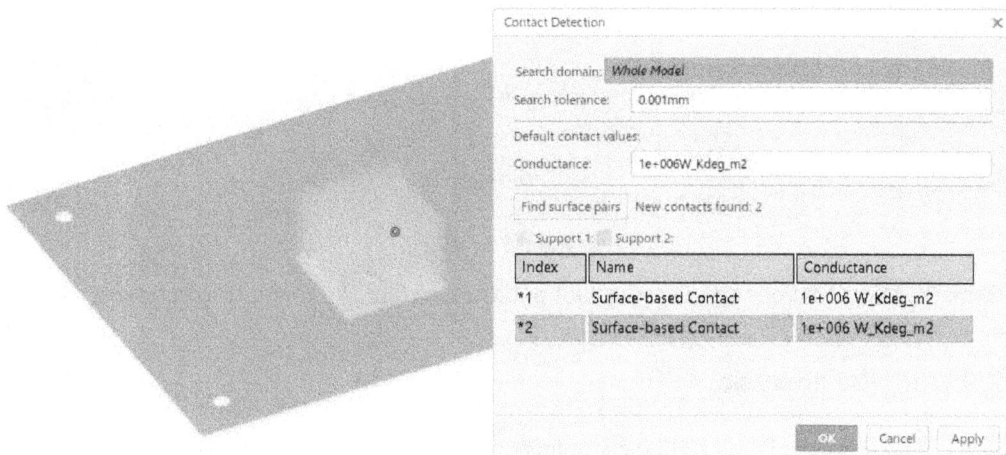

Figure 9–46

5. To modify the *Conductance* value for this contact, right-click it and select **Edit**, as shown in Figure 9–47.

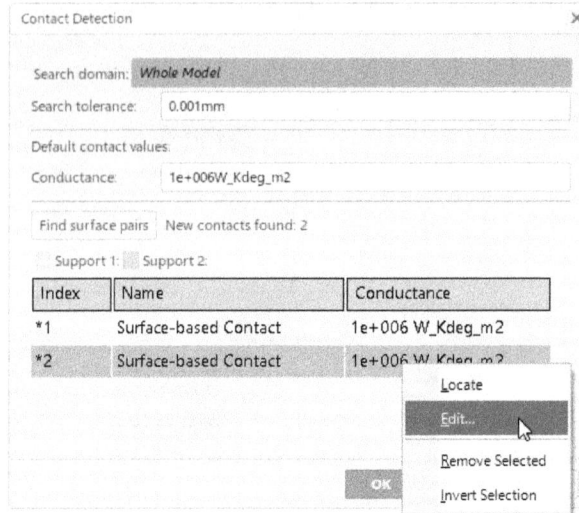

Figure 9–47

6. In the *Edit Contact* dialog box that opens, enter **200 W_Kdeg_m2** for the *Conductance* value, as shown in Figure 9–48.

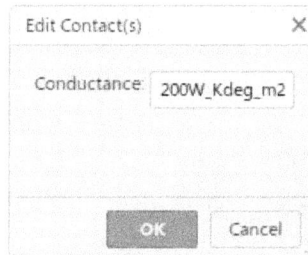

Figure 9–48

7. Click **OK** twice to close the *Edit Contact* and the *Contact Detection* dialog boxes.

Task 9: Run the analysis.

1. Run the analysis and wait until it completes.

Task 10: Display Temperature result plot.

1. Once the analysis completes, the **Temperature** result plot is automatically displayed, as shown in Figure 9–49. Note that the maximum temperature occurs in the IC part.

Figure 9–49

2. Zoom in on the **IC** part, as shown in Figure 9–50. Note how the top of the IC is cooled much better than the bottom (as it should be). The top of the IC transfers all of its heat to the heat sink through the almost perfect thermal bond, while transfer of heat from the IC to the PCB is impeded by the lower Conductance of this contact that you defined in Task 8.

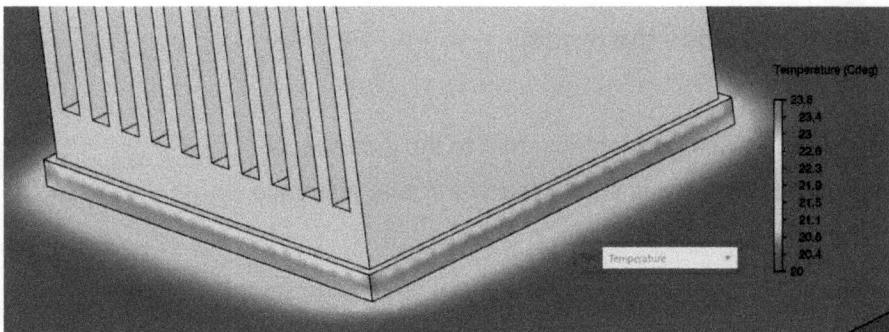

Figure 9–50

Task 11: Display Heat Flux.

1. Select **Heat Flux Magnitude** in the *Plot* drop-down menu. The result plot displays, as shown in Figure 9–51. Note that the maximum heat flow occurs at the bottoms of the fins, as it should. The heat flow from the bottom of the heat sink enters the fins through this area, before being dissipated through the convection on the fin surfaces.

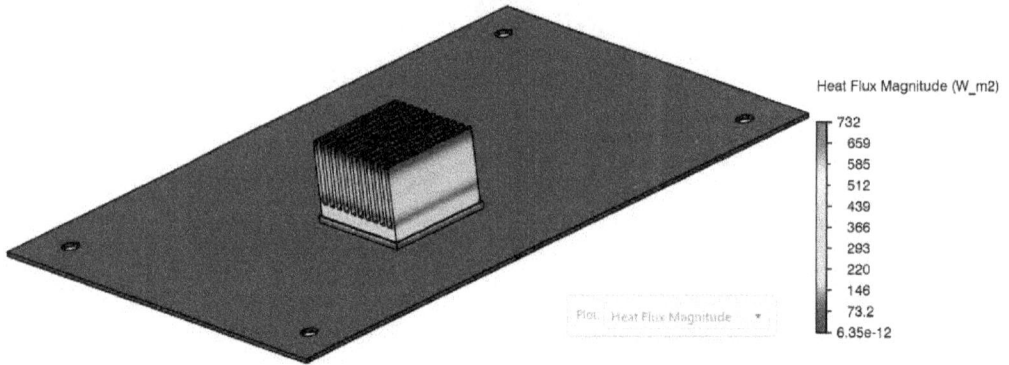

Heat Flux Magnitude (W_m2)

| 732 |
| 659 |
| 585 |
| 512 |
| 439 |
| 366 |
| 293 |
| 220 |
| 146 |
| 73.2 |
| 6.35e-12 |

Plot: Heat Flux Magnitude ▾

Figure 9–51

Task 12: Save and close the model.

1. Click (Result Visualization) to return to the model view.
2. Optionally, save the analysis and the part for future reference.
3. Close all windows.

End of practice

www.ingramcontent.com/pod-product-compliance
Lightning Source LLC
Chambersburg PA
CBHW080713220326
41598CB00033B/5402